CW00694035

Business as Partners in Development

Creating wealth for countries, companies and communities

Jane Nelson

The Prince of Wales Business Leaders Forum

in collaboration with
The World Bank
and
The United Nations Development Programme

We need to build a partnership of people who are engaged in the development business. Private investment has become of fundamental importance, and we need to see how effective we can become in meeting the needs of the private sector. One of my immediate priorities will be to accelerate and deepen our efforts to work with existing and new partners – with specific measures to reach out to the private sector, NGOs and civil society.

James D Wolfensohn
President
The World Bank Group

The global scourge of poverty can only be ended with a massive increase of employment and sustainable livelihoods generated primarily from enterprises in the private sector. In this age of globalisation and the increasing importance of transnational corporations, it is imperative that new partnerships be sought and formed with this vital sector, that promote innovations and investments to generate the economic opportunities fundamental to sustainable human development. Both public and private institutions have an obligation to ensure that poorer nations and poorer people benefit to a far greater extent than they have up to now from the new consensus on market-oriented approaches and globalisation.

James Gustave Speth
Administrator
United Nations Development Programme

ST. JAMES'S PALACE

The many environmental and social challenges of our time, where economic progress brings both opportunities and threats to the sustainable development of communities all round the world, require a new partnership approach. Business, which is now the key economic motor for development, has particular responsibility to balance profitability with concern for the long-term needs of future generations.

My Business Leaders Forum, through its "Partners in Development" programme, has embarked on a series of initiatives with the World Bank Group, United Nations Development Programme and other international agencies to review and spread good practice on how responsible business and local communities can work together to meet goals of sustainable development.

I hope that through reviewing good practice, visiting examples of sound partnerships in action around the world, sharing experience, making a commitment to continuous improvement in business practices, and working on initiatives to scale up experimental projects, all of us concerned with the long-term prosperity of our communities can make a greater impact on the thinking and practice of the managers and leaders of tomorrow.

HRH The Prince of Wales
President, The Prince of Wales Business Leaders Forum

Contents

Executive Summary

The following publication represents "work in progress". It has one overriding objective; to share some initial ideas and examples which will form the basis for a global learning and networking initiative which The Prince of Wales Business Leaders Forum will be conducting in collaboration with the World Bank, UNDP and other partners, as part of its *Partners in Development* programme. Launched in 1995, this programme identifies, analyses and promotes good practice by business as a partner in development, with the aim of encouraging replication and wider implementation. The programme focuses on partnerships between individual companies and amongst the business sector, government and civil society organisations. It emphasises the role that business can play not only in economic wealth creation, but also in widening economic opportunity and participation, investing in human capital, promoting environmental sustainability and enhancing social cohesion. It promotes the positive multiplier effect that business can have through the profitable, responsible and innovative performance of its core business activities, through its social investment and strategic philanthropy programmes, and through the advocacy and advisory role that the private sector can play in the public policy debate. Although the programme focuses on business activities in developing and transition economies, it also identifies partnership initiatives in OECD countries which have applicability elsewhere.

The Case for Public-Private Partnership

The first section of the publication sets out to make the case for public-private partnership:

- It illustrates the growing consensus within nations and between nations on the need for more sustainable patterns of development, emphasising not only the ecological, but also the human and social dimensions of the concept, which have gained greater attention in the four years since the Rio Earth Summit.

- It goes on to review the challenges of national governance and competitiveness in today's increasingly global and integrated world economy, emphasising the growing influence of the business sector and non-governmental organisations on the shaping and implementation of national policy agendas. In reviewing the key factors of international competitiveness, the paper touches on the debate between those that believe that economic globalisation and liberalisation, and the drive for international competitiveness has had, and continues to have, unacceptable and unsustainable social and environmental costs, and those that believe that economic competition is the ally, not the enemy,

There is a need to fundamentally reassess the way in which national wealth is defined and measured in order to include not only man-made capital but also natural, human and social capital.

of social progress. This tension between economic competitiveness and social cohesion lies at the heart of the debate on governance and on the shifting roles of government, business and civil society. It is a tension which is unlikely to disappear and there are few certainties about the outcome, other than the fact that partnership between the different sectors will be crucial.

- The section on *The Development Challenge* closes with a message about the need to fundamentally reassess the way in which national wealth is defined and measured. It identifies four key types of capital: man-made, natural, human and social, and reviews the ground-breaking work being undertaken by the World Bank and UNDP on the importance of human capital in the composition of national wealth, and the growing attention and analysis being focused on the concept of social capital.

- The publication moves from reviewing *The Development Challenge* at the level of nation-states, to a brief assessment of the closely related strategic management challenges facing individual companies. These include: globalisation and regionalisation of economic activity; unprecedented technological change; the growing importance of new markets; dramatic restructuring of organisations and work; changing demographics of the workforce; the transition from industrial to information-based societies; and the increasing demands for ethical behaviour being placed on business by a growing range of increasingly sophisticated stakeholder groups, including primary stakeholders such as customers and investors, as well as secondary stakeholders such as NGOs, governments and the general public.

- *The Corporate Challenge* goes on to review the evolving debate on corporate governance, and its shift from the narrow definition of the relationship between shareholders, management and Boards of Directors, to the broader definition of the relationships between the company and its wider stakeholders. It concludes that the focus on corporate governance will intensify rather than go away; that a reputation for good corporate governance can lead to competitive advantage; and that this calls for new types of partnership – both within companies and between companies and their stakeholders. A brief assessment of the current thinking on the sources of corporate competitiveness also emphasises the growing importance of partnerships and alliances, especially between companies and their primary stakeholders. The link between corporate competitiveness and partnerships with communities and other stakeholders however, is less clear, despite growing anecdotal evidence. This is an area which requires increased attention and research – especially the issue of how companies can create shareholder value through such partnership activities.

- The section on *The Corporate Challenge* closes by outlining "The Four Rs"; four core management strategies that companies must pursue in order to simultaneously achieve corporate competitiveness and good corporate governance. They are: reputation management; relationship management; responsiveness to systems and service needs; and resource efficiency and enhancement. All of these call for greater co-operation between functional divisions within a company, and between the company and its stakeholders.

- *The Case for Public-Private Partnership* closes by summarising some of the key benefits of such partnerships. From a societal perspective these are summed up as increased efficiency, effectiveness and equity. From a corporate perspective they are: enhancing reputation and "licence to operate"; managing, motivating and retaining quality employees; strategic market positioning; improving operational efficiency and quality; promoting better risk management; and investing in a stable society and healthy economy in which to operate.

The Contribution of the Business Sector

The heart of the publication draws on over 100 examples, from different industry sectors and countries, to illustrate *The Contribution of the Business Sector* to development.

- The first section describes how leading companies are managing their corporate contribution to meet wider societal and development goals. It looks at what we have defined as the 10 Ms: the key *Mechanisms and Models* by which a company can improve the quality and leverage of its activities to maximise their positive benefits to society (these activities are categorised as core business activities, social investment and philanthropy and engaging in the public policy dialogue); establishment of *Mission Statements* and *Methodologies* (or guidelines and codes of conduct); implementation of structures and systems to *Manage, Measure and Monitor* these activities; and development of incentives and capacity building initiatives to *Motivate* and *Mobilise* employees and other companies, and to *Mainstream* concepts of stakeholding and corporate responsibility into the core business process, rather than leaving them as "bolt-ons" in an isolated department.

- The second section looks at the impacts that business can have in the key areas which determine sustainable development: *Economic Development* – through increasing and spreading investment and income flows, employment, goods and services, infrastructure, technology, international business standards and practice, and local business development – emphasising the critical importance of increasing economic opportunities and participation, not just economic growth, and the role played in this process by backward and forward linkages and multiplier effects; *Human Development* – looking at workplace practices (in areas such as training, occupational health and safety, increasing opportunities for women and minorities and the issue of child labour), and investments in the wider community in education, training, health and nutrition and the application of information technology to this field; *Environmental Sustainability* – promoting cleaner production, sustainable consumption and biodiversity conservation; *Social Cohesion* – tackling social exclusion, crime and corruption, and supporting the development of civil society, cultural diversity and social entrepreneurship; *Integrated Community Development* – supporting participatory, integrated approaches to urban and rural development; and *Emergency and Disaster Relief.*

Multi-stakeholder Partnerships

The final section of the publication looks in more detail at 26 *multi-stakeholder partnerships* between international NGOs and business; international agencies and business; and between groups of companies themselves, all aimed at achieving the economic, human, ecological and social imperatives of sustainable development. It closes by summarising key lessons from "good practice" – a term which the PWBLF uses in preference to "best practice" due to the enormous complexity, stakeholder diversity and emotional content of partnership building, which exposes the label "best" to almost certain criticism. The key lessons are summarised under the broad themes of purpose, process and progress, and include: clear and common goals built on mutual benefit; the role of intermediary leadership; understanding and consulting all stakeholders, not just the partners; clarifying roles and responsibilities; understanding resource needs and capacities; communication; evaluating and celebrating success; and continuous learning and adaptation.

The challenge is about mobilising not only the social budgets and environmental policies of business, but the entire range of business skills, resources and networks that can beneficially impact the process of sustainable development, and can be leveraged through partnerships with other stakeholders.

The publication concludes that the critical organisational and managerial challenges which need to be tackled at both a societal and corporate level include: good governance and stakeholder-responsive leadership; the development of appropriate incentive structures and broader measurement systems (in both the marketplace and the public policy domain); and better cross-sector communication and dialogue.

It recommends that companies, NGOs, governments and international agencies place increased emphasis on: studying and rewarding corporate "good practice" in terms of both individual companies and their partnerships with others; joint efforts to raise awareness of the benefits and mechanisms of partnership; greater engagement in the public policy dialogue, to encourage government support for cross-sector partnerships; the identification and/or establishment of joint "demonstration projects"; a joint education and capacity building exercise based on experiential learning and aimed at educating development professionals, government officials, NGO and business managers; and similar initiatives aimed at educating some of the leaders of tomorrow.

This publication aims to take a few steps forward on several different journeys. It is first and foremost a societal journey; one which is taking countries, companies and communities into unchartered waters. Every group is struggling to get the navigation right. Although there is growing consensus that new forms of public-private partnership represent our common destination, no single nation, sector or individual has a monopoly on the charts and compasses for getting there. Each, however, has something to bring to the table, both in terms of vision and practical expertise.

It is also an organisational journey for The Prince of Wales Business Leaders Forum as we appreciate with ever greater clarity and urgency that our work is about mobilising not only the social budgets and environmental policies of business, but the entire range of business skills, resources and networks that can beneficially impact the process of sustainable development and can be leveraged through partnerships with other stakeholders. We are aware that visionary companies all over the world are also looking at these organisational challenges in the context of their own corporate success, and their changing public role as private enterprises. We believe that they should be rewarded and encouraged – with both positive feedback and constructive criticism where necessary. We also recognise that they represent only a tiny percentage of the world's 37,000 multi-nationals, let alone its millions of medium, small and micro-enterprises, and that there is a need to spread good practice much wider.

Finally, it is a personal journey for millions of people working in business, government and community organisations all over the world. A small fraction of these people and their activities are described in this publication. The publication is not intended to be strong on economic substance, or rigorous systematic analysis. It is an anecdotal, descriptive set of profiles about people, their organisations and their partnerships with others. None of their results are perfect, nor have they been easy to achieve. But it is impossible not to feel inspired by the passion, commitment and creativity that the vast majority of them are bringing to their search for solutions. I hope that the pages which follow will be a celebration of their vision and their efforts, offering a chance to debate, inspire and take action.

Jane Nelson, Policy and Research Director
The Prince of Wales Business Leaders Forum

THE DEVELOPMENT CHALLENGE

1. Economic growth alone is not sufficient, without the human, ecological and social dimension.

2. Governments alone are not sufficient, without empowering the private sector and civil society.

3. Sustainable development is a global imperative for action in every nation and at every level of society, not just developing nations and poor communities.

NATIONAL DEVELOPMENT CHALLENGES

FOUNDATIONS OF NATIONAL WEALTH
- ECONOMIC/MAN-MADE CAPITAL
- NATURAL CAPITAL
- HUMAN CAPITAL
- SOCIAL CAPITAL

NATIONAL GOVERNANCE

Requires increased cooperation and accountability between:.

a) Different levels of government

b) Different sectors

NATIONAL COMPETITIVENESS

Requires cooperation between public and private sector

– societal benefits –

THE CASE FOR PUBLIC PRIVATE PARTNERSHIP

– corporate benefits –

FOUNDATIONS OF CORPORATE WEALTH
- REPUTATION
- RELATIONSHIPS
- RESPONSIVENESS
- RESOURCES

STRATEGIC MANAGEMENT CHALLENGES

1. Globalisation
2. Technological change
3. New markets
4. Economic restructuring
5. Changing workforce
6. Growing importance of SMEs
7. From industrial to knowledge society
8. Increasing stakeholder demands

CORPORATE GOVERNANCE

Requires increased cooperation and accountability between:.

a) Management, directors and shareholders

b) Management and other stakeholders

CORPORATE COMPETITIVENESS

Requires cooperation between the company and its primary and secondary stakeholders

THE CORPORATE CHALLENGE

I The case for public-private partnership

There has never been a greater need for public-private partnership. Countries, companies and communities are all facing unprecedented change and complexity. At every level of society there is growing recognition that the economic, social and environmental challenges of today's world are too complex, and the financial, technical and managerial resources for tackling them are too scarce, not to search for new approaches; approaches which are more holistic than in the past, and which draw on the resources and strengths of other sectors alongside government. The following section looks at the key challenges facing nation-states and the corporate sector, focusing on their implications for governance and competitiveness, and then highlights some of the societal and corporate benefits of working in partnership.

Every few hundred years in Western history there occurs a sharp transformation. We cross a 'divide'. Within a few short decades, society rearranges itself – its world view; its basic values; its social and political structure; its arts; its key institutions. Fifty years later there is a new world. And the people born then cannot even imagine the world in which their grandparents lived and into which their parents were born. We are currently living in such a transformation. It is creating the post-capitalist society.

Peter Drucker

The Post-Capitalist Society, 1993

As in the Renaissance, it will be an exciting time, a time of great opportunities for those who can see and seize them, but of great threat and fear for many. It will be more difficult to hold organisations and societies together. The softer words of leadership and vision and common purpose will replace the tougher words of control and authority because the tough words won't bite anymore. Organisations will have to become communities rather than properties, with members not employees, because few will be content to be owned by others. Societies will break down into smaller units but will also regroup into even larger ones than now for particular purposes.

Charles Handy

Beyond Certainty: The changing worlds of organisations, 1995

1

The Development Challenge

The seismic societal changes of recent years have had an impact on almost every nation and every sector of society – positive and negative. Despite obvious and continued differences between different regions of the world, we are witnessing a remarkable convergence of opinion on the challenges and potential solutions facing the world's nations and their decision-makers at local, national and international levels. Above all, we are witnessing three key trends:

- A growing recognition – in both the public and private sector, and in OECD, developing and transition economies – of the crucial linkages between economic growth, human development, social cohesion and environmental sustainability. A set of complex and interdependent linkages which can best be summed up in the concept of sustainable development and in the increasingly clear message that economic growth is only part of the equation.

- An equally strong recognition that these challenges can no longer be tackled by yesterday's rules of governance; that government is only part of the solution.There is an urgent need to develop new ways of thinking and new approaches to governance – locally, nationally and internationally. Fundamental to this is the growing importance of the private sector, ranging from large multinational corporations to millions of small and micro-enterprises; and of civil society, ranging from international and professionally managed non-governmental organisations, to grassroots community-based organisations and individual citizens.

- A realisation that the old mindsets and terminology which placed the countries of the so-called "first, second and third worlds" in discrete and separate boxes are no longer justified or workable in today's interdependent world, where problems of poverty, unemployment, inequality, environmental degradation and social disintegration are impacting almost every nation to a lesser or greater degree. Whilst the absolute levels of each of these problems show enormous variations between OECD, developing and transition economies, the type of policies and participatory approaches needed for tackling them share much in common.

In short, the "development challenge" in today's world is one of complex and interdependent issues, which can only be tackled by co-operative, integrated and inclusive solutions, both within nations and between nations. The following section looks at these issues from the perspective of government and the nation-state, focusing on their implications for national governance and competitiveness. It concludes that multi-stakeholder partnerships are critical to national development; partnerships not only between different sectors – public and private – but also between different countries.

1.1 Sustainable Development: a growing consensus among nations

The 1992 United Nations Conference on Environment and Development (UNCED) was a defining moment in setting the agenda for the world's increasingly consultative approach to governance. UNCED's Secretary-General Maurice Strong had a vision to make this the first major UN Conference that would invite participation not only by governments, but also by business and civil society. His invitation was taken up by thousands of non-governmental and business organisations from more than 150 countries, including the creation of the Business Council for Sustainable Development which mobilised 48 of the world's most outstanding business leaders. The Rio Earth Summit became a rich kaleidoscope of environmental and social activists, bankers, industrialists and trade unionists, scientists and educators, religious and tribal leaders, journalists, diplomats, Presidents, Prime Ministers and Princes, even the occasional film star. For more than two weeks, 24 hours a day, they argued, debated and negotiated, and set in motion a new approach to development; one which aims to be more sustainable, more people-centred and more consultative. The world is far from achieving this goal, but some encouraging progress has been made.

I t is easy to forget that less than ten years ago Prime Minister Gro Harlem Brundtland of Norway and her UN-appointed World Commission on Environment and Development had yet to produce their seminal report "Our Common Future" and its call for a new approach to development which "meets the needs of the present without compromising the ability of future generations to meet their own needs."

Since that time the world has changed dramatically. More than 3 billion people have joined the world's market economies, technological change is revolutionising the way we live and work, and the impacts of globalisation are touching almost every society – for good and bad. Despite these changes, the Brundtland Commission's core message remains valid and has gained almost universal acceptance as a broad framework for development. The Commission's original message, which was based on consultations with thousands of people from around the world, was strengthened and endorsed by the 1992 Rio Earth Summit and Agenda 21 – Rio's blueprint for action. It has been further enhanced by five other global summits on population, human rights, social development, women, and cities, plus countless books and reports, mostly refining and enhancing rather than challenging the central theme. Most important of all however, it has been endorsed by action; by millions of new initiatives all over the world – some large-scale and international in scope, but most grassroots and local – which are all working towards the new paradigm for development.

Three key themes underpin this new paradigm of development:

a) Economic growth is not sufficient, and can in fact be detrimental, without appropriate linkages to the human, ecological, ethical and social dimension;

b) Governments operating alone are not sufficient, and can at best be ineffective, at worst detrimental, without empowering, building and working with the skills and resources of other sectors; and

c) Sustainable development is a global imperative for action in every nation and at every level of society, not just in developing nations and poor communities.

Human development is the end – economic growth a means. So, the purpose of growth should be to enrich people's lives. But far too often it does not. The recent decades show all too clearly that there is no automatic link between growth and human development. And even when links are established, they may gradually be eroded – unless regularly fortified by skillful and intelligent policy management.

UNDP Human Development Report, 1996

There is no – and can be no – delinking of economic reforms and effective social policy. Economic growth is crucial. No country has achieved sustained improvements in living without it. But investing in people to create human capital – which is the main attribute that people draw on in order to live more productive lives – is equally critical to raising living standards.

World Bank Annual Report, 1995

The links between the economic, social and ecological imperatives of sustainable development are captured by the diagrams below, developed by Ismail Serageldin and Andrew Steer from the World Bank's Vice Presidency for Environmentally Sustainable Development.

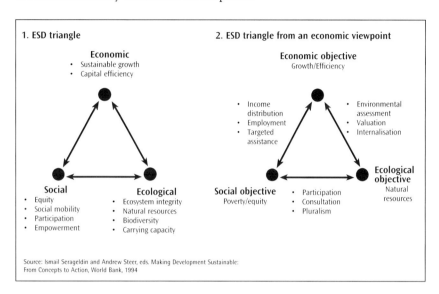

Source: Ismail Serageldin and Andrew Steer, eds. Making Development Sustainable: From Concepts to Action, World Bank, 1994

Equally important is growing consensus on the critical linkages between economic growth and human development, illustrated in the following diagram from UNDP's 1996 Human Development Report.

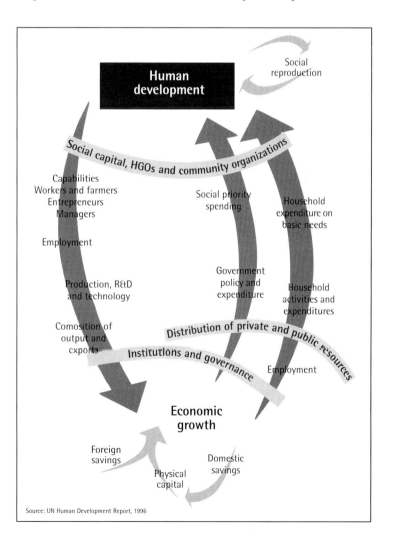

Source: UN Human Development Report, 1996

In its 1996 Human Development Report, the UNDP provides compelling evidence that despite spectacular economic advance for some countries, economic growth has failed for more than a quarter of the world's people, as illustrated in the following diagram:

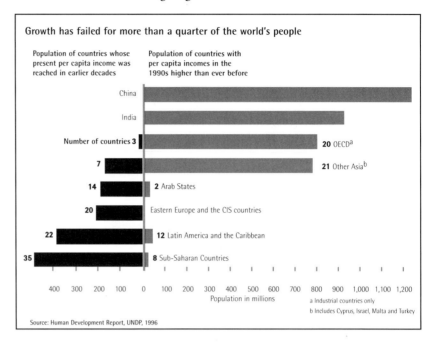

Growth has failed for more than a quarter of the world's people

Population of countries whose present per capita income was reached in earlier decades		Population of countries with per capita incomes in the 1990s higher than ever before
	China	
	India	
Number of countries 3		20 OECD[a]
7		21 Other Asia[b]
14		2 Arab States
20		Eastern Europe and the CIS countries
22		12 Latin America and the Caribbean
35		8 Sub-Saharan Countries

400 300 200 100 0 100 200 300 400 500 600 700 800 900 1,000 1,100 1,200
Population in millions

a Industrial countries only
b Includes Cyprus, Israel, Malta and Turkey

Source: Human Development Report, UNDP, 1996

Signs of increased inequality are causing growing concern in many countries. From the United States to Europe and Asia, people worry that a widening gap between rich and poor may worsen poverty and crime, causing serious social unrest. World Bank research shows that high levels of inequality are undesirable for another reason as well. In general, the less equal a country's distribution of assets, especially land, the slower its economic growth.

Michael Bruno, Chief Economist and Lyn Squire, Director Policy & Research, The World Bank

The report emphasises that quality and structure of growth are as important as quantity, if growth is to be sustainable and equitable. It goes on to identify five types of economic growth which may be achievable – and are being achieved – over short periods of time, but cannot be sustained in the long-term:

Jobless growth – where the overall economy grows but does not expand opportunities for employment. A type of growth being experienced in a number of OECD and developing countries.

Ruthless growth – where the fruits of economic growth mostly benefit the rich, leaving millions of people struggling in ever-deepening poverty. The UN has calculated that during 1970-1985, for example, global GNP increased by 40%, yet the number of poor increased by 17%. Rising income inequalities both between nations and within nations is an issue not only for many developing and transition economies, but also certain OECD countries.

Voiceless growth – where growth in the economy has not been accompanied by an extension of democracy or empowerment and/or by greater equality and participation for women, despite the fact that investing in women's capabilities is increasingly accepted as one of the surest ways to contribute to economic growth and overall development.

Rootless growth – which causes people's cultural identity to wither. The UN estimates that there are about 10,000 distinct cultures, but many risk being marginalised or eliminated by culturally repressive governments or other more economically powerful cultures, sometimes with violent results, as the tragedy in the Balkan states of former Yugoslavia demonstrates. The UN report uses Switzerland and Malaysia as examples of countries which have recognised the value of cultural diversity and implemented mechanisms to decentralise economic and political governance accordingly.

Futureless growth – where the present generation squanders resources needed by future generations. In many of the world's fastest growing economies – such as in East Asia – the combination of rapid industrialisation and urbanisation is placing enormous pressures on the environment through increased pollution, deforestation and natural resource depletion.

MULTILATERAL DEVELOPMENT AGENCIES
CREATING A SHARED VISION

The growing consensus on the key drivers of sustainable development is reflected at every level of the governmental process. At the international level, the multilateral and bilateral development agencies have started to refocus their priorities in similar directions. All of them are looking for ways to work with both non-governmental and private sector organisations, in order to be more effective in leveraging limited resources and reaching the communities they were established to help.

The lesson is clear: for economic advance, you need social advance – and without social development, economic development cannot take root. For the Bank, this means that we need to make sure the programmes and projects we support have adequate social foundations: by designing more participatory country strategies and programmes – reflecting discussions not only with governments, but also with community groups, NGOs, and private businesses; by putting more emphasis on social, cultural and institutional issues – and their interplay with economic issues – in our project and analytical work; and by learning more about how the changing dynamics between public institutions, markets, and civil society affect social and economic development. I see this as a critical challenge – in fact, the critical challenge before us.

James D. Wolfensohn
Address at 1996 Annual IMF/World Bank meeting

The World Bank, for example, identifies the following five major challenges as being crucial to future progress:

- **Pursuing economic reforms** that promote broad-based growth and reduce poverty;

- **Investing in people** through expanded, more effective programmes for education, health, nutrition and family planning – so that the poor can take advantage of the opportunities that growth creates;

- **Protecting the environment** so that growth and poverty reduction can be lasting and benefit tomorrow's generations as well as today's;

- **Stimulating the private sector** so that countries can become more productive and create jobs;

- **Reorienting government** so that the public sector can complement private-sector activity and efficiently undertake essential tasks such as human resource development, environmental protection, provision of social safety nets, and legal and regulatory frameworks.

While critics argue that the reality is a long way from matching the rhetoric, there can be no doubt that the World Bank has made, and continues to make, substantial managerial and organisational changes to support these imperatives. In 1993, for example, it created new Vice Presidencies in Environmentally Sustainable Development, Finance and Private Sector Development and Human Resources Development and Operations Policy, to spearhead and mainstream these issues through its operational divisions. It has set up innovative public-private partnerships in new fields, such as: The Consultative Group to Assist the Poorest (CGAP) to support and promote leading-edge micro-finance intermediaries; and Information for Development (InfoDev) to help developing countries benefit from the information revolution. It has established an Inspection Panel to increase accountability to non-governmental stakeholders; implemented systems to evaluate the environmental, and increasingly, the social impacts of World Bank projects, carrying out some 50 social assessments in 1994-95; launched a series of internal workshops and a source book on participatory development; established a Task Force on Social Development; and created internal cross-functional "learning networks' on issues such as human development and the private sector .

A number of other UN Agencies such as UNDP, UNEP, UNICEF and the ILO have adopted sustainable human development as one of their core goals and are implementing policies and programmes aimed at working more closely with the private sector and civil society organisations. The regional multilateral banks – the InterAmerican, Asian and African Development Banks and EBRD – are also pursuing, similar strategies aimed at a multi-sector approach to sustainable development. The 1996 report of the Development Committee Task Force on Multilateral Development Banks, for example, highlighted five areas for increased emphasis by these banks: reducing poverty; promoting effective government and a strong civil society; making development environmentally sustainable, investing in infrastructure and utilities; and encouraging private sector development, from microenterprises to multi-nationals.

Bilateral agencies speaking the same language

The imperatives of sustainable development have also become widely accepted among the bilateral development agencies, as the following three examples illustrate:

British ODA has revised its mission statement as follows:
To contribute to sustainable development and the reduction of poverty and suffering by:
• encouraging sound development policies, efficient markets and good government;
• helping people achieve better education and health and widening opportunities, particularly for women;
• enhancing productive capacity and conserving the environment; and
• promoting international policies for sustainable development and enhancing the effectiveness of multilateral development institutions.
One of ODA's programmes is its Joint Funding Scheme which offers matched funding to over 100 British NGOs working on some 1,800 projects, usually in partnership with local NGOs in host countries.

CIDA (The Canadian International Development Agency) identifies the following six priority areas in its aid programme:
• **Basic human needs:** to support efforts to provide primary health care, basic education, family planning, nutrition, water and sanitation, and shelter. Canada will continue to respond to emergencies with humanitarian assistance. 25% of ODA will be committed to basic human needs.
• **Women in development:** to support the full participation of women as equal partners in the sustainable development of their societies.
• **Infrastructure services:** to help developing countries to deliver environmentally sound infrastructure services – for example, rural electricity and communications – with an emphasis on assisting poor groups and building capacity.
• **Human rights, democracy and good governance:** to increase respect for human rights, including children's rights; to promote democracy and better governance; to strengthen the components of civil society, such as civic organisations and trade unions; and to ensure the security of the individual.
• **Private sector development:** to promote sustained and equitable economic growth by supporting private sector development.
• **The environment:** to help developing countries to protect their environment and to contribute to addressing global and regional issues.

The Japanese revised their ODA charter in 1992 to cite the following four guiding principles for the Japan International Co-operation Agency (JICA) and Overseas Economic Co-operation Fund (OECF):
• Environmental conservation and development should be pursued in tandem.
• Any use of ODA for military purposes or for aggravation of international conflicts should be avoided.
• Full attention should be paid to trends in recipient countries' military expenditures, their development and production of mass destruction weapons and missiles, their export and import of arms etc. so as to maintain and strengthen international peace and stability, and from the viewpoint that developing countries should place appropriate priorities in the allocation of their resources on their own economic and social development.
• Full attention should be paid to efforts for promoting democratisation and introduction of a market-oriented economy and the situation regarding the securing of basic human rights and freedoms in the recipient country.

It is easy to criticise these as mere mission statements, but in almost all cases, including those of other bilateral agencies in the European Community and countries such as Australia, there are substantive organisational changes underway to enable them to meet these objectives and to make the most effective and efficient use of increasingly tight aid budgets. As with the World Bank several bilateral agencies are placing much greater emphasis on working in partnership with NGOs to meet their objectives, and a few are moving beyond commercial contract and procurement relationships with the private sector to test more creative ways to leverage joint skills and resources. These organisations have undergone significant changes in direction in recent years, although the pressure is still strong to change faster and further, and to halt the erosion of aid budgets that is occurring in many donor countries.

THE SHARED AGENDAS OF NATIONAL AND LOCAL GOVERNMENTS

Even the "rich men's" clubs of the OECD, G7 and European Union are having to focus their attention not only on co-ordinating economic management and growth but also on the human, environmental and social dimensions of this growth. These dimensions cannot be ignored as their governments grapple with high levels of unemployment and economic insecurity, environmental challenges, growing inequality and social disintegration, rising crime levels, drugs and family breakdown. The 1996 UNDP Human Development Report calculates, for example, that there are now 100 million people in OECD countries living below national poverty lines. In recent years the politically explosive problem of youth unemployment and the waste of human potential and hope which it represents, has become a serious issue in a number of these countries.

These OECD governments are also realising that they face similar challenges to many of their counterparts in the world's developing economies. Despite marked differences in scale and in the availability of resources to tackle these challenges, governments all over the world are implementing similar policies, as illustrated by the anecdote opposite.

Indications of growing consensus are also apparent at the level of local government. Mayors and local authorities all over the world have mobilised resources and citizens for the implementation of Local Agenda 21. At the recent UN Habitat II Conference in Istanbul, the International Union of Local Authorities (IULA) brought together some 500 mayors and city leaders from around the world to review best practice and to build a global consensus for local action. There were clear parallels between the different cities at this unprecedented gathering, especially in the case of the world's megacities with populations of over 10 million people.

In summary, the international development debate is no longer about extreme alternatives – about communism versus capitalism, the free market versus state control, democracy versus dictatorship – but about finding common ground. It is about finding co-operative, integrated and inclusive solutions to complex and interdependent issues, both within nations and between them. It is about finding a balance between rights and responsibilities, between the individual, the community and the nation-state. It is about how to harness the economic potential of free markets, whilst accepting that there is much in society that cannot be run purely along free market lines. It is about strengthening civil society, whilst accepting that government has greater responsibility than ever before to create an enabling environment, to communicate its goals and to be accountable to an electorate struggling to cope with unprecedented change and uncertainty. It is about building new social structures and institutions to deal with new forms of insecurity, whilst recognising that the old sources of insecurity have not disappeared. It is about accepting that economic globalisation is creating losers as well as winners, both within nations and between nations, and that the winners cannot "win" indefinitely if the losers are excluded from the benefits and potential of economic opportunity. Most important of all, it is about creating enabling environments which give people more access to, and control over, resources and more opportunities to develop their own local solutions.

THE USA AND SOUTH AFRICA: Different Worlds, Same Challenges

President Bill Clinton's 1996 State of the Union Address elaborated on the eight key challenges that America faces – reinventing government and making it more responsive; bipartisan budgetary discipline; taking back the streets from crime, gangs and drugs; helping every American willing to work for it to achieve economic security; providing the educational opportunities needed for the new century; strengthening families; working for a cleaner and safer environment; and playing a global leadership role. A week later speaking in London, Mac Maharaj, South Africa's Minister of Transport, outlined six very similar imperatives for his own country – nation-building and agreeing a constitutional base for stable, responsive government; fighting crime; achieving economic growth with an emphasis on job creation; fighting poverty through better education, housing and health; maintaining fiscal and monetary discipline; and playing a regional leadership role in achieving Southern African integration. Two very different countries, at different stages of their political and economic development and yet with almost the same goals and challenges.

1.2 National Governance and Competitiveness

We in the United States have come to recognise that it is time to abandon our old model for combating poverty, based on heavy government intervention through massive bureaucracies. There was a time when these structures seemed essential to make our idealism productive. But their size, inflexibility and expense are now seen as obstacles to the purpose we still pursue. We are working now to create a more vital relationship between the government and the people.

Vice President Al Gore

UN Social Summit, March 1995

The World Bank has identified three distinct aspects of governance: (i) the form of political regime; (ii) the process by which authority is exercised in the management of a country's economic and social resources for development; and (iii) the capacity of governments to design, formulate, and implement policies and discharge functions

Governance: The World Bank's Experience, 1994

(i) NATIONAL GOVERNANCE REQUIRES PARTNERSHIP

From the United States to the Ukraine, national governments in industrial, developing and transition economies alike, are under increasing economic and political pressure to reassess their responsibilities and capabilities, and to share the mantle of governance with other players.

In industrialised countries, the share of government expenditure in national income has doubled since the 1930s creating increasingly unsustainable fiscal burdens, especially when the implications of aging populations are taken into account. As a result, welfare reform has become an imperative on both sides of the Atlantic and in Japan, with some governments proving more successful than others in tackling the political minefield of social expenditure cuts and structural changes that such reform entails. The pressure to privatise, or establish public-private partnerships in the provision of infrastructure and social services such as pensions, health care and higher education has probably never been stronger. Nor has the pressure to be more responsive and accountable to electorates who face increased economic and personal insecurity in a rapidly changing world, and who are becoming disillusioned with the ability of governments and established political parties to meet these concerns. In the transition countries of Central and Eastern Europe and the Former Soviet Union, the challenge amounts to a total transformation of the role of the state and even more fundamental restructuring in the relationship between the state, the market and civil society. In the developing countries as well, there is growing consensus on the need to scale down the economic role of the state, to make government more transparent and accountable, to cut extravagant military budgets, and to develop social services and safety nets for the millions of people who do not have them, in as effective and efficient a way a possible.

In short, all over the world, the capacity of the state to ensure good governance is being questioned and tested as never before. According to the World Bank, governance was a term rarely used in development circles until highlighted in the Bank's 1989 report, *Sub-Saharan Africa: From Crisis to Sustainable Growth*." Today it is not only a centrepiece of most bilateral and multilateral aid policies, but also a concept that is increasingly debated at both the national and corporate level in most industrialised countries.

Governance – that is, the control of an activity by some means such that a range of desired outcomes is attained – is not just the province of the state. Rather it is a function that can be performed by a wide variety of public and private, state and non-state, national and international institutions and practices.

Globalisation in Question: the international economy and possibilities of governance
Hirst and Thompson, 1996

REINVENTING GOVERNMENT

Ten principles towards a new way of thinking about governance and the nature of public leadership:

1 **Catalytic Government:** steering rather than rowing

2 **Community-owned Government:** empowering rather than serving

3 **Competitive Government:** injecting competition into service delivery

4 **Mission-driven Government:** transforming rule-driven organisations

5 **Results-oriented Government:** funding outcomes, not inputs

6 **Customer-driven Government:** meeting the needs of the citizen, not the bureaucracy

7 **Enterprising Government:** earning rather than spending

8 **Anticipatory Government:** prevention rather than cure

9 **Decentralised Government:** from hierarchy to participation and teamwork

10 **Market-oriented Government:** leveraging change through the market.

Source: *Reinventing Government,*
David Osborne & Ted Gaebler

The OECD's Development Assistance Committee cites the following factors as being critical in achieving good governance:

- legitimacy of government (degree of democratisation);

- accountability of political and official elements of government (media freedom, transparent decision-making, accountability mechanisms);

- competence of governments to formulate policies and deliver services;

- respect for human rights and the rule of law (individual and group rights and security, framework for economic and social activity, and participation).

Critically important goals, but difficult to achieve, especially in today's complex and rapidly changing world. Almost every function of national government, be it security, economic management, the provision of infrastructure and social services, or the establishment of appropriate legal and regulatory frameworks, has become more complex and more demanding at the same time as the ability of the state to fulfil these functions has declined. The emergence of a global economy, for example, is simultaneously making it more difficult than ever before for governments to control their national economies, but more important than ever before for them to provide an enabling environment for competitive markets and industries, and new learning and employment opportunities for citizens who are facing social dislocation and economic insecurity as a result of the same global economy. It will be impossible for the state to achieve its increasingly complex balancing act without drawing on the skills, resources and capacities of:

- **different levels of government** – ranging from local government to supranational structures; and

- **non-governmental players** – most notably the private sector (ranging from multi-nationals to micro-enterprises) and civil society (ranging from global NGOs to national citizen movements and local community groups)

It is increasingly apparent that there are many functions which national governments can effectively decentralise to the local level and others that are more efficiently and effectively carried out at the regional or even global level. Few countries, however, are close to getting the balance right between these different levels of government, and the process in most is likely to be fraught with political and practical obstacles, driven by a combination of vested interests, managerial and organisational challenges, and fear of change.

Likewise with the growing need for national governments to reach out to business and civil society organisations. This is being driven in large part by the fact that firstly, the collective power of people to shape their own future is greater now than at probably any time in history, and secondly, a growing level of resources are now controlled by the private sector. As a result, these two groups of actors are starting to play an important role in shaping and implementing local, national and international agendas; agendas which have previously been in the domain of government. The following pages look at the implications for national governance resulting from the evolving power of these two groups.

a) The emerging power of private enterprise

As far as the private sector is concerned, the dominant players in terms of national governance issues are the **multinational corporations** (MNCs), which have shown remarkable growth over the past ten years. There are now some 37,000 MNCs, controlling over 200,000 foreign affiliates worldwide. According to the UN, between 1980 and 1992 their sales more than doubled from US$2.4 trillion to US$5.5 trillion. As a group they control over a third of the world's productive assets, although they only employ around 5% of the global workforce, given their concentration in capital-intensive industries. The individual sales of some of these companies outstrip the GDP of many developing and developed countries. GM, for example, has revenues greater than the GDP of Indonesia and Norway, and only 30 countries have national GDPs higher than the 1995 revenues of the world's ten largest companies. The global marketing and production reach of many of these companies is also vast. Citibank, for example, operating in more than 95 countries, has trading rooms around the globe handling customer transactions and trading in millions of dollars in foreign exchange 24 hours a day; Coca-Cola, in 1995 sold 203.2 billion cans of coke in over 195 countries, and the "multi-local" company ABB employs over 200,000 people (the vast majority of them local nationals) in production and distribution plants in some 140 countries.

Three of the key issues in the debate on global corporations and national governance revolve around: the monitoring and control of corporate activities and ethics when they transcend national borders; the extent to which corporations should be expected to take on broader societal responsibilities normally shouldered by governments, such as building and running schools, roads and other forms of infrastructure where government cannot or will not take on the responsibility themselves; and the politically sensitive issue of whether corporations should or should not influence the public policy agenda in host countries and internationally.

- **Controlling and monitoring core business activities**: In many quarters these massive companies are still viewed with great suspicion. There is much debate in both governmental and NGO circles about if, and how, their activities should be monitored and controlled. And how they can be made more accountable. A growing number of the world's leading companies have joined this debate, and some have agreed to adhere to voluntary guidelines or Codes of Conduct, either developed by the company itself or by external organisations, as will be discussed in a later section. There is little doubt however, that the global economic system which these companies are a part of, is increasingly beyond the control of individual governments, or for that matter groups of governments. To blame the multi-nationals for this however, as a number of critics do, misses the point that they too are striving to understand how they manage and govern their activities in the new system and how business ethics can be properly applied to emerging markets. Whilst it tends to be the "cowboy capitalists", the abuses of corporate power and the "greed is good" stories that hit the media headlines, more and more business leaders are well aware of the challenges of responsibly managing their large, and increasingly decentralised enterprises in a fast moving, global environment.

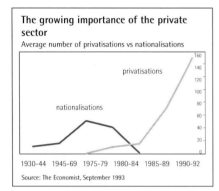

The growing importance of the private sector
Average number of privatisations vs nationalisations

privatisations

nationalisations

1930-44 1945-69 1975-79 1980-84 1985-89 1990-92

Source: The Economist, September 1993

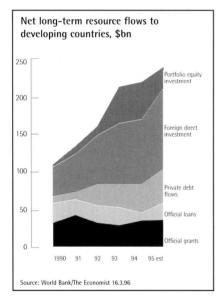

Net long-term resource flows to developing countries, $bn

Portfolio equity investment
Foreign direct investment
Private debt flows
Official loans
Official grants

1990 91 92 93 94 95 est

Source: World Bank/The Economist 16.3.96

Issues of accountability, responsibility and influence lie at the core of the debate on the relationship between the public and private sector, and the linkages between national governance and corporate governance.

- **Broader societal responsibilities**: In OECD, developing and transition economies, many companies are already taking on wider societal responsibilities, and examples of some of these initiatives form the core of this publication. Most business leaders, however, would argue that it is not their role to replace government in these functions, merely to add-value where necessary either for direct business reasons, i.e. if government-funded roads, training facilities etc. are not sufficient to meet core business needs, or for broader social investment reasons, driven by philanthropy or longer-term business interest. Most companies would agree that finding the right balance between public and private roles and responsibilities in social development, not to mention finding the right mechanisms to implement joint projects, is easier said than done, especially in developing countries. It is however an issue that is gaining increased attention, as this publication demonstrates.

- **Influencing the public policy agenda**: This is an especially sensitive area, raising issues such as bribery and corruption, the rights and wrongs of lobbying, and the moral responsibilities of multi-nationals operating in countries with repressive regimes and human rights abuses. While there are certain areas where, under no circumstances, should companies be allowed to influence the policy agenda, there are others where the private sector can play a valuable role in helping to shape the policy dialogue on issues such as the environment, education, training and employment, and many cases which fall somewhere between the two extremes. As with the other two governance challenges outlined above, there is no blueprint for the "right" level of corporate influence on public policy, but the issue is an important one which warrants further analysis.

POSTPRIVATISATION PERFORMANCE: Key Results from 61 Companies in 18 Countries

Indicator	Average change
Profitability	+45%
Efficiency	+11%
Investment	+44%
Output	+27%
Employment	+2,346(+6%)
Divident payout	+97%
Board turnover	46%

Source: The Privatisation Dividend, Viewpoint, Note no 68, The World Bank, 1996

In reviewing the changing impact of the private sector on national governance, mention should also be made of large **state-owned enterprises** (SOEs). These remain important players in many developing countries and raise a complex set of issues ranging from governance and accountability, to economic efficiency and environmental soundness. These issues have been well covered in the World Bank's 1995 report "*Bureaucrats in Business*" and will not be focused on in this publication. Suffice it to say, the commercialisation and ultimate privatisation of many of these state-owned enterprises presents a major political and economic challenge for national governments; one which would benefit from increased consultation and partnership with existing private sector enterprises and business associations. Although the research opposite and other empirical evidence suggests clear economic benefits from the privatisation of SOEs, issues such as competition and managerial accountability are equally as important as privatisation, in promoting economic efficiency. It is also becoming apparent in the transitional economies of Central and Eastern Europe and countries like China, that privatisation programmes must pay greater attention to social costs, such as job losses and the closing or downsizing of corporate social services which were often provided by SOEs under the old regimes.

Finally, although the focus of this publication is on large, mainly multinational companies, one cannot speak of the growing influence of the private sector without highlighting the critical importance of, and need to support, the millions of **small and micro-scale enterprises** which are the main vehicles of job creation and wealth generation in most countries – be they OECD, developing or transition economies. Here again, national governments working in partnership with donors, NGOs, large companies and the SMEs themselves, have a vital role to play in creating an enabling environment and support services for micro-finance intermediaries and small business.

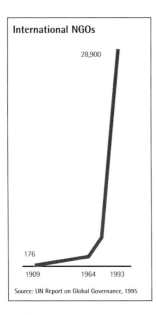

International NGOs

28,900

176

1909   1964   1993

Source: UN Report on Global Governance, 1995

b) The emerging power of civil society and NGOs

In recent years there has been phenomenal growth in the number of locally-led citizen movements and in the number and power of international NGOs and charities. According to the UN, in 1910 there were 176 international NGOs operating in more than three countries. Today, there are over 30,000, let alone the millions of small but often active and highly effective community-based organisations (CBOs) around the globe.

There has always been enormous social entrepreneurship, ingenuity and creativity to be found in local communities, but until recently vibrant civil society initiatives have been impeded in many countries by repressive governments, lack of access to resources and decision-makers, and difficulties in forming networks and communications. Democratisation and technological advances such as the Internet, have enabled thousands of these NGOs and CBOs to access and disseminate information at levels they could not have dreamt of previously, thereby increasing their participation in the national and international debate, and in many cases their power to influence it and take action.

A growing number of national and international **citizen movements** have emerged in recent years, in which business and in some cases governments are also participating, but which are led by individual citizens or citizen groups. In most cases these movements have been motivated by human rights and environmental issues. A few examples include:

- **The Brazilian Citizens' Hunger Campaign** which has mobilised millions of people, is described on the opposite page.

- Australia's national **Landcare** programme (which is profiled on page 196) was started by citizen action and is sustained by the mobilisation of thousands of volunteers, with government and business support.

- **"Clean-Up the World"** is a citizen movement which also started in Australia, but has now spread globally. Australian yachtsman, Ian Kiernan, was appaled at the pollution he saw in the world's oceans on a round-the-world race, and on his return to Sydney, set up a local campaign to clean up the Sydney harbour. After a few years this developed into a national campaign, with an annual "Clean-Up Australia" day supported by thousands of Australians. Today "Clean Up the World" is run in over 80 countries mobilising millions of individuals to clean up their local neighbourhoods, but at the same time to feel part of a global effort. It now receives extensive support from business and many governments.

- The **Greenbelt Movement** in Kenya, inspired by Wangari Mathaai, and the **Chipko Tree Movement** in India are two other well-known examples of individual citizens mobilising hundreds of others to fight a common cause against an indifferent and hostile public sector.

- The Swedish based **Natural Step** movement founded in 1989 by cancer researcher and physician Carl-Henrik Robert is another example of a citizen-led movement which is spreading globally from Sweden to countries such as the USA and South Africa. This visionary initiative is aimed at training business, government, educational and community leaders in natural systems thinking, so that their daily actions support the emergence of a sustainable economy. Many companies, including global players like Electrolux and Monsanto are now working closely with Natural Step to integrate this thinking into their business operations.

To develop an integrated approach to planning, governments must enable and stimulate rather than simply regulate, and leave room for solutions at the local or regional level.

Executive Director

Landcare Australia

THE BRAZILIAN "CITIZENS HUNGER CAMPAIGN"

Citizens in Action for Life, Against Hunger and Extreme Poverty, was initiated in 1993 by a group of Brazilian NGOs under the leadership of Herbert "Betinho" de Souza, the director-general of the Brazilian Institute of Social and Economic Analysis (IBASE) and a key player in the *Movement for Ethics in Politics,* which had been established to fight corruption during the Collor administration. Based on the recognition that nothing threatens democracy more than the existence of extreme poverty, this initiative has become a nationwide mass movement and an inspiration on what is possible through citizen action. Through the self-organisation of locally-based Committees of Citizens in Action (CCAs), millions of people all over the country, from the most diverse social origins and income levels, have participated in designing and implementing thousands of initiatives to increase the volume of human, financial and material resources in the fight against hunger. The campaign has been strongly supported by the media as the result of active collaboration between its organisers and the television networks, radio and press; well-known artists and celebrities have given their time and services; universities have agreed to undertake research in order to tackle the underlying causes of hunger and not just the symptoms; in May 1993 former President Franco established a ministerial-level National Food Security Council (CONSEA) to provide a nonpartisan public policy framework for the campaign, consisting of 9 cabinet ministers and 21 prominent citizens; and a large number of companies, including more than 30 of the major state-owned enterprises with thousands of branches and activities throughout the country, have supported the establishment of CCAs in the workplace. Banco do Brasil, for example, has had some 2,000 employee committees involved in the campaign. Some companies have offered under-utilised land for community food programmes, many others have donated products, time and financial resources. The greatest strength of the movement, its decentralised character based on self-organisation and local accountability, is an impediment to accurate assessment of its overall results. It is practically impossible to calculate the vast amount of resources which have been mobilised by the campaign to fight hunger, not to mention the broader impacts of attitudinal change and self-motivation. However, a 1994 survey by IBOPE (one of Brazil's largest polling institutions), showed that among people who were 16 years older or more, 62% of the population were informed about the campaign against hunger; 32% claimed to be participating or contributing to it in some form; and 11% were members of a CCA. In 1994 a second priority was added to the campaign – the drive for jobs – and in 1995 a third priority – access to land – both seen as critical factors underpinning poverty alleviation. President Cardosa has also established a new social action programme and citizens council to support the movement called the Comunidade Solidaria.

At the international level, the emergence of increasingly professional and powerful **non-governmental organisations** with a global reach has been another recent and important development. Although organisations such as the Red Cross have long had a global presence, there are now others which are establishing communications networks and delivery capabilities to match those of both multinational corporations and international donor agencies. They include organisations such as Greenpeace, The World Wide Fund for Nature, Oxfam, CARE International, Friends of the Earth, World Vision, AIESEC, and Save the Children.

Sometimes these organisations are mobilising their networks – of people, funds and technology – to confront government and/or big business. At others they are collaborating with government agencies and companies, and in many cases the same NGO is collaborating, or at least consulting with government and business on certain issues, and confronting them on others – Greenpeace providing a good example of this. The key point is that these organisations are increasingly capable of meeting both governments and large corporations on a "level playing field" which has critical implications for both national and corporate governance.

What do these other players mean for the role of government? The changing role of the state vis á vis other levels of government and other sectors of society, is an increasingly complex subject and one which requires greater analysis and attention. Despite some predictions that state-led governance is becoming irrelevant and/or ineffective, national governments are likely to continue playing a key role in guiding, catalysing, enabling and facilitating critical functions in society, even if more and more of these functions are actually delivered through the level of local government, supranational institutions, and/or non-governmental and private sector organisations. National governance in the 21st Century will require at the very least, increased consultation, and in many cases totally new forms of public-private partnership.

Down an unpaved side street in La Paz, Miguel
Gonzalez is running his mini-multinational
from the ground floor of his simple home. He
proudly describes his small graphics design
company as being, "part of the international
economy" and has every reason to do so. His
machinery and 90% of his raw materials are
imported – from France, Germany, the United
States, Brazil, Switzerland, and Japan. An Apple
Macintosh computer and laser printer have
pride of place in the bedroom, which doubles
as his office and design room. His customer list
includes the local subsidiaries of companies
such as VISA, Mastercard, Hansa-Siemens,
Toyota, Bosch and SONY. He got his initial
experience working for Coca-Cola, and started
his business with less than US$500, when the
country's largest beer company gave him his
first break, with a job of work and an advance
payment. FUNDES, a private organisation
headquartered in Switzerland, but operating
throughout Latin America to support small-
scale entrepreneurs, gave him his next loan.
Today he is part of the global business
community and a member of the burgeoning,
prosperous middle-class which is spanning the
globe – creating new markets and new
consumers.

Far removed from the streets of La Paz, New
Yorker Gerald Latymer has just become one of
several thousand of his colleagues to be made
redundant by the large multinational company
which has employed him for his entire working
life. A multinational company that could well
be one of Miguel Gonzalez's next clients as it
increases its level of operations and
investments in countries throughout Latin
America, Asia and the former communist
block. For Gerald, the future holds retraining,
uncertainty, the prospect of long-term
unemployment and a decline in his family's
standard of living.

In a chaotic colourful street in Nairobi, Faith
Kurmakini is selling fruit, in competition with
dozens of others who like her have come to
the city from rural homes where they can no
longer sustain a livelihood. She has seen the
large billboards advertising cars and mortgages
and soap. But she can't read them and even if
she could, she couldn't afford them.

(ii) NATIONAL COMPETITIVENESS REQUIRES PARTNERSHIP

The highly competitive, increasingly global economy has many faces. A few of them are described opposite; real people in real situations, who are either benefiting from economic change, facing increased uncertainty and potential hardship as a result of it, or still totally marginalised from it. Most policy-makers and business leaders agree that globalisation, liberalisation and privatisation are creating losers as well as winners; costs as well as benefits. Where the disagreement begins, is on the severity and allocation of the costs, and on the long-term prospects for those that have been adversely impacted by the drive for global competitiveness, such as Gerald Latymer, and those that are still excluded from the opportunities of the global economy, such as Faith Kurmakini. There are many eminent academics and policy-makers who believe that economic globalisation and increased competition have had, and continue to have, unacceptable and unsustainable social and environmental costs. Others believe that these processes are ultimately the ally, not the enemy of social progress, even though there may be human costs associated with the period of transition.

The more hopeful school of thought is illustrated by The European Commission's Competitiveness Advisory Group (CAG), a group of fourteen prominent Europeans drawn from industry, trade unions, academia and government. The passage below is taken from their first report to the President of the European Commission, Prime Ministers and Heads of State, and reflects the thinking of similar cross-sector advisory groups around the world:

> "Competitiveness is at times perceived as something of an obsession, undermining national cultures, displacing jobs, dividing peoples, encouraging social dumping by low-wage countries on more advanced nations. Far from all this, to the Competitiveness Advisory Group, competitiveness must be seen in its true light. Competitiveness implies elements of productivity, efficiency, profitability. But it is not an end in itself or a target. It is a powerful means to achieve rising standards of living and increasing social welfare – a tool for achieving targets. Globally, by increasing productivity and efficiency in the context of international specialisation, competitiveness provides the basis for raising peoples' earnings in a non-inflationary way. It increases value-added and growth potential, stimulating not only resource-saving innovation, but investment to expand capacity and to create jobs as well. Economic competition is thus the ally, not the enemy, of social dialogue."

European Competitiveness Advisory Group (CAG), June 1995

Less hopeful assessments point to the corporate downsizing, restructuring, takeovers, rising unemployment and inequality in countries which are struggling to be internationally competitive, and seriously question whether these are merely short-term transition costs or more alarming and systemic long-term trends. They fear the latter and argue that these trends will continue to perpetuate inequality, leading to a situation where the world is no longer divided simply along a geographic-based "third world-first world" axis of nation-states, but increasingly along a far more complex class-based "rich world-poor world" axis, where a global educated elite transcend national borders and cultures, sharing more in common with each other than with the poor and marginalised communities in their own countries. In the long run such a scenario would be socially and politically unsustainable. Writing on the subject of workers in the world economy in the June 1996 edition of *Foreign Affairs*, Ethan Kapstein, Director of Studies at the Council on Foreign Relations states: "The world may be

> **Consultative mechanisms between government and the private sector are proving to be an important means to generate clarity, focus and support for market reform. Consultation is hard and active work, but its rewards are manifold. Reforms can proceed faster and with greater consistency, once the combined effort and political capital of public and private sectors unite behind them.**
>
> Competition & Strategy Note 2
> The World Bank, 1996

moving inexorably toward one of those tragic moments that will lead historians to ask, why was nothing done in time?" Writing in the British magazine *Prospect* in July 1996, academic David Marquand asks: "will we have to chose between the free market and the free society?" They are not alone. More and more organisations and people are asking these questions, from the World Economic Forum to decision-makers and advisors in the public and private sector, especially in OECD countries, but also in the world's transitional and developing economies.

This tension between the drive for economic competitiveness and the maintenance of social cohesion lies at the heart of the debate on governance and on the shifting roles of government, business and civil society. It is a tension which is unlikely to disappear and there are few certainties about the outcome, other than the following:

- **Governments cannot tackle it alone.** There is a growing need for public-private partnership and the development of an enterprise culture in which private companies and business associations are co-operative as well as competitive, and capable of building local linkages and wealth, as well as global linkages and wealth. The increased attention being paid to cluster-based strategies for economic development and competitiveness illustrate this point. Research by the World Bank and others on industrial clusters in countries such as Germany, the USA, Italy, Malaysia, Colombia and Morocco, indicate that they can facilitate entrepreneurial networking and learning, enhance the relationships between public and private institutions, assist small and medium enterprises in benefiting from economies of scale, and provide joint resources for local education, training and community development.

- **Competitiveness is about much more than economics.** The determinants of competitiveness and the impacts that it will have on a society, are a complex mix of tangible and intangible factors which bridge the disciplines of macro- and micro-economics, management and organisation theory, public policy and the social sciences. In particular: a country's social infrastructure is equally as important to achieving competitiveness as its physical and economic infrastructure; and human performance – based on factors such as education, skills, knowledge, attitudes, entrepreneurship, creativity and health – is an increasingly critical component of economic performance.

The challenge for governments and business leaders everywhere is:

- to try and minimise the social costs of economic change;

- to spread the burden of adjustment so that it is not shouldered almost exclusively by the poor, the unemployed and the marginalised;

- to encourage social entrepreneurship, community enterprise, small and micro-enterprises and the strengthening of value chains in local economies; and

- to make the necessary investments in human development and social infrastructure that will facilitate lifelong learning, creativity, adaptability and greater equality of opportunity for as many people as possible, in a way that meets both social and competitiveness objectives.

None of these are easy to achieve. One thing, however, is certain. They will be close to impossible without public-private partnership. In today's world, no sector – government, business or civil society – controls on their own sufficient access to the different types of resources and capacities needed to achieve national competitiveness and social cohesion.

Competitiveness needs partnerships

The IMD's 1996 World Competitiveness Report defines competitiveness as: the ability of a country to create added value and thus increase national wealth by managing assets and processes, attractiveness and aggressiveness, globality and proximity, and by integrating these relationships into an economic and social model. It analyses the competitiveness of 26 OECD countries and 26 newly industrialised and emerging market economies against the eight factors illustrated below

Every single one of these eight factors is enhanced by the quality and extent of the partnerships in a country. These include not only public-private partnerships, and not only economic or commercially-driven partnerships, but multi-stakeholder partnerships at every level of society that help to determine the political, social, cultural and environmental strengths and opportunities of a country, and which ultimately underlie its economic strengths and opportunities.

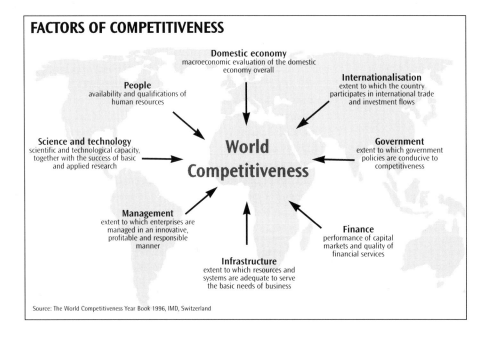

FACTORS OF COMPETITIVENESS

Domestic economy
macroeconomic evaluation of the domestic economy overall

People
availability and qualifications of human resources

Internationalisation
extent to which the country participates in international trade and investment flows

Science and technology
scientific and technological capacity, together with the success of basic and applied research

World Competitiveness

Government
extent to which government policies are conducive to competitiveness

Management
extent to which enterprises are managed in an innovative, profitable and responsible manner

Finance
performance of capital markets and quality of financial services

Infrastructure
extent to which resources and systems are adequate to serve the basic needs of business

Source: The World Competitiveness Year Book 1996, IMD, Switzerland

As the following statements illustrate, there is growing recognition that neither government nor business can achieve economic competitiveness on their own:

Government has an important influence on national competitive advantage, though its role is inevitably partial. Government policy will fail if it remains the only source of national competitive advantage. Successful policies work in those industries where underlying determinants of national advantage are present and where government reinforces them. Government, it seems, can hasten or raise the odds of gaining competitive advantage (and vice versa) but lacks the power to create advantage itself.

Michael Porter, The Competitive Advantage of Nations

A close and constructive partnership between government, business, labour and the broader community will be necessary to ensure the adoption of a coherent approach, geared for both development and competitiveness. This will translate across many different institutions and issues, including human resource development, technological capacity-building, small-enterprise development and industrial relations....Co-operation and co-determination will be essential.

Building a Winning Nation, The Consultative Business Movement, South Africa, 1994

The European Competitiveness Advisory Group is convinced that the creation of a learning society will be good for competitiveness. Key to the development of the learning society are the efforts of education institutions, but also of corporate management and the social partners working together.

Second European Competitiveness Report, December 1995

The competitiveness of a nation depends on many factors, almost all of which can be tackled most effectively by partnership between government, business and individuals.

Competitiveness: Creating the Enterprise Centre of Europe The British Government's White Paper on Competitiveness, 1996

1.3 Four types of capital: foundations of national wealth

Most definitions of sustainability imply that per capita wealth, broadly defined, should not decline. Surprisingly, no measures of wealth exist – despite the fact that much of economics, in theory and historically, is about the formation and distribution of wealth.

Monitoring Environmental Progress, The World Bank, 1995

One of the core messages that comes out of the debate on sustainable development, national governance and competitiveness is:

> The need to find new ways to measure national wealth which reflect more accurately the fact that societal well-being is based not only on economic growth, but also on human capabilities, ecological sustainability and social cohesion.

The World Bank and UNDP are two of a number of institutions currently undertaking pioneering work to develop such methods.

Ismail Serageldin, the World Bank's Vice President of Environmentally Sustainable Development (ESD), summarises the challenge as follows: "To get to the heart of the concept of sustainability we must expand our understanding of capital to include more than man-made capital as conventionally defined and accepted in the economic literature, to include other forms of capital that are every bit as important to our individual and collective well-being as man-made capital. There are at least four kinds of capital: man-made (the one usually considered in financial and economic accounts); natural capital (as discussed in many works of environmental economics); human capital (investments in education, health and nutrition of individuals) and social capital (the institutional and cultural basis for a society to function)." [1]

Three advances in this field which are particularly worthy of note are as follows:

(i) The World Bank's ground-breaking research on developing measures for a nation's productive wealth which encompass natural and human capital, as well as economic capital.

- According to the Bank's assessment of 192 countries, produced assets (man-made capital) represent only 16 percent to 20 percent of the wealth of most of the countries studied [2]. Astonishingly, with the exception of some raw material exporting countries, the value of human resources is equal to, or exceeds, both natural capital and produced assets combined, accounting on average for 64% of national wealth. Not only does this finding give credence to the growing consensus that development is best achieved by investing in people, but it also raises a major challenge for national governments the world over who, with a few exceptions, measure their wealth and focus their economic policies almost exclusively on measures of financial and produced assets.

- The findings also emphasise the fact that different types of capital are partially complements and partially substitutes for each other, and that sustainability does not require leaving to the next generation exactly the same amount and type of natural capital, but can involve the substitution of one type of capital for another. On this logic it will be worthwhile in certain cases to reduce some natural capital, such as the amount of oil in the ground, to invest in increasing human resources, by educating girls for example.

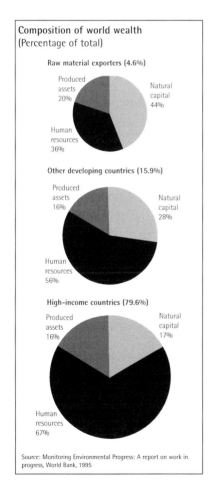

Composition of world wealth
(Percentage of total)

Raw material exporters (4.6%)

Produced assets 20%
Natural capital 44%
Human resources 36%

Other developing countries (15.9%)

Produced assets 16%
Natural capital 28%
Human resources 56%

High-income countries (79.6%)

Produced assets 16%
Natural capital 17%
Human resources 67%

Source: Monitoring Environmental Progress: A report on work in progress, World Bank, 1995

> The concept of human development is much deeper and richer than what can be captured in any composite index or even by a detailed set of statistical indicators. Yet is useful to simplify a complex reality – and that is what the HDI sets out to do. It is a composite index of achievements in basic human capabilities in three fundamental dimensions – a long and healthy life, knowledge and a decent standard of living. Three variables have been chosen to represent these dimensions – life expectancy, education attainment and income.
>
> The Human Development Report,
> UNDP, 1996

The World Bank emphasises that the measures underpinning this research are based on very crude estimates for individual country wealth measures, and that their numbers are only first approximations. Although they are likely to change, and although the Bank will not defend any individual country estimate without more in-depth analysis, it does not expect the overall regional patterns to change that much, and it is these overall patterns that are worthy of note. The Bank is also conscious of the numerous operational problems of measurement and evaluation which this initial research reflects and the fundamental limitation of equating people's well-being with the monetary value of their capital. Despite these *caveats*, this research is a pioneering step in the journey towards measuring the "true" wealth of nations and it sends an exciting and challenging message to the world's policy-makers and wealth-creators.

(ii) UNDP's Human Development Index and Human Development Report

In 1990, the United Nations Development Programme produced their first annual Human Development Report and launched the Human Development Index (HDI). Developed as a new way to measure human development and to assess national wealth using a statistic other than GNP, the HDI is a composite of three basic components of human development: *longevity* (which is measured by life expectancy); *knowledge* (which is measured by a combination of adult literacy and mean years of schooling); and *standard of living* (which is measured by purchasing power, based on real GDP per capita adjusted for the local cost of living – purchasing power parity). All three indicators are reduced to a basic measuring rod by setting minimum and maximum values for each dimension, which are reduced to a scale between 0 and 1; measuring a country's achievement in terms of the relative distance of each indicator from the desired goal; and taking a simple average of the three results. The result is that every country has a figure between 0 and 1 illustrating how far is has to travel to reach the maximum value of the HDI and allowing for intercountry comparisons. For example, the minimum adult literacy rate is 0% and the maximum 100%, so the adult literacy component for a country with an adult literacy rate of 75% would be 0.75. The minimum life expectancy set by the HDI is 25 years and the maximum is 85 years, so the longevity component of a country where life expectancy is 55 years, would be 0.5. These two figures, together with figures for income and schooling would then be averaged to come up with a single HDI for that country.

In every year since its introduction the HDI has been refined and enhanced to add extra dimensions and accommodate suggestions from policy makers and academics. Since 1993, for example, disaggregated HDIs have been developed for selected countries (such as Brazil, China, Egypt, India, Malaysia, Mexico, Nigeria, South Africa, Turkey, the Philippines and the United States) to highlight different levels of human development between different regions, racial and ethnic groups. In 1995, a gender-related development index was also introduced in order to adjust the HDI for gender inequality.

The HDI, and the comprehensive Human Development Report which accompanies it every year, offers a useful alternative to GNP for (a) measuring the socio-economic progress of nations; and (b)facilitating comparisons of human progress within certain nations and between them. Analysing the relationship between a country's HDI and its GDP is also useful for assessing equity and the extent to which the benefits of economic growth are translated into improvements in peoples' lives.

FOOTNOTES:

1　Ismail Serageldin, "Sustainability as Opportunity and the Problem of Social Capital" The Brown Journal of World Affairs. Summer/Fall 1996 Vol III, Issue 2, pp187-202

2　Monitoring Environmental Progress: A Report on Work in Progress, The World Bank, September 1995

3　Ismail Serageldin, Sustainability and the Wealth of Nations: First Steps in an Ongoing Journey, The World Bank, July 1996

4　Robert D Putnam, Making Democracy Work: Civic Traditions in Modern Italy. Princeton University Press 1993

5　Robert D Putnam, The Prosperous Community: Social Capital and Public Life, The American Prospect. Spring 1993 p35-42

The World Bank's East Asian
Miracle study found that growth
accounting models could only
"explain" 17-36% of the
difference in growth
performance between East Asia
and other parts of the world. The
unexplained difference is
attributed to factors such as
economic organisation,
innovation, absorption of
technology, and also institutional
arrangements for cooperation
and information exchange.

The East Asian Miracle,
The World Bank, 1995

(iii) Growing emphasis on the role of social capital

Increased attention is also being paid to the importance of social capital in determining a nation's wealth and the quality and effectiveness of its governance. In essence, the concept of social capital refers to the interpersonal relationships and the formal or informal networks and associations that help to build mutual trust, common purpose and a sense of civic community, thereby linking people together in a social compact which makes society more than the sum of its individuals.

Robert D Putnam, Director of the Center for International Affairs at Harvard University, has undertaken a landmark study: *Making Democracy Work: Civic Traditions in Modern Italy*[4], the essence of which is also summarised in his paper entitled: *The Prosperous Community: Social Capital and Public Life*[5] which makes a strong case for the causal relationship between the existence of civic community and the attainment of good governance, and sustained socio-economic development. Putnam describes a civic community as one characterised by active participation in public affairs, equal rights and obligations for all, solidarity, trust and tolerance; a set of norms and values which are in turn embodied in, and reinforced by, distinctive social structures and practices of co-operation. He emphasises the importance of voluntary, horizontal associations in contrast to formalised hierarchical associations (although others also see these as an important form of social capital) and provides compelling evidence that such associations influence not only how states operate, but also how markets operate.

Putnam's thesis on the centrality of civic community is increasingly reinforced by others – ranging from academic research in a number of universities, to best selling books such as Francis Fukuyama's *Trust: The New Foundations of Global Prosperity,* and Amitai Etzioni's *The Spirit of Community.*

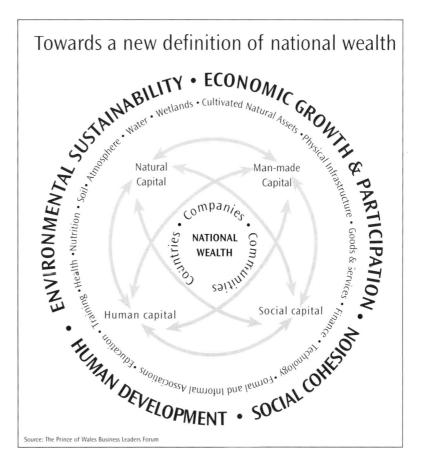

Towards a new definition of national wealth

Source: The Prince of Wales Business Leaders Forum

Differing views on global business in a global economy ...

A force for good... To meet the demands of an increasingly global operating environment, companies are moving towards partnership, teamwork, shared values and shared goals. They are beginning to focus less exclusively on shareholders and on financial measures of success – and instead to include all their stakeholder relationships, and a broader range of measurements, in the way they think and talk about their purpose and performance. It is this kind of inclusive approach which creates the opportunities companies need if they are to achieve competitive success, today and into the future.

The "Tomorrow's Company Enquiry"
United Kingdom, 1995

... or bad? Faced with pressures to produce greater short-term results, the world's largest corporations are downsizing to shed people and functions. They are not, however, becoming less powerful. While tightening their control over markets and technology through mergers, acquisitions, and strategic alliances, they are forcing both sub-contractors and local communities into a standards-lowering competition with one another to obtain the market access and jobs that global corporations control. The related market forces are deepening our dependence on socially and environmentally destructive technologies that sacrifice our physical, social, environmental and mental health to corporate profits. The problem is not business or the market per se but a badly corrupted global economic system that is gyrating far beyond human control. The dynamics of this system have become so powerful and perverse that it is becoming increasingly difficult for corporate managers to manage in the public interest, no matter how strong their moral values and commitment.

David Korten
When Corporations Rule the World, 1995

More responsible and accountable... The transnational, far from being "stateless" as some of the present commentary has it, is "many-stated," tethered in myriad ways to the nations and the local communities in which it operates. As corporations become globalised, they assume more responsibility, not less. The same forces of world competition that produce higher and increasingly common standards of quality and performance, produce higher and increasingly common standards of ethical behaviour.

Henry Wendt
Global Embrace: Corporate Challenges in a Transnational World, 1993

... or less? Corporations chartered in Delaware present themselves as American corporations when it suits their interests and emphasise their "statelessness" when it does not. Alliances struck between competing firms mostly based in the affluent regions of the industrialised world – North America, Europe, and East Asia – complicate the meanings of domestic and foreign, friend and foe, us and them. Twenty years ago the words "foreign capital" evoked images of dark, dirty, and dangerous mines, polluting refineries, airless electronics assembly operations, and plantations. All of these still exist, but they are less visible because they are enmeshed in complex transnational networks of many other sorts.

Richard J Barnett and John Cavanagh
Global Dreams: Imperial Corporations and the New World Order, 1994

2

The Corporate Challenge

The last chapter looked at issues of governance, competitiveness and wealth creation from the perspective of governments and the nation-state. This chapter summarises the corporate perspective on the same issues.

Business leaders, like their political counterparts, are facing a period of unprecedented change and complexity. Geo-political transformation and increasing integration of the world economy, accompanied by the emergence of new technologies, markets and competitors, are creating threats and opportunities for business which were unthought of ten years ago. At the core of these developments are two key challenges for corporate managers:

- **Increased pressures on corporate competitiveness**

  To survive in the new global environment companies are having to increase their competitiveness to satisfy investors and consumers who now have a global "smorgasbord" of options to chose from. This is placing intense pressure on companies to increase their efficiency, their productivity, their ability to innovate, their customer responsiveness and the quality of their products and services. In many cases this has been accompanied by corporate restructuring, re-engineering, downsizing and lay-offs, with the emergence of what many see as "leaner and meaner organisations" which are offering, and being rewarded for, good returns on the economic capital invested in them, but poor social returns.

- **Increased pressures on corporate governance**

  Partly in response to the above, but also as a result of the emergence of more participatory political systems, global communications technology and the flourishing of civil society, there is also growing pressure on companies not only to be more responsive to investors and customers but also to to be accountable to a wider group of stakeholders; a group which in many cases is growing in power and sophistication. Private enterprise is being called upon by both governments and the public, to operate ethically and to play a more proactive role in tackling the increasingly obvious social and ecological "downsides" of global economic competition. Even more fundamentally, people both within the business community and outside of it, are beginning to ask questions about the public role of the private sector and about the indicators against which companies currently measure their results and impacts. Just as a few visionary governments are starting to reassess the way they measure national wealth, visionary companies are reassessing how they manage, measure and present their contributions to sustainable development.

The following chapter reviews the strategic trends shaping the business environment, focusing on their implications for corporate governance and competitiveness, and concludes that multi-stakeholder partnerships are increasingly critical to corporate success. Partnerships not only between companies and their primary business stakeholders – financiers, employees, customers, and suppliers – but also between companies and the wider community, civil society and public sector.

2.1 Key strategic trends: new threats and opportunities for business

Business and society are in the midst of a revolution comparable in scale and consequence to the industrial revolution. Years from now people will want to know what it was like in the great business revolution of the late 20th Century. They will look back in awe at enormous changes – globalisation, the rise of networked information technology, radical new ways of organising work, the emergence of a knowledge-based economy – and how these converged in that historic period. They will wonder how you got through it!

Fortune Magazine,
November 1993

The strategic management challenges which business has started to face over the past ten years are well-known and increasingly well-documented. It is rare these days to pick up a newspaper, or business magazine, or listen to a business leaders giving an interview or speech, which does not make some mention of the dramatic changes facing the corporate world and their associated opportunities and challenges. What is less well-documented is how these changes are not only increasing the competitive pressures on business, but also the societal pressures.

Probably more than at any other time in history, the business community – especially in OECD countries – is being called upon to play a more proactive role in reconciling the drive for economic growth, material prosperity and technological progress, with the need for social equity, ecological sustainability and a renewed sense of humanity. Paradoxically, many of the strategic trends which are increasing the competitive pressures on companies are also increasing the need for new and creative forms of co-operation. Trends which are driving companies to be more efficient, innovative, productive and quality-driven are also driving them, albeit less directly and less clearly at this stage, but to be more responsive and responsible to an ever-widening and more demanding group of stakeholders. These complex and interdependent trends are irrevocably changing the world of business and they include the following:

STRATEGIC MANAGEMENT CHALLENGES FOR BUSINESS

1 Globalisation and/or regionalisation of economic relationships, resulting in new forms and sources of alliance and competition at the same time;

2 Unprecedented technological change, in the field of communications and information technology, as well as in other areas;

3 The growing importance of new markets, especially those in the emerging and transition economies, tempered by the fragility of their social, political and ecological systems;

4 Dramatic restructuring of organisations and work, in ex-communist, OECD and certain developing countries, sending out the clear message that there will be few – if any – jobs for life, and raising fundamental questions about the future of work as we currently know it;

6 Changing nature of the workforce in terms of both culture and gender in many countries;

5 Growing acceptance of the importance of entrepreneurship and of small-scale and micro-enterprise as the driving forces of wealth and employment creation;

7 Transition from an industrial society to a knowledge society, especially in the OECD countries, but also in economically significant sectors of transition and developing countries;

8 Increasing demands of a growing range and sophistication of stakeholder groups, including "traditional" core business stakeholders such as customers and investors, but also increasingly new and powerful stakeholders such as environmental, social and human rights activists.

It is beyond the scope of this publication to provide a detailed analysis of each of these trends, but some of their key implications for corporate governance, competitiveness and new forms of partnership are summarised in the following pages.

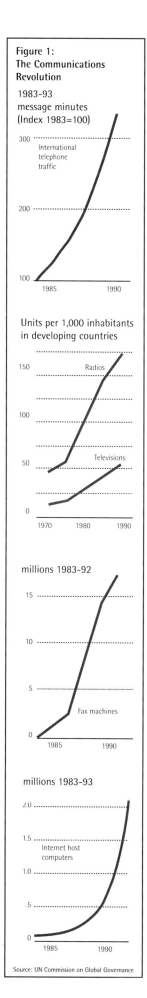

**Figure 1:
The Communications
Revolution**

1983-93
message minutes
(Index 1983=100)

International
telephone
traffic

Units per 1,000 inhabitants
in developing countries

Radios

Televisions

millions 1983-92

Fax machines

millions 1983-93

Internet host
computers

Source: UN Commission on Global Governance

1 Globalisation and/or regionalisation of economic relationships

The production, marketing, finance, human resource management, communications, research and development functions of companies are crossing borders in a manner and degree totally unprecedented. There is a growing perception that this process is making business more powerful and less accountable Corporations are seen to be increasing their global reach and impacting millions of people's lives around the globe, while at the same time dispersing their corporate activities, and the monitoring and control of these activities, across a wide range of different legal jurisdictions, making it difficult for even parent governments to monitor corporate responsibility, let alone less informed and often less interested host governments.

On the other hand, it could be argued that this process of globalisation is making individual companies responsible to more rather than less people and governments. This argument is underpinned by the fact that the activities of many multi-nationals in developing countries today go far beyond resourcing raw materials and/or exporting finished products, which was the pattern in the past. Successful multi-nationals are aiming to be 'local players' in the markets in which they source, produce, research and sell their products and services. It is what the Asea Brown Boveri Group calls "the art of being local worldwide". This requires being accepted and supported not only by host governments, but also (especially in countries becoming more open and democratic) by host communities and the public. This corporate drive to globalise on the one hand and to be a part of local communities on the other, has the potential of forcing business to become more responsible rather than less.

In practice, it is possible to find compelling evidence for both of these arguments.

Another key outcome of globalisation is the growing importance of alliances between companies – often former competitors – with the aim of sharing resources, skills and networks to gain access to new markets and technologies, to achieve larger economies of scale, or to develop new products and services which an individual company would be unable to resource alone. As a result, the language and practice of partnership and co-operation is gaining increased attention at the heart of corporate strategy, and competitiveness.

2 Technological change

Unprecedented in scope, magnitude and speed, new technologies are transforming the way we work, live, travel and communicate. They are providing new efficiencies and opportunities, and in many cases offering developing countries the chance to "leapfrog" stages in development. This is especially apparent in the telecommunications industry, which has the potential not only to help these countries enhance their economic growth and internationalise their economies, but also to help promote social cohesion and development as it allows the population to communicate, to work together and to share information, skills and knowledge. The graphs in Figure 1 opposite illustrate the rapid spread of new communications technologies around the world.

Technological change is, however, also leading to new socio-economic threats and ethical dilemmas. These include: the loss of jobs in many countries as a direct result of technology substitution; increased inequality as a result of the social and economic exclusion of people and communities who lack the education or resources to access new technologies;

undermining of local cultures; increased security risks due to criminals or terrorists accessing and abusing certain technologies; and a wide range of ethical dilemmas associated with biotechnology. One of the greatest challenges for both business and other leaders in the 21st century will be to harness the enormous potential of technology as a force for both corporate competitive advantage and common good, while controlling and sanctioning its potential negative impacts. A task which will be extremely difficult to achieve, but one which must be tackled.

> *We are being called as citizens and as corporations to new ways of thinking and acting in response to current technological trends. We must achieve greater clarity about what virtues and values we want our tools to serve. We have, for example, the choice of creating techniques that enhance environmental health, enlarge the range of human competencies, encourage personal initiative and creativity, and foster the development of our people. Equally, we can choose technologies that tend toward specialisation, institutionalisation, and centralisation, in which people are little more than accessories.*
>
> *H Maynard and S Mehrtens*
> *The Fourth Wave: Business in the 21st Century, 1994*

3 The rise and challenge of emerging markets

Some of the private sector's greatest commercial opportunities for the future, as well as some of its greatest social and environmental challenges, will be found in the world's emerging economies. The massive strategic shift by private investors into some of these emerging economies is now well documented. Figure 2 illustrates how private sector loans, foreign direct investment and portfolio investment in these markets have rocketed since 1987. The Institute of International Finance predicts that this figure will reach US$225 billion in 1996.

Countries averaging growth rates of 5-6% per annum, with large populations (including a burgeoning skilled and affluent middle-class in several cases), low wage rates and abundant natural resources, are offering production and marketing opportunities which cannot be ignored by business. This is especially the case for certain countries in Latin America and Asia whose real GDP growth is illustrated in figures 3 and 4.

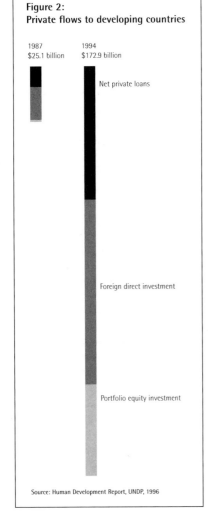

Figure 2:
Private flows to developing countries

1987
$25.1 billion

1994
$172.9 billion

Net private loans

Foreign direct investment

Portfolio equity investment

Source: Human Development Report, UNDP, 1996

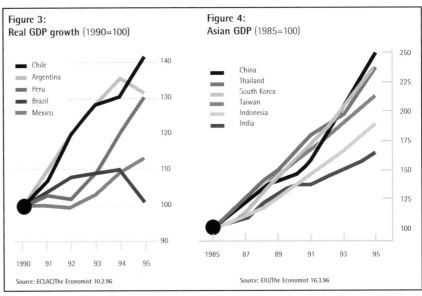

Figure 3:
Real GDP growth (1990=100)

Chile
Argentina
Peru
Brazil
Mexico

Source: ECLAC/The Economist 10.2.96

Figure 4:
Asian GDP (1985=100)

China
Thailand
South Korea
Taiwan
Indonesia
India

Source: EIU/The Economist 16.3.96

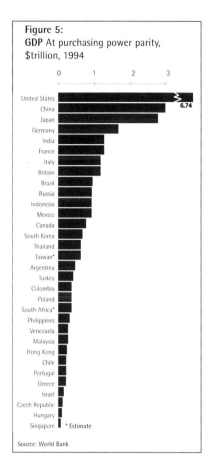

Figure 5:
GDP At purchasing power parity,
$trillion, 1994

United States — 6.74
China
Japan
Germany
India
France
Italy
Britain
Brazil
Russia
Indonesia
Mexico
Canada
South Korea
Thailand
Taiwan*
Argentina
Turkey
Colombia
Poland
South Africa*
Philippines
Venezuela
Malaysia
Hong Kong
Chile
Portugal
Greece
Israel
Czech Republic
Hungary
Singapore   * Estimate

Source: World Bank

Under the late Secretary Ron Brown, the US Department of Commerce established a major programme to focus on what it calls the ten Big Emerging Markets (BEMs): The Chinese Economic Area, India, ASEAN, South Korea, Mexico, Brazil, Argentina, Poland, Turkey and South Africa. The Commerce Department's 1996 Outlook and Sourcebook on these markets highlights the following points:

- Comprising half the world's population, the BEMs are expected to double their share of the world's imports to nearly 38% by 2010 and to double their share of global GDP from its current level of 10.2% to about 20.7% by 2015. In 1992 only four of the world's ten largest markets (based on the World Bank's evaluation of purchasing power parity) were BEMs, as illustrated in diagram 5. By 2020, six of the ten will be BEMs. No other category of markets has such dramatic growth potential.

- The BEMs have growing regional and global political influence and are making significant and rapid progress towards open market economies. Few other countries have undertaken economic reforms on such a broad scale in such a short period of time.

- If just three of the Asian BEMs – China, India and Indonesia – grow by an average of 6% a year until 2010 (well within OECD predictions), there will be approximately 700 million people in these countries with average income equivalent to Spain today. This dramatically expanded consumer market will be matched by plans for massive infrastructure projects totalling well over US$1 trillion in Asia over the next ten years, and at least half that much again in Latin America.

There are however two important caveats to this positive scenario:

(i) While the emerging economic potential and power of these big emerging markets cannot be ignored by business, nor can the fragility of their political and social systems and/or threats to their ecological systems.

(ii) There are still many developing countries, most notably in sub-Saharan Africa, which remain largely excluded from this process.

(i) Political, social and ecological fragility

In the transition economies of Central and Eastern Europe (CEE) and the Newly Independent States (NIS), although communism and centralised economic control have been found wanting, the benefits of capitalism have yet to be proven to large numbers of their populations. This is reflected in numerous opinion polls and the shift back towards the left in a number of recent national and local elections.

The World Bank's 1996 World Development Report highlights the uncertain and still unconvinced public attitudes towards political and economic reform in this region, as illustrated over page in Figure 6.

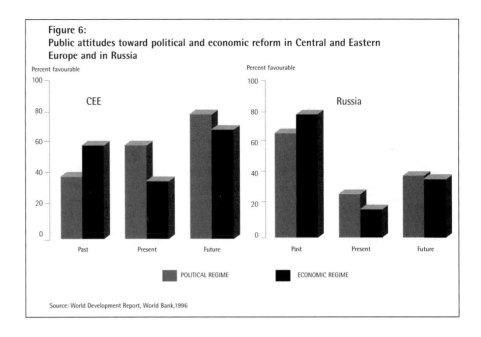

Figure 6:
Public attitudes toward political and economic reform in Central and Eastern Europe and in Russia

Source: World Development Report, World Bank,1996

These attitudes are reflections, at least in part, of rising inequality and poverty in many of these countries, as illustrated in Figure 7 using the Gini co-efficient, which ranges from zero (meaning that everyone has the same income) to 100 (one person receives all the income).

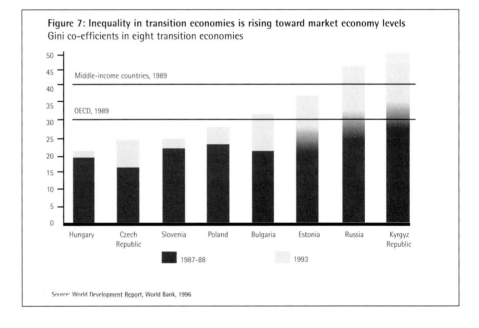

Figure 7: Inequality in transition economies is rising toward market economy levels
Gini co-efficients in eight transition economies

Source: World Development Report, World Bank, 1996

Three billion of the world's people – many of them living in these markets – still lack access to basic education, one billion lack sufficient food and agricultural technology, two billion need primary health-care and two and a half billion lack water and basic waste treatment facilities.

In the emerging economies of Asia and Latin America, although a large number of people are enjoying the material fruits of capitalism, this is tempered by severe and in some cases growing environmental degradation and social problems. These range from pollution levels that are growing at rates faster than the economy in certain Asian countries, to land degradation and deforestation, and large numbers of people who remain living in absolute poverty, especially in Latin America which has the world's most skewed income distribution. Three billion of the world's people – many of them living in these markets – still lack access to basic education, one billion lack sufficient food and agricultural technology, two billion need primary health-care and two and a half billion lack water and basic waste treatment facilities. These needs will never be met without economic

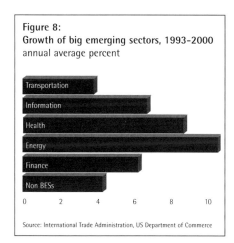

Figure 8:
Growth of big emerging sectors, 1993-2000
annual average percent

Source: International Trade Administration, US Department of Commerce

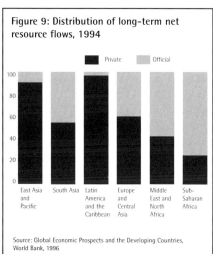

Figure 9: Distribution of long-term net
resource flows, 1994

Source: Global Economic Prospects and the Developing Countries,
World Bank, 1996

growth and dynamic markets, but nor will they met if the benefits of this growth are not shared more widely and produced more sustainably.

In their rush to capitalise on the economic opportunities of emerging markets, multinational companies cannot ignore the societal challenges presented by the forces of rapid political change, economic restructuring, urban growth and industrialisation. Companies operating in the key growth sector (see Figure 8) of: energy, infrastructure, tourism, information technology, healthcare, finance and environmental technology, will have a particularly important leadership role to play, as the way these sectors perform will be one of the most crucial factors determining each country's prospects for sustainable development. If business and governments can invest in these sectors in ways which optimise job and wealth creation and minimise environmental degradation, they will achieve much – but they can only do so if they work together with this as their common purpose.

(ii) The marginalised economies

The emerging markets which are attracting high levels of private sector capital are only a fraction of the world's developing countries. In 1995, for example, some 75% of private flows to emerging economies went to just 12 countries. About 50 countries received virtually no private investment at all. Many of these countries, most of them in sub-Saharan Africa, remain marginalised from the "global" economy and continue to show very low and/or negative growth rates. Figure 9 illustrates this skewed global distribution of private capital flows. Until these economies become more attractive to private enterprise – and this includes locally owned and managed businesses and small and micro-enterprises, as well as foreign investment – they have little chance of reversing this situation.

There are however, even in these countries, a number of large local businesses and multi-nationals (especially in the primary resource sector and food and beverages) which have a critical moral and economic leadership role to play. Working in partnership with national and local host governments, donor agencies and local and international NGOs, they can help to:

- influence appropriate government policy to create a more enabling environment for private enterprise; and

- support practical social, environmental and community initiatives.

As some of the case studies will illustrate, a number of companies are already doing so. Most of them see this as an important investment in their own long term success.

Today transnationals need far more than a developing nation's mineral resources. They need skilled labour, consumer markets, financial and commercial partners and continuing business opportunities into the near and distant future.

Julius Tahija, Chairman of the Board Caltex, Indonesia
Harvard Business Review, September – October 1993

4 Economic restructuring

In both ex-communist and OECD countries, the organisational structures which have characterised ways of managing work are undergoing dramatic change, usually resulting in more horizontal organisations, the downsizing of work forces, and higher workloads and responsibilities for those that remain.

Business leaders have a critical role to play in minimising the human costs of restructuring, including:

- the costs of unemployment (by planning for redundancy, minimising job losses and supporting those who have been made redundant, through counselling, advice and help in finding new work, self-employment etc.) and

- the costs and stress of dramatic change and uncertainty within the workplace – helping employees to understand new approaches and concepts such as re-engineering, total quality management, networked organisations, outsourcing etc.); empowering them to participate in the process of change; and investing in their training and skills enhancement to ensure greater "employability" even if companies can no longer guarantee "lifetime employment".

5 Changing nature of the workforce

Apart from helping employees cope with change, in many countries business managers are also having to deal with the fact that the workforce itself is changing in terms of gender, race and culture. Managing this diversity will also be a key challenge in the coming decades, not only for those companies operating internationally, but also domestic players in many countries.

6 The importance of small and micro-enterprise

There is increased recognition in OECD, developing and transition economies that small and micro-enterprises (SMEs), in both the formal and informal sector, have a critical role to play in ensuring long-term prosperity and employment creation. There is also a recognition that as large companies improve their environmental management it is increasingly these SMEs which are responsible for environmental degradation, often because they lack the technology, financial and managerial resources to tackle it.

Big business – both local and foreign – can play a vital role in supporting the development of a vibrant and responsible community of SMEs. For example, they can:

- assist and advise SMEs through technical, financial, managerial and marketing support with respect to both commercial and environmental management issues, delivered either directly or through intermediary organisations;

- create markets, by giving commercial business to SMEs through supplier contracts, franchises etc.; and

- help to develop an enterprise culture through education and awareness-raising programmes.

Businesses today have more responsibility not only to grow and do well, but to help in dealing with the dislocations and challenges this new era imposes on American workers, their families and their communities.

President Bill Clinton
Between Hope and History: Meeting America's Challenges for the 21st Century, August 1996

It is surely time to assess how we shift the emphasis in corporate ethos – from the company being a mere vehicle for the capital market to be traded, bought and sold as a commodity, toward a vision of the company as a community or partnership in which each employee has a stake, and where a company's responsibilities are more clearly delineated.

Tony Blair,
Leader of the British Labour Party
Speech on 'The Stakeholder Economy'
Singapore, January 1996

Industry is the main player in society… that's why we need to talk to them. Big corporations today have a responsibility that goes beyond their aim to make a profit. The focus is on social, moral and ethical obligations. There is a very progressive agenda. Our obligation is to say to industry "This is what you write. What is it you do?"

Thilo Bode,
Head of Greenpeace International
Financial Times, January 1996

7 Transition from industrial to knowledge society

Knowledge has become strategically powerful and is a key factor in ensuring the continuous innovation so critical to today's business success. It is now generally accepted that in the new information economy – both globally and nationally – the fundamental sources of wealth and competitive advantage are increasingly knowledge and communication, rather than natural resources and physical labour.

This places a growing pressure on the business sector to get actively involved in the education system and to support governments in establishing frameworks for "lifelong learning", in order to ensure that the future workforce has the necessary knowledge and skills to underpin future competitiveness.

8 Increasing stakeholder demands

The other sectors, organisations and individuals which are affected by, and in turn impact, a company's policies, decisions and operations are commonly referred to as its stakeholders. The stakeholder theory of business has been in existence for many years, but has recently come to the fore again on political, NGO and corporate agendas. This has been notable in the Anglo-Saxon countries, but is beginning to happen elsewhere as well.

Stakeholders range from:

- primary stakeholders which have a direct, market-driven and normally contractual link with the company – its investors, employees, customers, suppliers, distributors, alliance partners and competitors; to

- secondary stakeholders, which are other groups in society who are affected, directly and indirectly, by the company's activities and include: different levels of government; local communities; business associations; the media; social and environmental activist groups; education and research institutes; and the general public.

In practice there is an increased blurring of lines between these different groups, with so-called secondary stakeholders developing more direct, strategically important and sometimes contractual linkages with companies.

Also, as a result of economic globalisation, stakeholders are becoming much more dispersed geographically. Many American and British multi-nationals, for example, now face the situation where some 90% of their shareholders are in the USA or UK, but most of their turnover, their employees, their fixed assets, their operations and their goods and services are in other countries – in some cases close to 200 other countries!

In short, companies are facing a complex matrix of stakeholders who are becoming more varied, more demanding, more sophisticated and more international than at any other time in corporate history. As the following sections illustrate, this is raising major challenges for business in terms of: (a)corporate governance and (b)the policies and practices which companies are establishing for managing stakeholder relationships.

2.2 Corporate Governance and Competitiveness

THE CADBURY CODE OF GOOD PRACTICE

1) All listed companies registered in the UK should disclose the extent of their compliance with the code to maintain a Stock Exchange listing.

2) There should be a clearly accepted division of responsibility at the head of a company, ensuring a balance of power and authority.

3) Boards should include non-executive directors of sufficient calibre and number to carry significant weight in the board's decisions.

4) Non-executive directors should bring an independent judgement to bear on issues of strategy, performance, resources, including key appointments, and standards of conduct.

5) The pay packages of the chair and highest-paid director should be disclosed in the annual accounts, with separate figures for salary and performance-related elements.

6) Each board should have an audit committee composed wholly of non-executives.

7) Each board should have a renumeration committee composed largely of non-executives.

8) The directors should report on the effectiveness of the system of internal financial control.

9) The directors should report that the business is a going concern, with supporting assumptions or qualifying statements as necessary.

10) The audit committee should meet with the auditors at least once a year, without the presence of executive directors, to ensure there are no unresolved issues of concern.

(i) CORPORATE GOVERNANCE REQUIRES PARTNERSHIP

The last five years have seen a dramatic increase in the intensity and scope of the debate on corporate governance. Headline-grabbing news of financial crises and corporate collapses such as Barings, Maxwell's and BCCI; public disquiet over executive salary increases when thousands of employees are losing their jobs; "cowboy capitalists" roaming the world's emerging economies with no accountability and no responsibility other than to maximise short-term profit; aggressive corporate raiders; destabilising mergers and acquisitions; institutional investors focused on short-term financial results, often sitting in countries thousands of miles from where these results are actually being created; business fraud and corruption; political sleaze scandals linked to business; impressive advertising claims not met in practice... the list is alarming. It is hardly surprising that public distrust in the reliability and honesty of corporations and their leaders is widespread, as borne out by survey findings. This is unfortunate for the companies, Chief Executives and Boards of Directors that can demonstrate exemplary conduct and openness. It raises two important challenges for them:

- To the extent that the bad practice of the few can harm the reputation of the many, especially within the same industry sector, it is in the interests of the more responsible companies to actively engage in the growing debate on corporate governance in an attempt firstly, to develop frameworks and incentives that encourage ethical practice by all companies, and secondly, to communicate to the public and other stakeholders such as government and NGOs, the good practice that is already happening;

- Linked to this latter point, for individual companies that are exemplars of good corporate governance, there are potential competitive advantages to be gained from building a reputation with as wide a group of stakeholders as possible. In short, good corporate governance can enhance corporate competitive advantage, just as good governance in nation-states can enhance national competitiveness.

Both of these imperatives call for greater levels of dialogue and consultation, sometimes even contractual partnerships, with much wider groups of stakeholders.

The concept of corporate governance tends to mean different things for different stakeholders in different countries:

- In its narrowest definition, it is concerned solely with the relationships between a company's shareholders or owners, its management (led by the Chief Executive Officer) and the Board of Directors. Some of the most promising initiatives in improving corporate governance, such as the Cadbury Code of Best Practice in the United Kingdom, have focused on understanding and setting supervisory frameworks for this tripartite relationship. Even within this "narrow" definition, there are major differences between countries on how the issue of corporate governance is managed and monitored, reflecting different cultures, histories, political systems and ideologies.

Corporations determine far
more than any other
institution the air we
breathe, the quality of the
water we drink, even where
we live. Yet they are not
accountable to anyone.

Robert A G Monks
and Nell Minow
Power and Accountability, 1991

- More broadly, and increasingly important, corporate governance is defined as the relationship not only between these three groups, but also between a company's management and other stakeholders such as employees, customers, suppliers, creditors and the community, who also determine the performance and accountability of corporations, as well as being affected by it. In theory this more inclusive approach makes sense. In practice it is fraught with complexity and trade-offs, even for a company operating in only one country, let alone a company with operations and stakeholders in nearly 200.

In the case of both definitions, the key issues underpinning corporate governance are responsibility and accountability. The challenge facing companies is not only how to manage these two issues, but also how to measure and publicly disclose progress against them. Despite differing approaches to the subject several points are clear:

- The debate on corporate governance is not going to go away. It will become more intense and central to corporate reputation and success, not less so;

- The scope of the debate is likely to widen rather than narrow, to encompass a wider range of stakeholders, a wider range of issues and a wider range of geographies;

- Companies wishing to build reputation and competitive advantage from being exemplars in the field of global corporate governance will need to develop clear ethical codes and strategies, structures and systems for stakeholder management and public consultation, based on an active two-way dialogue rather than the one-way provision of information, which still tends to characterise most corporate external affairs departments;

- All of this calls for new types of partnership and collaboration – both within companies and between them and their stakeholders.

MANAGING CORPORATE GOVERNANCE IN EMERGING MARKETS

Excerpt from speech by Robert Davies,
CEO, The Prince of Wales Business Leaders Forum,
The Royal Institute of International Affairs, London, November 1995
Corporate governance is especially challenging for companies operating in emerging economies where national regulatory structures and monitoring systems may not be well developed, but where multinationals in particular are increasingly expected to follow international standards of corporate conduct. They must deal with issues such as: workers rights and representation, including the issue of child labour; advertising standards and consumer protection; controlling bribery and corruption; the representation of host country nationals in senior management, Boards of Directors and shareholder rosters; dealing with and/or operating in repressive regimes; improving public opinion and trust in business; and following internationally acceptable disclosure policies and practices. How can business leaders address these challenges in the emerging markets? An improved approach could take several pathways:

- Leadership from the top is demanded. Only the Chief Executive and Board can provide the vision and set the standards. Most importantly, those at the top must influence their peers in other companies, countries and cultures, recognising that while individual businesses demonstrate high standards, all business suffers from the bad practice of those who fail. It means playing an active role in industry, business or NGO organisations which are serving as intermediaries in

promoting these values, and encouraging local managers to get personally involved. It also requires engaging in discussions with international agencies and others on development, international security; and issues such as corruption.

- There must be a shift to greater public reporting by companies on social and environmental impacts, broadening the remit of reports on corporate governance – setting out values, measures of progress, reporting on activity and highlighting and rewarding the managers and employees who demonstrate leadership and enthusiasm.

- The crucial significance of building and strengthening civil society, where business and its stakeholders can play such an important and creative role must be recognised – contributing to stability, keeping cynicism at bay and building a society which recognises the interdependence of responsible business and sustainable communities.

- An enabling climate is required through which governments and international institutions underpin higher and uniformly enforced ethical, social and environmental standards.

Corporate governance in the changed global marketplace demands open minds and willingness to collaborate in partnership initiatives. It means taking a lead from the best, genuinely listening to stakeholders and setting standards with other sectors, with competitors and local communities, to provide the essential long-term conditions for good governance which safeguards long-term prospects for business.

WHAT THE "MANAGEMENT EXPERTS"
SAY ABOUT CO-OPERATION AND
COMPETITION

A firm adds value through the distinctive character of the relationships it establishes with its stakeholders – its employees, customers, shareholders and suppliers. That unique set of relationships gives the successful firm a distinctive capability – something it can do which its potential competitors cannot.

John Kay
The Foundations of Corporate Success, 1993

Business networks are not new, but their proliferation and visibility have increased their power... Networks presage the shape of future competition: not country against country, and not just company against company, but groups of companies joined in a network competing with other multi-company groups.

Rosabeth Moss Kanter
World Class, Thriving Locally in the Global Economy, 1995

Many of tomorrow's most intriguing opportunities will require the integration of skills and capabilities residing in a wide variety of companies. Competition for the future often takes place between coalitions as well as between individual firms.

Gary Hamel and C K Prahalad
Competing for the Future, 1994

Increasingly, to be globally competitive, multinational corporations must be globally co-operative.

Howard V. Perlmutter and David A Heenan
Global Strategies, 1994

Companies are just beginning to learn what nations have always known: in a complex, uncertain world filled with dangerous opponents, it is best not to go it alone.

Kenichi Ohmae
Global Strategies, 1994

(ii) CORPORATE COMPETITIVENESS REQUIRES PARTNERSHIP

In today's global and knowledge-driven economy, the ability to co-operate with other stakeholders is increasingly accepted as being critical to a company's competitiveness and success. The idea that competition and co-operation are mutually exclusive management strategies has never been totally accurate, but it is less valid today than at probably any other time. This is especially the case in terms of corporate relations with primary stakeholders such as customers, employees, investors and suppliers, but is also becoming a factor in terms of their broader stakeholder relations, with local communities and government.

Obviously a company's access to and/or ownership of resources, such as financial, human and natural capital, remain important to gaining competitive advantage. The critical factor, however, in today's highly competitive marketplace is "value-added" – the ability to use these resources efficiently and creatively, and to add value to them through processes such as total quality management, speed of response and delivery, product and service customisation and continuous improvement. All of these processes require the ability to organise and integrate different management functions so that a company can anticipate and respond quickly to change. Knowledge and competence are becoming strategic resources for business, and learning, organisational adaptability, entrepreneurship, innovation and the ability to manage change, complexity,and cultural diversity, are becoming the key competencies underpinning a company's ability to respond to customer demands, to add value and to become competitive.

As a result corporate managers are focusing more attention and effort on:

- using "best practices" as an important tool for understanding and benchmarking themselves against the processes, rather than the products of their competitors (on the *how* rather than the what); and

- building better linkages between different functions within their companies, and co-operative competitive strategies between their companies and other stakeholders – including traditional competitors.

Many types of relationship and many types of player

These co-operative competitive strategies encompass not only major strategic alliances, but also a myriad of other relationships – both contractual and informal – between a company and its primary stakeholders. These include joint ventures for specific projects, clustering, the establishment of business parks and the use of mechanisms such as outsourcing, management contracts, cross-licensing, franchising, and research and marketing consortia. It is also important to note that these strategies are not the monopoly of large companies, but are equally, if not more important for the countless small and medium-size companies which are also having to compete and survive in the global economy.

This growing emphasis on the competitive benefits of a company co-operating with its primary stakeholders is reflected in recent work by a number of leading management experts, ranging from Michael Porter and Rosabeth Moss Kanter at Harvard Business School, to John Kay at the London Business School, Kenichi Ohmae, Sumantra Ghoshal and C K Prahalad. A recent book by Barry Nalebuff from Yale and Adam Brandenburger from Harvard, is entitled "Co-Opetition" and building on Game Theory, describes co-operation strategies between companies and their myriad stakeholders as being the competitive force of the 21st Century.

THE IMPORTANCE OF BUILDING RELATIONSHIPS AND CONNECTIONS:
John Kay's Foundations for Corporate Success and Rosabeth Moss Kanter's 3 Cs

The work of John Kay on analysing the foundations of corporate success, and Rosabeth Moss Kanter on the characteristics of world class companies, both emphasise the competitive advantages that companies can gain by building relationships with their primary stakeholders.

John Kay describes a company's success as being defined by its contracts and relationships, and argues that value is added or competitive advantage achieved by the way in which the firm puts these contracts and relationships together. It is the unique way that the firm achieves this that determines its distinctive capability or source of competitive advantage. He has analysed ten successful European firms: Glaxo, Benetton, Reuters, Petrofina, Kwik Save, LVMH, Guinness, Cable & Wireless, BTR and Marks & Spencer, and concluded that they all offer examples of four distinctive capabilities.

- **Architecture** – a network of relational contracts within, or around, the firm. Firms may establish these relationships with and among their employees (internal architecture), with their suppliers or customers (external architecture), or among a group of firms engaged in related activities (networks);
- **Reputation** – which he describes as the most important commercial

mechanism for conveying information to consumers, but accepts that this capability is not equally important in all markets;
- **Innovation** – a process which he argues often involves complex interactions between firms, again raising the importance of relationships;
- **Strategic Assets** – which he describes as being of three main types: natural monopolies; cost structures of firms who have already incurred costs which new market entrants have not; and benefits from holding licences or regulatory approvals which competitors still need to obtain.

Rosabeth Moss Kanter describes world class, cosmopolitan companies as those that can harness and command the 3 "Cs", a set of intangible assets defined as:
- **Concepts** – leading-edge ideas, designs, or formulations for products and services that create value for customers;
- **Competence** – the ability to translate ideas into applications for customers, and to execute to the highest standards;
- **Connections** – alliances between businesses to leverage core capabilities, create more value for customers, or simply to open doors and widen horizons.

To-date, most of the research on co-operative competitive strategies has been focused on the advantages of relationships between companies and their primary business stakeholders – employees, customers, investors, suppliers and competitors. With a few exceptions, most notably in the environmental field, academics and management strategists have placed less emphasis on understanding the competitive benefits of relationships between companies and their secondary stakeholders such as local communities, environmental and social activists, and government entities. This situation is changing as the expectations and influence of these other groups increases and as companies, as well as politicians and community leaders, struggle to understand and manage the linkages between a company's competitiveness and its ability to contribute to the broader development needs of the countries and communities in which it operates.

Several of the world's most respected management experts are starting to address these issues, including Rosabeth Moss Kanter and Michael Porter. Although viewed from the perspective of the USA, their conclusions have resonance for other countries struggling to deal with the social dislocations of economic globalisation, and their central message of increased co-operation between profit-driven enterprises, civic associations and governments has wide applicability:

- Rosabeth Moss Kanter in her book *World Class: Thriving Locally in the Global Economy*, sets out the opportunities and some of the contradictions and difficult questions that are raised by economic globalisation. Writing in the *Harvard Business Review* she argues that, "Some see a basic conflict between social and community interests that are largely domestic or even local, and business competitiveness issues that often are international in scope," going on to say, "to avoid a clash between global economic interests and local political interests, businesses must know how to be responsive to the needs of the communities in which they operate even as they globalise. And communities must

> The new enterprise operates with fuzzy boundaries. Its processes, systems, operations and personnel are interactively and opportunistically linked to those of customers, suppliers and partners, even competitors. We call this new interactive organisation the "interprise". Its competitive advantage lies in creating value by leveraging relationships to the mutual benefit of all participants.
>
> Kenneth Preiss,
> Steven Goldman and Roger Nagel
> Co-operate to Compete, 1996

> Suddenly, the business world is undergoing massive, fundamental change. At the same time as global competition is raising the standards for quality, innovation, productivity and customer values, the scope of what a company can do alone is shrinking. In all industries, in every nation, firms have gained real power through cooperation around the world and the number of such efforts has risen by orders of magnitude within the past decade.
>
> Kenneth Jordan D. Lewis
> Partnerships for Profit, 1994

determine how best to connect cosmopolitans and locals and how to create a civic culture that will attract and retain footloose companies. The greatest danger to the viability of communities is not globalisation, but a retreat into isolationism and protectionism."

• Michael Porter's work is focused on tackling the economic and social distress of America's inner cities, by developing coherent, private sector-driven economic strategies that are supported by government social programmes, rather than led and subsidised by them. He outlines new roles for the private sector, government and community-based organisations for revitalising inner cities and helping to make them more competitive.

• Several of the business-led organisations which are profiled in later sections, such as the Social Venture Network, Business for Social Responsibility in the USA and Business in the Community in the UK, are also beginning to invest time and effort into developing a better understanding of the link between corporate competitive advantage and corporate community investment; as are a number of universities in the USA and UK such as Warwick University, Boston College and the University of Indiana.

• Although much of the work is being carried out in OECD-based institutions, some leading business schools in developing countries are also beginning to address the issue of corporate competitiveness and corporate contribution to development – these include the Asian Institute of Management in the Philippines, INCAE in Costa Rica and The University of Cape Town in South Africa.

There is no doubt however that this is an area which requires further research, aimed at developing answers to the following questions. Is corporate competitiveness best served by a company meeting only its minimal societal obligations of operating within the law and producing goods and services for customers, financial returns for investors, salaries for employees and taxes for governments? Whilst all of these are critically important functions of business, are they enough? In what other ways can business add value to the social, human and environmental capital that needs to be incorporated into a nation's definition of wealth? Are government regulations the only way to encourage profit-driven enterprise to add value in these others areas, and will they not make companies of one country less competitive than those of another which don't face these regulations? What about the role of government incentives, moral suasion and market influences exerted by customers and other stakeholders? And finally, how do all these answers impact and link with corporate competitiveness in a rapidly changing, highly complex and often uncertain global economy?

Where analytical research and empirical testing is still lacking, the anecdotal evidence of examples from around the world suggests that many leading companies, at the forefront of their sectors in terms of competitiveness and reputation, are already making these linkages. Further research will hopefully intensify this type of activity and give it analytical rigour. For now, however, visionary companies – be they big multi-nationals or smaller niche players – are doing what they've always done; looking at the realities they find in their markets of operation and then making the necessary organisational and operational changes, and taking the necessary risks, to respond to these realities. Such companies acknowledge that responding to a wider range of stakeholders than ever before is one of these new realities and that it is up to them to turn this reality into competitive advantage.

2.3 The Four Rs – Foundations of Corporate Wealth

For companies striving to simultaneously achieve both corporate competitiveness and good corporate governance, there are four closely interlinked cornerstones of success:

(i)   Reputation management

(ii)   Relationship management

(iii)   Responsiveness to systems and service needs

(iv)   Resource efficiency and enhancement.

Each of these is equally important whether one is considering the way the company manages its core business operations and its relations with primary stakeholders, or the way it manages its wider corporate governance challenges and stakeholder relations. If a company can manage these factors across all of its operational and support functions in an efficient, effective and responsible manner, it will be well positioned for individual corporate competitiveness and success, and also to make a broader contribution to economic progress, environmental sustainability and human development.

(i) REPUTATION

There is growing evidence, both anecdotal and empirical, of the importance that reputation plays in determining a company's competitive advantage and its long-term survival. Reputation is built on a complex base of intangible attributes such as reliability, quality, honesty, trust, social and environmental responsibility and credibility – which span the whole spectrum of a company's business and support activities. Despite this, and despite the fact that many managers agree that reputation does have value, most companies still adopt a fragmented and PR-driven approach to reputation management.

There are relatively few that have developed a company-wide, integrated management structure, let alone appointed someone with board level access as the corporate reputation director or chief reputation officer. All too often the business units which have a critical impact on a company's reputation, such as marketing and operations, and the support units such as health, safety and environment (HSE), government and community relations, investor relations, public relations, personnel and industrial relations do not work closely together, except when there is a crisis. This approach is beginning to change – most notably in the HSE area, with some companies starting to mainstream responsibility for environmental impacts and innovations to the business units.

(ii) RELATIONSHIPS

Closely linked to reputation are the relationships which a company maintains with its primary and secondary stakeholders – employees, customers, suppliers, investors, competitors, local communities, governments, social and environmental activist groups, research institutes etc. As has already been covered, in today's global economy these relationships are becoming increasingly complex, covering a wider range of organisations, issues and geographies than ever before. In order to respond to these trends, companies need to build more integrated and strategic approaches for

Many of the most exciting new opportunities require the integration of complex systems, rather than innovation around a stand-alone product. Not only does no single business unit have all the necessary capabilities, neither does a single company or country.

Hamel and Prahalad
Competing for the Future, 1994

building and managing stakeholder relations. In particular there is the need to move from one-way information provision to stakeholders towards the more difficult, but increasingly important process of two-way dialogue and genuine consultation.

(iii) RESPONSIVENESS
A company's ability to understand and respond innovatively to market trends, future opportunities and stakeholder needs, plays a key role in building reputation and competitiveness. Linked to this, there is a growing emphasis on "lateral thinking" and on systems approaches, aimed at building innovation around "service needs" or "customer benefits" rather than product specifications. Such approaches often require co-operation with non-traditional partners.

(iv) RESOURCES
Corporate reputation and competitiveness is closely linked to the way in which resources are obtained, used and enhanced. A company's ability to access high quality resources – be they human, natural, physical, financial or informational – and to adopt managerial and technical processes which add-value to these resources in an efficient and responsible manner, will influence the company's cost structure, the quality of its processes, products and services, its environmental impacts, its productivity, its ability to respond quickly to market needs and its relationships with business partners and other stakeholders.

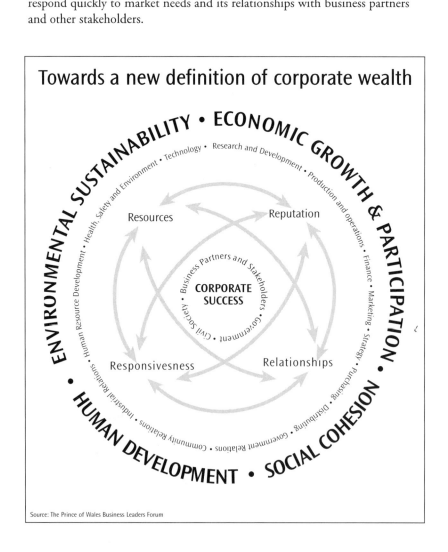

Towards a new definition of corporate wealth

Source: The Prince of Wales Business Leaders Forum

3

The Benefits of Partnership

The two preceding chapters have emphasised the critical importance of partnership between different sectors and different stakeholders as a building block in the drive towards:

- sustainable development at every level in society – local, national, regional and international;

- good governance, at both the corporate level and national level;

- competitiveness, at both the corporate level and national level; and

- a quality of national wealth creation which builds and nurtures not only economic capital, but also natural, human and social capital.

Multi-stakeholder partnerships are not an answer to every problem. Nor are they easy to achieve in practice. Despite the fact that partnership has become one of the "buzzwords" of our time, used by almost everyone from politicians and business leaders to community-based activists, many so-called partnerships are superficial and over-rated – powerful in theory, but complex, problematic and often disappointing in practice. Establishing and sustaining a mutually-beneficial partnership is rarely easy, especially with non-traditional allies. Enormous ignorance and/or distrust still exists between different groups and different sectors in many societies, and even with the best will in the world, there are numerous practical and cultural obstacles to overcome in building partnerships between organisations and sectors which have different characteristics, structures, methodologies and languages. This is the case even within nations, let alone building partnerships across national borders.

However, in the face of the world's increasingly complex challenges and scarce resources there are few other options. It is in the interest of all sectors in society, regardless of their differences, to at least give partnership a try:

- From a societal perspective, successful partnerships can be powerful catalysts for change and valuable mechanisms for delivering efficient, effective and equitable solutions to the challenges of development.

- From a business perspective, successful partnerships can enhance and leverage corporate resources, reputation, relationships, and responsiveness.

The following chapter reviews these societal and business benefits in more detail.

Multi–Stakeholder Partnership
Building Bridges Towards Sustainable Development

One of the major challenges facing the world community as it seeks to replace unsustainable development patterns with environmentally sound and sustainable development, is the need to activate a sense of common purpose on behalf of all sectors of society. The chances of forging such a sense of purpose will depend on the willingness of all sectors to participate in genuine social partnership and dialogue, while recognising the independent roles, responsibilities and special capacities of each.
Chapter 27, Agenda 21

Agenda 21 addresses the pressing problems of today and also aims to prepare the world for the challenges of the next century. It reflects a global consensus on development and environment co-operation. Its successful implementation is first and foremost the responsibility of governments.
Preamble, Chapter 1, Agenda 21

GOVERNMENT
- National, state, local
- Multilateral and bilateral governmental organisations

PRIVATE SECTOR/BUSINESS
- Corporations and multi-nationals
- Business and industry associations
- Small and micro enterprises

CIVIL SOCIETY/NON-GOVERNMENTAL ORGANISATIONS
- NGOs are diverse and multi-faceted, their perspectives and operations may be:
  - Local, national, regional or global
  - Issue, task or ideology oriented
  - Broad public interest or private
  - Small, poorly funded grassroots to large, professionally staffed bodies
  - Individual or networked

Business and industry, including transnational corporations and their representative organisations, should be full participants in the implementation and evaluation of activities related to Agenda 21.
Strengthening the role of Business and Industry, Chapter 30, Agenda 21

Non-governmental organisations play a vital role in the shaping and implementation of participatory democracy. Their credibility lies in the responsible and constructive role they play in society. Formal and informal organisations, as well as grassroots movements, should be recognised as partners in the implementation of Agenda 21.
Strengthening the role of NGOs, Chapter 27, Agenda 21

Source: Partnerships for Sustainable Development: The role of busines and industry. UNEP, Tufts University and PWBLF, 1994.

3.1 The Societal Benefits of Stakeholder Partnership

In today's world almost every function of government can be enhanced by greater dialogue and partnership with other public sector entities and other sectors; whether it is national security, the implementation of sound macroeconomic policies, social programmes and environmental policies, or the more intangible, but critically important responsibilities of good governance, accountability, empowerment of civil society and support for a vibrant and responsible enterprise culture.

Partnerships within government – between different functions and between different levels of government, from the local to the supranational – and partnerships between government and other sectors – most notably business and civil society, including NGOs, CBOs and individual citizens, can be useful both in setting the policy agenda and in implementing programmes.

Three areas of public-private partnership that offer particular potential are:

1 **Partnerships for leveraging resources** for specific programmes or projects – where "programmes and projects" could be either commercial or social or some hybrid, and where "resources" are not only financial capital, but also physical, technical and managerial resources;

2 **Advisory structures** to inform, debate and help to shape the policy agenda;

3 **Joint public-private communications campaigns** to inform, educate, motivate and in some cases, mobilise, the general public around specific public interest issues.

INCREASING EFFICIENCY, EFFECTIVENESS AND EQUITY

Public-private partnerships can help to achieve greater efficiency by:

- eliminating duplication of cost and effort
- pooling scarce financial, managerial and technical resources
- optimising "division of labour" and burden-sharing
- decreasing costs associated with conflict resolution and societal disagreement on policies and priorities
- creating economies of scale
- promoting technology co-operation
- facilitating the sharing of information
- overcoming institutional rigidities and bottlenecks.

They can also help to improve effectiveness by:

- leveraging greater amounts and a wider variety of skills and resources than can be achieved by different groups and sectors acting alone
- accommodating broader perspectives and more creative approaches to problem-solving
- addressing complex and interdependent problems in a more integrated and comprehensive manner
- shifting away from "command and control" to more informed joint goal-setting
- obtaining the "buy-in" of beneficiaries and local "ownership" of proposed solutions, thereby ensuring greater sustainability of outcomes
- offering more flexible and tailored solutions
- speeding the development and implementation of solutions

They can facilitate increased equity by:

- improving the level and quality of consultation with other stakeholders in society
- facilitating broader participation in goal-setting and problem-solving
- building the mutual trust needed to work through diverse, often conflicting interests, towards shared responsibilities and mutual benefit.

3.2 The Business Benefits of Stakeholder Partnership

Investing in stakeholder partnerships, with both primary and secondary stakeholders, can play a valuable role in enhancing a company's reputation, competitiveness, productivity, efficiency, risk management, innovativeness and long-term survival. Such partnerships can range from:

- **commercially-driven alliances and joint ventures**, such as management contracts, out-sourcing, cross-licensing and research and marketing consortia, to harness the opportunities and minimise the costs of entering new markets, developing new products and technologies, and dealing with structural change and global competition; to

- **socially-driven alliances and joint ventures** aimed at tackling broader societal issues such as crime, unemployment, poverty alleviation, environmental degradation, education, urban renewal and rural development, all of which also impact the corporate bottom-line, albeit normally less directly or immediately than market factors; and

- **ventures which combine both commercial and social objectives,** such as cause-related marketing.

A more partnership-driven approach to managing a company's stakeholder relations and community activities, can have the following benefits:

CORPORATE REPUTATION

Fortune Survey:	Financial Times Survey:	Asian Business
Survey: America's Most Admired Companies (1996)	Europe's Most Respected Companies (1996)	Asia's Most Admired Companies (1996)
Coca-Cola	ABB	Singapore Airlines
Procter & Gamble	British Airways	Samsung
Rubbermaid	Nestle	San Miguel
Johnson & Johnson	BMW	Siam Cement
Intel	Royal Dutch Shell	Charoen Pokphand
Merck	Siemens	McDonald's
Microsoft/Mirage Resorts	Marks & Spencer	Acer
Hewlett-Packard/Motorola	British Petroleum	Jollibee
3M	Unilever	Hewlett Packard
Pfizer	Roche	Coca-Cola
Walt Disney/McDonald's	Bayer	Pohang Iron & Steel
Gillette	Ericsson	Hong kong Bank
Levi Strauss	Danone	DBS Bank
Berkshire Hathaway	Air Liquide	Motorola
Home Depot	Philips	Hong Kong Telecom
Boeing	ING	Toyota Motor Co
Marriott	Saint Gobain	Daimler-Benz
Enron	Swissair	Hyundai
Albertsons	Nokia	Astra International
Pepsi Co	Berelsmann	BMW

(i) Enhancing reputation and "licence to operate"

There is clear evidence that a good reputation gains a company more customers, better employees, more investors, improved access to credit, and greater credibility with government. Almost all of the companies listed in the three surveys opposite invest substantial resources and senior management effort in building good relationships with a wide range of stakeholders, including local communities and governments. Of the multi-nationals listed, it is interesting to see some of them also listed in regions outside their home base.

The concept of "ethical capital" which is closely linked to reputation, is likely to gather credence as a mainstream assessment of a company's worth. In the same way that financial and intellectual "capital" gives a company strength in the marketplace, ethical capital accrued over a long period of time can ensure that a company will avoid costs from over-regulation or insurance against legal challenges. The difference between a company with ethical capital and one with an ethical deficit – perceived or real – can even determine their "licence to operate" in some emerging markets.

While governments have the most direct control and legal sanction over a company's "licence to operate", other stakeholders also influence this, for example, workers going on strike and customers boycotting products. Environmental and human rights groups are also beginning to play a greater role in challenging companies' "licences to operate" when they are perceived to be operating in an irresponsible manner or in sensitive areas. This has particular implications in certain developing countries where governments lack either the capacity, experience or motivation to provide a transparent and equitable framework for monitoring corporate governance to acceptable international standards.

(ii) Managing, motivating and retaining quality employees

Companies that work in partnership with their employees to: facilitate greater contribution by employees in decision-making and idea generation; provide safe, secure and family-friendly workplaces; invest in training and education; make a genuine commitment to minimise the social costs of downsizing when it has to occur; and encourage their employees to get actively involved in community volunteering and environmental initiatives, can reap clear human resource benefits in a number of areas:

- Recruiting, retaining and motivating top quality people;

- Promoting trust, pride, staff morale and loyalty;

- Breaking down internal barriers, both between departments and between managers and their staff, thereby promoting co-operation and teamwork;

- Helping staff to develop core competencies and lateral thinking through exposing them to opportunities and involvement outside their immediate job description;

- Making it easier for employees to accept and get involved in cultural change programmes; and

- Leadership training for high potential employees.

(iii) Strategic market positioning

In today's competitive markets, strategic market positioning is critical to success. In the short-term companies can leverage stakeholder partnerships to:

- gain market entry to new markets and countries;

- build or sustain market share and customer loyalty;

- promote and enhance brand image; and

- gain access to market intelligence.

A good overall reputation for quality, reliability and responsibility is important in achieving all of the above, but more proactive companies are also starting to invest in social or cause-related marketing, often in partnership with specific NGOs, and thereby creating more direct linkages between commercial benefits and social or environmental partnerships.

(iv) Improving operational efficiency and quality

Working in partnership with certain stakeholders (such as employees and suppliers) and improving relations with others (such as environmental groups and government agencies) makes it possible to:

- reduce input and transaction costs;

- increase process efficiency; and

- improve the quality of products and services.

(v) Promoting better risk management and access to financing

Companies which have established management systems for consulting and working with stakeholders tend to also develop sound internal control systems for monitoring governance issues and anticipating problems. They are better at controlling environmental risks and they usually have comprehensive systems in place, often in collaboration with local government and local communities, to deal with emergencies if they occur. They are also more likely to be "given a second chance" by customers and other stakeholders when problems do occur, if they have demonstrated a strong and genuine commitment to "due diligence". Increasingly, all of these factors have an impact on costs of capital.

(vi) Investing in a stable society and a healthy economy

Companies with a long-term vision cannot afford to ignore the adage that "islands of wealth cannot survive in a sea of poverty". Crime-ridden streets, marginalised and unemployed youth, high levels of pollution, large numbers of people who are excluded from participating in the market economy, potential consumers who are too poor to purchase goods and services in the formal sector, high levels of illiteracy in many countries, inadequate education levels for employment in the information era... the list is a long one, which affects many countries and which acts as a cancer not only on societal health, but also on the long-term prospects of the global free-market economy, and individual corporate survival. It is therefore in the best interests of business to invest resources in tackling these issues, and there will be long-term corporate benefits in doing so. There are many critics and sceptics, however, who would argue that it is the global market economy itself which is the cancer, that societal disintegration and environmental decline are inevitable outcomes of the current world system. To these critics, any community action by business is merely tinkering at the edges and unlikely to have any real impact on the systemic and structural problems of the global economy.

Somewhere between these two viewpoints individual companies must weigh up the direct benefits to their business, their resource availability, and their moral obligations as "corporate citizens", to decide if, and how, they can tackle some of these issues. There is the real danger of a "free-rider" approach by companies arguing that they cannot be expected as individual enterprises to tackle society's ills and assume that someone else – government, voluntary organisations, or other companies – will take care of these problems. Equally, there is the challenge for companies which do want to make a contribution, but which have very limited resources for doing so. However those that do tackle these issues – either in their individual capacity, or as part of a larger group of companies such as those profiled in Section III – demonstrate that they can help to achieve local societal improvements which **do** have a clear, and often direct benefit to their business – lower crime levels and improved school quality being obvious examples. Over the longer term such improvements also offer the best hope that business has for achieving the type of society in which the market and private enterprise have a central and prosperous position.

II The contribution of the business sector

A vibrant and responsible enterprise culture and a diversified private sector – ranging from micro-enterprises to multi-nationals – is one of the greatest sources of wealth a country can have. The business sector has the skills, resources, capacities and networks to be a valuable partner in development. Apart from operating within the law and contributing directly to economic growth, companies can make a contribution to development by: maximising the beneficial economic, social and environmental "spin-offs" of their core business activities, and minimising the negative ones; undertaking social investments and strategic philanthropy; and engaging in the public policy debate, locally, nationally and internationally. The following section describes firstly, how leading companies are managing these different approaches and secondly, specific examples from around the world of business contributions to development.

MANAGING THE CORPORATE CONTRIBUTION

1. **MODELS AND MECHANISMS**
   - core business activities
   - social investment and philanthropy
   - policy dialogue

2. **MISSION STATEMENTS AND METHODOLOGIES**

3. **MANAGING, MEASURING AND MONITORING**

4. **MOTIVATING, MOBILISING AND MAINSTREAMING**

THE CONTRIBUTION OF THE BUSINESS SECTOR TO COUNTRIES AND COMMUNITIES

1. **GENERAL OVERVIEW**

2. **ECONOMIC DEVELOPMENT**
   Aimed at increasing not only economic growth, but also economic opportunity and participation

3. **HUMAN DEVELOPMENT**
   Investing in education, training and health both in the workplace and in the wider community

4. **ENVIRONMENTAL SUSTAINABILITY**
   Investing in cleaner production and more sustainable patterns of consumption

5. **SOCIAL COHESION**
   Tackling social exclusion, crime and corruption and investing in civil society, social entrepreneuship and cultural diversity

5. **INTEGRATED COMMUNITY DEVELOPMENT**
   Supporting participatory development in urban and rural communities

6. **EMERGENCY AND DISASTER RELIEF**
   Improving emergency preparedness and helping out in natural and man-made disasters

DESCRIBING THE CORPORATE CONTRIBUTION

1 Managing the Corporate Contribution

There is growing acceptance of the central role that can, and must be played by the private sector in supporting not only economic growth, but also wider societal goals in OECD, developing and transition economies. Despite this, even the most outstanding companies are still at the first stages of developing appropriate structures and systems to manage their evolving roles and responsibilities in this new environment. Many more are only just defining these roles and responsibilities, let alone putting mechanisms in place to manage them. A survey of British business managers by the London-based Industrial Society in September 1996, showed that although the vast majority agreed with the modern business mantra that people are a company's most valuable asset, and more than 50% said that ethical standards had become a priority in the past three years, 40% of them admitted that they had never consulted their employees on ethics, or on a range of other major decisions affecting them – and this was despite the fact that 75% of them agreed that maintaining such standards had a positive financial effect. This, and other studies around the world, illustrate a clear gap between what managers know is good practice and what they actually see happening in their organisations and industry sectors.

The same can be said for the practice of public-private partnerships. Everyone is talking about them and although a growing number exist at the local level, formal nationwide public-private partnerships aimed at developing policies and mobilising joint resources for sustainable development are still relatively few. Some inspiring examples however do exist and serve as valuable models.

The following section looks at the management challenges facing companies in this area. It reviews some of the "good practice" in companies which are investing management time and effort to firstly, define their evolving role in society and how this relates to other sectors; and secondly, to establish internal structures and systems to manage this role. It looks at what we have defined as the 10 Ms:

- agreeing on the key **Mechanisms** and **Models** by which a company can improve the quality and leverage of its core business activities, its social investments and its policy dialogue, to maximise their positive benefits to society;

- establishing **Mission statements** and **Methodologies** (i.e. guidelines or codes of conduct) to reflect these objectives;

- implementing internal structures and systems to **Manage, Measure** and **Monitor** these activities;

- developing incentives and capacity-building initiatives to **Motivate** and **Mobilise** both employees and other companies, and to **Mainstream** these issues into the business process, rather than leaving them as "bolt-ons" in an isolated department.

None of these broader societal issues are easy for business people to deal with and not surprisingly there are unrealised expectations and in some cases cynicism on the part of certain stakeholders who remain unconvinced that the world of business is genuinely taking these issues seriously. There is no doubt, however, that a growing number of business leaders are determined to bridge the gap between rhetoric and reality, between good intentions and good management.

1.1 Mechanisms and Models

There are three main mechanisms through which a company can impact its stakeholders and manage its wider role and responsibilities in society. These are:

(i)   First and foremost, its core business activities

(ii)   Its social investment or philanthropic activities

(iii)   Its government relations and its engagement in the public policy dialogue.

The following section looks at these three mechanisms in more detail, highlighting a few of the models which leading companies are using to manage their societal impacts. The diagram on pages 96-97 captures the core elements of all three of these areas, and lists the main business functions through which companies can have an impact, as well as the company's primary and secondary stakeholders.

(i) CORE BUSINESS ACTIVITIES

One of the major challenges facing most companies is integrating or mainstreaming a strong sense of social and environmental responsibility through all business units and functions. At the very least, responsible companies must have systems in place to ensure that their commercial activities are conducted in a way which respects the law of the country in which they are operating. In the case of multi-nationals there is growing pressure, both internal and external, to operate everywhere to the standards and regulations set in their home country. Many are striving to achieve this, notwithstanding the very different regulatory, cultural and operational situations which a company faces when it is operating in 50-100 countries.

Leading companies are moving far beyond this base definition of corporate responsibility. Many of them are establishing systems to proactively address and manage not only their legal obligations, but also the potential impact (economic, social and environmental) of the total business operation on all its stakeholders, with the goal of maximising positive impacts and multiplier effects, and minimising negative ones.

To do this effectively requires an assessment or audit of every business function, including (not in any order of importance):

- **Corporate policy and strategy** – How can this be aligned to the objectives of promoting sustainable development and creating value not only for shareholders, but also other stakeholders?

- **Operations and production activities** – How safe are the company's operational processes and equipment? Is it developing policies and practices to promote cleaner production, focusing on both the inputs and outputs of the production process? What type of quality controls and assurance procedures are in place? Is the company investing management time and money in gaining quality standards such as ISO9000 and ISO7500? What are the social and environmental implications of the products being produced? What is the average product life, performance and packaging requirements?

- **Purchasing and supply chain management** – What is the percentage of locally manufactured components in the company's production process? Are suppliers, especially small-scale enterprises, being paid and

> There is more to our investment decisions than the expectations of profit... Today, a corporation must attend, not only to a single bottom line, but to multiple bottom lines – the social, environmental, political and ethical end results of the firm's actions and decisions. For a corporation has multiple roles to play in society as employer, user of resources, producer of goods, stimulator of consumption. Beyond its physical presence, it has social power and impact. Hence it must accept that there is a public responsibility to being a private corporation.
>
> Andreas Soriano III
> CEO, San Miguel Corporation

on time? How closely is the company working with its suppliers to develop joint efforts towards sustainable development? What type of training and management, financial and information support does it give to them? What types of social, environmental and quality standards does it set and how does it help suppliers to meet these? Are these standards applied internationally? The example of Levi Strauss's Global Sourcing and Operating Guidelines is provided on the following page.

- **Distribution and retailing** – How safe is the distribution process for a company's products? How close is the relationship between the company and its retailers? Is it working with them to improve the information and service given to end-users and customers – not only in terms of quality, but also in terms of social and environmental impacts. Where relevant, is the company making an effort to work with small-scale retailers?

- **Sales, marketing and customer relations** – Is the company offering a fair, safe and consistent deal to its customers, not only in its home country, but in all countries of operation? Is it providing adequate customer information? Is the information it provides through advertising and packaging honest and accurate? What procedures does the company have for responding to and managing customer complaints and consumer interests? How culturally sensitive is its advertising? Other than the obvious "communication" it has with its customers through the marketplace, and their purchase of goods and services, in what other ways is the company consulting with current and potential customers on their needs and interests? Is the company exploring opportunities for social or cause-related marketing, as a way of simultaneously meeting both sales objectives and wider social objectives?

> Social or cause-related marketing is a commercial activity by which a company with an image, product or service to market, builds a relationship or partnership with a 'cause' or a number of 'causes' for mutual benefit. When it works well, everyone wins, the company, the charity and the consumer.
>
> Business in the Community, UK

SOCIAL MARKETING

Social marketing is a 'growth industry' covering a wide range of activities from individual company programmes, to NGO campaigns involving groups of companies, and nationwide campaigns bringing together companies, NGOs, governments and the media. The highly successful IMAGINE campaign in Canada is an example of the latter, where the Canadian Centre for Philanthropy mobilised hundreds of companies to endorse the value of volunteering through the country's television, radio and print media, as well as in the packaging and marketing of their products and services. The model of this campaign has subsequently been adapted in Mexico as part of the MIRA campaign, which is also led by a group of companies.

NGOs such as the Red Cross, WWF, CARE International and WaterAid are some of the many that operate corporate-branding campaigns for fundraising. The Red Cross's recently launched HelpAd scheme, for example, encourages companies to advertise together with other brands that have synergy with their own. Many banks are operating credit card schemes in partnership with environmental and humanitarian NGOs. Companies such as Kelloggs are working with NGOs such as the Cancer Research Institute to promote healthier diets, and supermarkets in several countries are running customer loyalty programmes which provide computer equipment and books to customer's school districts. A number of retailing companies, such as Body Shop around the world, Pick n' Pay in South Africa and B&Q in the UK run in-store educational and awareness-raising campaigns about environmental and social issues. The list is long and growing. This is an area of great potential, but there are dangers for all partners involved if the different goals and approaches used to communicate different messages are not clearly understood by each party, and there is not a sincere and long-term commitment to creating accurate messages.

Levi Strauss & Co.
Global Sourcing and Operating Guidelines

Levi Strauss & Co. has a tradition of over 140 years of creating, manufacturing and distributing jeans and today, is the world's largest manufacturer of clothing. It employs more than 50,000 people in over 40 countries. Over the past ten years the company has been one of the world's corporate leaders in defining, articulating and managing a set of stringent criteria governing its selection of contractors, suppliers and business partners. The company has hired independent inspectors to audit its 600-700 suppliers worldwide, resulting in the termination of a number of supplier contracts and changes in the business practices of others. Levi Strauss has also been a leader in setting and following guidelines for country selection, and has backed these up by pulling out of Myanmar in 1992, and taking the decision in 1993 not to make any direct investments in China. The following two pages describe these guidelines as set out by the company itself.

Levi Strauss & Co.'s Global Sourcing & Operating Guidelines include two parts: the Business Partner Terms of Engagement, which address workplace issues that are substantially controllable by individual business partners; and the Country Assessment Guidelines, which address larger, external issues beyond the control of individual business partners.

Business Partner Terms of Engagement

The Terms of Engagement are tools that help protect Levi Strauss & Co.'s corporate reputation and, therefore, its commercial success. They assist us in selecting business partners that follow work place standards and business practices consistent with our Company's policies. As a set of guiding principles, they also help identify potential problems so that we can work with our business partners to address issues of concern as they arise.

Business partners are contractors and subcontractors who manufacture or finish our products and suppliers who provide raw materials used in the production of our product. We have begun applying the Terms of Engagement to business partners involved in manufacturing and finishing and plan to extend their application to suppliers.

Specifically, we expect our business partners to operate work places where the following standards and practices are followed:

1. **ETHICAL STANDARDS**
   We will seek to identify and utilise business partners who aspire as individuals and in the conduct of all their businesses to a set of ethical standards not incompatible with our own.

2. **LEGAL REQUIREMENTS**
   We expect our business partners to be law abiding as individuals and to comply with legal requirements relevant to the conduct of all their businesses.

3. **ENVIRONMENTAL REQUIREMENTS**
   We will only do business with partners who share our commitment to the environment and who conduct their business in a way that is consistent with Levi Strauss & Co.'s Environmental Philosophy and Guiding Principles.

4. **COMMUNITY INVOLVEMENT**
   We will favour business partners who share our commitment to contribute to improving community conditions.

5. EMPLOYMENT STANDARDS

We will only do business with partners whose workers are in all cases present voluntarily, not put at risk of physical harm, fairly compensated, allowed the right of free association and not exploited in any way. In addition, the following specific guidelines will be followed:

- **Wages and Benefits:** We will only do business with partners who provide wages and benefits that comply with any applicable law and match the prevailing local manufacturing or finishing industry practices.

- **Working Hours:** While permitting flexibility in scheduling, we will identify prevailing local work hours and seek business partners who do no exceed them except for appropriately compensated overtime. While we favour partners who utilise less than sixty-hour work weeks, we will not use contractors who, on a regularly scheduled basis, require in excess of a sixty-hour week. Employees should be allowed at least one day off in seven.

- **Child Labor:** Use of child labor is not permissible. Workers can be no less than 14 years of age and not younger than the compulsory age to be in school. We will not utilise partners who use child labor in any of their facilities. We support the development of legitimate workplace apprenticeship programs for the educational benefit of younger people.

- **Prison Labor/Forced Labor:** We will not utilise prison or forced labor in contracting relationships in the manufacture and finishing of our products. We will not utilise or purchase materials from a business partner utilising prison or forced labor.

- **Health & Safety:** We will utilise business partners who provide workers with a safe and healthy work environment. Business partners who provide residential facilities for their workers must provide safe and healthy facilities.

- **Discrimination:** While we recognise and respect cultural differences, we believe that workers should be employed on the basis of their ability to do the job, rather than on the basis of personal characteristics or beliefs. We will favour business partners who share this value.

- **Disciplinary Practices:** We will not utilise business partners who use corporal punishment or other forms of mental or physical co-ercion.

Country Assessment Guidelines

The diverse cultural, social, political and economic circumstances of the various countries where Levi Strauss & Co. has existing or future business interests raise issues that could subject our corporate reputation and therefore, our business success, to potential harm. The Country Assessment Guidelines are intended to help us assess these issues. The Guidelines are tools that assist us in making practical and principled business decisions as we balance the potential risks and opportunities associated with conducting business in a particular country.

In making these decisions, we consider the degree to which our global corporate reputation and commercial success may be exposed to unreasonable risk. Specifically, we assess whether the:

BRAND IMAGE would be adversely affected by a country's perception or image among our customers and/or consumers;

HEALTH AND SAFETY of our employees and their families, or our Company representatives would be exposed to unreasonable risk;

HUMAN RIGHTS ENVIRONMENT would prevent us from conducting business activities in a manner that is consistent with the Global Sourcing Guidelines and other Company policies;

LEGAL SYSTEM would prevent us from adequately protecting our trademarks, investments or other commercial interests, or from implementing the Global Sourcing Guidelines and other Company policies;

POLITICAL, ECONOMIC AND SOCIAL ENVIRONMENT would threaten the Company's reputation and/or commercial interests.

In making these assessments, we take into account the various types of business activities and objectives proposed (e.g. procurement of fabric and sundries, sourcing, licensing, direct investments in subsidiaries) and thus, the accompanying level of risk involved.

Levi Strauss & Co. is committed to continuous improvement in the implementation of its Global Sourcing & Operating Guidelines. As we apply these standards throughout the world, we will acquire greater experience. As has always been our practice, we will continue to take into consideration all pertinent information that helps us better address issues of concern and update our Guidelines.

What makes top performing companies different, I would urge, is their organisational arrangements. Specifically, they are better organised to meet the needs of their people, so that they attract better people than their competitors do and their people are more greatly motivated to do a superior job, whatever it is that they do...

... What motivates people? In talking to workers, managers, top executives, psychologists, and career counsellors, I found a number of common factors, including the need to feel in control, to believe in the value of their work, to be challenged, to engage in lifelong learning and to be recognised for their achievements. Top-performing companies seem to honour these needs.

Robert Waterman,

The Frontiers of Excellence:

Learning from companies that

put people first

- **Human resource development and employee relations** – Does the company have clear guidelines and management systems for: occupational health and safety; wages and benefits which comply with legal requirements or prevailing national and industry practices; equal job opportunity; working hours; employee privacy; and disciplinary procedures? How effectively are these guidelines communicated to employees? Is the company committed to increasing the economic stake and participation of employees in the company through profit-sharing, employee share ownership schemes and so on? How does the company tackle the issue of child labour? What systems does it have for respecting, and indeed, celebrating gender, ethnic and racial diversity in the workplace? Does it have policies and practices specifically aimed at improving the employment and advancement of minorities and women? Are there systems to enable job flexibility for working mothers and other people who do not work full-time? What rights and benefits do part-time or contract workers have? How much time and money is invested in employee education and training to help develop a person's "employability", even if lifetime job security can no longer be guaranteed in most companies? How do companies deal with the difficult process of restructuring and downsizing in a way that minimises the resulting unemployment, human costs and stress? How closely and creatively do they work with trade unions and labour organisations, not only on traditional issues of working conditions and conflict resolution, but also on issues such as achieving cleaner production standards and joint investments in local communities where employees and their families live? What is the level of information sharing and consultation between management and employees? Does senior management make genuine attempts to ensure employee participation and empowerment in decision-making? Are employees encouraged to get involved with volunteer activities in the community? What sort of incentive systems are there to reward employee initiative and leadership in terms of quality, environmental and social responsibility?

- **Financial management and investor relations** – How is the drive for profitability and growth aligned to corporate governance issues such as: the composition of boards of directors, division of responsibility at the head of a company, pay-packages of senior executives, independence of auditing and renumeration committees, integrity of internal financial controls, disclosure policies etc.? How often, and in what ways, does the company communicate with its investors? How is it dealing with tax obligations on an international scale and what is its position on transfer pricing? How seriously and creatively is the company approaching issues such as full-cost accounting, measuring economic value-added, developing financial and accounting measures for externalities and social and environmental value-added? What is the company's position on bribery and insider training?

Investing in employees

Two of a growing number of nationwide initiatives to encourage greater corporate investment in the well-being and future potential of the workforce, are the UK's Investors in People programme and President Clinton's Principles of Corporate Citizenship. The latter has formed the basis for a series of consultations between the President and corporate CEOs, and the recent launch of an award scheme, *The Ron Brown Awards for Corporate Citizenship*, which aims to emulate the approach of the Malcolm Baldridge Total Quality awards. An interesting aspect of both schemes is the message that government is also an employer, the biggest employer in many countries, and should undertake the same responsibilities to invest in its employees as the business sector. Although these are both OECD-based initiatives, they have applicability elsewhere.

Investors in People

Investors in People is open to all sizes of employing organisations in the UK in all sectors of the economy, including the public and private sectors. It was developed by the government's Employment Department and the National Training Task Force, working with major national business and employee organisations such as the Confederation of British Industry, the Trade Union Council, and various professional institutes and Chambers of Commerce.

The core elements of the programme are based on good practice examples and experiences from the country's most successful organisations – both small and large. Organisations which apply to become Investors in People undergo a process of auditing, action planning and assessment. Once they have been recognised as an Investor in People they can use this fact on all their corporate materials and promotional literature for three years, after which they must apply for re-assessment.

President Clinton's Principles of Corporate Citizenship

Employers and employees must do their part....as they are doing in many of our finest companies – working together, putting the long-term prosperity ahead of the short-term gain. As workers increase their hours and their productivity, employers must make sure they get the skills they need and share the benefits of the good years, as well as the burdens of the bad ones.

President Clinton,
State of the Union Address, January 1996

The President's five corporate citizenship challenges are as follows:

1. FAMILY-FRIENDLY WORKPLACES
Create workplaces that allow workers to be both productive workers and caring and responsible family members. Family friendly policies can range from flexible work schedules, to help with child and elder care, to time off for parent-teacher meetings. Companies that recognise our broader obligations as parents, family members and citizens off-the-job, get more committed employees on-the-job.

2. HEALTH AND RETIREMENT SECURITY
Provide the security that a living wage, health-care and pension benefits can bring.

3. SAFE AND SECURE WORKPLACES
Protect the health and safety of employees through management commitment and employee involvement.

4. INVESTMENT IN EMPLOYEES
Recognise that investments in your employees are every bit as important as investing in factories and equipment. Provide broad opportunities for education and training, both in and outside the firm, for new skills and advancement.

5. PARTNERSHIP WITH EMPLOYEES
Give employees a voice in the workplace and share the burdens and benefits of good times and bad. When restructuring and layoffs are essential to a company's long-term health be open, be helpful, be fair. Productive companies need committed employees.

- **Research and development** – How much does the company invest in research and development? Is it paying increased attention to integrating social and environmental issues into its R&D processes? How much consultation does it undertake with stakeholders outside its primary marketplace to determine the future direction of research and development? Is it establishing R&D operations in developing and transition economies and building R&D capacities in these markets? If relevant, what is its position on animal testing?

- **Government relations** – Are these managed in an open, transparent and accountable manner? What is the company's position on bribery? How does it manage its lobbying activities with host governments and its contributions to political parties? How closely does it work with government agencies to develop sound and realistic regulations for employment, environmental standards, competition policy and so on? What type of input does the company, or its industry associations give to public policy through research, analysis and public-private consultations? Are they establishing and participating in joint business-government advisory groups and joint ventures for the delivery of public goods and services? What is the relationship of the company with local government authorities?

- **Other stakeholder relations** – How does the company manage its community relations activities, public affairs activities and media relations? What systems does the company have in place for crisis prevention and management, especially emergency preparedness at the community level? How open is the company and its facilities to local communities? Does it have formal structures in place for regular community consultation about the company's core business activities?

- **Environmental management** – How does the company manage its environmental impacts? Does it have an environmental policy and management information system? Is there someone with Board level responsibility for environmental issues? Does the company carry out environmental impact assessments for new projects and products? Does it subscribe to any external environmental management standards and systems such as ISO1401 and the European EMAS (Eco-management and Audit Scheme)? Does it report publicly on its environmental impacts? Is this reporting verified by an external third party organisation?

In Norwegian the word for profit is 'fortjeneste' which translates into the words 'for service'. And this is the way we should look at profit. Something that business achieves 'for service' not only to our shareholders, but to society at large.

Erling Lorentzen, Chairman,
Aracruz Celulose

These questions give an indication of the wide range of issues which can determine the societal impact of a company's core business operations; and whether this impact is positive or negative. They also illustrate the fact that good corporate citizenship is a concept which touches every aspect of business performance and is not simply a question of community relations or philanthropic activities – although these are also important as outlined in the following pages.

(ii) SOCIAL INVESTMENTS AND PHILANTHROPY

After managing the impacts of their core business activities, the second major mechanism companies have for addressing wider social, environmental and economic issues is through their community investment or social investment programmes. A discussion paper prepared by the US Council on Foundations in September 1995 for the Corporate Citizenship in Asia conference, defines Corporate Community Investment as:

The non-revenue generating engagement of the enterprise in external relations with social, community or governmental organisations designed to create a benefit to the external entity, or a mutual benefit to the corporation and external organisation.

A large number of companies still do not have dedicated community relations departments, running these activities instead through the public relations or corporate affairs function. More and more, however, are establishing separate management functions for community relations, and/or setting up social foundations. In some cases these departments are "bolt-ons" – with separate objectives, strategies and management systems to the company's core business activities. In others – notably in companies which have outstanding reputations, which have already taken a lead in the area of environmental management, and which are competitive leaders in their industry sectors – there has been a fundamental shift in the way corporate community investment (CCI) or corporate social investment (CSI) is perceived and managed. It is moving beyond *ad-hoc*, and often reactive philanthropy, to proactive impact assessment and stakeholder management more closely aligned to core business objectives. This trend is not only changing the nature of community investment programmes, but is also influencing the management of mainstream business activities.

The shift is being driven by the two apparently conflicting trends outlined in the section on *The Corporate Challenge*, namely: increased pressures on corporate competitiveness and on corporate governance. Global competitiveness is placing intense pressure on business to be more productive, efficient and innovative, and essentially to deliver "more with less" whereas the increasingly sophisticated demands of a growing number of external stakeholder groups is putting intense pressure on business to be more responsive and responsible, and essentially to deliver "more to more".

Therefore on the one hand, the pressure on companies to develop management structures for CCI has probably never been greater; but neither has the pressure to do so in a more strategic, professional, targeted, measurable and efficient way – in a way that gets maximum return for resources deployed (be they financial, human, technical or physical) and which clearly "adds-value" to core business objectives and strategies. Forging partnerships with other companies, non-governmental organisations (NGOs), community-based organisations (CBOs), local authorities, national governments and donor agencies is one of the most effective mechanisms for meeting these dual challenges of delivering "more with less" and "more to more".

As a result of these trends companies are paying increased attention to:

- developing a more **strategic approach to philanthropy** and in some cases removing the term altogether and replacing it with terms such as community investment or partnership;

- creating win-win situations and **mutual benefit**, which offer the company a return on its investment, rather than *ad hoc* charitable donations;

> In many companies there has been a fundamental shift in the way corporate community investment is perceived and managed. In these companies, it is moving beyond ad-hoc, and often reactive philanthropy, to proactive impact assessment and stakeholder management more closely aligned to core business objectives.

- applying the **core competencies** of the business to social investment, especially the skills and energy of its employees, but also products and services, instead of simply making cash donations;

- linking CCI to **mainstream business strategy and interests**, instead of it being a "bolt-on". This is most noticeable in the growing emphasis being placed on education, training and human resource development (which are the major focus of CCI activities in most companies, be they in the USA or South Africa, UK or the Philippines); and

- **global strategies** with **localised delivery**, reflecting a similar trend in the core business functions of many multinational companies.

Leading CCI strategist David Grayson, has developed a framework to illustrate the trends or different waves in CCI. This work has been added to by others, such as Mark Vermilion in the USA and PACT's Corporate Community Investment Network in the USA. The following diagram summarises these different contributions:

	1st Wave	2nd Wave	3rd Wave	4th Wave
PURPOSE	Philanthropy	Strategic philanthropy	Community investment	Healthy business environment
MOTIVE	Morality	Long-term self-interest	Long-term/ direct self-interest	Direct self-interest
STRATEGY	Ad Hoc	Systematic	Strategic	Organisational ownership
STAFF	Administrator	Manager	Entrepreneur/ consultants	Ingrained at all management levels
STRUCTURE	Detached from business activities	Detached, but linked to business interests	Part of line structure	Integrated with business functions
INITIATIVE	Passive	Responsive to requests in target areas	Initiating	Integrated into daily decision-making
CONTRIBUTION	Mainly cash of goods	Cash and donations skills and cash	Business resources,	Embedded in profit and growth goals
DRIVERS	Chairman's whim	Guidelines in place	Business-linked guidelines in place	Part of business strategy
SUSTAINABILITY	One-offs	Assistance on specific issues	Nurturing and capacity building of NGOs	Ongoing part of business management/goals and appraisals

It should be apparent from the above that there are numerous ways in which companies can manage their community relations and investment activities. Most companies employ a combination of approaches and organisational structures for undertaking these activities. They include:

a) **Company specific or company "branded" programmes** – Most major companies will have their own community investment programmes and some of them have developed global "brands", such as BP's Science Across the World; American Express's Travel and Tourism Academies; Shell's LiveWire programme; and Grand Metropolitan's KAPOW programme, which are all profiled in later sections.

b) **Corporate foundations** – Many American companies, but also a number of European multi-nationals and large national companies in countries such as Brazil, the Philippines, India and South Africa, have established foundations, which are usually funded according to company profits – either via direct cash transfers or by the allocation of shares to the foundation, with foundation income derived from dividends. Some of these foundations are funding foundations, others operating foundations, and some a combination of both.

c) **National Philanthropy or Foundation Centres** - In some countries national coalitions of corporate foundations or centres of philanthropy have been established. For example: the US Council on Foundations, which has played a global role in spreading good practice on the creation and management of corporate foundations; the South African Grantmakers Association; The Canadian Centre for Philanthropy and similar initiatives in Mexico and Colombia.

d) **Working through industry associations** – The representative bodies of business, such as Chambers of Commerce, Confederations of Industry and Trade Associations, are also beginning to set up units to address broader societal issues. Many of these representative bodies now have environmental task forces or policy groups (especially in OECD economies, but also increasingly in developing and transition economies). Most also look at issues of human resource development and education, albeit normally from the perspective of how they relate directly to the workplace and to business competitiveness. A few are also looking at the wider role of business in areas such as business-education partnerships, AIDS, rural development, corruption, crime prevention and so on. The Confederation of Indian Industry is one of the outstanding business associations in this field, and is profiled on page 72 The efforts of CII and other industry associations are absolutely critical in terms of mainstreaming these issues onto the business agenda and their growing number is a positive indication of where the trend is going.

e) **Public interest business partnerships** – There are growing examples of groups of companies joining forces to tackle a specific social or environmental issue or range of such issues. Some of the most outstanding multi-issue corporate partnerships are profiled in section III of the publication. Corporate-led partnerships aimed at specific issues, such as education, crime prevention, urban regeneration and the environment, are profiled in the section on *Describing the Corporate Contribution.*

f) **Strategic NGO-business partnerships** – Some companies are also developing strategic partnerships with one, or a small group of international NGOs, to work together on a longer-term, international level. Examples of nine of these partnerships are profiled in section III.

The following examples look at some of these approaches to managing community investment activities in more detail, focusing on the role of corporate foundations, centres of philanthropy, industry associations and public interest business partnerships.

CENTRO MEXICANO PARA LA FILANTROPÍA (CEMEFI)

The Mexican Centre for Philanthropy is a non-profit, membership organisation that is supported by the mexican private sector and several US Foundations. Its goal is to encourage social responsibility, in the corporate sector and society-at-large, and to strengthen civil society institutions. The centre undertakes a range of campaigning, research and institutional development activities to meet these goals. One of its major initiatives has been the **MIRA** campaign; a nationwide social marketing programme aimed at encouraging companies and individuals to contribute their time, talents and money to community development. It encourages companies to contribute 1% of pre-tax revenue and individuals to donate 1% of gross income to community activities; and calls on all mexicans to offer one hour of volunteer work a week.

Inspired by the successful IMAGINE campaign in Canada and "Give Five" campaign in the USA, MIRA consists of national advertising and promotional activities, public relations and information dissemination, sponsorship and research projects, and specific programmes targeted at companies and individual citizens. The founding funders of the initiative were Coca-Cola, Grupo Cifra, Fundacion Ampara and Alberto Bailleres, with other companies, foundations and individuals offering smaller amounts of support. Operationally, the campaign works through four networks: NGOs; business; the media; and opinion leaders.

To date more than 200 institutions have become members of MIRA and the campaign has received extensive media coverage - close to 100 articles since its launch in May 1994, 60 interviews on 15 stations, and regular 30 second promotions on 20 stations. At the end of the first three years in 1997, an analysis will be made on the programme's effectiveness in changing attitudes and behaviour of both companies and individuals.

FOUNDATIONS FOR DEVELOPMENT
The role of corporate foundations

Corporate foundations play a valuable role in supporting community development in many countries. Although there are numerous variations in terms of how these foundations are funded, structured and operated, they all share common characteristics of:

- being supported primarily by the private sector, although some of the larger and more established ones now act as a channel for government and donor agency funding as well, and

- bringing the managerial and organisation skills and the financial discipline of the private sector to wider national development needs.

Some of these corporate foundations undertake activities which are closely linked to the core business interests of the parent company. For example, the Citicorp Foundation which is supporting a US$10 million project on micro-financing and the Glaxo-Wellcome Foundation which focuses on supporting projects related to health care. Others have less of a direct link, but most of them are focused in one way or another on education and/or community development and the creation of livelihood opportunities.

Many corporate foundations, especially those in developing countries, are closely linked to family companies. Even in the OECD economies a number of leading foundations were originally established by individual entrepreneurs or corporate founders – the Ford and Kellogg Foundations being two examples. In a number of countries, groups of foundations have joined forces to establish national centres of philanthropy or national foundation councils aimed at sharing expertise and providing a common voice in campaigning for charity and influencing the policy dialogue. The following pages profile Mexico's national Centre for Philanthropy, three corporate foundations from developing countries (the Ayala, the Hope and the Odebrecht Foundations), plus some examples of the work being undertaken by four multinational corporate foundations in Africa (IBM, Coca-Cola, Kellogg and RTZ-CRA).

The Ayala Foundation in Asia Pacific

Established in 1961, with a mission "to improve the quality of life of the Filipino by contributing to the eradication of poverty in all its forms", the Ayala Foundation is supported by the Ayala Group, the largest holding company in the Philippines. Over the years it has evolved into a fully fledged development institution, combining all the vital elements of project management from planning and management to monitoring and evaluation. The foundation plays a valuable intermediary role between foreign and local development agencies and grassroots people's organisations. Its programmes are structured to encompass both socioeconomic and cultural dimensions, and it emphasises ventures which empower the poor on a more permanent basis than is achievable under traditional philanthropy-driven approaches. The foundation's programmes include:

- *an integrated community development programme*, which offers relocated squatters the opportunity to own a home and develop livelihood activities. The programme encompasses social and organisational development support, training in leadership, team-building, resource management, conflict resolution and institutional capacity-building. It is carried out in different communities around the Philippines and supported by different Ayala Group companies, donor agencies and a few other companies, such as Levi Strauss Phils. Inc.

- *a scholarship and market-driven skills training programme*, which offers vocational and technical training scholarships and equips out-of-school youth and unemployed adults with specific skills needed by various industries.

THE HOPE FOUNDATION IN THE MIDDLE EAST AND AFRICA

Established in 1992 by Hani Yamani, the Hope Foundation is an example of one entrepreneur's vision to share the profits of his work with others. Yamani donates 20% of the income of his businesses to the foundation which is active primarily in the Middle East, Africa and Bosnia Herzegovina, although it also supports projects in Bangladesh, Nepal, Pakistan, Cuba, Albania, Chechnya and Germany. Projects to date have concentrated on medical services, child care initiatives, relief activities in war-torn countries, aid to the poor and the promotion of Islamic values. They include: a variety of projects with the International Islamic Relief Organisation, ranging from a blindness prevention programme to the production of children's books based on Islamic principles to help children understand the true teachings of this religion; capitalisation of the Hope Foundation in Namibia and support for sending Namibian students abroad for technical studies; an agricultural programme in Bosnia Herzegovina aimed at increasing food and jobs self-sufficiency; support for the Water Well Drilling project in Africa, with a focus on Chad and Mali; and a blindness prevention campaign in Cuba. The foundation is also supporting research on public-private partnerships and a study on the development role of leading multinational and national companies being undertaken by the World Bank Group and The Prince of Wales Business Leaders Forum.

The Odebrecht Foundation in Brazil

Established in 1965 by the Odebrecht Corporation, one of Brazil's largest privately-owned conglomerates, the Emilio Odebrecht Foundation (FEO) is a non-profit organisation aimed at promoting social programmes of public interest. The Foundation supports programmes in various parts of Brazil, with a focus on the state of Bahia, where the Odebrecht Group has its headquarters. Its main focus is on improving the quality of basic schooling in the country and educating young people with life skills. FEO has made a strong commitment to working in partnership with state government, local authorities, NGOs and grassroots community organisations in implementing its programmes.

The foundation's *Education: An Exercise in Citizenship* project illustrates its approach. The project was aimed at educating teenagers and preparing them to be more responsible members of society. It helped to introduce participatory education methods and important youth issues to an antiquated public school system in Salvador, as well as revitalising information and techniques in public health organisations working with youth. The project included the founding of 10 centres for student-teacher interaction and the training of over 2,000 people. In five medical centres throughout the city, health professionals were taught new techniques on how to deal more effectively with troubled youth. A play was also created that dealt with a variety of youth issues and which helped to raise public awareness and foster community spirit. The city government played a key role in ensuring access to both the city's education and health systems and worked closely with FEO on project implementation. FEO has also been working on a joint project with UNICEF entitled *Only Schools Can Make Brazil Right*.

FOUNDATIONS operating in Southern Africa

A book produced in 1995 by Myra Alperson, of the US Conference Board, entitled *Foundations for a New Democracy* offers a useful overview of some of the major corporate foundations operating in South Africa. These range from those established by local South African companies such as the Liberty Life and Southern Life Foundations, to those set up by foreign investors such as Colgate-Palmolive and Toyota. Many of these are funding entities, making donations to NGOs and CBOs although some, such as the Gencor Development Trust, have developed into fully operational development agencies. Other foreign investors have chosen to support community activities in South Africa and elsewhere in the region through their international foundations, instead of establishing locally registered entities. Examples include Citicorp, American Express, IBM, the Kellogg Company, and the Coca-Cola Company. In 1994, an organisation called the South African Grantmakers' Association was established to enable corporate foundations, trusts, development funds and community social investment officers to network and collaborate on a more systematic basis.

Although there is much less corporate wealth to the north of South Africa, a number of local and foreign-owned companies have foundations which are operating in the region, such as those described below and opposite.

- **The Kellogg Foundation** has been operating in the region since 1986 with an emphasis on human development. Its grants are aimed at building the capacity of people and helping them to acquire the skills, knowledge and leadership needed to solve their own problems. Approximately half of its grants to the region go to education, health and rural development projects. The foundation also offers bursaries and international study grants and runs the Kellogg International Leadership Programme, which selects fellows from around the region and gives them support for their personal development and community activities. Since 1987, more than 300 study grants have been awarded to mid-career professionals in southern Africa. In South Africa, the Kellogg Foundation is working with the International Youth Foundation (IYF) on a variety of projects which are profiled on page 228.

- **The IBM Foundation** since 1985 the IBM Foundation has invested some US$24million in South African projects aimed at supporting education and the country's overall economic development. In 1994, it established the *Reach & Teach* programme aimed at helping to improve the quality of elementary and secondary education and employment opportunities in the country. Through this initiative two job training centres have been established and a variety of education projects supported. In Zambia, Tanzania and Nigeria the foundation has provided financial and technology support to the *Communications for Better Health* initiative run by the Health Foundation.

- **The Coca-Cola Foundation** has established a variety of education projects and enterprise development initiatives in the region. In Zimbabwe, where young people under the age of 20 constitute more than 60% of the population and youth unemployment is soaring, the Coca-Cola Foundation, in partnership with IYF, is supporting skills training and youth enterprise development. It is working with the Chitungwiza Youth Survival Programme , which provides young people with relevant training through apprenticeships, to incorporate business and leadership skills into their programme and to reach a larger number of young people. It is also supporting the Zimbabwe Association of Community Theatre to support train-the-trainer workshops throughout the country in implementing youth-run cultural and performing arts groups. In Kenya and Zimbabwe, the foundation has established the Coca-Cola Forum in Management and Marketing to support entrepreneurship and small-scale business, as profiled on page 116.

> For all of corporate South Africa, the time is ripe for an evaluation of new directions and models of corporate social investment, and that's what *Foundations for a New Democracy* aims to do through its profiles. It tries to show how companies with vision and courage – and the people behind them are making CSI an inclusive, developmental process which at its best is a "win-win" situation for the companies and the constituencies that benefit from their investment.
>
> Myra Alperson

RTZ-CRA in Zimbabwe, Namibia and South Africa

••••••••••••••••••••••••••••••••••

British-based RTZ-CRA, one of the world's major mining companies, has taken a decentralised approach by creating three foundations in southern Africa which are directly linked to, and mainly funded by, its subsidiaries in the region rather than head office. As a result, there has always been a strong sense of local ownership and identity, and each of the foundations – The Rössing Foundation in Namibia, The Palabora Foundation in South Africa and the Rio Tinto Foundation in Zimbabwe – has developed in a slightly different way according to local needs and capacities.

The Rio Tinto Foundation, which is profiled on page 206, is primarily a funding foundation – selecting strategic projects to support, and then paying to bring in appropriate individuals or organisations to run them.

The Palabora Foundation is a "hands-on" operating foundation, running projects in the areas surrounding the Palabora mine and one major project near Johannesburg - the Reef Training Centre. Although the Reef Training Centre receives funding and in-kind support from other companies, as profiled on page 144, the Foundation itself is funded by the company.

The Rössing Foundation, on the other hand has evolved into something akin to an independent, nationwide development agency, which is funded not only by the company, but increasingly acts as an intermediary organisation for channelling funds from international donor agencies, government and other companies, to NGOs and community-based organisations (CBOs). It currently manages more than N$10 million in external funds, enabling donors to use the Foundation's infrastructure and expertise to allocate funds to specific projects in return for which the Foundation normally charges a management fee. This offers an interesting model which harnesses the managerial efficiency and financial discipline of a corporate entity to meeting national development needs at a level and scope of activity that no individual company or its foundation could handle alone.

The Rössing Foundation has been an operational and funding entity since it was first established in 1978. Starting with an initial focus on adult education and training, the programme has broadened to provide support for income and employment creation projects in agriculture and other sectors in order to assist people in using the skills they acquire. The Foundation currently runs 12 educational and agricultural centres around the country offering a range of vocational courses and associated support programmes for small businesses.

These projects include:

- **The Khomasdal Education Centre** in Windhoek, which offers courses in vehicle maintenance, basic technical skills, commercial and secretarial skills, English, textile design, needlework and environmental education, as well as serving as a community centre and library;

- **The Luderitz Centre** in the south of the country, which is now managed by the Namibian government and has been supported by a combination of public-private funding from Namibia and donor agency funds. It is a maritime training centre offering a wide range of courses to support the Namibian fishing industry;

- **The Okashana Centre** in the north of the country, which has carried out crop trials of staple foods, in co-operation with the International Centre for Research in Semi-Arid Tropics and which also services as a conference centre;

- **The Gibeon Folk Arts Project** which involves a group of some 20 rural women producing applique art. The Foundation provides technical assistance and manages marketing and finance, including export promotion, whilst a members' committee manages production. Local NGOs are training the producers to take over responsibility for financial management and marketing. The project has brought tangible benefits to the women and their families in an area where few income generation options are available. The Foundation has entered into partnership with the Norwegian Aid Agency (NORAD) and the New Zealand High Commission for funding purposes; and

- **The Okombahe Development Project** which assists small farmers in developing irrigated commercial vegetable production and family gardens. The Foundation in addition to managing the project and providing technical assistance, has brought in other partners. The government provided the land, two private companies and foreign governments provided finance and equipment, and one of them provides a market for the produce.

The three RTZ-CRA Foundations in southern Africa serve as useful models for the company's operations elsewhere in the world and for other companies and donor agencies.

INDUSTRY ASSOCIATIONS
Representing commercial and "business in society" interests

Industry Associations, representing specific industry sectors or business in general, play a critical role in any vibrant and healthy market economy. They help to build the "corporate social capital" which enables even the fiercest of competitors to come together to tackle issues of common interest. It is useful to differentiate between representative industry associations (such as Chambers of Commerce and specific trade bodies) and public interest business partnerships. The former are established primarily to represent their members' commercial business interests (although of course in today's world this increasingly means looking at wider societal issues) whereas the latter are established with the specific purpose of mobilising business to tackle broader societal and development issues.

Industry Associations have been around for many years at both national and international levels. The International Chamber of Commerce, for example, was established in 1919 and many national Chambers of Commerce even earlier. What has changed for these bodies in recent years, is a growing focus on environmental and social issues, especially the former. In both OECD and developing countries more and more industry bodies are establishing environmental units and/or task forces (some of these are profiled in the section on environmental sustainability). A few industry associations, although not nearly enough, are establishing task forces or units to look at the broader role of business in society. One of the leaders in this field is undoubtedly the Confederation of Indian Industry (CII).

THE CII

In 1995 the CII recently celebrated its 100th Anniversary. It represents more than 3,000 Indian companies, both large and small-scale, public and private, which between them account for a turnover of some US$35 billion and represent about 38% of the total workforce. CII covers a wide range of industry sectors and business issues and assumes a variety of roles, including promotional, advisory, catalytic, consultative, and facilitative. It organises site visits and inward and outward trade missions, runs training workshops and consultations between business and other sectors, and produces publications and information on a large databank. Over the past decade it has greatly increased its focus on services looking at issues such as total quality management, industrial relations and environmental management. It has also established a Corporate Citizenship Council, which covers the following issues:

- Education and literacy
- Health and family welfare
- Rural development
- Consumer affairs
- Sports
- Bharitya Yuva Shakti Trust (a youth development programme);
- HIV/AIDS.

CII's recently launched Programme on HIV/AIDS Prevention and Care is supported by a large number of companies – both Indian and multinational. HIV/AIDS is spreading faster in India than in any other country, and WHO estimates that at current trends, by 2050 there will be more HIV positive people in India than the rest of the world combined. This obviously has serious implications for business.

The CII programme is a major communications and education and training initiative, aimed at: making the "business case" for corporate involvement in HIV/AIDS prevention and care; and providing companies with the information and tools that they need to take action.

Literature sponsored by United Distillers, among others, is being disseminated to companies throughout the country, which will be followed by workshops and a range of support services. The task force, consisting of international leaders in this field, such as Levi Strauss, has tested the programme for efficacy, affordability, ease of implementation and accessibility and it is now being rolled out on a national basis.

PUBLIC INTEREST BUSINESS PARTNERSHIPS
Building corporate networks for societal action

● ●

Business is the most powerful force in our society today, especially if we are willing to accept some moral and civic leadership, as well as financial leadership. Business has the tools, the energy, and the will to fill the growing vacuum of leadership.

Arnold Hiatt, Former CEO of
Stride Rite Corporation
and SVN member

If you think you are too small to make a difference, you must never have spent a night with a mosquito in your room...

Anita Roddick, Founder of
The Body Shop International
and SVN member

The number, profile and scope of public interest business partnerships, established specifically to tackle broader societal issues, has grown dramatically in recent years. There are numerous examples throughout this publication of such partnerships at both a national level and a local level, established to tackle a wide range of societal issues from rural development and urban renewal, to education and environment. The vast majority of these did not exist ten, or even five years ago.

The final section of the publication profiles some of the most outstanding nationwide public interest business partnerships. There are also a few business partnerships of this type operating internationally. They include: The Prince of Wales Business Leaders Forum; The World Business Council for Sustainable Development; the World Business Academy; The Caux Roundtable; and the Social Venture Network (SVN). The latter is profiled below, with the others being described elsewhere in the publication

THE SOCIAL VENTURE NETWORK

SVN is an interesting example, as it illustrates that global networking and action is not the preserve of large multi-nationals alone. Although it has some major companies as members, such as Levi Strauss, the SVN is primarily a network of individual entrepreneurs with the vision and business acumen to create a better world.

Founded in the USA in 1987, the SVN Mission states:

"We are an international network of socially and environmentally engaged entrepreneurs and business leaders, dedicated to changing the way we and the world do business. Our goal is to integrate the values of a socially and environmentally sustainable society into day-to-day business practices. To do this, we strive to develop ourselves personally and professionally. We provide a supportive environment in which we challenge ourselves and each other to develop our enterprises to be both commercially successful and socially and environmentally responsible. Our network creates opportunities for learning and facilitates both transactions among members and the start-up of new organisations and ventures."

Since 1987, true to its mission, SVN and its members have helped to create a number of offspring organisations and initiatives. For example: SVN Europe which was established in 1993 and has now been launched in about 10 European countries; Business for Social Responsibility in the USA; and Students for Social Responsibility, which brings together business school students from around the USA. In the UK, with the leadership of the Body Shop, the New Business Academy has been established to run executive seminars and workshops and to develop case studies demonstrating that "doing good makes good business sense."

(iii) PUBLIC POLICY DIALOGUE

The third and final mechanism through which business can impact sustainable development, after its core business activities and its social investment and philanthropy activities, is through its engagement in the public policy debate. This can be a sensitive and potentially difficult area, as there is sometimes a fine line (or even no line at all) between:

a) **efforts by industry associations, or even individual companies, to lobby government with the goal of achieving direct commercial advantage or protecting direct commercial interests, sometimes at a cost to the environment or to society at large; and**

b) **efforts to engage with government specifically to develop common solutions to wider societal issues, which benefit may benefit business, but have the public interest as their core motivation.**

There is obviously a link between the two which will be stronger in some situations and on some issues than others. It is not necessarily a negative link. The "zero-sum" attitude that suggests that lobbying for commercial advantage automatically leads to environmental or societal disadvantage, is an increasingly out-dated one, borne of an era where confrontation characterised public-private dialogue rather than co-operation. This is not to suggest that such situations do not occur. They do and they do so too frequently. There is however a trend towards finding win-win solutions and joint approaches, which meet commercial needs, but also tackle broader social needs and national issues. A few examples of this approach include:

South Africa's National Economic Development and Labour Council
Launched in February 1995, Nedlac is a formal vehicle for dialogue on social and economic policy between the South African government, business, labour and community interests, aimed at jointly pursuing goals of growth, equity and participation. Despite a number of difficulties and disagreement on certain issues, by June 1996 Nedlac had been able to conclude seven formal agreements, including the labour relations bill, mine health and safety bill and agreements regarding the establishment of institutions to promote small and medium-sized enterprises. It operates through an 18-person Executive Council which meets quarterly, and a 16-person Management Committee which meets monthly, with members drawn from all sectors, and an annual National Summit for about 300 delegates. Four chambers cover the issues of public finance and monetary policy; trade and industry; the labour market; and development, and meet on a frequent basis.

The UK Government Advisory Council on Business and the Environment
Established by the Department of the Environment and the Department of Trade and Industry in May 1991, to engage in greater and more systematic dialogue with business on environmental policy, looking at issues of both an immediate interest and of a longer term nature. ACBE is composed of about 25 business leaders from a variety of sectors, who serve in their individual capacities for a two year period. They consult with government officials and report back formally with policy recommendations to the Minister of the Environment and the President of the Board of Trade and Industry. Working groups have included: global warming; environmental management; recycling; commercial and export opportunities in the environmental area; and the financial sector.

For all involved in Nedlac, the period from its launch until now has been an intense and challenging experience. We are building a social partnership between government, labour, business and the community, while at the same time engaging in policy debates on issues on which there have been sharply contested interests and views. Nonetheless, is the short space of fifteen months, there have been several achievements, while further challenges also need to be addressed.

Jay Naidoo,
Executive Director, Nedlac,
May 1996

The President's idea of appointing 'industry' and 'environmental' co-chairs to a council that included members of his Cabinet as well as leaders from many sectors of society presented us with an unusual challenge. We hardly knew each other when we started. The 'environmentalist' had experience as a regulatory official, environmental litigator and sharp critic of the company in which the 'industrialist' had spent his professional life. Now we had to agree – and learn to trust each other – to be able to lead the Council.

Jonathan Lash and David Buzzelli,
Sustainable America

The U.S. President's Council on Sustainable Development

Established in June 1993, the 25-member PCSD was a ground-breaking partnership drawing high-ranking representatives from government, industry, labour, environmental and civil rights organisations, charged with developing bold new approaches to integrate economic, social and environmental concerns into the nation's policy and regulatory processes.

The PCSD was jointly chaired by Jonathan Lash, President of the World Resources Institute and David Buzzelli, VP Environment, Health and Safety and Public Affairs at the Dow Chemical Company. It spent two years undertaking research and public hearings all over the country, on behalf of the President. Eight task forces were established to manage this process, covering: eco-efficiency; energy and transport; natural resources management and protection; principles, goals and definitions; population and consumption; public linkage, dialogue and education; sustainable agriculture; sustainable communities and an interim team to look at climate change. Over the two year period the PCSD had an outreach to several thousand people, held more than 50 public meetings and hundreds of informal meetings, produced newsletters and public comment surveys, and consulted with about 450 experts. Their final report to the President recommended 154 specific actions and 38 major initiatives in areas from economic and regulatory policy, to education and international policy.

The Canadian Business Council on National Issues

Established in 1976, to help strengthen the country's economy, its social fabric and its democratic institutions, this is a non-partisan, not-for-profit organisation composed of the chief executive officers of 150 leading Canadian corporations, representing every major sector of the economy, employing some 1.4 million people and accounting for a turnover of more than CDN$450 billion.

The Council is active in key areas of public policy and is committed to effecting economic, social and political change. Over the past 15 years task forces drawn from among the Council's membership have dealt with issues such as: sustainable development; international competitiveness; education reform; social policy; employment; youth unemployment; international trade and investment; foreign policy and international security; political reform and the Canadian constitution; monetary policy; fiscal reform; competition policy; energy policy; defence policy; and corporate governance.

Government must share its responsibilities by coordinating macro-economic policy and microeconomic reforms with the business community

Mission Statement of Peru 2021

Peru 2021

Peru 2021 was established in 1995 by a group of Peruvian business leaders, representing national and foreign companies, and supported by the Confederacion Nacional de Instituciones Empresariales Privadas (CONFIEP). The goal of Peru 2021 is to promote a new national vision of business leadership working in partnership with the government, to develop the policies and projects needed to create a modern, internationally competitive economy and a decent quality of life for all Peruvians by the year 2021, when the country celebrates its bicentennial. The initiative has identified a set of key themes for which it is developing vision statements for the year 2021, consultations and focus groups, surveys and joint public-private action plans. These themes include: leadership; education; the economy; the environment; technology; society; government and business.

1.2 Mission Statements and Methodologies

The Johnson & Johnson Credo:

We believe our first responsibility is to the doctors, nurses and patients, to mothers and fathers and all others who use our products and services. In meeting their needs everything we do must be of high quality.
We must constantly strive to reduce our costs in order to maintain reasonable prices. Customers' orders must be serviced promptly and accurately. Our suppliers and distributors must have an opportunity to make a fair profit.

We are responsible to our employees, the men and women who work with us throughout the world. Everyone must be considered as an individual. We must respect their dignity and recognise their merit. They must have a sense of security in their jobs. Compensation must be fair and adequate, and working conditions clean, orderly and safe. We must be mindful of ways to help our employees fulfil their family responsibilities. Employees must feel free to make suggestions and complaints. There must be equal opportunity for employment, development and advancement for those qualified. We must provide competent management, and their actions must be just and ethical.

We are responsible to the communities in which we live and work and to the world community as well. We must be good citizens – support good works and charities and bear our fair share of taxes. We must encourage civic improvements and better health and education. We must maintain in good order the property we are privileged to use, protecting the environment and natural resources.

Our final responsibility is to our shareholders. Business must make a sound profit. We must experiment with new ideas. Research must be carried out, innovative programs developed, and mistakes paid for. New equipment must be purchased, new facilities provided and new products launched. Reserves must be created to provide for adverse times. When we operate according to these principles, the stockholders should realise a fair return.

As outlined in preceding pages, a company can contribute to sustainable development through its core business activities, its social investment activities and through public policy dialogue. Its willingness and ability to make a positive impact through any of these areas will depend crucially on:

- **its guiding values and principles as a company i.e. its mission and operational guidelines; and**

- **its management structures and systems for implementing these guidelines, measuring and monitoring impacts, motivating and mobilising employees and mainstreaming good practice into the core business agenda.**

Most major companies have a mission statement. Not surprisingly, an analysis of these statements shows a strong correlation between the companies with an outstanding reputation and the mission statements which talk about the wider responsibilities of business in society. A number of companies are now putting concepts such as sustainable development and stakeholders into their missions. This marks a change from three years ago, when more than 100 examples in a 1993 book entitled *101 Great Missions Statements*, showed only one company – IBM – that explicitly used the word stakeholder (although many others listed different groups with a stake in the company) and none that used the concept sustainable development.

Although it is easy to dismiss mission statements as merely "pieces of paper" or public relations exercises, the process of employee and stakeholder consultation that some companies go through to develop and/or adapt their mission statements says a great deal about their commitment to being responsible corporate citizens. One of the classic mission statements is the 45 year old Johnson & Johnson Credo, which is as relevant today as ever.

Closely linked to mission statements are methodologies – operating guidelines or codes of conduct. These can be of many types, depending on who has developed them and for what purpose. For example:

(i) **Voluntary/self-regulatory corporate guidelines. These may be guidelines developed by an individual company for managing its own performance; or industry sector guidelines produced by trade associations in consultation with their members; or general business guidelines not specific to a particular industry.**

In the last six years there has been dramatic growth in all three of these areas. At the individual company level many multi-nationals now have internal health, safety and environment (HSE) guidelines and aim to apply these on a global basis. Some also have ethical guidelines and a small, but growing number have specific guidelines for their investments and sourcing activities in developing countries, such as Levi Strauss and Ciba.

There has also been a dramatic increase in industry sector guidelines and charters, especially for environmental management. A 1996 analysis of these carried out by UNCTAD, lists about 26 industry associations which have established such guidelines, the vast majority of them since 1990. The best known of the sector-specific guidelines is the chemical industry's which is

RESPONSIBLE CARE

The best-known and most developed sector-specific initiative is the chemical industry's Responsible Care programme. This was launched by the Chemical Manufacturers Association in 1988 in response to public concerns about the manufacture and use of chemicals. The programme requires member companies to: improve their performance in health, safety and environmental quality; listen and respond to public concerns; assist each other to achieve optimum performance; and report their progress to the public. Two aspects of Responsible Care are especially notable. Firstly, all member companies of the Chemical Manufacturers Association must participate in Responsible Care as an obligation of membership. CMA has about 175 member companies which account for more than 90% of the basic chemical productive capacity in the USA and Canada. Many of these companies are multi-nationals and are playing a key role in spreading Responsible Care around the world and getting it adopted by national chemical associations in other countries. Secondly, the public is directly involved in shaping the initiative through a Public Advisory Panel.

Although the detailed implementation depends on local circumstances, the overall philosophy and goal of continuous improvement is international. All members of the CMA pledge to manage their businesses according to a set of ten Guiding Principles. They put these principles into action through adherence to six Codes of Management Practice which are: the Community Awareness and Emergency Response Code (CAER); the Pollution Prevention Code; the Process Safety Code; the Distribution Code; the Employee Health and Safety Code; and the Product Stewardship Code. Performance measures are being adopted for each of these codes, and members undertake self-evaluation, reporting annually to CMA on their progress. Responsible Care is also developing a Management Systems Verification Process with appropriate third party involvement and relies on regular input from an independent public advisory panel composed of leading environmentalists and health and safety experts. The programme relies heavily on the concept of mutual assistance and networking among members, and also supports a partnership programme for companies and trade associations which are not members, but have contact with chemicals or the chemical industry.

described opposite. Of the national industry associations one of the most interesting is the **Keidanren's Environmental Guidelines for Japanese Companies Operating Abroad**, described on the following page. This is one of the few initiatives that specifically sets out overseas obligations for members of a national industry association. The best known of the non-sector specific, international environmental guidelines is the International Chamber of Commerce (ICC's) **Business Charter for Sustainable Development**, which was launched in 1991 and has been signed by hundreds of companies around the world. This charter has provided a useful framework against which many national and sector-specific guidelines have since been developed and is profiled on page 80.

Less developed are industry association guidelines for social responsibilities – at home and abroad. The most comprehensive international guidelines in this area are the **Caux Principles**. These were developed by the Caux Roundtable, a group of business leaders from Japan, Europe and the USA, with support from the Minnesota Center for Corporate Responsibility. Although they are not produced by a representative industry association such as the ICC, this does not detract from their value as a framework for corporate action. Their main principles are summarised on page 81. Business for Social Responsibility in the USA has also started to work on social and human rights guidelines for American companies operating abroad.

(ii) Voluntary Guidelines for corporate responsibility established outside the corporate sector by NGOs and government agencies.

There has also been an increase in this type of guideline in recent years. One of the oldest models was the Sullivan Principles for American companies operating in South Africa during the apartheid era. A more recent example which is focused on environmental management, is the **CERES Principles,** created by a coalition of ethical and institutional investors in the USA with more than US$150 billion in assets under management. More than 100 companies, including General Motors, have signed these principles, which among other requirements, commit signatories to publicly report on their progress on environmental management. **The Council on Economic Priorities** is also developing Sourcing Guidelines for American and European companies which source products from developing countries, as are a number of other non-governmental organisations such as Oxfam and Fair Trade.

The US Department of Commerce has recently launched a set of principles for American companies operating abroad, illustrated overpage, and both the **ILO** and **OECD** have established guidelines for multinational enterprises, covering a wide range of the non-commercial activities of corporations operating in foreign countries. Although not guidelines *per se*, the **EBRD's Transition Indicators** for project appraisal are also a useful statement against which companies can evaluate their impacts.

It is clear that activity in this field is growing, driven by both business and other stakeholder groups. If given support by CEOs and senior managers, such guidelines can form the basis for a comprehensive management and measurement system and provide valuable frameworks against which companies and their stakeholders can evaluate progress. The challenge of course is actually implementing and adhering to them. Often it is not the major multinational companies which fail to achieve this, but national companies, which lack either the managerial, technical or financial resources, or the regulatory incentives to do so.

The Keidanren's ten-point Environmental Guidelines for Japanese Enterprises Operating Abroad

1. Establish a constructive attitude toward environmental protection and try to raise complete awareness of the issues among those concerned.

2. Make environmental protection a priority at overseas sites and, as a minimum requirement, abide by the environmental standards of the host country. Apply Japanese standards concerning the management of harmful substances.

3. Conduct a full environmental assessment before starting overseas business operations. After the start of activities try to collect data and if necessary, conduct an assessment.

4. Confer fully with the parties concerned at the operational site and co-operate with them in the transfer and local application of environment-related Japanese technologies and know-how.

5. Establish an environmental management system, including the appointment of staff responsible for environmental control. Also try to improve qualifications for the necessary personnel.

6. Provide the local community with information on environmental measures on a regular basis.

7. Be sure that when environment-related issues arise, efforts are made to prevent them from developing into social and cultural frictions. Deal with them through scientific and rational discussions.

8. Co-operate in the promotion of the host country's scientific and rational measures.

9. Actively publicise, both at home and abroad, the activities of overseas businesses that reflect our activities on the environmental consideration.

10. Ensure that the home offices of the corporations operating overseas understand the importance of measures for dealing with environmental issues, as they establish their overseas affiliates. The head office must try to establish a support system that can, for instance, send specialists abroad whenever the need arises.

Source: The Keidanren

The US Government's Model Business Principles

Recognising the positive role of US business in upholding and promoting adherence to universal standards of human rights, the Administration encourages all businesses to adopt and implement voluntary codes of conduct for doing business around the world that cover at least the following areas:

1. Provision of a safe and healthy workplace.

2. Fair employment practices, including avoidance of child and forced labour and avoidance of discrimination based on race, gender, national origin or religious beliefs; and respect for the right of association and the right to organise and bargain collectively.

3. Responsible environmental protection and practices.

4. Compliance with US and local laws promoting good business practices, including laws prohibiting illicit payments and ensuring fair competition.

5. Maintenance, through leadership at all levels, of a corporate culture that respects free expression consistent with legitimate business concerns, and does not condone political coercion in the workplace; that encourages good corporate citizenship and makes a positive contribution to the communities in which the company operates and where ethical conduct is recognised, valued and exemplified by all employees.

In adopting voluntary codes that reflect these principles, US companies should serve as models, encouraging similar behaviour by their partners, suppliers, and subcontractors.

Adoption of codes of conduct reflecting these principles is voluntary. Companies are encouraged to develop their own codes of conduct appropriate to their particular circumstances. Many companies already apply statements or codes that incorporate these principles. Companies should find appropriate means to inform their stakeholders and the public of actions undertaken in connection with these principles. Nothing in the principles is intended to require the company to act in violation of host or US law. This statement of principles is not intended for legislation.

Source: US Department of Commerce

The CERES Principles

1. Protection of the Biosphere – reducing emissions and making continual progress towards eliminating the release of any substance that may cause environmental damage.

2. Sustainable Use of Natural Resources – including water, soils, and forests and conserving non-renewable resources.

3. Reduction and Disposal of Wastes – eliminating waste through source reduction and recycling and handling all wastes responsibly.

4. Energy Conservation – improving energy efficiency, using environmentally safe and sustainable energy resources.

5. Risk Reduction – minimising health, safety and environmental risks to employees and communities.

6. Safe Products and Services – reducing the use, manufacture or sale of products and services that cause environmental damage.

7. Environmental Restoration – promptly and responsibly remedying environmental problems; redressing injuries caused to individuals; restoring environmental damage.

8. Informing the Public – timely notifying those affected by environmental mishaps; seeking advice and counsel with community members; not punishing whistle blowers.

9. Management Commitment – bringing the board of directors and chief environmental officer into key environmental decisions and policy.

10. Audits and Reports – conducting an annual self-evaluation; completing and publicly disclosing an annual CERES report.

Source: The Coalition for Environmentally Responsible Economies (CERES)

The EBRD's Transition Indicators for Project Appraisal

Competitive interactions and the competitive environment

1. To what extent does the project utilise local suppliers/domestic inputs? (backward linkages i.e. commodity and services)

2. To what extent are such inputs supplied at non-distorted prices? (backward linkages)

3. To what extent does the project utilise downstream marketing and/or processing activities? (forward linkages)

4. To what extent does the project directly contribute to the formation and expansion of SMEs?

5. To what extent does the project contribute directly to the private sector provision of facilities or services?

6. To what extent does the project contribute to the development of more rational infrastructure pricing, effective collection and/or effective regulation in the sector?

7. To what extent does the project directly improve the competitive environment and/or reduce market distortions in the sector?

8. To what extent does the project involve privatisation or other means of improving effective corporate governance of enterprises in ways that increase market orientation?

Learning and discovery

9. To what extent does the project create or transfer skills relevant to a market economy? (e.g. management, marketing, financial and banking skills, specialised technical skills etc.)

10. To what extent does the project directly support export-oriented activity, including trade facilitation such as export finance and insurance?

11. To what extent does the project contribute to the development of new financial instruments by local financial institutions?

12. To what extent does the project directly enhance financial intermediation by creating new types of intermediary? (e.g. insurance company, stock market, venture capital company etc.)

13. To what extent does the project create a new and easily replicable line of activity? (demonstration effects e.g. in manufacturing or finance).

Source: The European Bank for Reconstruction and Development (EBRD)

The ICC Business Charter for Sustainable Development: Linking social good and commercial potential

Principles for Environmental Management

1. Corporate priority
To recognise environmental management as among the highest corporate priorities and as a key determinant to sustainable development; to establish policies, programmes and practices for conducting operations in an environmentally sound manner.

2. Integrated management
To integrate these policies, programmes and practices fully into each business as an essential element of management in all its functions.

3. Process of improvement
To continue to improve corporate policies and environmental performance, taking into account technical developments, scientific understanding, consumer needs and community expectations, with legal regulations as a starting point; and to apply the same environmental criteria internationally.

4. Employee education
To educate, train and motivate employees to conduct their activities in an environmentally responsible manner.

5. Prior assessment
To assess environmental impacts before starting a new activity or project and before decommissioning a facility or leaving a site.

6. Products and services
To develop and provide products or services that have no undue environmental impact and are safe in their intended use, that are efficient in their consumption of energy and natural resources, and that can be recycled, reused, or disposed of safely.

7. Customer advice
To advise, and where relevant, educate customers, distributors and the public in the safe use, transportation, storage and disposal of products provided; and to apply similar considerations to the provision of services.

8. Facilities and operations
To develop, design and operate facilities and conduct activities taking into consideration the efficient use of energy and materials, the sustainable use of renewal resources, the minimisation of adverse environmental impact and waste generation, and the safe and responsible disposal of residual wastes.

9. Research
To conduct or support research on the environmental impacts of raw materials, products, processes, emissions and wastes associated with the enterprise and on the means of minimising such adverse impacts.

10. Precautionary approach
To modify the manufacture, marketing or use of products or services or the conduct of activities, consistent with scientific and technical understanding, to prevent serious or irreversible environmental degradation.

11. Contractors and suppliers
To promote the adoption of these principles by contractors acting on behalf of the enterprise, encouraging and, where appropriate, requiring improvements in their practices to make them consistent with those of the enterprise; and to encourage the wider application of these principles by supplies.

12. Emergency preparedness
To develop and maintain, where significant hazards exist, emergency preparedness plans in conjunction with the emergency services, relevant authorities and the local community, recognising potential trans-boundary impacts.

13. Transfer of technology
To contribute to the transfer of environmentally-sound technology and management methods throughout the industrial and public sectors.

14. Contribute to the common effort
To contribute to the development of public policy and to business, governmental and inter-governmental programmes and educational initiatives that will enhance environmental awareness and protection.

15. Openness to concerns
To foster openness and dialogue with employees and the public, anticipating and responding to their concerns about the potential hazards and impacts of operations, products, wastes or services, including those of trans-boundary or global significance.

16. Compliance and reporting
To measure environmental performance; to conduct regular environmental audit and assessments of compliance with company requirements, legal requirements and these principles; and periodically to provide appropriate information to the Board of Directors, shareholders, employees, the authorities and the public.

The Business Charter for Sustainable Development was adopted by the 64th session of the ICC Executive Board on 27 November 1990 and was first published in April 1991.

The Caux Round-Table – Principles for Business

SECTION 1: PREAMBLE

The mobility of employment, capital, products and technology is making business increasingly global in its transactions and its effects.

Laws and market forces are necessary but insufficient guides for conduct.

Responsibility for the policies and actions of business and respect for the dignity and interests of its stakeholders are fundamental.

Shared values, including a commitment to shared prosperity, are as important for a global community as for communities of smaller scale.

For these reasons, and because business can be a powerful agent of positive social change, we offer the following principles as a foundation for dialogue and action by business leaders in search of business responsibility. In so doing, we affirm the necessity for moral values in business decision-making. Without them, stable business relationships and a sustainable world community are impossible.

SECTION 2: GENERAL PRINCIPLES

Principle 1
The responsibilities of businesses: beyond shareholders, towards stakeholders.
The value of a business to society is the wealth and employment it creates and the marketable products and services it provides to consumers at a reasonable price commensurate with quality. To create such value, a business must maintain its own economic health and viability, but survival is not a sufficient goal.

Businesses have a role to play in improving the lives of all their customers, employees, and shareholders by sharing with them the wealth they have created. Suppliers and competitors as well should expect businesses to honour their obligations in a spirit of honesty and fairness. As responsible citizens of the local, national, regional and global communities in which they operate, businesses share a part in shaping the future of those communities.

Principle 2
The economic and social impact of business: towards innovation, justice and world community.
Businesses established in foreign countries to develop, produce or sell should also contribute to the social advancement of those countries by creating productive employment and helping to raise the purchasing power of their citizens. Businesses also should contribute to human rights, education, welfare and vitalisation of the countries in which they operate.

Businesses should contribute to economic and social development not only in the countries in which they operate, but also in the world community at large, through effective and prudent use of resources, free and fair competition, and an emphasis upon innovation in technology, production methods, marketing and communications.

Principle 3
Business behaviour: beyond the letter of law towards a spirit of trust.
While accepting the legitimacy of trade secrets, businesses should recognise that sincerity, candour, truthfulness, the keeping of promises, and transparency contribute not only to their own credibility and stability but also to the smoothness and efficiency of business transactions, particularly on the international level.

Principle 4
Respect the rules.
To avoid trade frictions and to promote freer trade, equal conditions for competition, and fair and equitable treatment for all participants, businesses should respect international and domestic rules. In addition, they should recognise that some behaviour, although legal, may still have adverse consequences.

Principle 5
Support for multilateral trade.
Businesses should support the multilateral trade systems of the GATT/World Trade Organisation and similar international agreements. They should co-operate in efforts to promote the progressive and judicious liberalisation of trade and to relax those domestic measures that unreasonably hinder global commerce, while giving due respect to national policy objectives.

Principle 6
Respect for the environment.
A business should protect and, where possible, improve the environment, promote sustainable development, and prevent the wasteful use of natural resources.

Principle 7
Avoidance of illicit operations.
A business should not participate in or condone bribery, money laundering, or other corrupt practices: indeed, it should seek co-operation with others to eliminate them. It should not trade in arms or other materials used for terrorist activities, drug traffic or other organised crime.

SECTION 3: STAKEHOLDER PRINCIPLES

A set of principles for corporate relationships with customers, employees, owners/investors, suppliers, competitors, and communities.

1.3 Managing, Measuring and Monitoring

Commitment to the community must be an integral part of our business strategy. What's more, it can no longer be seen as the responsibility of one centralised department. Community involvement should be managed and delivered on a company-wide basis; it has to be run by the people who run the business. I also believe that, to be effective, SB's community and charitable activities must be aligned with our strategic intent and relevant to the needs of our business. In everything we do for the community we must reach the same high standards of excellence that we achieve in all other parts of our business. Our charitable activities must be customer-driven, innovative and cost effective, so that we can achieve maximum positive impact for both SB and the communities we serve.

Jan Leschly,

Chief Executive Officer,

SmithKline Beecham

The old adage, "if you can't measure it, you can't manage it" and vice versa, is becoming increasingly central to the philosophy and practice of corporate social and environmental responsibility. Mission statements and guidelines are only as good as their implementation. CEOs and directors can, and must, give guidance and direction, but the actual implementation can only be carried out by the people in the company who are making the products, delivering the services, carrying out the R&D, purchasing the inputs, marketing the outputs, managing the financial books, running the training, co-ordinating health, safety and the environment, and managing the community relations activities.

In a fairly typical multinational company this means thousands of people, in hundreds of locations, carrying out millions of tasks and interacting with millions of stakeholders every single day. It is an enormous management challenge to inculcate both the mindset and the methodologies which will result in each of these people thinking about the social and environmental implications of their daily work. It is however a management task worth investing in, as more and more evidence illustrates the positive impact on company morale and productivity when employees feel that they are participating in the company's wider contribution to society.

To make this happen in practice it is necessary not only to have mission statements and guidelines, but also to develop management systems which include the following processes:

a) Undertaking baseline studies/audits to ascertain current situations;

b) Setting targets based on this information and on stakeholder feedback;

c) Developing external and internal performance measures and standards, against which to measure progress towards the stated targets;

d) Assigning responsibilities and resources for training/motivating/ implementing/monitoring/reporting;

e) Reporting, both externally and internally; and

f) Monitoring performance against internal and external benchmarks.

Much like the approach to total quality management (TQM), these stages should be viewed as parts of a circle and with an emphasis on continuous improvement, which is one of the underlying principles of TQM. Regular and consistent stakeholder consultation and analysis – both internal and external – is absolutely fundamental to every stage of this process.

SmithKline Beecham is one of a small number of companies which is devoting time and resources to developing a coherent global strategy for managing its community investment activities. The following profile offers a brief summary of the approach the company is taking and the following pages look specifically at developments in the area of measuring and monitoring social and environmental impacts.

SmithKline Beecham
Building a global strategy for corporate community involvement

SmithKline Beecham is one of the world's leading health-care companies, discovering, developing, manufacturing and marketing pharmaceuticals, vaccines, over-the-counter medicines and health-related consumer products, and providing health-care services including clinical laboratory testing, disease management and pharmaceutical benefit management.

The company has a reputation in many of its countries of operation as a good corporate citizen. Like the vast majority of multi-nationals, however, until recently SmithKline Beecham has not managed its corporate community activities on a global basis. In April 1995, under the co-sponsorship of Jan Leschly the company's Chief Executive Officer and James Hill, Director & Senior Vice President of Corporate Affairs, a cross-sector, cross-functional task force was established. Its goal was to develop a new worldwide strategy for community and charitable activities, aligned to the company's corporate objectives, and capable of adding value to its global business and achieving measurable results.

The task force included ten senior executives representing each sector of the business, each region and a variety of disciplines. The task force members were assisted in their task by external experts in corporate community involvement and have undertaken a number of outreach activities with internal and external stakeholders, to review good practice and to survey attitudes.

One of the first actions they took, for example, was to consult with Grand Metropolitan, a recognised leader in the field of corporate community involvement. This consultation took the form of a visit to a school active in GrandMet's KAPOW programme, profiled on page 139, and a meeting with Lord Sheppard, GrandMet's Chairman and Geoffrey Bush, Group Community Relations Director. The task force also had access to benchmark studies of its competitors, as well as other leading corporate citizens. An external audit of SB's existing programmes in the UK and USA was undertaken and existing survey research on customer expectations in this area was compiled. A survey of targeted SB managers was also carried out, to get their views on the company's charitable and community activities. One of the strongest messages which came out of this survey was the fact that 92% of respondents supported the company's corporate responsibility programme, and substantial percentages (over 80% in each case) believed that SB should contribute resources other than cash, including SB products, management skills and employee skills.

Through a process of discussion and consultation the task force came up with a set of recommendations for: a new mission statement and strategic focus; close alignment with core business values; centralised policy and strategic direction-setting, combined with decentralised management and accountability – achieving a management structure which would enable the company to "think globally and act locally"; employee involvement; and communications and measurement.

One of the key elements of the company's emerging strategy is to align its community involvement with its core business by focusing on health-care and SB's five 'Core Values' as a company: customer; innovation; performance; people; and integrity.

As an example, the Community Partnership Management Team for SB International decided that health education and mobilisation would be the key strategic focus for its activities. The Team is currently in the process of developing a more consistent, customer-orientated approach by seeking the input of leading practitioners through a series of regional stakeholder workshops in China, Latin America, Africa and the Far East. The aim is to draw on the expertise of NGOs, healthworkers and others to assess key health education needs in each region, and respond with optimum deployment of SB's resources - products, people and cash. SB's strategy rests on the premise that the most effective and sustainable results will be achieved through active collaboration with local players.

SmithKline Beecham recognises that community involvement is a long-term activity; one which brings benefits over years rather than months, but one in which the company is committed to investing and to achieving continuous improvement.

> Social auditing and reporting is not just an ethically desirable activity, it is also a driver for improved effectiveness of the organisation and enhanced inclusion, and thus support from stakeholders.
>
> The Body Shop

MEASURING & MONITORING SOCIAL & ENVIRONMENTAL IMPACTS

The measurement of social and environmental impacts is becoming an increasingly sophisticated, complicated and important process. Management tools such as accounting and auditing, impact assessments, stakeholder analysis, reporting and benchmarking are being applied by more and more companies as they try to make sense of their wider impacts in society. Although most of them are still at the stage of tackling this agenda internally, a growing number are beginning to report externally on their impacts. This is especially the case with respect to environmental impacts, but a few companies are also producing reports on their social or community activities. In the latter case, a small number of companies have produced externally verified social audits, although most are still at the stage of providing either descriptive overviews of their social and community activities, or unaudited statistics.

There is clearly a long way to go before companies are in a position to report comprehensively on audited assessments of their overall contribution to sustainable development. This should not, however, detract from the progress that has been made in the field of auditing and reporting – especially on the environmental front – in the last five years. The following "snap-shots" look at a few encouraging initiatives in this field. They are followed by a "guest article" written by Dr Simon Zadek of the New Economics Foundation (NEF), which is one of the organisations playing a leading role in developing new measures and indicators for sustainability.

- In 1990, Norwegian company **Norsk Hydro** was the first company in Europe, and one of the international pioneers in this field, to produce an environmental report. Today there are in the region of 300-400 companies around the world producing such reports. This is still a tiny fraction, but the quality and depth of these reports is improving and a strong body of "good practice" and useful lessons is being developed for other companies to follow.

- The major accountancy firms are beginning to offer not only environmental auditing services, but social auditing as well. One of these is **KPMG** which has established a business ethics service in the USA aimed at helping its clients to create, "moral organisations – which have established effective compliance and control, developed ethical sensitivity in their employees and adopted business practices that are grounded in good ethics." In South Africa, the company is developing a reputation for its work on social auditing structured to help clients measure and improve their activities in areas such as: affirmative action; employee participation; community investment; environmental management and stakeholder consultation. With a global network on more than 1,000 offices in over 100 countries around the world, a professional service organisation such as KPMG can make a valuable contribution to spreading good standards and business practices.

- In September 1994, a group of large British companies joined forces to form the **London Benchmarking Group**, with the aim of working together to better define measures of efficiency and effectiveness in all types of community involvement activity by using benchmarking techniques. They are British Petroleum, Grand Metropolitan, IBM UK, Marks & Spencer, National Westminster Bank and Whitbread – six of the leading British companies in this field.

- In 1996, **The Body Shop** published *The Values Report* – a set of documents covering the company's performance in three areas of ethical concern: the environment, animal protection; and social practices. In doing so it became one of a small group of companies around the world to undertake a verified social audit.

- In its 1996 Annual Report, **Monsanto** placed sustainable development as one of the company's three core strategies for the future and commenced a series of stakeholder consultations to define what this commitment means for the management and future direction of all its business units.

These examples and others like them are a tiny fraction in comparison to the large number of companies which are doing very little in the field of measuring and reporting on their social and environmental impacts. However, the fact that they are some of the world's most visionary and commercially successful companies is a hopeful sign that this is the way of the future.

ENGAGING STAKEHOLDERS

A unique international programme run by SustainAbility, the United Nations Environment Programme (UNEP) and the New Economics Foundation (NEF) has done much to track progress in this field. SustainAbility is a British-based think-tank and consultancy which works with major companies in different parts of the world helping them to realign their corporate strategy to the sustainable development agenda. It promotes the concept of the "Triple Bottom Line – economic, environmental and social" and is playing an influential role in moving the corporate agenda in this direction.

The Engaging Stakeholders programme began in 1995, building on earlier work carried out by SustainAbility and UNEP in the area of corporate environmental reporting. It was based on the active support of 16 sponsoring companies, and more than 12 stakeholder organisations – ranging from stock exchanges to institutional investors and governments – whose work increasingly involves using the environmental reports produced by companies worldwide.

The programme has had a triple focus:

- the growing need for business to engage a range of internal and external stakeholders in developing, implementing and improving environmental and sustainable development programmes;

- the role of environmental disclosure and reporting in building the necessary credibility, trust and other forms of 'social capital' needed to ensure real, sustained stakeholder relationships which genuinely add value to a particular business; and

- more specifically, the role of the corporate environmental report (CER) in addressing both these areas of need.

The result of the programme is two separate, but linked reports: Volume 1 is entitled The Benchmark Survey which looks at the issues from the corporate perspective; and Volume 2, The Case Studies: looks at the issues from the stakeholders' perspectives.

- The Benchmark Survey – Second International Progress Report on Company Environmental Reporting, focuses on the latest developments in company environmental reporting, taking forward the existing UNEP/SustainAbility work in this field and mapping out the likely landscape for reporting over the next 5-10 years. It contains a 5-Stage reporting model, characterising various styles of CER and mapping out the possible elements of sustainability – or Stage 5 – reporting. Volume 1 also features a revised set of 50 reporting elements – or ingredients – and presents the findings of SustainAbility's 1996 CER benchmarking survey of 40 leading report-makers. The report emphasises the role of external stakeholders, such as markets and public authorities, in achieving sustainability – or so-called 'Stage 5' – reporting and in setting reporting boundaries. Accountability and stakeholder engagement, the report argues, will become increasingly important. It concludes with a discussion of 10 key transitions in environmental management and reporting, outlining the emerging agenda for report-makers.

- The Case Studies - 12 Users Respond to Company Environmental Reports, accompanies and illustrates Volume 1, arguing that better understanding of emerging stakeholder expectations and agendas is a vital starting point for expanding and improving the reporting process. In particular, the issue of how to create demand for CERs and widen their appeal needs to be tackled if companies are to continue reporting and if the resulting data is to be of real value in helping to manage the transition to sustainable development. Volume 2 explores the perspectives of 'report-users' by means of a collection of 12 stakeholder case studies, ranging from the Danish Environmental Protection Agency and Greenpeace to the Thai Stock Exchange. In addition to setting out what these stakeholder groups really want to know, the report gives key recommendations to report-makers on how to better target and engage their stakeholders.

For further information contact SustainAbility Ltd at: 49-53 Kensington High Street, London W8 5ED, Tel:+44 0)171 937 9996, Fax:+44 (0)171 937 7447, Email: info@sustainability.co.uk

An overview of contemporary developments in corporate social auditing

Dr Simon Zadek, *Research Director, New Economics Foundation*

The last decade has seen the practice of corporate social auditing – the measurement of, and reporting on, organisations' social performance in relation to their aims and those of their stakeholders – converging with principles first set over half a century ago. Companies in many countries have increased their investment in identifying, understanding, reporting on, and improving, their social performance, including their environmental footprint. One study by the Centre for Environmental and Social Accountancy Research found that major British companies, for example, have on average quadrupled their volume of social reporting over two decades, albeit in a fragmented way. This increase in 'silent accounting' throughout the corporate sector has been largely voluntary, although in a number countries there has been an increase in mandatory social reporting.

The increasing engagement of companies in social and ethical accounting and auditing is happening because of their recognition of the need to earn and sustain 'licenses to operate' by demonstrating their practice of responsible corporate citizenship. As the Chairman of British Telecom, Sir Iain Vallance, states, "I believe that in today's society, companies not only need to operate in an ethical manner, but also need publicly to demonstrate that they are doing so". In some instances this is understood in terms of risk and reputation management, and in others as a part of corporate affairs and marketing. In all cases, companies that have chosen to invest in this area have seen the imperative to have comprehensive information, regular disclosure, and systematic stakeholder dialogue, covering a range of issues that had hitherto been poorly understood, and inadequately dealt with in key decision-making processes.

The most innovative experiences have moved beyond fragmented reporting towards more systematic, comprehensive, rigorous, and externally verified methodologies for exploring, disclosing, and improving corporate social performance. The 'social audits' carried out by The Body Shop, Traidcraft in the UK and now Ben & Jerry's in the USA, the 'ethical accounting' undertaken by Sbn Bank and other companies in Denmark, and the 'social balances' of Co-op Italia, all offer practical, powerful, lessons for the corporate sector. For example, the social audit method developed and practised by the New Economics Foundation and others has drawn from best practice in benchmarking, stakeholder dialogue, management and quality assurance systems, external verification procedures, and the principle of continuous improvement.

The future of corporate social auditing depends on establishing agreed standards that allow quality of practice to be assessed, and for recognised training to be developed for social auditors and other key service providers. As for financial and environmental accounting and auditing, this will require professional institutes working to develop protocols, regulations, and accreditation systems based on negotiations between key parties and drawing on the emerging body of practical experience. As Alice Tepper Marlin of the US-based Council on Economic Priorities states, "...there is an urgent need for agreement on methods for gathering and analysing data so as to facilitate trend analysis and comparisons amongst companies, and to render the reports amenable to audit procedures".

> ...[social auditing] is an obvious way by which the public may be informed of the manner in which a large business... is discharging its social responsibilities... In the case of big companies it would provide a useful safety-valve for criticism. But it is essential that the social audit, when it comes, be made not only in the area of work and human relations, but also in that of the company's dealings with its customers, suppliers, and the community."
>
> **George Goyder, 1961**

One particular area where agreed systems and processes are rapidly developing is for monitoring and auditing corporate performance against agreed codes of conduct for working in developing countries, particularly covering labour standards. NGOs and companies are now active in developing monitoring systems, processes, and institutional standards that will meet the imperatives of comprehensiveness, transparency, and independence. For example, key NGOs – including the Catholic Institute of International Relations, Christian Aid, the Fair Trade Foundation, the New Economics Foundation, Oxfam, and the World Development Movement have formed a Working Group on Corporate Monitoring to establish the key design parameters and institutional needs for effective monitoring.

The Institute of Social and Ethical Accountability

One critical step in this direction has been the establishment of the Institute of Social and Ethical AccountAbility, an international professional body that aims to develop and promote best practice standards and accreditation procedures in social and ethical accounting and auditing. As the Chief Executive of The Body Shop, Anita Roddick, states, "The future of social auditing will depend on today's innovations becoming tomorrow's standards. The Institute of Social and Ethical AccountAbility exists to make this happen".

AccountAbility's membership already extends across key stakeholders in this process, including companies and consultancies, non-profit organisations, business schools and the accountancy and quality assurance professions. AccountAbility aims to evolve a federal learning and governance structure, and in this vein has supported the development of the first national body for social auditing, the Institute for Social and Ethical Auditing of South Africa. This Institute, with its Secretariat handled by the policy and institutional development NGO, the Development Resources Centre in Johannesburg, aims both to develop an understanding of what constitutes appropriate standards in South Africa on a platform of examining international and national experience, and national needs and circumstances, and also to influence the evolution of international standards in this process.

Contact: The New Economics Foundation
(Peter Raynard: neweconomics@gn.apc.org).

All quotes taken from AccountAbility Quarterly (No.1 Summer 1996), the journal of the Institute of Social and Ethical AccountAbility.

MONITORING

Individual companies which have adopted and/or established their own Codes of Conduct and operating guidelines usually have internal systems in place to monitor their progress against these guidelines. In a few cases, such as the chemical industry's Responsible Care programme and the European Eco-management and Audit Scheme (EMAS), there is an obligation to report externally on progress. This tends to be the exception however, rather than the norm. In the absence of public disclosure it is difficult for external third parties, such as investors, customers, NGOs, government bodies or the general public, to monitor corporate impacts and progress. This in turn makes it extremely difficult for them to make informed investment and consumption decisions that reward socially and environmentally responsible companies and penalise the less responsible ones.

In recent years there has been a sharp increase in efforts to monitor corporate, social and environmental impacts for investment purposes, spearheaded by the ethical fund management movement and some of the major American institutional investors, and supported by the progress made by companies in publicly reporting on these impacts. Initiatives such as the CERES Principles have been launched and other monitoring systems have been developed in both the USA and Europe. To-date, however, there has been little focus on monitoring corporate impacts outside the USA and Europe, especially in developing countries. Two of the initiatives that are starting to look at this are the Corporate Monitoring Group described on page 87 and the New York-based Council on Economic Priorities (CEP).

THE COUNCIL ON ECONOMIC PRIORITIES

First launched in 1969, CEP has been a pioneer in the field of social and environmental monitoring. Alice Tepper Marlin, CEP's Founder and Executive Director, was a young securities analyst with a money management firm when she saw the potential of providing investors with factual research on corporate practices which influence the quality of American life. She realised that once investors had this information they would be better positioned to encourage corporations to exercise greater social responsibility. Over the years CEP's mission has extended from informing investors to informing all corporate stakeholders. In its first quarter century the organisation has published thousands of pages of factual research on corporate social responsibility, the environment, and security and conversion; has been the subject of thousands of articles in the media; has testified before numerous governmental bodies; and has been able to influence corporate behaviour in many ways.

CEP co-operates wherever possible with business, but is ready to criticise and publicise social and environmental offenders where deemed necessary. This "stick and carrot approach" is best exemplified by CEP's well-known annual Corporate Conscience Awards and its equally well-known Campaign for Cleaner Corporations. The first honours companies for outstanding achievements in a number of areas of social responsibility (including global ethics) and the latter publicises the companies that CEP researchers have identified as environmental offenders, while at the same time offering them practical recommendations for improvement.

CEP's research team currently track more than 700 United States companies and 200 foreign-based companies operating in the USA, and rate them against: 12 areas of corporate environmental performance; women's advancement; minority advancement; charitable giving; community outreach; family benefits; workplace issues; disclosure of information; military contracts; and animal testing. This information forms the basis for CEP's SCREEN service for investors and for its *Shopping for a Better World* guide. The latter has gained national acclaim and has had a measurable influence on buying decisions, which in turn has encouraged major companies to work with CEP on improving their performance and ratings.

In 1994 CEP convened a Business Advisory Council to increase awareness within the business community of corporate social responsibility issues and to advise CEP on research criteria, new programmes and ways to increase disclosure. It also collaborated with the British-based New Consumer organisation in producing a pioneering series of "good practice" case studies on multi-nationals operating in developing countries. In the past year it has launched a *Partnership for Responsible Global Sourcing* in the USA for companies with suppliers based in developing countries, and is currently reviewing the potential for a similar initiative in Europe.

1.4 Motivating, Mobilising and Mainstreaming

Despite the important role that they play, mission statements, guidelines, codes of conduct and systems for managing, measuring and monitoring, are only "tools". The greatest opportunity for harnessing the power and potential of business as a partner in development lies firstly, in motivating and mobilising the talents and energies of the millions of people who work in the business sector and secondly, in mainstreaming a greater sense of innovation, entrepreneurship, individual responsibility and social and environmental awareness into their daily working lives.

It is not surprising that companies which have outstanding reputations for motivating their employees are not only commercially successful, but also leaders in the field of social and environmental responsibility. In his 1994 book, *The Frontiers of Excellence*, Robert Waterman profiles a small number of American companies which have a track record of excellence in terms of inspiring, empowering, challenging and valuing their employees. Several of these companies: Levi Strauss, Rubbermaid, the AES Corporation, Merck, Motorola and Procter & Gamble are renowned internationally for their leadership in the field of social and environmental responsibility. They also offer some of the best examples in the world of companies which have established win-win partnerships with suppliers, customers, NGOs and local communities that benefit both the company and its stakeholders. Levi Strauss for example, is quoted in almost every study of good corporate citizenship, with good reason, for its commitment to responsible global sourcing, employee involvement and a variety of community investment activities ranging from support for HIV/AIDS initiatives to youth issues and local economic development programmes. Merck has been responsible for two of the most innovative international corporate responsibility projects in the world: its partnership with INBio in Costa Rica, aimed at a mutually beneficial programme of biodiversity prospecting, and its Mectizan Donation Programme, launched in 1987 to supply a drug which combats river blindness to affected populations in developing countries. AES has forged innovative partnerships with NGOs such as Oxfam, Care International, the Nature Conservancy and the World Resources Institute, to establish carbon offset projects in Latin America, and both Motorola and Procter & Gamble have well-regarded community investment activities in different parts of the globe.

In almost every case it is the employees of these companies who have mobilised their skills and energies behind the company's social investment activities. Five of the key factors underpinning the motivation and mobilisation of these employees are as follows:

(i)   **Leadership from senior management**

(ii)   **Experiential learning and capacity-building**

(iii)   **Employee volunteering programmes**

(iv)   **A corporate culture of consultation**

(v)   **Incentive systems.**

The leadership paradigm of
Control, Order, and Predict
no longer works. It seems to
me that CEOs are telling us
that the new paradigm for
success has three elements:
Align, Create and Empower.
This trilogy is what effective
leadership is all about.

Warren Bennis,
Leaders on Leadership,
Harvard Business Review

The leader of the past was a
person who knew how to
tell. The leader of the
future will be a person who
knows how to ask...

Peter Drucker,
The Leader of the Future,
The Drucker Foundation

(i) LEADERSHIP FROM SENIOR MANAGEMENT

Throughout history, the progress of organisations and societies has been closely linked to the courage, vision and integrity of their leaders, and no more so than today. In an increasingly multi-polar and multi-stakeholder world, where traditional structures of governance are giving way to a more complex tapestry of interactions between different cultures, sectors and organisations, leadership is needed at all levels of society – in government, business and voluntary organisations. As the business sector adjusts to a radically different environment from the one it faced even five years ago, corporate leadership and vision is critical. Its presence or absence will be fundamental in determining how employees adapt and respond to the challenges described in earlier chapters.

Clearly, leadership styles vary dramatically from country to country, company to company and person to person. Despite this, companies with a strong culture of responsible leadership and employee motivation often share common traits. They invest heavily in leadership development programmes (including training, experiential learning and volunteering) and in employee consultation and communication processes aimed at developing a sense of common purpose. Many of them also have frameworks and systems specifically aimed at inspiring and incentivising their employees. And in almost all of them, senior managers from the Chief Executive downwards are open and accessible to their staff – equally ready to listen as they are to direct. At the same time they also have a clear strategic vision and an ability to articulate it, even if they do so in different ways.

One of the clearest examples of a company articulating its approach to leadership is Levi Strauss. The company has a Mission Statement, like most other successful companies. It also has a Code of Ethics and Global Sourcing and Operating Guidelines, but what really sets it apart is its Aspirations Statement. This statement captures the company's sense of purpose and its leadership imperatives, and in doing so, goes much further than a mission statement in describing how it will motivate and mobilise its employees.

(ii) EXPERIENTIAL LEARNING AND CAPACITY-BUILDING

Apart from inspiring employees through good leadership, companies can also invest in training activities to help their current and future employees develop the practical skills and mindsets needed to be more entrepreneurial, innovative and responsible. There is a great difference between training and human resource development programmes which are classroom or theory-based and those that enable people to actually experience what it is that they are learning about. There is also a difference between programmes that focus on building a person's level of information and those that focus on building a person's capacities to apply and use that information. There is a growing emphasis on the latter approaches to management development, both within companies themselves and in leading management education institutions.

Some of the management education organisations which are applying these approaches and integrating social and environmental responsibility into their programmes include:

- **The University of Michigan's Corporate Citizenship programme** is an initiative consisting of lectures, project visits, volunteering and internships, in which all its MBA students and managers on selected executive management programmes participate.

LEVI STRAUSS & CO.

Mission Statement

The mission of Levi Strauss & Co. is to sustain responsible commercial success as a global marketing company of branded casual apparel. We must balance goals of superior profitability and return on investment, leadership market positions, and superior products and service. We will conduct our business ethically and demonstrate leadership in satisfying our responsibilities to our communities and to society. Our work environment will be safe and productive and characterised by fair treatment, teamwork, open communications, personal accountability and opportunities for growth and development.

Aspiration Statement

We all want a Company that our people are proud of and committed to, where all employees have an opportunity to contribute, learn, grow and advance based on merit, not politics or background.

We want our people to feel respected, treated fairly, listened to and involved.

Above all, we want satisfaction from accomplishments and friendships, balanced personal and professional lives and to have fun in our endeavours. When we describe the kind of Levi Strauss & Co. we want in the future what we are talking about is building on the foundation we have inherited: affirming the best of our Company's traditions, closing gaps that may exist between principles and practices and updating some of our values to reflect contemporary circumstances.
What type of leadership is necessary to make our aspirations a reality?

NEW BEHAVIOURS

Leadership that exemplifies directness, openness to influence, commitment to the success of others, willingness to acknowledge our own contributions to problems, personal accountability, teamwork and trust. Not only must we model these behaviours, but we must coach others to adopt them.

DIVERSITY

Leadership that values a diverse workforce (age, sex, ethnic group etc.) at all levels of the organisation, diversity in experience and diversity in perspectives. We have committed to taking full advantage of the rich backgrounds and abilities of all our people and to promote greater diversity in positions of influence. Differing points of view will be sought; diversity will be valued and honesty rewarded not suppressed.

RECOGNITION

Leadership that provides greater recognition – both financial and psychic – for individuals and teams that contribute to our success. Recognition must be given to all who contribute: those who create and innovate and those who continually support the day-to-day business requirements.

ETHICAL MANAGEMENT PRACTICES

Leadership that epitomises the stated standards of ethical behaviour. We must provide clarity about our expectations and must enforce these standards throughout the corporation.

COMMUNICATIONS

Leadership that is clear about Company, unit and individual goals and performance. People must know what is expected of them and receive timely, honest feedback on their performance and career aspirations.

EMPOWERMENT

Leadership that increases the authority and responsibility of those closest to our products and customers. By actively pushing responsibility, trust and recognition into the organisation, we can harness and release the capabilities of all our people.

> Business must now start to develop and deliver new (training) programmes: management training is not enough. New technology can bring us massive quantities of information. But as we look towards a future in which training courses can be delivered electronically, we must set priorities that link technical learning with personal growth and the new responsibilities of global citizenship.
>
> John O'Neil,
> How to Make a Leader,
> World Link Magazine,
> February 1995

- **Harvard Business School's recently launched "Social Enterprise Initiative"** which is co-chaired by Jim Austen, a pioneer in the field of management in developing countries and Kasturi Rangan, an expert on social marketing. This initiative was driven in part by a growing recognition of the need to develop the managerial skills and financial self-sustainability of the voluntary sector, but also by a survey of graduates from the business school – most of whom are now working in the business sector – which showed that over 80% of these business leaders dedicate significant time, money and effort to social enterprises. It is envisaged that all future MBA students will be required to take courses in this area.

- **Stanford Business School's Public Management programme** involves about 100 MBA students every year in extra-curricular activities dedicated to public service. It focuses on a specific public policy topic such as global sustainability, education partnerships and urban development, and places MBA students in public service/non-profit internships and volunteer programmes.

- **The Asian Institute of Management** has integrated corporate responsibility issues and sustainable development into its management programmes and also runs community support initiatives and management training for development professionals in Asia.

- **The New Business Academy** was founded in 1995 by Anita Roddick, CEO and Founder of The Body Shop International, with the goal of developing the kind of business education required for socially and ecologically responsible business. It is researching best practice case studies and developing programmes for current and future business executives in subjects such as social and ethical auditing, eco-management, socially responsible business, international trade and human rights and renewing corporate governance.

- **The Prince of Wales Business Leaders Forum's INSIGHT programme** brings together people from the business, government and voluntary sectors to participate in workshops, secondments, and local and international visits to partnership projects, in areas such as education, community-based development and crime prevention. The goal of the programme is to raise awareness, share experiences and build links between different sectors and countries aimed at increasing partnership between business and other groups in society.

- **AIESEC's Educating Tomorrow's Global Business Leaders programme.** Launched in 1995 in partnership with the PWBLF and supported by British Airways, BP and American Express, this programme has surveyed the attitudes of nearly 8,000 business and economics students in 28 countries on their attitudes towards the role of business in society. Consultations are now being set up in seven developing and OECD countries between corporate human resource specialists, academics and students to increase the focus of corporate responsibility in the university curriculum.

- **The Management Institute for Environment and Business BELL programme** (Business Environment Learning and Leadership) is supported by more than 25 business schools in the USA and is also being implemented in Latin America, with the goal of bringing together companies and universities to "green" management education.

- **Students for Responsible Business** is a US-based network of business students and alumni committed to effecting social change through business, through campaigning, networking and internships.

- **The Rockefeller Foundation's LEAD (Leadership for Environment and Development) programme** brings together policy makers and business people from more than 15 developing and transitional economies in a part-time 18-month programme of lectures, study tours, project visits and internships. Its primary objective is to establish a global network of decision-makers, numbering more than 1,000 by the turn of the century, with the multi-disciplinary and cross-sectoral skills to steer a path towards sustainable development in their countries.

(iii) EMPLOYEE VOLUNTEERING

Employee volunteering programmes offer an increasingly popular form of management development which relies heavily on experiential learning and capacity building. They also fulfil a joint objective of motivating and mobilising employees to take direct action on social and environmental projects in a way that benefits the employee, the company and the community.

In the USA in particular, but also in the United Kingdom and increasingly in other countries, companies have established comprehensive programmes to encourage their employees to get involved in community volunteering either on company time, or with company funding and in-kind support. In some companies this type of involvement is a required part of management objectives. In the UK, for example, the highly respected retail chain Marks & Spencer requires all of its store managers to take a leadership role in a community initiative. In other companies volunteering is a key element of in-house management training and development, as is the case with Hindustan Lever in India, profiled on page 205, which sends all its young executives to work on community projects. Both BP and Hewlett Packard are examples of companies which have sent teams of managers to Africa to work on community development projects as part of personal development and team-building exercises.

Nationwide campaigns to encourage employee volunteering are in operation in both the USA, through the Points of Light Foundation, and UK, through Business in the Community which is profiled on page 268. These models have much potential in other countries. Studies in both countries demonstrate that employee volunteering programmes can help to: meet strategic business goals; build the quality, skills, experience and motivation of the workforce; build corporate reputation; and provide clear community benefits by offering not only the cash of business, but also the managerial and technical skills and energies of its employees. There is mounting evidence that employees who get involved in such programmes are more motivated in their regular jobs as a result, as well as being more aware of the role that both they as individuals and their companies can play in society.

As with the dissemination of other "good business practices" multinational companies are playing a valuable role in spreading the concept and practice of employee volunteering to developing and transitional economies. It can be argued that the severe shortage of management skills in many of these countries make it extremely difficult to establish comprehensive employee volunteering programmes, given that managers are often already fully stretched taking care of urgent business priorities. However, even under these circumstances, well-structured and targeted volunteer programmes can usually reap more benefits, than they cost in terms of time and money.

THE POINTS OF LIGHT FOUNDATION

The Points of Light Foundation is a private US-based non-profit organisation which seeks to engage the public in meaningful community service aimed at alleviating some of the USA's most serious social problems. Its Principles of Excellence programme is targeted specifically at business leaders and aimed at encouraging them to mobilise their employees in community volunteering initiatives. The initiative is based on a set of three guidelines – A Plan to A.C.T. These call for companies to: Acknowledge that the corporation's community service involvement and its employee volunteer efforts contribute to the achievement of its business goals; Commit to establish, support and promote an employee volunteer programme that encourages the involvement of every employee and treat it like any other core business function; Target community service efforts at serious social problems in the country. The initiative is supported by companies throughout the United States accounting for thousands of employees and thousands of hours of community service.

The power of corporate volunteering efforts cannot be underestimated. Even one day of volunteering time can have a remarkable impact on local communities. In California, for example, during a recent initiative to bring information technology into schools, some 100,000 engineers and other volunteers with technical expertise helped to wire 9,000 schools to the Internet on one day. As part of the same national initiative, 80% of the schools in Connecticut were also wired by volunteers in one day's worth of work. Millions of skilled employees in thousands of companies around the world offering the equivalent of just one day of volunteer time to local community projects could make a valuable contribution.

> What I have learned is how to manage with the consensus of all employees. I've come to believe strongly in the value of consensus, and I've come to believe that it is becoming a prerequisite in the 1990s for almost every corporation. There are national surveys that show there is less trust in leadership than ever before - political leadership, business leadership, you name it. That alone should be clue enough that it is important that we communicate with all our people and justify what we're doing to all our people.
>
> Gerald Greenwald, CEO of United Airlines which is owned 55% by its employees
>
> Fortune.Magazine, October 1996

America's 1995 Corporate Conscience Awards

Community Involvement:
Colgate-Palmolive Company
The Timberland Company

Environmental Stewardship:
New England Electric System

Employee Responsiveness:
Polaroid Corporation

Equal Employment Opportunity:
The Coca-Cola Company

Global Ethics:
Merck & Co.

(iv) CORPORATE CULTURE OF CONSULTATION

Another key factor in motivating and mobilising employees is regular and genuine consultation with them on matters relating to their jobs and immediate workplace, as well as the wider role of the company in society.

An example of how one company is tackling the latter is **Monsanto's Sustainability Team**. Monsanto has taken a major step in placing sustainable development, together with operational excellence and growth, as one of its three strategic corporate goals. To-date it is one of the relatively few companies to articulate a commitment to sustainable development in its corporate annual report. In support of this commitment a cross-functional team of employees has been established, divided into seven subteams: the eco-efficiency team; the full-cost accounting team; the index team; the water team; the new products/business team; the global hunger team; and the education/communications team. The Sustainability Team has undertaken a variety of company-wide initiatives to inform, educate and learn from employees about the importance of sustainable development to Monsanto's strategic goals, and to encourage them to get actively involved in one of the subteams or other sustainability initiatives.

BHP, the large Australian mining and petroleum company, is another company which has recently launched an employee and community consultation initiative. Called *Common Ground*, the initiative is lead by an independent Council and will fund environmental projects related to the petroleum industry, which have been identified by employees, their families, the community and people with specific knowledge of the environmental issues associated with the oil and gas industry, such as academics, geologists, marine biologists, engineers and environmentalists. The goal of the initiative is to increase employee awareness of environmental issues and to make a clear commitment to both employees and the community about the company's readiness to respond to concerns and to improve the quality of environmental care.

(v) INCENTIVE SYSTEMS

The use of financial and non-financial incentives – such as awards and recognition programmes – play a useful role, both in motivating employees and in mainstreaming corporate responsibility issues into core business functions. Some companies, such as Kodak, are developing innovative systems for aligning bonuses to environmental performance, and many others operate internal award programmes, such as the BP Chairman's Award described opposite.

High profile external award programmes and media coverage also serve to shine the spotlight on good practice, motivating the companies and individuals responsible. These include:

- America's Corporate Conscience Awards, run by the Council on Economic Priorities;

- The US Business Enterprise Awards, run by the Business Enterprise Trust, a national non-profit organisation led by prominent leaders in business, academia, labour and the media, which seeks to identify and celebrate exemplary acts of socially-concerned business leadership;

- President Clinton's recently launched Corporate Citizenship Awards;

- The World Environment Center's Gold Medal Award;

The BP Chairman's Award

The BP Chairman's Awards are designed to recognise achievement in Health, Safety and Environmental care. Everyone who works for the company is encouraged to enter. Whether they are employees or contractors, are HSE professionals or not, whether they have made an individual contribution or worked as part of a team, whether they work on a BP site or for a BP joint venture company. The judges look for projects that have been completed and have delivered results, not ideas or projected schemes. Each entry is assessed on four criteria as follows:

- Performance - did the activity make a contribution to the Group's performance?

- Reputation - has it enhanced BP's HES reputation?

- Innovation - is the activity an innovative solution to a longstanding problem?

- Transferability - can the activity be applied to other regions or businesses within BP?

The level of interest and recognition that the programme generates within the company is high. In 1996, some 800 people teamed up to submit a total of 199 entries from 24 different countries and numerous different operating units. The ten winners ranged from a ground-breaking initiative in Norway to re-inject produced water resulting in substantial economic and environmental advantages, to the use of solar panels in Colombia and the environmental management of used oil in South Africa.

- the UK-based WorldAware awards for British companies operating in developing countries;

- AmCham Brazil's national Eco-awards which are made to both Brazilian and multinational companies;and

- UNEP's Global 500 Awards which to-date have been awarded to a small selection of outstanding companies which include: Golden Hope Plantations in Malaysia; Bamburi Portland Cement in Kenya; and Alcoa Aluminium in Australia.

The press can also play a critical role. National newspapers in South Africa, the Philippines, India, and Zimbabwe, for example, run annual supplements on corporate citizenship and Colombia's *El Tiempo* runs a regular column on the subject. However, much more could be done in this field.

Conclusions on managing the corporate contribution

Managing the multitude of economic, social, environmental, cultural and political impacts that a large company has on the many countries and communities in which it operates is a complex, but not impossible task. As more corporate leaders develop a vision for their company's role in contributing to sustainable development, and motivate and mobilise their employees to share that vision, the tools and systems for managing, measuring, reporting and monitoring this contribution (many of which are currently being pioneered) will hopefully come into their own and help to put the vision into practice for many more companies. The following section looks at some of the companies around the world that are already trying to put such a vision into practice. None of them are perfect, but they offer some idea of the myriad ways in which business can be a partner in development.

The contribution of the business sector

COMPANY MANAGEMENT FUNCTIONS

- policy and strategy

- finance and investor relations

- control

- production and operations

- sales and marketing

- purchasing

- distribution and retailing

- human resource development and industrial relations

- health, safety and environment

- research and development

- public affairs

- community relations

- government relations

- corporate foundation/ philanthropic giving

BOARD OF DIRECTORS

⟵——————————————⟶

CHIEF EXECUTIVE OFFICER

A. CORE BUSINESS ACTIVITIES

The principal contribution of business to development is through the efficient and ethical pursuit of its core business activities. It can however, maximise the beneficial spin-offs and multipliers of these activities – especially through promoting local economic participation and sharing core competencies and business practices with host countries and communities:

1. INVESTMENT AND INCOME FLOWS
- portfolio and direct investment
- taxes
- salaries
- foreign exchange earnings

2. EMPLOYMENT
- direct and indirect job creation
- minimising the social cost of restructuring and downsizing

3. GOODS AND SERVICES
- meeting needs/offering choice
- marketing and advertising
- consumer rights issues
- fairtrade

4. HUMAN RESOURCES
- training and management development
- occupational health and safety
- promoting workplace diversity, supporting women and minorities
- child labour issues
- employee share ownership and incentive schemes

5. INFRASTRUCTURE
- physical – transport, communication, housing, utilities
- institutional – financial, legal, trading and distribution, business associations

6. TECHNOLOGY TRANSFER AND CO-OPERATION

7. STANDARDS/BUSINESS PRACTICES
- corporate governance/ethics
- health, safety and environment
- product and process management
- stakeholder management i.e. guidelines for suppliers and contractors; industrial relations and conflict resolution procedures etc.

8. LOCAL BUSINESS DEVELOPMENT
- promotion of an enterprise culture
- creating forward and backward linkages
- promoting small-scale and micro-enterprises

BUSINESS ASSOCIATIONS

⟵——————————————⟶

- Representative bodies
- Issue-driven coalitions

BOARD OF DIRECTORS

⟷

CHIEF EXECUTIVE OFFICER

COMPANY STAKEHOLDERS

B. SOCIAL INVESTMENT AND PHILANTHROPY

In surrounding communities, which can range from immediate localities to nationwide or even foreign communities where the company has an interest, the company can make social investments or philanthropic donations to improve human, social and environmental conditions. This can be achieved through the company's own community relations programme, or by creating a corporate foundation, or by establishing strategic public interest partnerships with other stakeholders such as other companies, NGOs and government entities, or by working through existing industry associations.

A company can offer:

1. **PEOPLE** – advisors, volunteers, secondees, trustees

2. **MONEY** – grants, loans, venture capital, equity

3. **PRODUCTS AND SERVICES** – donations, "at cost", social marketing

4. **COMPETENCIES** – technical, managerial, training courses, work experience

5. **FACILITIES** – premises, equipment

6. **ACCESS TO BUSINESS NETWORKS** and decision-makers

C. POLICY DIALOGUE

Business can contribute to the formulation and implementation of policy – locally, nationally and internationally – by acting in a transparent way to share experience and competencies with public institutions, regulators and agencies.

1. NATIONALLY
- developing appropriate regulatory, institutional and incentive structures
- tackling obstacles to private investment
- contributing to content of education, training, local economic development, employment, environment policies

2. INTERNATIONALLY
- developing "level playing fields" for social and environmental policies and regulations
- developing global codes of conduct

COMPANY STAKEHOLDERS

- investors/creditors

- employees

- customers

- suppliers

- trade unions

- distributors/retailers

- local communities

- general public

- activist/campaigning groups

- other NGOs

- media

- academic and research institutes

- government
  - local
  - national
  - supranational

BUSINESS ASSOCIATIONS

⟷

- Representative bodies
- Issue-driven coalitions

© The Prince of Wales Business Leaders Forum, September 1996

MANAGING THE CORPORATE CONTRIBUTION

1. **MODELS AND MECHANISMS**
   - core business activities
   - social investment and philanthropy
   - policy dialogue

2. **MISSION STATEMENTS AND METHODOLOGIES**

3. **MANAGING, MONITORING AND MEASURING**

4. **MOTIVATING, MOBILISING AND MAINSTREAMING**

THE CONTRIBUTION OF THE BUSINESS SECTOR TO COUNTRIES AND COMMUNITIES

1. **GENERAL OVERVIEW**

2. **ECONOMIC DEVELOPMENT**
   Aimed at increasing not only economic growth, but also economic opportunity and participation

3. **HUMAN DEVELOPMENT**
   Investing in education, training and health both in the workplace and in the wider community

4. **ENVIRONMENTAL SUSTAINABILITY**
   Investing in cleaner production and more sustainable patterns of consumption

5. **SOCIAL COHESION**
   Tackling social exclusion, crime and corruption and investing in civil society, social entrepreneurship and cultural diversity

5. **INTEGRATED COMMUNITY DEVELOPMENT**
   Supporting participatory development in urban and rural communities

6. **EMERGENCY AND DISASTER RELIEF**
   Improving emergency preparedness and helping out in natural and man-made disasters

DESCRIBING THE CORPORATE CONTRIBUTION

2 Describing the Corporate Contribution

The preceding section reviewed some of the approaches that companies are using to manage their wider role in society. It emphasised three broad areas of corporate action which determine a company's contribution to development:

- **core business activities**
- **social investment and philanthropy**
- **policy dialogue.**

The following section draws on more than 100 examples from around the world to describe some of the positive impacts that these three areas of activity can have on host countries and communities where companies are operating. It reviews the contribution of specific companies and/or corporate-supported partnerships to the following interlinked areas, all of which are critical to the achievement of more participative and sustainable wealth creation. Some of the contributions, for example technology co-operation, are relevant to almost all areas:

- **Economic Development** – emphasising not only the economic growth contributions that the formal business sector can make, but also ways in which it can try to minimise the human costs of restructuring, and can promote broader economic participation and business development, especially through supporting small, medium and micro-scale enterprises (SMMEs);

- **Human Development** – this looks at ways in which companies can develop the skills and capacities of their own employees in the workplace, but also at corporate community programmes outside the company's immediate business activities targeted at education; training and skills development; health and nutrition; youth development; and the application of information technology to social development;

- **Environmental Sustainability** – the corporate contribution in this area has received wide attention and analysis since the Rio Earth Summit. It is briefly overviewed here, looking at a range of business-led initiatives at the international, national and sectoral levels;

- **Social Cohesion** – this looks at examples of business helping to tackle problems of social exclusion (many of which are a direct result of corporate downsizing and economic restructuring), private sector efforts to tackle crime and corruption, and initiatives to support a healthy civil society and social entrepreneurship which underpin the achievement of social cohesion;

- **Integrated Community Development** – in reality, none of the above happen separately or in a vacuum, and this looks at some localised initiatives in both urban and rural settings where business is playing an important and beneficial role in a more integrated approach to participatory community development;

- **Emergency Relief and Disaster Planning** – is another field where the private sector is becoming more active, both in terms of being better prepared for industrial accidents and in helping out at times of natural and man-made disasters such as earthquakes, famine and war; and

- **Developing Innovative Financing Mechanisms** – in all the above areas, financing is a critical and often scarce resource. One of the contributions that business can make is helping to develop mechanisms that maximse the efficiency, effectiveness and accessibility of scarce public and private funds for community development, social programmes and environmental projects.

2.1 A General Overview

Prior to looking at specific examples and case studies of the business contribution to development, three points are worth noting:

(i) THE IMPORTANCE OF MEDIUM, SMALL AND MICRO-ENTERPRISE

The following examples are drawn mainly from the formal, large-scale business sector – both multi-nationals and local companies. This is just a starting point, reflecting the core types of companies with which the PWBLF works, and in no way suggests that medium, small and micro-enterprises (SMMEs) – from both the formal and informal sector – do not make a valuable contribution to sustainable development. Indeed, they are often, and justifiably, referred to as "the backbone" of national economies.

From the economic powerhouses of East Asia and the rapidly emerging economies of Latin America, to the industrialised nations of the European-North American-Japanese triad and the countries of sub-Saharan Africa, SMMEs account for the vast majority of enterprises and provide a substantial amount of employment and output. In the European Union, for example, enterprises of less than 10 people constitute nearly all enterprises, provide about 33% of all jobs and nearly 25% of output. Enterprises from 10-500 employees represent a further 42% or so of employment and some 47% of output, compared with only 25% of employment and 30% of output by large firms. In Latin America, more than 95% of all enterprises employ less than 50 people and these enterprises, many of which are in the informal sector, account for an estimated 35-40% of GDP. They are usually far less capital intensive than their large and medium size counterparts, and so account for a smaller percentage of investment, but their contribution to employment and output cannot be ignored. Nor can their dynamism, and agility when it comes to seeking out and filling new market niches – all of which are critical to wealth creation and competitiveness.

The contribution of SMMEs to human development, social cohesion and community-level investment is also important. OECD-based organisations such as Business for Social Responsibility in the USA and the Social Venture Network, offer many excellent examples of medium and small-scale companies developing creative and proactive solutions to community problems. In many cases these smaller companies offer a bigger percentage of their employee time and/or profits to social investment than their larger corporate peers. In poorer countries and communities, SMMEs, many of which are family-owned and operated, are often the wealth-creating "glue" that, together with non-profit civil society associations, holds many communities together. When government services fail, or do not even reach these communities, the entrepreneurs of the informal enterprise sector often develop ingenious, and admittedly not always legal solutions. Harnessing this ingenuity and entrepreneurship and mainstreaming it into the formal economy where it is legal, is one of the great challenges for governments; one in which the large-scale, formal business sector can play a valuable role. In many cases these SMMEs serve as subcontractors, suppliers, distributors, and franchisees to larger companies and there is therefore a potential business link that can be created between the two, not to mention a myriad of other ways in which big business can support the development of a healthy and vibrant SMME sector, some of which will be described in the next section. One important area is sharing and supporting cleaner production technologies given that the SMME sector, rather than large scale business, is often the source of industrial environmental problems.

> There are an increasing number of people throughout the developing world who are looking for jobs, opportunities and optimism. Neither charity nor development assistance can provide opportunities on the scale necessary. Neither can government schemes, though the schemes of government are inevitably of crucial importance. Small businesses, in their millions, can provide the opportunities.
>
> Stephan Schmidheiny,
> *The Cutting Edge: Small Business and Progress*, 1994

(ii) DIFFERENT CONTRIBUTIONS FROM DIFFERENT SECTORS

In describing the impact of large-scale companies, it should go without saying that there are enormous differences in contribution between different industry sectors. The primary resource industries: oil and gas; mining; forestry and agribusiness, for example, obviously have a very different set of impacts and contributions to make to host countries and communities, than fund managers making portfolio investments, or retail companies sourcing and distributing products and goods, and consumer goods companies selling foodstuffs, beverages, pharmaceuticals and other household products. While these sectoral differences are worthy of further study and comparison, the following section attempts to draw examples from a wide range of sectors and does not analyse specific sector characteristics.

(iii) THE IDEOLOGICAL AND PRACTICAL CHALLENGES OF ASSESSING CORPORATE CONTRIBUTIONS

There is still misunderstanding and even mistrust of the private sector amongst certain governments, NGOs and civil society associations. This is not without some justification. It will always be possible to find examples of corrupt, unethical, unclean and destructive business practices on the part of large companies, and not only in developing countries. Even within individual companies that have an outstanding reputation for being socially responsible, there will always be examples where they have made mistakes, where a local plant in one country has an appalling record of environmental mistakes, arrogance or lack of community consultation, or even where one individual, or small group of individuals, has been highly unethical. The power of the global media and the growing information networks of the NGO community are combining to ensure that such cases are brought to the public attention. This is a useful role to ensure better corporate governance, but it is not always accurate in its provision of information, and even when it is, it tends to detract from the many positive things that companies are doing. Good news doesn't make the headlines – often not even the "back-pages" let alone the "front-pages" of the world's newspapers.

It is for this reason that the following examples attempt to focus on the "good news" and the good practices of companies. They do so in the knowledge that most of them have not been independently evaluated and verified in terms of their impacts on all possible stakeholders. This raises another challenge that companies face in the minefield of global corporate responsibility; even when they think they are doing things well or making a positive contribution, there will often be someone to point out the shortfalls. From a purely practical perspective it is not always easy for companies to "prove" that their impacts are beneficial or benign to society, or that they are striving to make them so. One of the main reasons that a number of leading companies are undertaking and reporting on externally verified environmental impacts, and considering how they can do the same with their more complex social impacts, is to substantiate the good practice that they genuinely believe they are doing. Even when they have such studies done, it is clear that the issues are so complex and interdependent that certain impacts are almost impossible to measure, let alone verify, with any certainty. However the will to try is increasingly there, and the field of environmental, and social evaluation and reporting is likely to grow in importance. There is also great potential for the development of impact indicators, which companies can measure their impacts against, and use to describe their contributions to development. The framework developed by the EBRD and summarised on page 79, is one example of such indicators.

> While there has been almost universal movement towards a private sector approach to development, there are still many countries in which government officials have only a grudging intellectual acceptance of the need for private sector growth. There is still much misunderstanding, even mistrust, of the private sector on the part of many African governments.
>
> Creating the Action Agenda
> UNDP, 1996

At the more global, systemic level, almost every single private sector contribution that is described in the following pages can be looked at from a positive and negative perspective, depending on the viewer. For example:

- **Technology transfer** – new technologies can have a dramatic impact on economic growth and can benefit specific industry sectors by: facilitating the production of new goods with a higher value-added; ensuring cleaner production processes; increasing production efficiency and product quality; improving management techniques; and even increasing equity and access to economic opportunities. There are, however, also the obvious examples of high social costs when technology displaces human resources, the ethical questions raised by biotechnology and genetically enhanced organisms, and many criticisms of technology being inappropriate to local needs, because it undermines local production or because it is too costly, too capital intensive, too strongly protected through exclusive patents or too difficult to maintain.

- **The production of goods and services** – in many cases the production of a wider range of goods and services has benefits to host countries and communities, but there are many who question their appropriateness, their cost, their displacement of locally produced products, the way in which advertising creates unnecessary needs and unsustainable consumption patterns, the ethics of western advertising in poor countries where few can afford to purchase the goods, the immorality of selling products banned in parent countries, the unfairness of trade relations, and the environmental dangers of "a billion Chinese buying fridges", to give one of many consumer challenges on the environmental front. The need to produce products which will have a minimal environmental impact through their entire life-cycle – from "cradle to grave" – is one of the greatest responsibilities and potential market opportunities facing industry.

- **Finance and tax systems** offer other examples of the positive and negative impacts of the private sector. Companies are major contributors to government taxes, yet in almost every country, including many OECD ones, there are valid criticisms of corporations finding "loopholes" through which they can legally avoid paying tax, not to mention too many examples of illegal evasion. Private-driven portfolio investment has played a major, and usually beneficial role in the development of emerging stock markets, but many would criticise its short-term imperatives and the instability that can be created by massive inflows and outflows, as Mexico experienced in early 1995. Others would criticise the fact that the multi-trillion dollar global banking industry which is capable of developing ever more complex and sophisticated financial instruments, is uninterested and unwilling to develop systems and services for micro-credit.

These are all valid concerns, and are issues that national and multinational companies, as well as governments in OECD, developing and transition economies, must seriously consider in the drive towards sustainable development. Each of the different types of impact described in the following pages is probably worthy of detailed debate and analysis along the above lines, let alone the debate referred to in earlier sections about the impact and sustainability of the free-market, global economy in general. The following pages, however, take as their starting point the existence of this global economy – warts and all – and attempt to capture some of the ways in which individual companies and groups of companies operating within this global context are contributing to the public good, while at the same time focusing on their private profitability and the bottom-line.

2.2 Economic Development

It is obviously through its contribution to economic development that the private sector has its most immediate and major impact. This is an area which has been extensively and comprehensively studied and will not be covered in detail here, other than to summarise the major private sector contributions to economic development and to elaborate on a few key points. The contributions can be listed as follows:

Economic development is in part about increasing economic growth but equally important it is about increasing economic participation and opportunity for as many people as possible.

(i) INVESTMENT AND INCOME FLOWS

The private sector is the major source of both portfolio and direct investment in a growing number of countries; it is also a key contributor to government taxes, directly and indirectly through corporation tax, value-added and income tax; it mobilises financial risk capital and the nation's savings, adding value and circulating it through the economy via loans and equity investments, employee salaries, supplier contracts, investor returns and so on; it influences the Balance of Payments through visible and invisible imports and exports; and generally facilitates the increasingly complex and vital flow of financial capital within national economies and between them. This in turn underpins the investments in industrial development, infrastructure, technology and people that are so critical to national wealth creation.

None of the above can occur however, or will not occur efficiently and effectively, without a stable macro-economy and an enabling environment built on: sound and clear legal and regulatory systems; responsive, transparent and accountable public institutions; a solid and diversified financial and banking structure; and incentive and risk-sharing mechanisms for certain long-term investments, such as infrastructure, urban regeneration and social services (to the extent that the private sector is starting to provide these in many countries). Governments, despite their diminished economic power in the global economy, play a fundamental role in providing all of these, and the need for public-private partnership to ensure the maximum efficiency and effectiveness in each area is paramount.

(ii) EMPLOYMENT

The business sector creates jobs, both directly and indirectly. Surrounding even the smallest of companies is a network of service providers and suppliers of goods and products; a complex multiplier effect that ripples through the economy, with one enterprise and one sector linking to another, even beyond national borders. Obviously, as recent experience in a number of countries demonstrates, the private sector also destroys jobs and/or fundamentally changes them to keep up with dramatic technological change, creating enormous economic insecurity, stress and social dislocation. The way that individual companies deal with this process of restructuring, in as humane and yet efficient a way as possible, is one of the major challenges business is facing in many OECD and transition economies. So too is the related challenge of education and training, which will be covered in the section on human development.Another employment issue of growing importance in OECD countries is greater employee

TACKLING THE CHALLENGE OF RESTRUCTURING IN CENTRAL AND EASTERN EUROPE

The pressures for industrial change are more intense and more complex in central and eastern Europe than probably anywhere else. In this region, the dramatic political changes and movement from a planned, centralised economy to a free market are superimposed on the global challenges which business is facing everywhere, such as technological change, increased competition and the shift of jobs from manufacturing to service industries. In the last six years, companies throughout the region have been seeking ways to improve their economic performance and management and to rapidly change the entire structure of their operations and the culture of their employees. They have often worked in partnership with foreign investors to achieve this by establishing joint ventures; shadow management programmes; mixed management teams; consultancy contracts, and supplier assistance initiatives. Grants and loans from bilateral and multilateral agencies have also been critical in enabling managers from these companies to undertake business management training.

Whichever path a company chooses, change is inevitable and is often linked to the need to shed employees, which poses obvious social problems. Strategies and management systems therefore need to be developed to:

a) plan for redundancies and minimise job losses – for example by early consultations with trade unions and employees, and steps such as: cutting external recruitment; reducing the use of contractors and temporary staff; reducing overtime; retiring those eligible for a pension; retraining employees to fill vacancies for skills in short supply; and redeploying staff where possible; and

b) support those who have been made redundant – for example by offering redundancy packages of financial help, counselling and advice, covering a wide range of areas from counselling to overcome shock, to career options advice and training on job search methods, how to prepare CVs, letters, interviews, counselling on self-employment and retiring, and advice on claiming various state benefits.

Promoting self-employment and supporting the emergence and/or strengthening of small to medium-scale businesses is one of the key areas that can alleviate some of the social problems of massive industrial restructuring. ABB in Poland, for example, during the restructuring process that followed some of its early investments in the Polish market, established a programme to "spin-off" almost 40 non-core business

functions, in areas such as cleaning, maintenance, canteen management, building and carpentry, welding and plumbing, and to assist over 600 employees to move to and manage these newly established small-scale companies. After having a guaranteed market from ABB initially, many of these companies are now expanding their customer base and their businesses.

Much of the industrial restructuring of central European companies has benefited from access to western expertise through commercial joint ventures, take-overs and consultancy. However for many of the largest companies in heavy industry, such as the coal mines and steel industry, these commercially viable options are not readily available. These are also the companies which often need to shed most labour, leading to unemployment and major social problems. The western aid programmes have recognised this problem and have subsidised the provision of advice to these companies. This support has been supplemented by western companies operating in the region, who recognise the long-term importance of helping central and eastern Europe to make as painless a transition as possible to a market economy.

One such programme was a joint initiative in Hungary between The Prince of Wales Business Leaders Forum (PWBLF), and several British companies, supported by the Know-How Fund. British Petroleum seconded John Cox, one of their experts on restructuring, to the PWBLF, who set up a series of workshops and study exchanges. Groups of Hungarian managers came to the United Kingdom to learn about the highly regarded outplacement training programme that British Coal Enterprise (BCE) had developed to deal with pit closures. After visits to job shops and training centres, and opportunities to shadow BCE staff at work , the Hungarians were able to apply some of these lessons to their own situation. The DIMAG steel works, for example, opened a job shop and the first managed workspace in Hungary based on their experience. BCE also benefited from the exchange in that it won a government contract to train redundancy experts throughout Hungary. Working with a team of experts from British business, local authorities and government, the PWBLF also ran four Restructuring Workshops in different Hungarian cities, attended by several hundred Hungarian managers from the coal, steel, chemicals, rubber and textile industries. Similar workshops were held in the Czech Republic, with technical and financial assistance from companies such as Coopers & Lybrand, ABB, and the Rover Group.

participation in (a) decision-making, through structures such as quality circles, employee consultation groups and works councils; and in (b) benefiting from the economic results of the company through employee share ownership programmes and profit-sharing schemes.

Again, government has a critical role to play, working in partnership with business and the trade unions (where they exist and enabling them to develop where they do not), to work out employment policies which ensure:

- a combination of fairness, flexibility and openness in the workplace for those that have jobs in the formal sector, and

- access to training, advice, information, credit and work experience, for those that do not.

(iii) GOODS AND SERVICES

The private sector, especially a competitive, innovative and efficient private sector, can greatly increase the quantity, quality and variety of goods and services in society. These in turn can have beneficial impacts in numerous ways. For example, in fields such as health-care, agriculture, information technology, and insurance and other financial services, to name just a few, new products and services can help to improve nutrition, health standards, savings, entrepreneurial opportunities and access to information. Three of the key challenges associated with the production of goods and services are: their impact on environmental sustainability; their availability to the poor; and the distribution of benefits between producers and consumers, both when they are located in the same country and in different countries. The latter relationship is one which is the focus of the growing fair trade movement.

FAIR TRADE

Trade can play a critical role in enabling developing and transition economies to increase economic growth and employment, and to alleviate poverty. Unfortunately, efforts by these economies to export their goods and services to OECD economies are often met by protectionism, especially when value has been added such as in the processing of primary commodities. There is the associated problem of subsidised OECD products being dumped in developing countries, which can undercut local food production. Another trade-related challenge is the uneven terms-of-trade that may exist, as a result of which producers in developing economies, especially primary producers, only earn a fraction of the final price that consumers pay for the end-products. Linked to this, there is the issue of exploitation that can occur in producing goods for export; ranging from environmental degradation to appalling working conditions, sometimes in the factories and/or plantations of foreign-owned companies, let alone local ones.

Governments, NGOs and the private sector all have a role to play in tackling these issues and ensuring that trade is mutually beneficial to both producers and consumers. At the inter-governmental level the issues are starting to be addressed by the World Trade Organisation, especially in the environmental sphere. Voluntary organisations and multinational companies – both those producing in, and sourcing from developing and transition economies – can play a role in two main ways. Firstly, in campaigning for fair trade, and secondly, in practising fair trade. Recent years have witnessed the emergence of Alternative Trading Organisations (ATOs) in the USA, Canada and a number of European countries. Some, such as Oxfam Trading, are linked to existing development NGOs, others have been established specifically to promote fairtrade. These organisations, together with NGOs which do not have their own trading initiative, are playing a key role in raising awareness of fair trade issues, promoting the adoption of sourcing guidelines for major companies and, in the case of the ATOs, also demonstrating in practice that fair trade is economically viable and socially and environmentally beneficial. Companies such as the Body Shop and Starbucks have built successful businesses around fair trade and the vision of "trade not aid". These different fairtrade organisations have also encouraged major retail chains and supermarkets, especially in textiles, footwear and foodstuffs, to stock socially and environmentally sound products from developing countries, for example the coffee called cafédirect in the UK. The major change, however, will only come when these large companies implement comprehensive fair trade policies as part of their everyday business practice, as opposed to one-off promotional activities. A few, such as B&Q in the UK which is profiled on page 208, have started to implement management systems to do this.

As with investment and employment, there is a need for public-private partnerships even in the area of goods and services. While it is not the role of governments to interfere in the immediate production and marketing processes of business per se, the two sectors can work together on:

- financing and promoting research and development, which is crucial to innovation and to the development of cleaner products and processes which have less of a negative environmental impact;

- developing guidelines for advertising standards that allow companies room for creativity and flexibility, while protecting consumer interests;

- running joint national education and awareness campaigns to promote more responsible consumption patterns, encouraging people to reduce, recycle and reuse products; and

- looking at ways to jointly develop distribution mechanisms that can deliver basic goods and services, such as medicines and micro-credit, to the poor.

(iv) INFRASTRUCTURE

There are two broad categories of "infrastructure" which are critically important to economic development, both of which the private sector, working in partnership with the public sector, can contribute to:

a) Physical infrastructure

b) Institutional infrastructure.

a) Physical infrastructure

The last few years have seen an unprecedented increase world-wide in private participation in infrastructure financing, construction and management. Until recently public monopolies have been largely responsible for providing telecommunications, transportation systems, water and waste management services, electricity, and housing in many countries – OECD, as well as developing and transition economies. Few governments today, however, can afford this approach and they are looking towards the private sector as a partner and provider, as well as seeking a greater level of community participation, especially in finding local, low-cost solutions to urban infrastructure needs in poor communities.

The existence of infrastructure which is efficient, clean and widely accessible (from both a physical and financial perspective) is critical to achieving economic development, increased competitiveness, environmental protection, improved standards of living and poverty alleviation. The scale of the challenge is enormous. A large percentage of the world's population still lack access to the most basic services of clean water and sanitation; economic activities in many developing countries suffer delays and unnecessary costs because of electricity cuts, traffic congestion, and inadequate telecommunications systems; and even in some of the so-called developed countries, the decaying urban infrastructure of inner-city areas and insufficient public investment in transportation, power and telecommunications, is creating both economic and human problems.

The World Bank estimates that developing countries currently spend an estimated US$200 billion a year on infrastructure – a figure beyond the means of both governments and multilateral agencies. East Asia alone may need to spend more than US$1 trillion on infrastructure between now and the end of the decade. Achieving private sector participation is a critical, but complex and difficult process. The combination of: sunk costs; large economies of scale and scope; complexity of financing and construction; potential costs of clean-up and rehabilitation; high long-term risks, ranging from commercial to political and environmental; and the non-tradable character of most infrastructure assets, require specialised approaches to encourage private financing and provision of these services. Given the public nature of these services, there are also issues of competition and regulation that must be tackled, together with societal concerns about reaching the poor, equitable pricing, the environment and resettlement.

Publications such as the World Bank's paper entitled *The Business of Sustainable Cities: Public-Private Partnerships for Creative, Technical and Institutional Solutions*, and the IFC's paper *Financing Private Infrastructure Projects*, offer useful guidelines and examples of approaches for tackling some of these challenges; involving partnerships between the public and private sector, local governments and communities, aimed at developing efficient, clean and accessible physical infrastructure.

TELECOMMUNICATIONS
Infrastructure for economic and social progress

In today's information-based environment, inadequate communications infrastructure is a major limiting factor for developing countries wanting to participate more equally in the international economy, and also for remote communities wanting to participate more equally in the national economy. Poor communications systems reflect and perpetuate inequality, both internationally and nationally. The governments of most developing countries have ambitious plans to expand and upgrade their telecommunications systems, but this requires large amounts of capital, modern and innovative technology, and skilled expertise.

In the past decade many multinational telecommunications companies have forged creative and mutually beneficial partnerships with other international and local players, in some of the world's most challenging communications markets. In doing so they have:

• helped these countries to overcome some of the capital, technology and skills obstacles which they face;

• enabled them to upgrade and expand their communications capabilities, to the benefit not only of their economies and emerging business sectors, but also to the benefit of some of their poorer, more remote regions;

• built long-term relationships and a base on which to develop further business and investment opportunities, both for the telecommunications sector itself and other industries.

b) Institutional infrastructure

Closely linked, and equally important to physical infrastructure is the network of institutional structures that underpin an efficient and transparent market economy, which can interact with its trade partners using a common business language and clear and open "rules of engagement". These structures range from financial, legal and regulatory systems, to business associations and support services for things like trade and investment promotion.

Numerous multinational companies have played a key role in helping transition and developing countries to establish and/or strengthen such structures in recent years. Often this support has been commercially provided – either direct to host governments, or on contract to the multilateral and bilateral development agencies. However, in a number of cases, companies have also undertaken *pro bono* work and offered work placements for managers from transition and developing economies, enabling them to learn from experience. Some of the contributions have been as follows:

- Many of the world's leading **professional firms** in fields such as accountancy, consulting and the law, including Price Waterhouse, KPMG, Coopers & Lybrand, Clifford Chance, and Sherman and Stirling, have played an important role in advising developing and transition economies, on the establishment of financial, accounting and regulatory systems, which match international business standards and also encompass important issues such as environmental and labour law. A critical element of this process in most countries has been training local employees to attain internationally recognised professional qualifications and offering a wide range of *pro bono* services, often in partnership with organisations such as The Prince of Wales Business Leaders Forum, the World Business Council for Sustainable Development, and local business associations and chambers of commerce. These have included seminars and workshops, work placements, and offering volunteer advice and leadership to help establish small-scale enterprise support agencies and initiatives such as Hungary's Environmental Management and Law Association.

- **Commercial and investment banks** have worked in partnership with the multilateral banks and bilateral donor agencies, to provide technical assistance to developing and transition countries in establishing local stock exchanges, setting up banking regulations and supervision structures, and deepening and broadening the capital markets to ensure the more efficient mobilisation of savings and their allocation to the most productive investments. Although this assistance has normally been on a commercial basis, paid for by host governments and development agencies, many banks have also offered wider *pro bono* support in areas such as raising awareness on the environmental risks associated with banking and training local government officials, as illustrated by the example opposite.

- **Foreign companies** have established their own **Chambers of Commerce**, such as the American Chamber of Commerce, in many countries which have had a valuable demonstration effect, as well as fulfiling important networking and support roles for member companies and their local business partners. They have also supported the establishment of local business and trade associations, such as Bankers' and Hotel Associations. As described in other sections, more of these business associations are starting to develop environmental programmes and guidelines for their members, as well as initiatives on education, health, rural development and broader social development goals.

EBRD's Banking and Environment Advisory Committee

An example is the banking advisory committee established by the EBRD in the early 1990s to help it to develop a programme for Central and East European banks providing them with guidelines, training seminars and information on what western banks were doing to manage environmental risk and reporting procedures; and to develop internal environmental management programmes. Leading British and American banks such as Bank of America, National Westminster Bank and Lloyds Bank, plus some 50 other banks from Germany, Hong Kong, Switzerland, the United States, Spain and Japan, worked together with the EBRD and local Bankers Associations and individual banks in the region, on this project.

> Technology co-operation is a complex game, with many players: businesses in industrial and developing countries; the governments of these countries; schools and training bodies; and non-governmental organisations, with pressure from the media and consumers to maintain the movement towards sustainable development.
>
> World Business Council for Sustainable Development, *Changing Course*, 1992

(v) TECHNOLOGY CO-OPERATION

From multi-million dollar pollution prevention systems in electrical power plants in India, to simple processing facilities for small-scale mining operations in Zimbabwe, the development of a country's technological capacity has a vital role to play, not only in terms of improving its productivity, competitiveness and living standards, but also in enabling it to find efficient, effective and equitable solutions to both social and environmental challenges.

The concept of technology co-operation has therefore come to play a central role in the drive for more sustainable patterns of development. It is a concept which recognises the importance of countries, companies and communities being able not only to access, but also to adapt, use and maintain, environmentally sound and socially beneficial technologies. To achieve this the concept places a heavy emphasis on the development of human skills and capacities, and makes a clear distinction between one-way technology transfer between suppliers and recipients, and the two-way dialogue and partnership-building process which underpins technology co-operation.

The requirements for successful technology co-operation are varied and numerous, depending on a wide range of technical, financial, managerial and cultural factors, plus the scale and purpose of the technology in question. Some common factors however, underpin the success of almost all types of technology co-operation. These include:

- **A supportive policy framework** which promotes direct private investment and environmentally and socially responsible products and production processes at different levels in the economic system, from large-scale business to micro-enterprise;

- **Access to capital** including private sector funds and innovative public-private and community-based financing mechanisms;

- **Access to information** through improved information networks and databases, which are structured to meet the actual operational needs of enterprises, and which can be accessed by SMMEs as well as major players, depending on the relevance of the information to these different groups;

- **Development of technological, managerial and organisational skills**, which can be applied to adapting, maintaining and innovating new technologies.

None of these requirements can be met without forging mutually beneficial partnerships between a wide range of institutions. Multinational companies play a critical role in promoting technology co-operation through their global networks of subsidiaries, joint ventures, local agents and suppliers, and especially in building the local competencies, networks and standards needed to optimise the usage and benefits of modern technology. Business associations also play a vital role by promoting standards and providing information, advice and guidelines for local companies, especially small and even micro-enterprises. Non-governmental organisations, such as the UK-based Intermediate Technology group, and local community-based organisations are essential in helping to build capacity at the community level for small-scale appropriate technologies in fields such as manufacturing, agriculture and mining. Finally, the input of governments and international agencies is important to ensure appropriate policy frameworks and funding structures.

Technology Co-operation and Capacity Building: the Oil Industry Experience

Technology partnerships can range from local, low-cost, labour intensive initiatives between a few small-scale organisations, to international high-cost, capital-intensive initiatives amongst a large number of players, with many variations in between. The following profile illustrates how this spectrum applies to technology cooperation in the oil and gas industry.

In 1995, UNEP's Industry Office collaborated with IPIECA (the International Petroleum Industry Environmental Conservation Association) to produce a series of case studies on the technology co-operation and capacity building activities of eleven of the world's major oil and gas companies to assess the contribution they were making to Agenda 21. The companies reviewed were Amoco, British Petroleum, Canadian Occidental, Chevron, Elf Aquitaine, Esso, Imperial Oil, Mobil, PT Caltex, Shell and Total, and the case studies covered a wide range of countries, including Russia, Colombia, Canada, the Yemen Republic, Papua New Guinea, Malaysia, Indonesia, and Senegal. They also looked at a variety of commercial, governmental and non-governmental partners, and at different stages of the value chain. Some of the examples included:

- Co-operation between Amoco and its Russian partners – Nadym Gasprom, Komi Research Institute, the Institute of Agriculture for the Northern Urals and American and Russian scientists – to develop effective methods for the revegetation of severely degraded parts of western Siberia;

- A partnership between Chevron Niugini Pty. Ltd., its joint venture partners in Papua New Guinea (BP Exploration, Ampolex (PNG Petroleum), BHP Petroleum, Japan PNG Petroleum, Oil Search Ltd. and Petroleum Resources Kutubu Pty. Ltd.) and the government of Papua New Guinea, local landowners, community-based organisations and environmental organisations, including the World Wide Fund for Nature. The purpose of this partnership is to develop innovative technologies and management systems to minimise negative environmental impacts of the oil consortium's large-scale development in an environmentally fragile and isolated part of the country; and to ensure active community consultation and participation to enable the commercial partners, the government and local communities to benefit from the economic returns of the project;

- In the Yemen Republic, Canadian Occidental worked in partnership with the government and technical experts to undertake a detailed Environmental Impact Assessment (EIA), despite the fact that there was no environmental regulatory framework in place in the country at the time of the project's conception. CanadianOxy ensured that their pre-construction investigations utilised Yemeni authorities from a number of disciplines, providing them with an opportunity to learn about EIA processes and technology, and facilitating the replication of this approach in other industrial developments in the Yemen Republic.

- In Senegal, Total worked in partnership with Totalgaz, the Senegalese government, the European Development Fund, about 50 distribution companies, local metal workers and local communities, to develop and market efficient, cost-effective and safe butane cookers. These have had an impressive impact on reducing demand for woodfuel, which was leading to severe deforestation and desertification in parts of the country.

- In Malaysia, at the other end of the technology spectrum in terms of sophistication, Shell has worked in partnership with Mitsubishi, Petrona, and the State government of Sarawak to introduce state-of-the-art technology in establishing the Shell Middle Distillate Synthesis (SMDS) plant which is able to convert natural gas into liquid fuels of high purity. A strong commitment has been made to capacity-building local employees to manage this process. Of the 330 staff who run this sophisticated technology, 244 are Malaysians. 90% of them are recruited locally and trained both locally and internationally by the consortium partners.

IPIECA was created in 1974 with special responsibilities for global environmental issues related to the oil industry. Its members include over 20 of the world's major oil and gas companies and more than 10 other associations related to the petroleum industry. Through this network IPIECA is able to mobilise some of the most experience scientists and environmental experts that the oil industry can provide. It also works closely with the United Nations and other intergovernmental organisations. IPIECA is active in five main areas: oil spill response, global climate change, biodiversity, transportation and technology cooperation.

Intermediate Technology:
Working with the world's small scale producers

Find out what people are doing, and help them to do it better. Dr EF Schumacher

Intermediate Technology (IT) is an international non-governmental development organisation, registered in the United Kingdom, which works with small-scale producers in Africa, Asia and South America. Founded in 1966 by Dr EF Schumacher, author of the book *Small is Beautiful*, IT propogates approaches to managing technical change that are effective in enabling resource-poor people to work their own way out of poverty.

Most of the world's poorest people earn their incomes from small-scale enterprises in households, fields or workshops. Small-scale producers rely on small-scale technology and IT believes that these enterprises can be made more secure, more productive, more competitive and more capable of surviving rapid economic change, through the use of improved technology. The organisation operates in that "intermediate" area between the technological frontier of large-scale production of the global economy, and those technologies of traditional subsistence that are no longer viable. It helps small producers to combine their local knowledge and skills with other scientific and technological knowledge from the wider world.

IT operates with some 250 staff working from interlinked offices in the UK, Peru, Bangladesh, Sri Lanka, Sudan, Kenya and Zimbabwe, all of which work with partner organisations in each country to gain fuller understanding of peoples' lives and to build sustainable local capacities. The Group maintains high levels of technical competence in six broad areas of small-scale production: energy, transport, manufacturing, food production, food processing, building and shelter. Its annual income exceeds UK£7 million, and is sourced from individual donations and grants from foundations, trusts, companies, international organisations and governments.

The organisation is engaged in a wide range of activities including research, technology development, field testing and commercialisation, technical assistance,

training and advocacy. Only rarely does IT provide assistance in the form of money. Through its practical project work it is involved at all stages of helping small-scale enterprises to develop, adapt and share the technical knowledge, experience and skills required to meet their needs.

IT also operates several subsidiaries:

- IT Publications Limited, which is a wholly-owned publishing company with an international reputation for publishing high quality material on technology and development, with some 300 titles currently in print;

- IT Consultants Limited, which offers professional advice and assistance world-wide on the use and application of improved technologies and the management techniques required to ensure their success.

One of the many technology co-operation projects that IT has worked on is a partnership in Zimbabwe between The Small-Scale Miners Association of Zimbabwe (SSMAZ), a non-profit association of mainly poor black miners, and Industrial Mining and Farming Ltd. (IMF), a medium-sized, white-owned company producing and marketing mining and agricultural equipment for the local market. IMF worked closely with IT and the SSMAZ to develop mobile milling machines and other basic extraction equipment, and to establish a regional custom milling centre, which could be used by a large number of small-scale miners to achieve more productive, cleaner and efficient methods of extracting and processing the gold which these miners have panned from alluvial deposits.

This is one of countless examples where locally-based medium and small-scale enterprises can co-operate for mutual benefit. Success however depends very much on a combination of:

- access to technologies that are appropriate in terms of cost, scale, complexity and local conditions; and

- participation of the people who have to use and control these technologies, at every stage of the process.

The gift of material goods makes people dependent. The gift of knowledge makes them free. Dr EF Schumacher

(vi) STANDARDS AND BUSINESS PRACTICES

One of the most valuable, but intangible, contributions that foreign investors can offer to a country is helping to spread internationally accepted standards and internationally competitive business practices in a wide range of areas. Also within countries, large companies working in partnership with smaller companies can achieve the same impact. This does not only apply to OECD-based companies investing in transition or developing economies, but is equally applicable for investment flows between countries at similar stages of economic development. German and Japanese companies investing in the United Kingdom, for example, have had a valuable impact in terms of providing new ideas and new methods of management and vice versa.

These impacts can be achieved in a myriad of ways: companies requiring internationally accepted quality standards from local suppliers, agents and contractors; companies applying higher standards for occupational health and safety, and for labour relations and employee benefits than those that exist in the local regulatory environment; the application of stringent environmental management standards, not only in a company's own processes and products, but also those that it demands of its suppliers; and emphasis placed on inculcating high standards of ethical behaviour and good corporate governance in local staff, subsidiaries and business partners. Equally beneficial is the sharing and application of business practices such as Total Quality Management (TQM), just-in-time manufacturing, employee innovation circles, innovative financing mechanisms and so on.

Even in this area of relationships between a company and its commercial partners, governments have a role to play in agreeing on national and international frameworks of mutually acceptable rules and regulations within which companies can disseminate different business practices and standards. The United States, for example, has strict regulations on bribery and corruption, which all American companies operating internationally are legally required to adhere to. However few other OECD governments place such constraints on their home-based multi-nationals, with the result that even if American companies are spreading high standards of ethical behaviour, there are companies from other countries which may be doing the opposite.

(vii) LOCAL BUSINESS DEVELOPMENT

Linked to all of the above, an important contribution that any company can make when moving operations to, or sourcing materials and products from, a new country or community, is to maximise the potential for local business development in that location. One of the key "mechanisms" for achieving this is backward and forward linkages along the company's value chain. For example, how many indirect jobs can be created by a certain level of investment? Or how many local businesses can benefit from a certain level of investment? The nature of this investment, especially its capital or labour intensity and the complexity of the value chain in that particular industry sector, are important determinants of how much local business can be developed.

The multiplier impact of the Coca-Cola system in Poland and China is profiled on the following pages and offers an excellent example, not only of the wide range of economic benefits that a multinational can bring to host countries and communities, but also the leadership role that Coca-Cola has played in opening its operations up to independent external analysis and impact assessment.

Development means using local people as contractors, consultants and suppliers, even when taking the business elsewhere seems easier and less expensive. In the long run, the company will benefit as much as the community from its commitment to local business.

Julius Tahija,
PT Caltex, Indonesia
Harvard Business Review,
September-October 1993

MEASURING THE IMPACT: Two university studies on the Coca-Cola system in Poland and Romania, and China

The Coca-Cola Company is the world's largest beverage company and owner of the world's most recognised trademark and best-selling soft drink, which is now available in more than 195 countries. Its global system consists of three partners, executing distinct, yet highly interrelated roles:

- The Coca-Cola Company develops brands and produces concentrates;
- Its bottlers manufacture and distribute finished products and undertake local marketing; and
- Its customers – for example retailers, who present the company's products to the public.

The company's bottlers and customers represent thousands of individual enterprises throughout the world, the vast majority of which are locally-owned and managed enterprises in host countries and communities. Many on the retailer side represent small and micro-enterprises, and they reach several billion consumers.

In March 1995 a research team of international business and economics professors from the University of South Carolina, completed a major study on foreign direct investment in Poland and Romania focusing on the impact of Coca-Cola's investment. In December 1995, the Faculty of Economics and Politics at Cambridge University published a similar study on Coca-Cola's impact in China. The following profile summarises some of their conclusions;

1. Foreign Direct Investment in Transition Economies: The Coca-Cola System in Poland and Romania

Interviews and surveys explored both quantitative and qualitative impacts, and the economic multiplier process was traced through its real connections in the two economies. The study found that the new bottling operations had an immediate, strong economic impact and introduced competitive business practices at a

critical juncture in the transitional period. Although the following profile focuses on Poland, it is worth noting that in Romania, Coca-Cola helped to create more than 20,000 small-scale retail operations, establishing an entire entrepreneurial class.

The Coca-Cola system was responsible for the largest flow of foreign direct investment to Poland during the early period of economic transition. Starting from a low base, the company embarked on an aggressive investment programme and achieved market leadership by 1994, together with a significant multiplier impact especially through backward (supplier) linkages. Some of the key impacts of this multiplier were as follows:

- The total employment supported by the backward and forward multiplier was significant – with more than ten jobs being created for every direct job;

- All major inputs for the production of soft drinks were found locally. Coca-Cola bottlers bought sugar from a local (foreign-owned) refinery, which in turn was supplied with beets grown by Polish farmers. Although sugarbeets had been an important product in pre-communist Poland, the productivity and quality had fallen far behind Western standards like most of the country's agriculture. Coca-Cola was responsible for helping to re-establish the domestic sugar refining industry, indirectly supporting 6,400 jobs in the private agricultural sector and encouraging Polish beet farmers to adopt efficient production methods for the first time in decades in order to meet Coca-Cola's quality standards;

- Two years after launching its expansion, Coca-Cola purchased all its other major supplies in Poland, from bottles to advertising materials. This created further employment multipliers, creating over six jobs for every direct job. As with the beet farmers, local suppliers were required to meet the company's global quality standards, which was not easy at first, but

To put it very directly, it is the remarkable power of the multiplier effect that makes capitalism the economic system that can best satisfy the needs and wants of people. ...First, we create jobs for the employees of our system. Second, we support the people and businesses who supply us with goods and services. Third, we help our customers to make money. And fourth, we help create standards that raise the general quality of life in the places where we do business.

Roberto C Goizueta, Chairman and CEO, The Coca-Cola Company

they were supported by the company to reach the acceptable levels;

- The company's investment also created forward linkages in the retail sector – not only in terms of jobs created, but also in terms of training and skills development. The company established a training programme specifically for shop owners and managers, covering topics such as planning, financial control and merchants' procedures;

- This and other initiatives also helped to develop the business support infrastructure in the country, including the establishment of a Chamber of Commerce for the Food Retail Trade;

- Although not possible to quantify, it is clear that the company's high-profile investments in Poland in the early days of transition also helped to legitimise economic reforms and convince other foreign investors to take the risk;

- In the larger society, the company acted as an agent of goodwill during a trying period. It showed what businesses could contribute beyond production and sales and became actively involved in local community projects, sponsorship of public events and innovative community programmes, such as an integrated city-wide recycling programme in Brwinow. This initiative brought together the soft drinks producers, packaging manufacturers, local authorities, education institutions, the media and consumers, to establish a recycling system in the city and a widespread environmental education programme.

The impact of the Coca-Cola system in Poland can be summed up in a few words: multiplier effect and transfer of competencies. The company's investments not only created economic multipliers for the country, but also helped to introduce globally competitive standards of production, marketing, retailing and management.

2. Joint Ventures and Economic Reform in China: A case study of the Coca-Cola business system, with reference to the Tianjin Coca-Cola plant

The research carried out by Dr Peter Nolan and others at Cambridge University analysed the micro-economic impact of the growth of the Coca-Cola business system in China since the mid-1980s. The paper's primary conclusions were that the general effect has been positive to the Chinese economy, especially because of China's impoverished conditions; its evolving technical position; and its transition from communist administrative "planning". In particular, the Coca-Cola system has played a role in:

- **Modernising Chinese Industry** – the construction and refurbishment of Coca-Cola plants has improved the efficiency and quality of both production processes and products; decreased the wastage of inputs and outputs;

improved hygiene; and created strong linkages to the local economy through increased purchase of building materials, factory furniture and construction labour;

- **Building Indirect Up-Stream Employment** – it is estimated that for every job at the Coca-Cola plant, six additional jobs are created in the Chinese economy. Up to 5,000 "full-time equivalent" workers are engaged in supplying materials to a single plant such as Tianjin, putting the number at tens of thousands of suppliers in the economy as a whole. This is larger than would be the case with indigenous soft drink producers, given the greater complexity and range of inputs required to meet international quality standards;

- **Increasing Indirect Down-Stream Employment** – there are between 40,000 and 70,000 retailers estimated to be selling products under the Coca-Cola trademark, many of them small-scale enterprises which the company helps with the provision of equipment, credit and training;

- **Increased Labour Productivity and Employment Standards** – when renovation of the Tianjin plant was completed output rose by 274% and profits per worker increased 389% from 1990 to 1994. This productivity gain was achieved through the investment in modern equipment; improved technical and business training programmes; improved wage levels and work conditions; average benefit levels double those for comparable situations in the local states sector; and more open, merit-based criteria;

- **Changing Chinese Soft Drinks Companies** – local companies have also restructured their operations and marketing to be more efficient and quality-driven;

- **Increasing Profitability and Tax Revenues** – the company's superior business organisation and greater cost consciousness has helped joint-venture plants to greatly increase their profitability and increased both value-added and income taxes paid to the government;

- **Advancing Standards of Production and Management** – Coca-Cola has shared important business practices throughout its network of suppliers and retailers, ranging from marketing skills, cost reduction, pricing, product quality, punctuality and technical progress;

- **Trend toward Domestic Sourcing of Raw Materials and Fixed Assets** – by 1994 some 98% of all materials necessary to produce a bottle of Coca-Cola were sourced locally;

- **Improved Quality of Suppliers** – the quality demands placed on suppliers have rippled through several tiers of the supply chain. Enterprises that meet the company's exacting international standards typically advertise this fact and this helps them to build their reputation and increase sales to other customers.

(viii) BUILDING BRIDGES BETWEEN LARGE AND SMALL-SCALE BUSINESS

The following section looks at one of the key ways in which large companies can increase not only economic growth, but also economic participation; through supporting the development of small and micro-enterprises, and helping them to get access to markets, finance, training, physical infrastructure and business support services. Large-scale companies can support linkages with small and micro-enterprises through their core business activities, their social investment or philanthropic activities, and their influence on the public policy agenda.

a) CORE BUSINESS ACTIVITY

Clearly, one of the most valuable and potentially sustainable types of support that large companies can offer SMMEs is to form business relationships with them as suppliers of raw materials, goods and services; sub-contractors; franchisees; distributors; and retailers.

- **SMMEs can offer a wide variety of products and services**, ranging from basic office and factory supplies to printing services, office cleaning, grounds and premises maintenance, plumbing, welding and canteen services. Many large-scale companies have established small-business units to facilitate this process, as illustrated by the example of South Africa's Anglo American Corporation profiled on page 118.

- In the forestry and agribusiness sectors SMMEs can be part of **small-scale outgrowers schemes**, such as those run by Aracruz Celulose in Brazil (see page 202) and Mondi and Sappi in South Africa in the forestry area, and agricultural outgrowers schemes such as the Mumias sugar scheme in Kenya, profiled on page 203, and the San Miguel shrimp programme profiled on page 118. There are many other such examples: Cadbury's sourcing coca from small-scale producers in India; Starbucks sourcing coffee from small-scale producers in Latin America; the Body Shop sourcing products from indigenous producers all over the world as part of its Fairtrade programme; Nestle developing small-scale indigenous dairy enterprises in Thailand and Indonesia, and SmithKline Beecham and Hindustan Lever doing likewise in India, to name a few. These relationships usually occur at a local level, but in a growing number of cases they occur at an international level, driven by the Fair Trade movement, which is in turn being driven by the combination of visionary entrepreneurs and increased social awareness amongst the world's more wealthy consumers.

- Certain types of companies can also **subcontract parts of their manufacturing processes** out to SMMEs. The clothing sector is an obvious example of this, with subcontracting happening on both an international basis – as illustrated by companies such as Levi Strauss and the Gap working with subcontractors in South Asia and Latin America – and on a local basis. In Zimbabwe, for example, Truworths which is one of the country's leading clothes manufacturing and retailing chains, has established systems to ensure that a high percentage of its "cut, make and trim" activities are undertaken by small-scale, indigenous manufacturers who receive a wide range of support services from the large company. Jonee Blanchfield, the company's Managing Director and one of the country's outstanding female entrepreneurs, has made a conscious management decision to develop as many small-scale business linkages as possible and to improve opportunities for women in the workplace.

BMW AND W.I.P. MOTORS IN SOUTH AFRICA

In mid-1995 a pioneering BMW dealership opened in central Johannesburg, representing a partnership between one of the country's largest car dealerships and a group of women entrepreneurs. W.I.P. motors is a joint venture between Imperial Motor Holdings, one of South Africa's foremost retail groups with more than 30 dealerships country-wide, and the Women Investment Portfolio (W.I.P.), is a consortium of black women investors using their purchasing capacity to negotiate economic empowerment and independence. W.I.P.'s mission is to foster entrepreneurship among women, facilitate the incorporation of women in economic initiatives, and create and distribute wealth among its members.Brought together by BMW these two groups can each offer something valuable to the partnership and obtain mutual benefit. Imperial will provide the expertise and experience that comes from being one of the most successful retail groups in the motor trade, while W.I.P, representing the interests of some 30,000 black women, will use their influence and contacts to broaden BMW's customer base, while at the same time ensuring that economic empowerment continues beyond the dealership by outsourcing and subcontracting work to small-scale entrepreneurs.

- Many large-scale companies moving into the transition economies of central and eastern Europe and the NIS have been faced with the high social costs of downsizing bloated, inefficient state entities and have set up programmes to **unbundle and outsource non-core activities**, by setting employees up in their own businesses, such as the initiative outlined earlier by ABB in Poland. This is an activity which is also happening with increased frequency in South Africa, as large companies strive to increase productivity and international competitiveness, while at the same time creating jobs to tackle high levels of unemployment.

- On the **distribution and retail side** there is also much that can be achieved to widen the opportunities for economic participation. Coca-Cola is one of the companies which has been highly successful around the world in working with millions of small, locally-owned and managed distributors and retailers, offering them management assistance, credit, mentoring support and the marketing benefits of the Coca-Cola brand name for their tiny shops in many of the world's poorest and remotest communities. The multiplier impact of the Coca-Cola system in Poland and China is profiled on page 112. In Zimbabwe and other countries throughout Africa the company has set up small-scale distributorship schemes, and in Asia in 1993, the Far Eastern Economic Review estimated that the Coca-Cola system created jobs for more than 85,000 people, of which only 1,600 were paid directly by the company. Other companies with large-scale distribution requirements, such as South African Breweries the world's fourth largest brewer, also have successful owner-operator driver programmes which not only support small-scale entrepreneurs, but also have clear business benefits for the company. SAB is one of the most competitive, low-cost brewers in the world, a performance which is due in part to the fact that the company produces 75% of its beer in glass returnable bottles which are sent out every morning via its network of small-scale distributors who deliver them to their own networks of customers, returning at the end of the day with truckloads of empties to be filled up and sent out again.

- The area of **franchising and leasing** is also of growing importance in linkages between large companies and SMMEs, especially medium-scale, or the more sophisticated end of the small-scale business sector. In many countries the major oil companies, such as British Petroleum and Shell, have programmes to help indigenous entrepreneurs operate service stations which they either own or lease, while the company provides them not only with petrol, but with a package of support services, such as administrative and book-keeping software, training and advice on business management, environmental management, marketing and retailing. Other retailers and service companies are setting up similar franchise arrangements around the world, such as McDonald's and the Body Shop. The Mexican company DEMASA is another example. It operates franchises in several Central American countries, producing tortillas and other foodstuffs, where it owns and helps to maintain the machinery, sells raw materials to franchisees at wholesale prices, provides a comprehensive package of quality control training, credit and advice services and the benefit of its national advertising budget, whilst giving small-scale producers the opportunity to run their own production processes and maximise their sales opportunities in their own localities.

- The provision of **commercially viable credit and savings services to SMMEs** is a critically important area which has gained increased attention in recent years. Case studies on this include the Citicorp Foundation on page 119, CGAP on page 232 and ACCION International on page 224.

b) SOCIAL INVESTMENT

Companies can also support SMMEs, without having direct business relationships with them. This can be done via the following types of social or community investments:

- **Offering basic business training** – Volunteer programmes by the managers of large companies, or business school students, can be a valuable way of sharing time and expertise with small-scale entrepreneurs to give basic lessons in skills such as book-keeping, marketing, costing, pricing etc. One such example is Business Skills South Africa (BSSA), which is a national programme, established as a partnership between Coopers & Lybrand and the National Industrial Chamber, one of the country's business associations. BSSA runs integrated courses for small-scale entrepreneurs at different skill levels. Many of the affiliates of the ACCION and FUNDES networks in Latin America run training programmes with volunteer input from large-scale companies. In Poland, a group of multi-nationals are working with the Business Leaders Forum in Poland on a series of master classes for small-scale enterprises (see page 262). In Kenya, Botswana, South Africa, Brazil, Colombia and the Philippines, business students from the AIESEC organisation (see page 230) working in partnership with large companies, offer business training and advice to small and micro-entrepreneurs. The list of examples is long, but there is potential for much greater activity in this field.

- **Offering technical and vocational training** – This area is equally important. The Reef Training Centre in South Africa profiled on page 144 and the BOC welding school in Poland profiled on page 142 are two of many examples where companies have either opened their established facilities and in-house training programmes to non-employees, or have made major social investments to establish vocational or technical training programmes specifically for the wider community;

- **Volunteering management time** – Many business leaders from large companies serve as advisors and trustees on the boards of microfinance intermediaries and NGO organisations which have been established to support SMME development. Certain companies encourage their managers to volunteer for activities in this field and a few offer secondments to these intermediary support organisations.

- **Donating premises, equipment, discards or off-cuts** – Some companies offer the use of premises or equipment to SMMEs, and others donate off-cuts which can be used efficiently and effectively by the informal sector – benefiting not only their businesses, but also the environment, by cutting down waste and increasing recycling of industrial products. These can range from discarded stainless steel products to industrial rags.

- **Innovative financing techniques** – There are numerous ways in which financial sector companies, and others, can work with intermediary organisations to establish innovative funding structures to leverage capital for SMME loans and equity investments – these range from simple community investment funds to the creation of banks to serve micro-enterprises, such as BancoSol in Bolivia.

- **Establishing and supporting intermediary organisations** – This is a critically important role that large companies can play. Many of the above services can be offered through such organisations, for example, KMAP and the Alexandria Business Association profiled on page 121. Large companies can also establish incubator workshops for SMMEs, such as the Kecskemet example in Hungary profiled opposite.

THE COCA-COLA FORUM IN MANAGEMENT AND MARKETING IN AFRICA

This initiative has been established in Kenya and Zimbabwe by the Coca-Cola Company to expand its contribution to Africa's economic development. The broad objectives of the Forum are to improve the abilities of Africa's small and medium enterprises to manage their businesses,and market their goods and services; support government assistance programmes to SMEs; help to cultivate entrepreneurship, especially among students; support women's business endeavours; widen employment opportunities in the private sector for university students; and support teaching and research activities in the field of SME development and entrepreneurship. The initiative is coordinated by Coca-Cola's regional offices in two countries, in collaboration with the University of Zimbabwe and the University of Nairobi. Clark Atlanta University in the USA has been closely involved with the design and initiation of the curriculum. The Coca-Cola Forum involves a wide range of activities, including: public seminars; training materials and workshops; radio programmes; applied research; networking;student internships; and the establishment of small business aid clinics.

- **Research and Development** – This is another area which large companies can support on a *pro bono* basis, establishing university chairs and research programmes to focus on SMME development.

- **Enterprise Education** – Companies can reach out to schools to teach students about entrepreneurship and the world of business. Many such programmes exist in the OECD countries and there is potential to apply them elsewhere, as is being done by Partners for Growth in Zimbabwe, and via the work of US-based Junior Achievement and UK-based Young Enterprise, throughout central and eastern Europe.

c) THE POLICY AGENDA

Finally large-scale companies and their business associations can use their influence to encourage national governments to create a more enabling environment for SMMEs. They can call for and support:

- the improvement of tax and other incentives for SMME development;

- the development of legislation to cut late payments, which is often a major problem for SMMEs dealing with large companies;

- the commitment of government departments to source services and supplies from SMMEs, which is an area of immense, but rarely tapped potential in many countries; and

- the establishment of institutional and physical support structures, which are driven by business needs, not by government bureaucracy.

A nationwide example of this has been the *Business Links* programme established throughout the United Kingdom. This is a national network of one-stop-shops to advise SMMEs, which is co-ordinated by the government's Department of Trade and Industry, but builds on numerous local initiatives and works closely with business support associations and individual companies throughout the country, to ensure locally appropriate design and delivery. The private sector, and public sector business partnerships such as Business in the Community (see page 268) have played an important role in helping the government to develop this programme. Some of the lessons and experiences gained in the establishment of *Business Links* have been shared with developing and transition economies, through information and exchange programmes supported by British ODA.

A more localised example, albeit one which has potential for replication elsewhere, is the way in which government authorities in Hungary, at both the local and national level, and the British ODA, worked with the private sector in establishing the Keckskemet workshops described opposite.

The following pages offer brief profiles of:

- four individual companies – United Biscuits, Anglo American, San Miguel and Citicorp – which are supporting the development of SMMEs in some of the countries and communities where they are operating; and

- six collaborative public-private partnerships in sub-Saharan and north Africa aimed at SMME development.

THE KECSKEMET BARRACKS PROJECT

In 1990, member companies of The Prince of Wales Business leaders Forum were approached to help convert a former Red Army Barracks, in Kecskemet, Hungary, into small-scale incubator workshops. The project started in 1991 with a feasibility study, partly financed by the British Know How Fund and drawn up by Hackney Business Venture. A new organisation, the British Hungarian Small Business Foundation was set up to manage the project. It brought together representatives from the county of Kecskemet, and member companies of the PWBLF and the Hungary Business Leaders Forum. They appointed Lancashire Enterprises Limited to carry out the work, based on its reputation for building local development partnerships between the public and private sector. Funding for the initiative was provided by the Know How Fund, the European Union's PHARE programme, British Petroleum; Cable & Wireless; and ARCO. The first incubator units were ready for occupation in 1993. Today the Kecskemet Barracks are a central focus point for small-scale entrepreneurs in the region, offering not only workshop spaces, but also a range of training and support services and useful networking opportunities.

SNAP-SHOTS OF CORPORATE ACTION

UNITED BISCUITS in Hungary

The transition from communism to a free market economy is undoubtedly a tough one for central Europeans – the Gyor Centre is intended to help the people of the town who are trying to set up small businesses to make this quantum leap.

**Sir Robert Clarke,
Chairman, United Biscuits**

In 1990, as part of Hungary's privatisation programme, British-based United Biscuits (UB) bought Gyori Keksz, a food processing company in Gyor. As a second phase investment, UB chose a greenfield site at Gyor Industrial Park to manufacture potato chip products for the central and east European market. Apart from the direct economic benefits of these investments, UB wanted to make sure that local people, as well as its employees, could share the benefits. The result was the establishment of a business advice centre for SMMEs, which has become one of the most highly regarded of its type in the region. Building on its extensive experience from supporting the local enterprise agency network in the United Kingdom, UB approached the local authorities in Gyor and enlisted the support of other major companies, such as Associated Newspapers, IBM and donor agencies such as the British Know How Fund.The centre was opened in April 1992, and today offers a comprehensive range of services, designed to provide practical business assistance and training to small-scale enterprises. The centre is run by Hungarians, trained in the United Kingdom and locally. Since 1992, the Centre has supported more than 300 Hungarian entrepreneurs and done much to enhance the company's reputation both locally and nationally.

ANGLO AMERICAN in South Africa

The Anglo American Corporation and De Beers were pioneers in South Africa in establishing a unit to promote and manage direct business linkages between the groups' operating companies and small-scale business. Established in 1989, the programme is called The Anglo American and De Beers Small and Medium Enterprise Initiative (SMEI). The SMEI has experienced significant growth with more than three hundred business opportunities having been created, employing over 4,000 people. Since its inception, the unit has conducted more than R 200 million worth of business with the SMME sector. It undertakes three main programmes:

- Contracting services to, and purchasing goods and materials from, small black-owned businesses, including the outsourcing of activities previously carried out in-house, such as canteen and cleaning services. This process has involved streamlining the company's tendering and payment formalities, giving contractors access to Anglo's bulk purchasing facilities, which can save up to 80% on the cost of materials, offering transport and storage facilities, and advice and mentoring;
- A venture capital company called the Labour Intensive Industries Trust Limited which takes minority equity stakes in small business enterprises and makes loans; and
- Advisory Centres located in different towns to identify investment, contracting and purchasing opportunities and to offer training, advice and mentoring to the SMEI's small-scale business partners and others.

The programme has not only helped to establish many viable SMMEs, but has also resulted in significant cost savings for the company, and valuable reputation enhancement. In 1993, the interest from SMEI's lending and dividends from LITET investments enabled the initiative to become self-funding.

SAN MIGUEL in the Philippines

We're trying to take our community relations beyond PR. The service co-operative scheme, where our plants link up with people's organisations to do essential tasks such as harvesting and simple processing of prawns, goes a long way towards local community development.

**Joey Guillermo, San Miguel's
Community Relations Group**

San Miguel Corporation is the industry leader in large-scale prawn production in the Philippines. In 1990, San Miguel's agribusiness division worked in partnership with the Negros' Economic Development Foundation (NEDF) to establish a Co-operative Service Contracting Scheme (CSCS) to subcontract the harvesting and processing of shrimps to locally-owned and managed peoples' organisations. The NEDF acted as an intermediary in helping San Miguel to identify the initial six co-operatives, and to co-ordinate a programme of linkage building, technical assistance, financial assistance and other support services between the company and its sub-contractors. The company funded most of this activity and also supplied the necessary processing equipment.

BANKING ON ENTERPRISE
Citicorp's $10 million small business creation initiative

Citicorp is one of the world's largest and most successful banks, with operations in over 95 countries and activities in a wide range of financial markets and instruments. However, like almost all of its counterparts in the commercial banking sector, until recently the company has had very little to do with the world of micro-finance and community enterprise – especially in developing countries. That situation has started to change as a result of a US$10 million initiative launched by the Citicorp Foundation in 1995. Although the initiative is run through the bank's community investment arm as opposed to its mainstream business, it offers hope not only to its immediate beneficiaries, but also to the longer-term process of educating bankers about the commercial potential and socio-economic importance of small and micro-enterprise.

The key objective of the five year initiative, *Banking on Enterprise*, is to seed innovative micro-lending programmes in Citibank markets around the globe, with the aim not only of infusing new capital into the field of micro-enterprise, but also providing a vehicle for disseminating information on successful programmes and developing leadership in this growing field.

The foundation is achieving these goals in a number of ways:

- The core of the initiative is a grant process, offering in the region of US$50,000 each to micro-lenders in some of Citicorp's key markets;

- The Foundation has also made a special "success transfer" grant to ACCION International to support the expansion of ACCION's successful lending programmes and the development of new financial services in Latin America and the USA. Citibank's mainstream business units also work closely with ACCION in helping to manage and leverage its innovative Latin American Bridge Fund;

- The Foundation is working with Citibank's Private Bank division to develop a training programme on financial management and services for micro-lenders;

- It is sponsoring the Micro-Credit Summit to be held in Washington in February 1997, which will be the first step of a decade-long campaign to ensure that 100 million of the world's poorest people, especially women, will be receiving credit for self-employment by 2005.

The grant programme has already distributed funds to micro-finance intermediaries operating in Mexico, India, Kenya, Indonesia, Poland, South Africa, Argentina, Bangladesh, Chile and Egypt, as well as low income neighbourhoods in New York, San Francisco, Washington DC, Chicago and Miami. These intermediaries include: the Trickle-Up Program created 16 years ago and now operating in 108 countries; the more recently created Environmental Enterprise Assistance Fund which is a non-profit venture capital organisation seeking to provide the capital investments needed to grow small-scale environmental businesses in markets such as the Philippines and Indonesia; PRIDE Africa which is headquartered in Kenya; the American Trust for Agriculture in Poland, which has launched a fund for Women in Rural Enterprise Development; the Pan American Development Foundation in Mexico, which is part of the Mexican Foundation for Rural Development; EQI in Cairo and Shared Interest in South Africa. Each microfinance intermediary is using the funds in different ways, some for capitalising existing loan funds, and others for training, technical assistance and workshops. PRIDE Africa is setting up an innovative loan guarantee mechanism with commercial financial institutions in a pilot initiative to facilitate loans to micro-entrepreneurs, and at the same time, to raise awareness about the commercial potential of such loans in the banking sector.

The next challenge for the Citicorp Foundation is to start educating its own commercial bankers about the world of microfinance and the commercial opportunities of dramatically scaling-up financial services to this sector. Citibank's operations in Colombia have already started to play a role. RepFin SA., a wholly-owned subsidiary of the bank, has made a US$500,000 equity investment in the Colombian micro-finance intermediary FinanceSol. Cititrust has also agreed to underwrite, on a best efforts basis, a US$3.5 million equity instrument for FinanceSol to be placed in Colombia. This has been partly in response to severe funding problems faced by FinanceSol, but also reflects the long-term potential that this branch of Citibank sees in the field of micro-finance.

UNITING ENTREPRENEURS

Programmes linking large and small-scale businesses in sub-Saharan and North Africa

● ●

1 PARTNERS FOR GROWTH in ZIMBABWE

Established in 1995, Partners for Growth (PfG) is an initiative by more than 40 Zimbabwean business leaders to provide a network and focus to increase their companies' involvement in – and contribution to – SMME development. Its initial establishment was supported by funding and advisory input from The Prince of Wales Business Leaders Forum and the British ODA. The German government also offers some support, but the core funding comes from member company subscriptions. Member companies include a mixture of multinational and local companies such as: Anglo American, Apex Corporation, Ashanti Goldfields, Astra Corporation, Barclays Bank, BP, Coca-Cola, Coopers & Lybrand, Costain, Dunlop, Edgars Stores, Farmers Development Trust, Fincor, Industrial Development Corporation, KPMG, Lever Brothers, Lonrho, Lyons Brooke Bond, Meikles, Nestle, Old Mutual, Olivine Industries, PG Industries, Radar Ltd, Rio Tinto, Southampton Assurance, Standard Chartered Bank, Truworths, TSL, Zimbabwe Leaf Tobacco Co., and Zimbabwe Sugar Refineries.

The main objective of *Partners for Growth* is to encourage the establishment of direct business linkages between large-scale companies and small indigenous enterprises. There are a number of strands to this, such as: helping to set up new small businesses and reinvigorating existing ones; helping to build the capacity of development agencies and NGOs; sharing experiences and communicating examples of successful partnerships within Zimbabwe and internationally; and improving the quality and opportunities for entrepreneurship. Members of *Partners for Growth* are embarked on a practical agenda to achieve these aims. Many are already sub-contracting services and off-loading non-core operations to small indigenous enterprises. These range from transport, the maintenance of premises and equipment, the supply of raw materials and consultancy services, to commercial operations previously undertaken "in-house". Many are also nurturing their small business partners with financial, technical, marketing and training support. PfG produces a biannual publication of "good practice" case studies from Zimbabwe and around the world, and member companies come together regularly in small Development Teams to share experiences, to co-ordinate their involvement with other organisations, and to listen to international speakers.

Working in partnership with Prince Edward, one of the country's leading government schools, PfG has recently launched an Enterprise Education programme in a group of 9 pilot schools. The programme is modelled on similar initiatives in the UK and USA and the long-term goal is to expand its implementation throughout the country's school system.

2 THE KENYA MANAGEMENT ASSISTANCE PROGRAMME in KENYA

The Kenya Management Assistance Programme (K-MAP) was founded in 1987 by Victor Pratt, a local businessman, and the large-scale business community in Kenya who wished to contribute their skills and experience to assist the development of Kenyan entrepreneurs. K-MAP's membership consists of 180 large and medium scale companies, including a number of multi-nationals such as Barclays Bank, Coca-Cola and Citibank, who pay subscriptions and, most importantly, donate executive time to counsel and train the organisation's small business clients. Apart from this private sector support, K-MAP has also received substantial donor assistance, initially from USAID and more recently the British ODA. A small proportion of funds is also generated from membership fees, and operations such as training workshops and publications.

Business Counselling is K-MAP's core activity and is the *raison d'etre* of the organisation, using volunteer counsellors from K-MAP's member companies. In 1995, K-MAP had some 400 registered counsellors and 900 registered SMME clients. Other activities include training workshops, publications, tapes and a magazine. ODA funding has supported the development and the provision of courses in business growth, women's enterprises and business survival.

3 AMSCO AND THE AFRICAN PROJECT DEVELOPMENT FACILITY (APDF)

These two initiatives have been spearheaded by the IFC, but are also supported by multinational companies, UNDP, USAID and other donors. They operate in a number of African companies, focused on supporting medium-scale and more advanced small-scale enterprises, with investments ranging from a few hundred thousand dollars to US$7 million, and a combination of consultancy and business support services. The AMSCO initiative is profiled on page 241

4 EMPRETEC in GHANA

This programme is co-ordinated on a world-wide basis by a partnership between UNDP, UNCTAD and various other UN agencies and the business community. It has been highly successful in Ghana, and is profiled on page 236.

5 GET AHEAD FOUNDATION in SOUTH AFRICA

The Get Ahead Foundation (GAF) is one of several SMME intermediary organisations in South Africa which receives support from the large-scale business sector. It was established in 1984 by Archbishop Desmond Tutu and Dr Nthato Motlana, under the directorship of Don McRobert, with the goal of empowering people in the informal sector, through loans and training, to become self-sufficient entrepreneurs. It is based on the philosophy of mutual responsibility and on delivering services which reflect the full cost of their provision, thereby ensuring long-term sustainability.

The GAF targets four main types of clients (and it sees its beneficiaries very much as clients, rather than recipients of "charity hand-outs"): street hawkers (who receive about half the loans available); informal "back yard" manufacturers, retailers and service providers; entrepreneurs operating in business hives and other supported environments; and self-contained businesses which are close to being formal. It offers these clients a combination of: micro-loans (ranging from R200 to R2000 per person); training and advice in basic management training (book-keeping, marketing, pricing etc); and technical skills (e.g. sewing, knitting, woodwork, motor mechanics, welding).

Its loan system is based on the "group lending" approach pioneered by the Grameen Bank in Bangladesh – where groups of up to five borrowers act as each others' "collateral" thus overcoming the lack of collateral assets which often impedes micro-entrepreneurs, and ensuring repayment rates in the range of 87-90%. Since its creation The Get Ahead Foundation has made thousands of loans and helped to create hundreds of formal and informal enterprises and thousands of jobs, both full-time and part-time. It receives private sector funding and also works with a number of major companies, such as South African Breweries, Rio Tinto's Reef Training Centre and Middleburg Steel and Alloys, to establish direct business and training linkages between large and small-scale enterprises.

Other SMME intermediaries in South Africa which receive support from, or work with the large-scale business sector include: the Triple Trust Organisation, the Opportunity Trust's Izibuko Foundation and the Equal Opportunity Foundation.

6 ALEXANDRIA BUSINESS ASSOCIATION in EGYPT

The Alexandria Business Association (ABA) began its activities in 1983 as a Chamber of Commerce to support and promote the interests of Alexandria's formal sector business community. ABA soon expanded its activities to include community welfare, with members contributing time, money and resources towards various community and social development programmes. With the support of USAID and the co-operation of businesses such as the Environmental Quality International, the ABA developed The Small & Micro Enterprise Project (SMEP) to provide credit and technical assistance to micro- and small-scale enterprises in the Alexandria region.

Since its inception, the ABA/SMEP has divided its portfolio between micro-enterprise owners employing five or less employees and small enterprise owners employing between six and fifteen employees. Between 1990-1995, the ABA/SMEP has worked with over 17,000 SMMEs, which account for over 45,000 jobs. Loan repayment rates are in the 90% category. Initial seed money provided by USAID (in US$) is held in the name of the project in several commercial banks. The banks then make a line of credit available to the SMEP for lending in the equivalent amount of Egyptian pounds.

The ABA/SMEP established the Alexandria Small Business Centre (ABSC) to address the non-financial needs of its client micro-entrepreneurs. The ABSC provides several business development and training programmes in areas such as accounting, marketing, quality control, licensing and taxation. In addition, the ABSC provides a technical library and showroom.

Evidence that human
capital development is
critical for overall economic
and social development is
not new. What is new is that
the awareness of its
importance has gone
beyond the confines of
academic scholars and
social reformers and has
entered into the thinking of
mainstream decision
makers.

World Bank Annual Report, 1995

2.3 Human Development

Recent research by the World Bank's Vice Presidency for Environmentally Sustainable Development, which concludes that on average human capital accounts for 64% of national wealth and becomes increasingly important as countries develop, sends a strong message that human development is crucially important and requires increased attention and investment.

There is now overwhelming evidence that investments in people, and specifically in their education, training, health, nutrition and family planning, yield high returns and are fundamental to poverty alleviation and sustainable development. Although the absolute needs are greater in the world's developing countries, this strategy is equally important in the OECD and transition economies, where rising levels of inequality can only be tackled by people-centred investment policies and programmes.

The growing importance attached to human resource development is reflected in:

• The increased resources being allocated to it by international agencies. The World Bank's lending for human capital development, for example, has increased more than five-fold in nominal terms over the last decade (see figure 1);

• The central position that issues such as education and training and family welfare are attaining on a growing number of national policy agendas – from Brazil to Britain; and

• The fact that almost every survey undertaken on the social spending of companies, from the Philippines, to South Africa, to the USA, demonstrates an increasingly strong focus on education and other activities to build human capital.

In its recently published report entitled *Poverty Reduction and the World Bank: Progress and Challenges in the 1990s*, the World Bank argues that basic education is a key element in developing the human capital of the world's poor, and that three areas are particularly crucial: early childhood development; primary education; and educating girls. The Bank is also giving particular focus to two areas of primary health care: improving maternal and child health; and raising the nutritional standards of the poor, especially women and children. The World Bank's direct support for nutrition, for example, has increased tenfold since 1990. It has also broadened in scope from traditional population, health and nutrition programmes to a more holistic integration into other sector programmes, such as agriculture and food, security, education and industry projects.

So what does this all mean for the business sector, not traditionally associated with interventions on these issues? There is no doubt that the private sector has a critical role to play in all of the above areas. Many companies have been playing a role for a long time, although this has not always been recognised, and a large number of them are beginning to take a more strategic and holistic approach to human resource development, both for direct business interests and broader social motivations.

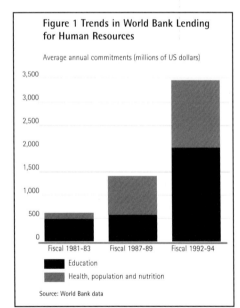

Figure 1 Trends in World Bank Lending for Human Resources

Average annual commitments (millions of US dollars)

Fiscal 1981-83   Fiscal 1987-89   Fiscal 1992-94

■ Education
▓ Health, population and nutrition

Source: World Bank data

Business has a role in global development not only through capital investment, but more importantly, by investing in human capital and providing local people with the tools to drive their own economic development forward.

As with most of the business contributions described in this publication, there are three main ways in which companies can contribute to human resource development:

- Through their core business activities all companies can make a direct impact in the workplace, by making investments in their employees and their employees' families. Certain companies, for example those in the agriculture, food, health care, publishing and information sectors, can produce goods and services which, if made more accessible to the poor, could help to improve health and nutrition levels, access to books, information and so on;

- Through their social investment and philanthropy activities – as mentioned above, many companies are already spending the largest percentage of their community investment budgets on education and other human development activities; and

- Through their influence on public policy, for example by encouraging governments to undertake education reforms which make curricula more appropriate for the needs of the global economy, giving advice on education management and financing etc.

The following section overviews business contributions in a few of these areas. It looks initially at some key issues in employee relations and human resource development in the workplace; and then goes on to look at the type of social investments and policy interventions that a sample of companies and business associations are making in the critical area of education, before briefly overviewing some examples of corporate contributions to training and skills development (outside the immediate workplace); health and nutrition projects; youth development; and the application of information technology to social and environmental projects.

(i) INVESTING IN HUMAN DEVELOPMENT THROUGH WORKPLACE PRACTICES

Four key human development issues are overviewed in the following two pages:

a) **Employee education and training**

b) **Occupational health and safety**

c) **Increasing opportunities for women and minorities**

d) **Child labour.**

a) Employee Education and Training

In a rapidly changing world where there is growing acceptance of the need for "lifetime" learning, companies have a major impact on the education and training of their employees, and on the regular enhancement of their skills and capacities. The training budgets of many multinational companies run into millions of dollars and work hours – an area which warrants further research if only to demonstrate the critically important impact and multiplier effects that this can have, especially in developing countries.

The majority of the companies profiled in this publication are exemplars in this area, and many of them are investing heavily in the development of their employees in developing and transition economies. They are doing so not only through direct employee training and management development programmes, but also through technology co-operation, especially in environmental technology, and in the more general transfer of business

ABB: BUILDING LOCAL SKILLS AND MANAGEMENT CAPACITIES

ABB is one of the outstanding examples in the employee education and training field. It now employs in the region of 70,000 people in developing and transition economies, a threefold increase since 1990, and since this date has made investments in these markets in the region of US$260 million. In Poland, as one example, ABB has invested more than US$1 million in a Management Development Centre at Falenty, which is focused on improving employee skills in finance, economics, communications, leadership and teamwork. Some 4,000 people have been trained at this centre between 1993 and 1996. The Falenty Centre is used to bring together ABB staff from around the region, to improve regional co-operation and cultural understanding. It also runs courses for non-ABB employees and is operated as a profit-centre, with incentives to improve both the quality and quantity of its service, both internally to ABB and externally.

The company also has management training centres in Brno, in the Czech Republic and in Moscow, and has established a number of partnerships with other companies, international agencies and academic institutions to leverage the training it provides for its own employees, to the employees of suppliers and other business partners. One of these projects is a management leadership programme in Russia, which is profiled on page 244. Other examples include the ABB/INSEAD Asia-Pacific Business School and the ABB/Duke University Management Programme for the Americas. In a large number of its developing and transition operations the company's entire management team, as well as lower level employees, consists of local people. In Egypt, for example, there are only five expatriates among 1,500 permanent staff and almost the entire country management team are locals. Local nationals are also country presidents in numerous locations.

practices and management know-how which comes from working together. The ripple effects of these activities can be enormous. For example, well-trained employees often move on to senior positions in local companies and sometimes government, spreading the impact of their training and giving local people the tools to drive their own economic development forward. A number of companies also offer scholarships, funding or full school facilities for the children of their employees.

b) Occupational Health and Safety

Two of the key issues companies face in this area are risk management and safety in the workplace, and dealing with the spread of HIV/AIDs among workers. The latter issue is covered in the section on health.

As far as occupational safety is concerned, there have been a growing number of initiatives to develop employer codes of conduct and guidelines in recent years. Many of these have been undertaken by companies themselves and their trade associations (most notably the chemical industry), others by trade unions, NGOs and international organisations such as the ILO and UNEP. Governments in many countries have also increased regulations in this area, although there are often problems of implementation and monitoring.

There are three main ways to reduce risk in the workplace. Companies can:

- Minimise risk at source by ensuring that dangerous equipment, materials and operational procedures are kept to a minimum and are carefully labelled, controlled and monitored;

- Establish clear operational guidelines and management procedures to ensure that safe practices are implemented and adhered to; and

- Train, equip and empower workers to take responsibility for personal safety in their activities.

Obviously a good system combines elements of all these approaches. Placing a heavy emphasis on the establishment of sound management procedures and continuous training and empowerment of employees, is especially important. A World Bank study of industrial chemical accidents, for example, concluded that some 80% of industrial accidents were due to managerial inadequacies, and only 20% were attributable to equipment failure or worker error.

The following profiles look at how a collaborative effort by chemical companies, suppliers, farmers' associations, and end-users is helping to improve the use of agrochemicals in Africa, and how BOC Gases and British Petroleum are transferring international standards and management systems for occupational safety around the world.

Multinational companies can play a valuable role in transferring sound health and safety processes from one country to another.

A case study produced by New Consumer in 1995 illustrates how BOC, one of the world's five largest producers of industrial gases with operations in more than 60 countries, transferred South Africa's highly regarded NOSA (National Occupational Safety Association) system from its South African company AFROX to its operations in Pakistan. This has resulted in: a dramatic improvement in the company's incident/accident record in Pakistan; emulation of the programme by other companies; increased

THE AGRICULTURAL CHEMICAL INDUSTRIES ASSOCIATION IN ZIMBABWE

Despite their important contribution to increased agricultural productivity, the production, distribution and use of agrochemicals pose numerous environmental and health risks. These risks are particularly difficult to manage in an African context of: minimal legislation and/or controls and monitoring systems; lack of information; low literacy and education levels; severe economic constraints on both governments to implement controls and on businesses to follow them, especially medium and small-scale enterprises; and inadequate technologies and/or facilities to ensure safe use i.e. instructions to "wash with soap and water" or "keep in a cool place" are meaningless if water is scarce and there is no electricity; likewise the recommendation to "dispose of used containers" when villagers have no other containers to carry water.

Maximising the efficiency of agrochemical production and use, while minimising the risks, requires a multi-disciplinary and holistic approach, with partnership and technology co-operation at its core. The Agricultural Chemical Industries Association (A.C.I.A.) in Zimbabwe, provides an example of such an approach. The A.C.I.A. was established to bring together all the importers, suppliers, stockists and end-users of agrochemicals in the country, with the overriding objective of ensuring the sound use of these chemicals in the workplace.

The organisation is aided in its task by a relatively clear regulatory framework which guides its activities nationally and influences chemical use in

agricultural exports. Zimbabwe is also a signatory to the International Labour Organisation convention on safety in the use of chemicals at work. Local suppliers and stockists provide comprehensive training and extension services in partnership with government extension organisations. They are also paying increased attention to training and informing farmers on the concept of Integrated Pest Management.

To promote safe chemical usage, the A.C.I.A. has developed a comprehensive labelling system and education programme. Apart from requiring very detailed labels, even more important, given low literacy levels among many farm workers and peasant farmers, is the use of colour coding and in some cases pictograms. All agrochemicals in the country are colour coded according to the relative level of toxicity and all suppliers are now required to use the same codes, and labels have to be put on every packet, regardless of its size. Instructions to dispose of containers are also well-documented on the labels and their destruction is strongly encouraged, although extremely difficult to enforce when so many poor people use these containers for carrying water and foodstuffs. The chemical companies work closely with various farmers' unions and agricultural extension services to run training courses, which cover issues such as levels and reduction of risk exposure; hygiene; protective clothing; measuring, mixing and loading equipment; disposal of pesticide waste; drift reduction and emergency measures in the case of pesticide poisoning. They also have public relations and awareness campaigns via radio programmes, magazines and charts.

employee morale; reputation enhancement; and invitations by the Pakistani government to advise them on safety standards and policies. The company has also transferred this system to its operations in a number of other developing countries in Asia and Africa. The NOSA system is based on a management by objectives approach and provides not only a managerial framework for companies, but also a public rating system, which enables companies to benchmark their performance and to build reputation for responsible practices.

Road safety is an important issue for British Petroleum, which has drivers transporting millions of tonnes of petrol, often on poorly maintained roads in different parts of the world. Throughout Africa, for example, the company insists on its drivers conforming with international standards. They must be properly trained, their vehicles must be properly maintained, and their performance must be regularly monitored. This focus is extended to community awareness programmes on road safety, with the result that in pursuit of the company's commercial objective it is also helping to save lives on African roads.

c) Increasing opportunities for women and minorities

Despite the fact that women now account for almost half the workforce in many countries, even in OECD economies there are still extremely few women in senior management positions, let alone in developing economies. The situation is the same for minority groups in most countries. More companies are implementing policies and programmes to change this situation, but there is a long way to go. In some countries groups of companies have joined forces to establish campaigns aimed at increasing support for women and minorities in the workplace. Examples include, Opportunity 2000 and Race for Opportunity, run by Business in the Community in the UK and profiled on page 268.

Such campaigns are recognising the need to focus not only on the workplace, but also on the education system, and companies can play a valuable role in supporting education activities which help girls and ethnic minorities to develop their full potential.

d) Child Labour

One of the most sensitive issues that many companies face if they are manufacturing, or subcontracting their manufacturing, in developing countries is the prevalence of child labour. The ILO estimates that there are between 100 and 200 million children below the age of 14 working around the world, 95% of them in developing countries.

Levi Strauss has been one of the corporate leaders in tackling the issue of child labour in a way that sets clear standards for its subcontractors to follow, as described on page 60, but at the same time takes a realistic view of the economic conditions that drive many children to work. For example, it discovered that one of its subcontractors in Bangladesh was employing young girls under the age of 14 on a full-time basis, some of them the only wage earners in their families. The company made an agreement with the contractor that it would establish a school on the site and pay for uniforms and books if the contractor would continue to pay the children's salaries while letting them go to school until the age of 15. Reebok is another company that has taken a strong position on the issues of child labour and human rights in the workplace.

The ILO and several international and national NGOs have also started to work on a consultative rather than confrontational basis with companies to find workable solutions to the issue of child labour. These initiatives include:

- The Council on Economic Priorities (CEP) which has established a Partnership for Responsible Global Sourcing in the USA and is working on a similar initiative in Europe, plus a Child Labour Handbook with the ILO;

- The International Youth Foundation and its *Companies Caring for Children* campaign which is profiled on page 228;

- The Human Rights programme of US-based Business for Social Responsibility (profiled on page 266); and

- The innovative Abrinq Foundation in Brazil, which is profiled on page 151.

> The problem of child labour persists – along with stubborn poverty, its root cause. Reaction to the issue is visceral, but responses are often fragmented and divisive. Finding solutions will require sustained collaboration among corporations, governments, international organisations, and trade unions, as well as other groups in civil society in industrialised and developing countries alike.
>
> Deborah Leipziger,
> Council on Economic Priorities

A country's performance in the global game does not begin with its corporations. Rather, it begins in the mind-sets of its people – how people are taught to think, to deal with one another, to work together. In other words, the race begins in school. The first clues to what makes a nation tick – its distinct core values – can be seen in how children are educated.

Hedrick Smith,
Rethinking America, 1995

Studies have found that a one year increase in schooling can augment wages by more than 10% and raises GDP significantly. In Peru, for example, it was found that if farmers had an additional year of schooling, it increased their probability of adopting modern farm technology by 45%. In Thailand, farmers with four years of schooling were three times more likely to use new fertilizers and other inputs than farmers with one to three years of school. It is also evident that education promotes entrepreneurship. Someone once said: "The road to success is paved with education."

Mark Mobius,
The Investor's Guide to the
Emerging Markets, 1994

(ii) EDUCATION

Apart from their contribution to education and training in the workplace, more and more companies are targeting their social investment activities at improving education in society as a whole. This trend reflects: a)a growing recognition of the central role of education – socially, politically and economically – in both developed and developing countries; and b)a direct business interest in having a future workforce with the quality of education and skills necessary to compete in the global, knowledge-based economy.

The wide range of challenges associated with achieving a quality education system can be summarised under the two broad headings of accessibility and applicability:

- Firstly, education must be accessible to the largest number of people possible and increasingly on a flexible and lifetime basis. This raises issues of equity and efficiency in the provision of education; the importance of early childhood development (including an integrated approach that tackles nutrition needs as well as learning needs); a sound universal basic education system; cost of delivery; outreach; location of facilities; availability of books, teachers and equipment; the access to learning opportunities for girls; availability of adult education programmes; and the balance between formal and informal education; and basic, higher and lifetime learning.

- Secondly, education must be applicable to the needs and local conditions of people, but also relevant to their country in the global economy. This raises issues such as the effectiveness of education; the link between education and labour market needs; the relevance of the national curriculum to today's global economy; the identification of core competencies that children and adults should develop beyond reading, writing and reasoning (and obviously the critical importance of having these three skills); the growing need for a sound education in maths, science and information technology; the need for education in environmental issues and cultural understanding; the importance of teacher development and training; the importance of cultural relevance; the design, attainment and measurement of national standards or benchmarks; and threaded through all of these, the need for quality in the management and delivery of education.

A recent World Bank report entitled *Priorities and Strategies for Education* concludes that reforming education financing and management requires redefining the role of government in six main ways, with appropriate policies depending on country circumstances. These are:

- a higher priority for education in general;

- a greater attention to the linkages between learning and labour market outcomes;

- focusing public investment on basic education, coupled with more reliance on private financing for higher education;

- increased attention to equity issues;

- greater involvement at the household level to improve accountability of educational systems; and

- more autonomous institutions.

> **Operations in the education sector can be greatly improved by increasing the participation of government officials, education professionals, local communities and the private sector. Such participation can increase the relevance and quality of education, improve ownership and build consensus, help to reach remote and disadvantaged groups, mobilise additional resources, and build institutional capacity. Participatory operations involve risks and costs, however, and certain preconditions are necessary for success.**
>
> Participation in the education
> and training sector
> The World Bank, 1995

All of these issues have relevance for the business sector. There are a number of "leverage" or "influence" points where companies can make a particularly valuable contribution to tackling some of the above challenges. These are:

- Co-operation with governments and educationalists in debating and implementing systemic educational reform;

- Providing advice, funding and managerial support to improve the efficiency and effectiveness of the governance, financing and management of the education sector and/or specific schools;

- Supporting training and relevant experiential learning for teachers;

- Contributing to curriculum development; and

- Supporting initiatives that directly reach schoolchildren, ranging from the provision of equipment, materials and after-school study facilities, to mentoring programmes, nutrition programmes and exposure to the world of work.

The following profiles look at some collaborative and individual company programmes which address some or all of the above issues, and all of which have potential application in other countries.

Collaborative corporate initiatives
The first three, Aim High, EQUIP and AmCham Brazil are targeted at improving quality in education. Goals 2000 is an example of a government-led, but business supported, programme for systemic education reform. The Conference Board of Canada illustrates how companies are working with other stakeholders to develop ethical guidelines for business education partnerships.

Individual corporate initiatives
The first two profiles illustrate how two companies – KPMG and 3M are offering management advice and training to teachers. Investing in early learning is a crucial issue being addressed by BMW and TRW. Some examples are given of companies investing in physical infrastructure for education in Egypt and South Africa. BP and Toyota provide illustrations of companies investing in science and technology education, and GrandMet and American Express offer examples of how companies can help to prepare children for the world of work.

The Aim High Programme in the United Kingdom

BRITISH COMPANIES AIMING HIGH FOR EDUCATION

- Marks & Spencer supports **Compact Plus** programmes in over 150 schools, supporting young people at risk from 15-18 years old;

- NYNEX Cables support **Learning Centres** in a number of cities;

- Toyota has established a **Science and Technology Education Fund** which is distributing grants in excess of UK£1.2 million to over 2,000 schools;

- The Royal Insurance company has developed a **Core Skills Portfolio**, enabling 20 pilot schools to audit their progress against a core set of skills;

- Cadbury Schweppes is spearheading a group of 50 companies to look at the potential for **Cause-Related Marketing** in supporting schools; and

- KPMG is operating a **Mentoring Support Programme** between KPMG partners and head teachers in inner-city schools.

Aim High is a campaign run by Business in the Community in the UK (profiled on page 268) which aims to encourage companies to work with schools and colleges to help raises levels of achievement in the British education system. Although the United Kingdom is world-class for the one in three people who get to university, it underachieves by some 20% for the middle band of students and there are about 150,000 young people who leave school every year functionally illiterate. Many will not be able to find jobs and this sets in motion a cycle of deprivation and social exclusion that is increasingly difficult to break out of. It has been estimated that the costs to British business of trying to rectify this situation through training and other programme, is in the region of UK£8 billion. More and more British companies have recognised the threat that this situation presents to the long-term competitiveness and prosperity of their businesses. As a result, about 150,000 companies support the Aim High campaign, which operates through a nationwide network of 160 business-education partnerships in 25,000 schools and colleges.

One of the key principles of Aim High is that each company should develop an education programme appropriate for the company culture and structure, and relevant to the needs of the school and community it is working with. The campaign has developed 10 Pathways to Achievement as the best ways for companies to help raise students' aspirations and performance. These pathways can be applied to countries all over the world and are as follows:

• **Compacts** – supporting agreements between young people, their schools and local businesses, which set goals and incentives for course completion and achievement, and provide support for young people at risk of failing or dropping out;

• **Curriculum Development for teachers and students** – providing materials, equipment and employee expertise, opening sites for placements and visits by students and teachers to enable them to understand the world of business better;

• **Mentoring** – encouraging employees at all levels in the company to help young people to set goals, plan career paths and achieve more with their lives;

• **Key Skills** – helping to develop employment competencies through personal challenges, problem solving and enterprise education;

• **Parents and Governors** – encouraging experienced staff, especially parents, to become more involved with schools as school governors; supporting parent/school contracts, advisory services, self-help groups for parents;

• **Work Experience** – providing challenging placements, with quality preparation and review, so that young people aged 15-19 experience a range of work tasks which develop the skills and qualities needed by employers. In the UK today, as a result of Aim High and other programmes, some 93% of all 15 year olds go on a two week experience;

• **Teacher and Management Development** – helping teachers at all levels to learn from business through placements, access to in-house courses and training, and helping senior teachers, especially heads of schools to improve their management skills;

• **Careers** – supporting careers education and guidance programmes and promoting national records of achievement;

• **Out-of-School Support** – working with schools and the community to improve access to books, homework and study support centres or after-school clubs; and

• **14-19 Education** – helping young people to achieve advanced or Level 3 qualifications through bursaries, recognition schemes and support of vocational courses.

Educational Quality Improvement Programme (EQUIP) in South Africa
• •

EQUIP is a programme of the National Business Initiative for Growth, Development and Democracy in South Africa (NBI) which is profiled on page 246. Its objective is to support education quality improvement initiatives aimed at enhancing schooling conditions in South Africa's most depressed areas. The programme aims to work with education authorities at national and provincial levels, as well as involving private companies, aid agencies and donors, NGOs and other service providers, and most importantly, school governing bodies, and the schools and local communities themselves.

EQUIP works directly with selected schools and helps them to build local capacity to identify their own needs; develop proposals to meet these needs; mobilise resources to implement these proposals; and take accountability for showing quality improvements. Some of the possible quality improvement activities highlighted by EQUIP are:

- Refurbishment of existing facilities;

- Supplementary facilities and/or resources;

- In-service teacher education;

- Leadership training for school principals and staff;

- Parental education programmes;

- Extra-mural activities for pupils and out-of-school youth;

- Establishment of effective school governing structures.

A number of pilot schools have been identified and EQUIP is providing finance to up-grade these and is working on developing mechanisms that can be applied nationally, such as incentives and tax exemptions, to get private companies more involved.

THE JOINT EDUCATION TRUST

One other major business-led initiative in South Africa is the Joint Education Trust. Established in 1993 by a partnership of leading companies, teacher and labour unions, business associations and political organisations, JET provides funding to organisations which: improve the quality of teaching via teacher upgrading projects; provide adult basic education, and meet the education needs of out-of-school and unemployed youth. Its founders committed R500 million to the Trust over five years, and also apply their knowledge, skills and influence to the issues which the Trust addresses.

Initial results in pilot schools have demonstrated a decline in drop-out and failure rates, parents and teachers have increased their involvement with schools, test results have improved and the low per student cost has made the project a useful model for educational authorities around the country.

AmCham's Quality in Education Institute in Brazil
• •

It is estimated that only 12% of the economically active population in Brazil is being sufficiently prepared for a technologically modern society. Although 95% of students have access to primary school, only 18% complete their primary education, only 2 in every 100 seventh grade students assimilate more than 70% of the required math content and given current trends it will be 3080 before Brazil will reach a 90% high school graduation rate. The Sao Paulo-based American Chamber of Commerce, with some of its multinational and Brazilian member companies, recognised the lack of results-orientated educational projects in the country. It has therefore established a programme aimed at developing and testing a methodology for improving education quality, at a cost low enough to ensure the possibility of dissemination throughout the public school system.

The programme, operated through the Quality in Education Institute, has set the educational objective of ensuring that 70% of maths students in pilot programmes assimilate 70% or more of the basic maths and Portuguese skills, as defined by the Secretariat of Education. The programme is focusing on developing the key skills of: reading, writing and analysing texts; applying basic maths operations; and resolving problems. It is supported by some 90 local and multinational companies, including the Brazilian subsidiaries of American Express, Arthur Andersen, Bank of Boston, Chase Manhattan, Ciba, Dow Chemical, Goodyear, Hoescht, ING Bank, Johnson & Johnson, Kodak, McKinsey, Monsanto, Oracle, Philips, Siemens, TRW, Unisys and Xerox.

Goals 2000 in the United States of America

American companies have a long-standing tradition of business-education partnerships. A 1994 research report by The Conference Board, entitled *Business and Education Reform: The Fourth Wave*, illustrates how corporate involvement in schools has evolved from:

1. **ad hoc business-support programmes for individual schools, to;**

2. **the application of sound management principles in schools, by training teachers and administrators in Total Quality Management and outcome-based performance approaches; to**

3. **advocacy and pressure for public policy initiatives, such as school choice and national standards; to**

4. **a more integrated approach with elements of all the above, based on collaboration for more systemic reform, and focusing on working with key stakeholder groups to achieve reform from within and without schools, and enhance school curriculum development and performance.**

An example of this more strategic approach is the support that business has given for President Clinton's Goals 2000 initiative. The *Goals 2000: Educate America Act* was signed into law in March 1994, to provide the framework for a new and supportive partnership between federal, state and local governments, business, educators, parent organisations and communities. The initiative is a reflection of the fact that despite more than a decade of educational reform in the USA, American students and schools are not measuring up to the high standards required to support a strong democracy and competitive economy.

States participating in the Goals 2000 initiative are required to develop comprehensive strategies for: upgrading curriculum and assessment standards; improving the quality of teaching; expanding the use of technology; strengthening accountability for teaching and learning; promoting more flexibility and choice within the public school system; and building strong partnerships between schools, families, companies and others in the community. Each state is asked to demonstrate that it has developed its strategy with broad-based, grass-roots involvement from other sectors. States that participate in Goals 2000 receive seed money to help launch and sustain their reform efforts, which they are expected to use for leveraging other funding sources, including from business.

The federal government has developed a range of campaigning and informational materials, plus guidelines to encourage greater business participation in education. An example is its initiative *Building Business and Community Partnerships for Learning*, which covers a wide range of actions that business can support in the following areas:

- **In the classroom** – through curriculum development, enhancing teacher efficacy, and motivating students for learning;

Business Support for Goals 2000

The US Business Roundtable and the Chief Executive Officers of individual American companies have played a key role in helping the government to shape and implement the Goals 2000 initiative. Companies are engaged in supporting systemic education reform at both the Federal and State level of government. The work of TRW is one example.

From 1993 to 1996 Joseph Gorman, TRW's Chairman and CEO, chaired the Business Roundtable Education Task Force. During this period, he testified before Congress and led delegations of business leaders to meetings with the Secretary of Education, and President Clinton to promote bipartisan support for the Goals 2000 initiative. Despite the shift in political leadership in the US Congress after the November 1994 election, the business community supported a sustained effort to prevent federal funding cuts of Goals 2000.

TRW has major operations in both California and Ohio, and in both States, as well as other parts of the country, it has played a leading role in supporting comprehensive education reform at the State level, through the involvement of locally based senior managers following the lead of the Chief Executive at the national level.

- **In the school** – through helping teachers and administrators to define their missions and set objectives, and to develop leadership and change management skills;

- **In the district** – by supporting school-based restructuring; student assessment standards and school accountability; and setting up communication and resource networks;

- **In the community** – by building local consensus for reform; connecting families and schools; and linking community resources, for example by supporting the use of schools for local activities after school hours;

- **In the policy arena** – by supporting incentive structures to reward performance improvements; funding research to reassess rules and regulations; and supporting government funding and physical improvement programmes.

In each of these areas the federal government provides detailed suggestions for how companies can get involved by giving funding, providing material and human resources, or undertaking advocacy and campaigning activities.

Other collaborative business education initiatives

Nationwide education improvement programmes led exist in a number of other countries. In the Philippines, for example, Philippine Business for Social Progress, which is profiled in detail on page 252, has an Education Consensus Group, which engages in policy dialogue with the government and runs campaigns to involve companies in practical programmes focused on: promoting science, mathematics and English teaching; industry-school linkages; management improvement in the education sector; and the supply of books, equipment and information technology to schools. In Jamaica companies are working in partnership with other sectors to improve the use of technology in classrooms, as profiled on page 234, and UK-based Warwick University co-ordinates an International Partnership Network for people and organisations from all sectors involved in business-education partnerships. Many Chambers of Commerce and Confederations of Industry are also establishing programmes to look at the increasingly important question of business engagement in education.

Individual business education initiatives

Countless individual company-school partnerships exist around the world, ranging from small, local level initiatives, to nationwide and even global programmes. More and more multinationals are beginning to replicate education programmes which they support in one country to other countries. Some examples of this approach are described in the following pages, together with some examples of individual corporate education projects in one country.

Ethical Guidelines for Business-Education Partnerships

The Conference Board of Canada co-ordinates a multi-stakeholder forum, with some 30 members from different sectors, committed to promoting ethical and effective business-education partnerships. It has developed a set of 14 Ethical Guidelines for such partnerships in consultation with the Corporate Council on Education and more than 200 representatives from business, education institutions, teachers' organisations, student groups, and government departments across Canada. These guidelines are aimed at supporting partnerships which safeguard learners' interests, build trust and mutual respect between partners, regulate themselves, and facilitate the making of informed decisions.

Offering management advice and training for teachers: KPMG and 3M

Advising head teachers on management issues has proved a really effective way for KPMG partners and senior staff to apply their business expertise in the community and develop their own management skills to help organisations undergo change.

Michael Fowle

Partner, KPMG

KPMG, the international accountancy and management consultants, are working with Business in the Community in the United Kingdom to establish a major support programme for the professional development of head-teachers in inner-city schools. The model being developed is also being considered by KPMG's South African office for adaptation to that country. In the UK, 15 senior professionals and managers from KPMG are working as mentors with head-teachers, meeting them once or twice a month, and providing on-going advice and support on the increasingly complex management issues of running their schools. The mentors commit to support a school for about a year, and the matching process between the company and the school is facilitated by Business in the Community, with the help of the National Association of Head-teachers. The mentors are trained before the programme by KPMG's Career Consulting division. Their involvement not only enables them to support educational improvement, by helping head-teachers tackle management problems, but also gives them useful exposure to working with small, complex organisationswhich are subject to public accountability and financial restraint, and which are under pressure to improve performance.

3M is one of a number of companies around the world in partnership with the environmental NGO, Earthwatch, to support the training of school teachers on environmental issues. The 3M programme is called the 3M Earthwatch Environmental Teaching Awards, and every year it enables 20 teachers to take part in field research in areas such as maternal nutrition and women's health in Africa (Masvingo Province, Zimbabwe) and resource management projects in Russia and parts of central and eastern Europe. The award scheme offers winning teachers the opportunity to: expand their personal horizons through active participationin scientific research; gain a clearer understanding of the role of science in everyday life; work with leading scientists; and pass on the benefits of their experience to their students, colleagues and local communities.

Investing in early learning: BMW in South Africa and TRW in the USA

BMW spends more than R3 million a year in South Africa on a variety of community programmes, mainly in the fields of education; small business development, including being one of the four founder members of the Technical Business Development Trust (with Shell, Hoescht and Nedcor); local community support; and crime prevention (see profile on page 173).

The Early Learning Centre

One of the projects for which BMW is best known is its Early Learning Centre. This child care centre – which caters for the pre-school children of about 100 employees – is very much employee-motivated and driven, with support from management rather than vice versa, and offers an excellent example of internal partnership between management and workers.

The company provides the premises and staff salaries for the centre, but BMW employees take full responsibility for the operating costs. They hold successful and highly participatory raffles on a regular bi-monthly basis which cover food, equipment and upkeep of the centre. Employees/parents also direct the content, management and fee structure of the centre and there is a strong sense of "ownership" and pride in its achievements.

The centre provides:

a) a stimulating and safe environment for employees' children, with experiential learning opportunities and sensitivity to the country's nine languages;

b) a mechanism to motivate management and employees around a common mission of joint responsibility; and

c) a resource for the wider community. For example it offers: consulting services to other companies and communities on what has worked and what has not in establishing and running the centre; a teaching practice venue for formal educational institutions; workshops (on request) for local teachers, field workers and parents; weekend courses for local teenagers on life-skills and leadership.

TRW's Foundation distributed nearly US$6.5 million to selected education, health and welfare initiatives in the USA and internationally in 1995. TRW has a particular interest in early childhood education. The following profiles look at two of the programmes that it supports in the USA which have relevance elsewhere in the world.

stART smART

TRW provides financial assistance to stART smART, a programme of the Wolf Trap Foundation for the Performing Arts. The grant supports the institute's work in 23 cities throughout the United States where TRW employees live, with a focus on underprivileged children. Recently, TRW earmarked a portion of its stART smART funding for international purposes. In October 1996, the programme will be initiated in the United Kingdom. The primary goal of stART smART is to ensure that all children enter school ready to learn. The Wolf Trap Institute accomplishes this by placing professional performing artists in pre-school classrooms. These artists train teachers to use the performing arts as powerful teaching tools and active learning experiences which help children master a variety of important life and academic skills.

Early Childhood Intervention Alliance

In 1993, TRW instituted the Early Childhood Intervention Alliance (ECIA). The ECIA programme is conducted by the internationally known Cleveland Center for Research in Child Development. Through TRW funding, the programme promotes high quality day-care through the professional development of day-care staff. This is accomplished by placing professionally trained child development specialists in day-care centres across the country. These specialists provide on-going assistance to the directors and staff of the participating day-care centre and assist the care-givers in forming meaningful relationships with children through one-on-one intervention and in-service training. Currently six TRW communities are benefiting from this project. And while each community is different, the common thread is that the TRW investment is helping to ensure each child achieves mastery in self-care and personality development.

Physical infrastructure and improvements in Egyptian and South African schools

One of the biggest challenges to improving the quality of education in many developing countries is the lack of, or at best, poor condition of classroom facilities, teaching aids, computers and even books and paper for children to read and write on. Almost all the major multinationals operating in remote regions of the world, such as mining, oil and gas companies, invest in community infrastructure when they set up operations in these places and this usually includes schooling facilities for the families of employees and often the wider local community. A number of companies have also made physical improvements to schools not only near their own operations but on a nationwide basis.

Sami Saad, a construction and engineering company headquartered in Egypt, is one example. Over the past few years the company has helped to build and equip a number of schools around the country.

In South Africa physical improvements to schools in the townships and rural areas has also received increased attention from companies in recent years. One innovative solution to meeting the lack of facilities has been the use of old shipping containers. For example, Coca-Cola has worked in partnership with Safmarine, which supplied 29 used containers, the mining company JCI, which paid to have the containers refurbished and transported to the site, and Eskom, the national power company which electrified the site, to build a school in Zonkisizwe, near Johannesburg. The local community also participated in the programme by carrying out all the negotiations with local and state government to get teachers and operating licences, by laying the school's foundations, finding furniture, and taking responsibility for the on-going maintenance and up-keep. In an area notorious for vandalism and high crime rates, the school, which has minimal security, has to-date suffered no damage or burglaries. Since 1993, Coca-Cola's 'Partners in Education" programme has placed more than 300 container facilities in different schools.

Gencor, another large South African company, has embarked on an even more ambitious joint venture with Eskom, the Department of Education and local communities to build and fully equip 15 schools, costing in the region of R4 million each and structured to double as community centres, in disadvantaged areas of the country. Each partner has a key role to play. Gencor acts as the overall project facilitator, Eskom undertakes the electrification, the government provides the teachers and an allocation of state funds and the local community provides the labour to undertake not only the construction, but also the design and management of the schools, thereby creating local jobs and ensuring that the local community participate in and "own" the project.

Investing in science, maths and technology education: BP and Toyota

BP's Science Across the World

The British Petroleum Company is involving more than 700 schools in 40 countries on four continents, in one of the most innovative global corporate community projects in the world. Its *Science Across the World* programme is an innovative approach to education that promotes and facilitates collaboration on a range of scientific issues. between students and teachers around the world.

The company has operations in Europe, the USA, Australasia and parts of Africa, and an expanding presence in other regions, notably SE Asia, South America and the former communist bloc. Its global community investment activities are targeted at community development, environment and education, with science and technology education being an important area of focus. The *Science Across the World* programme has enabled the company to leverage its global network and communications expertise in a way which meets these community investment objectives, and at the same time offers a unique multi-cultural dimension.

The programme is structured to encourage active participation and communication between students, and materials are designed to be flexible and easy to use. The project's key objectives are to:

- **raise awareness among students of the ways in which science and technology interact with society, industry and the environment;**

- **raise awareness of different ways of life, perspectives, cultures and traditions;**

- **share ideas and activities relating to issues of common concern, such as energy supply and water quality;**

- **develop communications skills; and**

- **enhance the role and quality of teaching by stimulating schools in different countries to examine different approaches to particular issues.**

The programme was initiated in 1990 as *Science Across Europe* – which is a partnership between BP and the UK-based Association for Science Education (ASE), with support from schools and educators throughout Europe. In 1991 BP in Asia formed a similar partnership with

RECSAM, a Malaysian-based regional science and mathematics education centre and various regional and national government organisations, to launch *Science*

Across Asia. Modelled on its European counterpart, but adapted to local needs and issues, the Asian programme has now been followed by an American initiative, co-ordinated by John Carroll University in Cleveland, where BP's US headquarters are located, and in 1995 *Science Across Africa* was launched. Co-ordinated by the University of the Witwatersrand in South Africa, the African programme has been implemented in South Africa, Namibia, Zimbabwe, Zambia and Botswana. By the end of 1995 some 300 schools in 20 European countries were participating in the European programme and 450 schools from 10 Asian countries in the Asian programme. These projects are reaching thousands of young people between the ages of 14-17 years old.

The initiative demonstrates two key lessons:

- **the ability of multinational companies to use their global networks and resources to spearhead community projects that reflect the adage of 'thinking globally and acting locally' and**

- **the potential of replicating 'good practice' and successful projects through a multinational company's corporate network.**

The involvement of BP has been crucial in the development of the project not only from the point of view of funding, but also because the company's presence across the world has provided the global links between and within regions.

The NGO Partners of
Toyota Teach

The NGO Partners of Toyota Teach

- **The Centre for Cognitive Development** – established in 1986 to encourage democratic and learner-centred education for school teachers, principals and inspectors;

- **The RADMASTE Centre at Wits University** – which focuses on Research and Development in Mathematics, Science and Technology Education;

- **READ** – (Read, Educate and Develop) was established 14 years ago in response to the lack of libraries and other reading facilities in black communities. It has activities throughout South Africa, working with more than 2,000 institutions and training over 70,000 people through courses and workshops during this period. Its goal is to help the people of southern Africa to read, write and speak with greater competence and it is supported by a wide range of companies, education authorities, teacher associations, community organisations and employee bodies;

- **Primary Science Programme of Natal** – a nationwide initiative aimed at improving the quality of science teaching and learning;

- **Natal College of Education** – which offers distance education and professional up-grading opportunities for teachers;

- **The Umlazi College for Further Education** – a distance learning institution.

Toyota Teach in South Africa

Toyota, the world's third largest automaker, has a long-standing reputation as a leader in corporate social investment in South Africa. In 1989, the company formed The Toyota South Africa Foundation which is jointly funded by Toyota Motor Corporation of Japan and Toyota South Africa. The company also requires its divisional line managers to get personally involved in community projects, and in 1993 was the first company in the country to produce a full disclosure corporate social investment report.

The company's flagship project in South Africa is "Toyota Teach". The Natal-based initiative is a teacher up-grading programme, targeted at developing innovative maths and science teaching skills for primary school teachers. One of its most interesting features is the fact that Toyota brought together six NGOs and academic institutions to actually develop and run the programme on a collaborative basis under the directorship of a retired school principal. The six NGOs are listed opposite:

Each NGO contributes something different to the programme and they meet together on a regular basis to discuss progress. The actual programme consists of:

- **workshops to increase teaching competence and the involvement of school principals;**

- **seminars to increase student, teacher and parent interest in maths and science eduction;**

- **materials development;**

- **advocacy for policy changes at both the school and government department level.**

To date the programme has reached close to 40 primary schools, over 1,000 teachers and directly some 45,000 students. Evaluations indicate marked improvements in teachers and students who have been exposed to the programme.

Toyota provides funding support from both Japan and South Africa, as well as in-kind resources, such as premises, paying for the programme director and NGO networking etc. Many of the students impacted by the project are from communities where Toyota factory employees live, which has obvious benefits for the company, not to mention the brand recognition that has come with the project's success and national coverage. It is an excellent example of how one company has worked with a diverse, well-established and experienced group of NGOs (all of whom get support from other companies on other projects) in a way that gives this particular project a very clear company brand.

- **The UK Travel and Tourism Programme** is in 430 schools with 6,000 students. It offers the only industry-sponsored course to be officially recognised as part of the UK national curriculum and has been set up as a separate foundation. There are four business partners. A related programme is taught in Scottish schools.

- The **US programme** is in 64 schools in 40 cities in 21 states, reaching 3000 students.

- The Academy programme in **Ireland** has grown from two pilot schools in 1990 to 180 schools in 1996 with 6,000 students and has been incorporated into a government agency. There are five business partners.

- The first non-English language programme started in November 1991 in **Mexico City** where it is in two schools. There are 12 business partners. Another programme is under development in Puerto Vallarta.

- In **Hong Kong,** the local educational authorities implemented a programme in 28 schools in 1994, since then 13 more schools have joined the Programme for a total of 41 schools with 2,600 students. The curriculum is taught in Chinese and English, and the course is recognised as an official exam subject. The programme is run by a separate foundation. There are six business partners.

- In **Hungary,** 33 schools offer the Travel and Tourism Programme, with over 1,000 students enrolled. It is taught in Hungarian and English. There are 20 business partners. The course has been officially recognised as an elective by the education authorities.

- An Academy programme in the Sao Paulo State in **Brazil** is under development in one school. There are 34 business partners.

- In 1994 the Travel and Tourism Programme opened in three schools in St Petersburg, **Russia** and has now expanded to five.

- A pilot programme started in Paris, **France** in autumn 1994 is now in three schools. Programmes opened in four schools in three provinces in **Canada** in September 1995 and in **South Africa** in January 1996 in 16 schools with over 800 students.

Educating children about work: American Express and GrandMet

American Express's Academies of Travel and Tourism

Since its founding in 1850, American Express has served the travel and financial needs of business and leisure travellers around the world. Today the company operates over 1,700 travel offices in more than 120 countries and offers American Express Cards in local currencies in over 30 countries. In approaching its social investment and philanthropic activities, American Express looks for initiatives which are relevant to its business and through which it can leverage other sources of funding and support, from both private and public sector partners.

Long-term involvement with the development of the travel and tourism industry is a natural focus for the company. It is a focus which has potential benefits for thousands of communities and millions of people around the globe, given that travel and tourism is now the world's largest industry, contributing more than 10% to global GNP and employing one out of every nine people. It is an industry that also has growth potential in the world's developing and transition economies, but its long-term sustainability depends on the social and environmental health of local communities. This in turn depends partly on the skills and integrity of people working in the industry. Developing such a workforce is the focus of the American Express Academies of Travel and Tourism.

The Travel & Tourism Programme is a one or two year academic course of study taught in existing secondary schools by teachers who have received special training. The curriculum, which is developed by professional educators working with industry specialists, introduces young people to the travel and tourism industry. Work experience in the industry is an important component.

The initiative dates from 1986 when, with American Express Foundation support, pilot programmes commenced in the UK under the name Travel and Tourism Programme and in the US under the name Academy of Travel and Tourism. In both the US and internationally, industry partners have joined American Express to provide additional funding and work experience for students, as well as assist in teacher training. The reach and replication potential of the programme is illustrated by the examples profiled on this page.

GrandMet's KAPOW programme

Today, KAPOW operates in 16 US states, through 26 partnerships with GrandMet subsidiaries and local schools. Over 4,500 students have participated in the programme, which has mobilised 400 company volunteers and 200 educators.

In 1994, KAPOW was piloted in the United Kingdom, and there is potential for GrandMet to adapt it to some of the other countries where the company is operating around the world.

Grand Metropolitan is one of the world's leading branded consumer goods businesses, with a portfolio of international brands which include Pillsbury, Burger King, Häagen-Dazs, Smirnoff, J&B Rare and Bailey's. Whilst continuing to build its well-known brands in the developed markets, in recent years the group has also undertaken international expansion into emerging markets such as India, Vietnam, China, Argentina and Russia.

The company spends approximately 1.5% of worldwide trading profit, less interest costs, on community involvement and is a recognised leader in the field. It was one of the first companies in the United Kingdom, for example, along with BP and British Airways to produce a descriptive report of its world-wide community investment activities. The strategic focus of the group's community action is helping people to help themselves, i.e. empowerment. Most of its community work is done through education, training and enterprise programmes which offer opportunities, particularly to young people, to achieve self-sufficiency. Its stated strategy in its community activities is fourfold:

- to be innovative;

- to set a good example for others to follow and to act as a catalyst;

- to be at the forefront of issues and to take ownership of all these or projects with which GrandMet is associated; and

- to work as an active participant with public, private and voluntary sector partners to create projects that meet shared goals and leverage resources.

The partnership with the National Child Labour Committee has been valuable in providing both expertise and credibility to the project. It offers a good example of how a company and NGO can build on each others' strengths and core competencies.

In 1991, GrandMet commissioned a gallup poll of 907 eight to twelve year olds in the USA, which showed that only 23% believed that education leads to a successful career. In response to these poll results, GrandMet worked with America's non-profit National Child Labor Committee, which promotes the rights, dignity and well-being of children and youth as they relate to work and working, to design KAPOW (Kids and the Power of Work). The programme is aimed at enabling young people to see a clear connection between what they learn in class and the skills they need to succeed in a career and in life.

One of the key elements of KAPOW is the establishment of strong partnerships between GrandMet's subsidiaries and specific schools, combined with the mobilisation of employee volunteers. Each company assembles a team of volunteers who range from fork-lift truck operators to lawyers and marketing vice-presidents. These volunteers receive professional training to prepare them for their roles and are then assigned to specific classes to help deliver a professionally developed curriculum. The curriculum enables volunteers and educators to show children the world outside the classroom, to teach teamwork, good behaviour, and decision-making skills. It is also designed to combat age, race and gender stereotypes. During the academic year KAPOW students also visit their partner company to see and participate in business activities.

Another factor underpinning the programme's success to date, has been its careful implementation. Pilot projects are completed and evaluated before further roll-out and adaptation to other environments and cultures.

TELECURSO 2000
Mobilising television for training

In a country famous for its *telenovelas*, where some 75% of homes have television sets, and where there is a desperate need to provide training for the millions who failed to complete formal schooling, an innovative private sector partnership has combined the entertainment value of the *telenovela* with the powerful reach of the television network, to tackle the critical national need for improved education and vocational training. This initiative is a joint venture between the Roberto Marinho Foundation (FRM) – the private foundation of the large Globo TV network, the Federation of Industries of Sao Paulo (FIESP), which have both provided millions of dollars worth of funding, and the National Industrial Training Service (SENAI). Together they have developed a television programme called *Telecurso 2000*, which is broadcast by Globo TV every morning just before the popular "Good Morning Brazil" programme, and again during the day on educational channels, using well-known actors and applying education and training concepts to everyday situations that Brazilians face. The TV programme is supported by materials made widely available through newsagents, and by an accreditation process through government supported examinations. Hundreds of companies throughout the country have established *telesalas* – training rooms with trained facilitators – for their employees to use, and similar training rooms have been set up in community centres, churches and even buses. Peter Knight, Chief Executive of the World Bank's Electronic Media Center, writes in his paper *Destined to Leapfrog: Why a revolution in learning will occur in Brazil, Russia and South Africa*, that in the period since the programme was launched, some 1,517 organised telesalas have been established with trained facilitators, reaching more than 40,000 people. The foundation of the large Bradesco Banking network will be helping to establish more than 500 extra telesalas and many more companies are joining the initiative. The *Telecurso* programmes also reach many more people who are not part of organised study groups.

(iii) TRAINING AND SKILLS DEVELOPMENT

The growing need for "lifetime learning" requires that initial education and skills are continuously developed and enhanced by individuals, by their employers (if they are employed), by government supported programmes and/or by public-private partnership initiatives. For some people there is the need to develop vocational and technical skills, for others managerial and professional skills, and for most, interpersonal skills, such as good written and oral communication, numeracy, team-working, personal effectiveness and so on.

Despite many outstanding examples of corporate-funded training, most companies around the world do not invest enough resources in this area. AS a result, there is still insufficient up-skilling or re-skilling occurring for many of those that are employed, let alone for those that are not. This places a growing demand on business, not only to increase in-house training, but also to explore ways to:

- leverage existing in-house training facilities to be used by people or organisations not working directly for, or with the company;

- invest in training programmes in local communities as part of the company's individual social investment activities;

- develop collaborative efforts with other companies and training institutions to leverage resources and/or work through existing business associations to offer training programmes;

- advocate for government policies and programmes that: a)offer tax or other incentives to companies that are investing in training for both their own staff and others; b)provide joint funding for such programmes; andc)support institutional structures to increase the accessibility, appropriateness and effectiveness of training.

There are numerous companies that are engaging in some or all of these activities, and the following examples review a small fraction of these. The profile opposite is an outstanding example of how information technology is being mobilised to dramatically widen the reach, and lower the cost, of vocational and technical training in Brazil. The other profiles look at ways in which companies have either shared their own in-house facilities with a wider audience, or established major training initiatives as part of their longer-term business and social investment strategies, or collaborated together on joint *pro bono* initiatives. These examples are: the Toyota and LA Urban League's joint venture Automative Training Centre in Los Angeles; BOC's welding school in Poland; the Shanghai Business Leadership 2000 programme; U S WEST's Russian Centre for Business Education and Training; The Palabora Foundation's Reef Training Centre in South Africa; the Japanese Executive Management Training Programme for managers from Central and Eastern Europe; and the Institute for Integrated Learning in Management located in India. Another collaborative training partnership is profiled on page 244, where ABB, Tetra Laval, Norsk Hydro and several other leading Scandinavian companies have joined forces with the Scandinavian bilateral development agencies to establish a management leadership training centre in Russia. Another key area where companies can support training initiatives is the field of SME development.

Any successful job training programme must include a winning combination of people and institutions – both profit-making businesses which possess technical expertise, financial and in-kind resources, and an effective community-based organisation possessing professional expertise in counselling and job placement. Most importantly, the community organisation must have credibility with the constituency to be served and a sensitivity to their needs, frustrations, hopes, aspirations and untapped abilities.

John Mack, President of the Los Angeles Urban League

Toyota and the LA Urban League's Automative Training Centre in the USA

In response to the 1992 civil unrest in Los Angeles, Toyota and the Urban League established the Los Angeles Urban League Automative Training Centre. The Urban League is a 74 year old private, non-profit organisation which has advocated and advanced equal opportunities for African Americans and increasingly other minorities, especially Latinos. It works closely with the private sector in planning and implementing job training and placement programmes.

Toyota agreed to commit US$3 million to the Automative Training Centre (ATC) over a three year period, during which time operations have gradually been handed over to the Urban League, which will ultimately assume full financial and administrative responsibility for the facility. Toyota's commitment however has gone far beyond this grant.

The company's senior management have assumed a leadership role in the initiative; it has seconded a technical training professional to manage the facility and its trainers; and it has strongly encouraged its suppliers and other partners along the business value-chain to get involved. As a result a wide range of other companies, ranging from large multinationals to medium and small-scale local players, have offered funding, equipment, supplies, work experience placements and renovation services to the initiative, as well as full-time jobs to its graduates. Some of these companies include: AT&T, Sears, Midas Muffler, Hawthorne Furniture, Tune Up Masters and Smog Pro.

The ATC provides entry-level training and job placement in the automative service field to young unemployed people, at no cost to themselves. They are obliged however to undertake individual responsibilities and the centre focuses as much on personal skills development and team-working, as it does on providing a technical skill and qualification.

In its first two years of operation the Centre has successfully trained more than 200 unemployed individuals and placed 82% of them in automative repair jobs. The project's premises are bright and clean, and an strong sense of energy and purpose permeates right through it – a very different picture to the anger, hopelessness and despair that features in the lives of so many inner city residents in Los Angeles.

BOC Gases' Welding School in Poland

BOC Gases' welding school, in the Polish town of Wroclaw, is an example of how the company's technical skills and resources are being deployed to meet both local and national community needs, as well as some of the company's own training requirements.

In May 1993, The BOC Group made a significant investment in Poland by acquiring the major part of the former Polish state gases supplier, Polgaz. In A new company called BOC Gazy was formed, in partnership with the Polish State Treasury, with operating sites in the major industrial centres of Siewierz, Poznan and Wroclaw.

> One way for us to bring together the aspirations and needs of the local community with our business experience, is by helping in the education and training process – in our case, by teaching people to weld.
>
> John Filer,
> Chief Executive, European Gases,
> BOC Ltd

BOC has an active involvement with The Prince of Wales Business Leaders Forum, through the participation of CEO David John on the PWBLF's Board, the active engagement of John Filer, the company's Chief Executive of European Gases, and through the position of Janusz Golebiowski, from BOC Gazy, who is chairman of the PWBLF's Polish affiliate in Poland (which is profiled on page 262). In discussion with the PWBLF's representatives, the idea of establishing a welding school was developed, as a way in which the company could make a mutually beneficial investment in its new host country and community. The challenges of youth unemployment and training are serious in Poland and BOC realised that there was potential to help a group of young people to develop useful skills for the future, while at the same time training a pool of local people who would be potential employees for the company. BOC Gazy also realised that it could make a contribution to Poland's relentless drive to transform its technology base from traditional to world-class.

The school was opened in July 1995, staffed by two BOC Gazy fabrication specialists who have undergone extensive training at the Polish Welding Institute. With twelve fully-equipped welding bays, the centre has the potential to train up to 20 students at any one time. It currently offers two main types of courses: one to teach young unemployed people the fundamentals of welding so as to give them a basic skill (which is provided free of charge) and the other to introduce experienced, fee-paying Polish welders to the most technologically advanced equipment and processes, which will not only enhance the skills base for BOC, but the country in general, as well as substantially increasing safety standards and quality.

BOC Gases has also undertaken major investments in China in recent years. Apart from the establishment of a co-operative venture with a local university to offer MBA-style training for BOC's Chinese managers, the company has also been a key supporter of the Shanghai Business Leadership 2000 programme.

The Shanghai Business Leadership 2000 programme

Shanghai Business Leadership 2000 is a programme which has been established by The Prince of Wales Business Leaders Forum, as a partnership between the Mayor of Shanghai, Shanghai Jiao Tong University and a group of major international companies operating in China, including Coopers & Lybrand, BOC Gases, ERM, McKinsey, Coca-Cola, Sedgwick, DHL, John Swire & Sons, Marks & Spencer, and G. Melchers & Co.

Chinese Business Leaders of the Future

The Chinese companies which sent senior managers to participate in the initial pilot of this innovative programme employ many thousands of workers. The companies were:

China HuaNeng Group • Shanghai HuaNeng United Co • Shanghai Chemical Conglomerate (holding) Co • Shanghai Hardware and Machinery Corp • Shanghai HuChang Iron & Steel Co Ltd • Shanghai Medical Administration Bureau Co • Shanghai No 1 Cotton Textile work • Shanghai Petro-Chemical Stock Co • Shanghai Plastic Industrial Co • Shanghai Squibb Pharmaceutical Co Ltd • Shanghai Textile Conglomerate (Holding) Co

The programme's mission is to promote cross-cultural understanding among Chinese and Western business leaders and to help them manage dramatic economic and social change. It is hoped that the alumni group can work effectively together to promote good corporate citizenship in Shanghai. At the programme's core is a two-way process of mutual learning which recognises the value of the business practices that western managers can share with their Chinese counterparts, whilst at the same time recognising the strengths of Chinese culture and society.

The programme is an intensive, short-term, part-time initiative developed for senior managers from international companies and their counterparts in Chinese state-owned enterprises. During the eight weekly sessions of the programme, the emphasis is on comparative Western and Chinese approaches to problem solving and management. Seventeen business leaders participated in the pilot programme which was held in the first half of 1996 and is currently being evaluated.

Sessions focused on issues such as: cross-cultural business challenges in key business disciplines; new approaches to human resource development; leveraging information technology; global marketing; total quality management; corporate governance; and business environmental management issues. Case studies relevant to China were discussed and the managers participated in joint project visits.

U S WEST's Centre for Business Skills Development in Russia

U S WEST International is a Fortune 35 company, serving millions of customers and employing approximately 60,000 people in the USA and internationally, including developing countries such as Russia, Brazil, Hungary, India, Indonesia and Malaysia. It has been a major telecommunications player in Russia, opening a Representative Office there in 1990. In 1993, as part of its commitment to Russian business development, U S WEST founded the Russian Centre for Business Skills Development (CBSD).

The CBSD provides relevant, "hands-on" business training with the goal of bringing Russian managers to a market economy level and to support the process of transition in the country. Its overriding mission is to bring world-class quality business education to Russia.

U S WEST provided more than US$700,000 to develop the core curriculum for the CBSD, working with a development team of Russian and western professionals. In particular, the company worked with the Strategic

Management Group, a consulting group composed of professors from the prestigious Wharton Business School, and the Academy of National Economy, which is a premier institute of higher education in Russia. These two partners played a key role in developing a curriculum which was of high quality and relevant to local needs and capacities. Another partner in establishing the programme was Apple Computer, which offers one of the best software platforms in the world for education and training.

Subjects covered by the CBSD include: orientation to business in a market economy; business ethics; customer service; fundamentals of marketing and sales; fundamentals of finance; communications; professional skills; and basic computer and applications literacy. CBSD has operational training centres located in Moscow, St Petersburg and Nizhny Novgorod. Almost three years after its launch, U S WEST is starting the process of handing over management to local Russians and encouraging the transition of CBSD into a self-financing, fully-fledged business college.

The Reef Training Centre in South Africa

• •

The Reef Training Centre (RTC) is a project of the Palabora Foundation, which was established by The Palabora Mining Company, a subsidiary of RTZ-CRA, in 1987. The Company contributes 3% of its after-tax profits annually to the Foundation and the value of its endowment currently stands at approximately US$4 million. The Foundation has two major programmes, one to support community development in the Phalaborwa area of Northern Transvaal and the other to run a Vocational Skills Training Centre (the Reef Training Centre) servicing the Gauteng region of South Africa (Pretoria, Witwatersrand and Vereeniging).

Shumane Ratshibvuma comes from a small village in the former homeland of Venda. Only a few of his fellow villagers have access to electricity, most use candles and cook on an open fire. At 21, Shumane has a vision of changing this way of life for his people. Graduating from the Reef Training Centre as an electrician has enabled him to take one step towards achieving that vision by enabling him to set up his own electrical business when he returns home. Now that he has the skills and a potential market, the challenge will be to find credit for his micro-enterprise.

Although initially funded 100% by the Palabora Foundation, the RTC is increasingly drawing support from other companies – a model which has enormous potential for replication. It is an interesting combination of a technical training centre and wildlife sanctuary – offering courses in both artisan trades and environmental issues.

Its trade courses focus on automative repairs, panel beating, electrical wiring, welding and building, supported by entrepreneurial education and life-skills development. Trainees are drawn mainly from neighbouring low-income communities, but as the centre's reputation grows more people are coming from other parts of the country. They include unemployed youth and returned exiles, as well as self-employed tradesmen who require additional training. A modular system has been developed to permit flexibility in completing the programmes. The use of well-graded and highly practical training methods, and rigorous testing and certification at the end of each course means that the centre has established a strong reputation with potential trainees and employers. Average enrollment is 120 trainees a day, and 850 trainees graduated from courses at the centre in 1995 (in courses ranging from 9 to 16 weeks). The centre also achieved 1,000,000 accident free hours and a four star rating from NOSA – the National Occupational Safety Association.

The Palabora Foundation enters into partnerships with corporations (there are currently 12 corporate partners) and NGOs, to finance the provision of infrastructure and support for trainees. More than a third of the RTC's costs are now covered by these partner organisations. The preferred partnership arrangement is a joint venture in which the corporate partners provide financial support and expertise and participate as members of a Project Steering Committee to assist the development of a specific training programme. Some of the key corporate partners participating in specific programmes include: Afrox (BOC's South African subsidiary), which supports the centre's welding and metalwork division, Caltex, which supports the business skills training unit; Castrol, the motor mechanics division; and P.G. Glass, the glazing division. Other corporate partners provide annual donations to the Trainee Bursary Fund or provide business skills training, for example First National Bank, Honeywell, Coca-Cola, Standard Bank, BP, Shell and the Joint Education Trust all gave financial support in 1995.

NGO partners such as the Get Ahead Foundation and the Soweto Builders Forum identify and support trainees from their associated projects and ensure placement on completion of training. In a very creative partnership the Gateway Fund (which supports handicapped people) manages the Centre's greenhouses providing employment for the handicapped and food for the trainees. The RTC also works with the Department of Labour as a training contractor for unemployed people.

The Wildlife Sanctuary is used as an environmental education resource for school-children – often mixing children from different race groups and socio-economic strata – to enable them to learn both about each other and their natural environment. Some 600 children visit the centre every month, many of whom have never seen a wild animal before. Nestle SA and British Petroleum SA are partners with The Palabora Foundation in this initiative, together with local education authorities.

Japanese Executive Management Training Programme
• •

The Japanese Executive Management Training Programme (EMTP) was launched in 1991. Co-ordinated until recently by IBM Japan, it is a unique transnational partnership between the government, business and NGO sectors, including:

- Japanese and multinational companies operating in Japan. Over the past five years sponsor companies have included AMP Japan Ltd., Amway Japan Limited, ASCII Corporation, Daishowa Paper Manufacturing Company, Dentsu Inc., DIAL Service Co. Ltd., DISCO Inc., IBM Japan Ltd., ITEC Inc., LBS Co. Ltd., OMRON Corporation, PASONA, TAIYO Electric Corporation and Tokyo Electric Power Co. Ltd.;

- young Japanese business leaders, who attended the initial meeting with The Prince of Wales in 1990 which led to the establishment of the programme;

- the Government of Japan, through the Ministry of International Trade and Industry (MITI) and its Association for Overseas Technical Scholarships (AOTS) – which has trained close to 100,000 people from 150 countries since 1959; and

- the PWBLF and its local affiliated organisations in the Czech Republic, Hungary, Poland and Slovakia.

During a visit to Japan in 1990, The Prince of Wales made an invitation to a group of young Japanese business leaders to demonstrate good corporate citizenship in the global business economy, by helping to support the development of management skills in the fledgling free market economies of central and eastern Europe.

A young Slovak businessman shares his experience

In the beginning of 1992 I got a chance to travel to Japan thanks to Japanese companies and the PWBLF. At the time I was working in a state enterprise. My stay in Japan and participation on the training course confirmed my ideas with respect to my personal realisation and I decided to start working in the private sector... I have created space for my broader personal realisation, and I could undertake several activities in various directions. Moreover, I could more effectively fulfil my ideas about not-for-profit activities, whose base was laid down during my stay in Japan. Social feeling, which I saw in Japan everywhere, enabled me to better understand the goals and importance of the third sector, a sector unknown and strange to me before. In reality, I have set up an AOTS association in Slovakia. Activities of this association are oriented on selecting and sending managers mainly from private sector on training courses to Japan and Europe. This fulfils not only my personal ambitions, but is also a kind of 'installment' to those who enabled me to visit Japan and by means of gained experiences there to change my life. This work is very important and successful. The seminar we are organising this week is bringing to the Slovak managers the way of Japanese Total Quality Management. It is an international seminar organised in co-operation with Sony from Japan and the PWBLF.

Mr Lubor Lazar,
Director of CLAVIS Ltd. and AOTS Slovakia

A pilot programme, designed to provide one month's management training and experience in Japan to young CEE business leaders was held in 1992 and since then a one month programme has been held every year.

Focusing on leadership enhancement, broadening perspectives, and understanding of market economies and practical management experience, the EMTP consists of: a rigorous selection process undertaken by the PWBLF's local affiliates in central and eastern Europe; an orientation stage in CEE when the PWBLF ensures that all successful applicants are fully briefed on the background to the programme, Japanese culture and sponsor companies; followed by one month in Japan on the management training course, developed and conducted by AOTS, which includes programmes hosted by young Japanese business leaders involving study visits and individual placements with host companies. From 1996 the co-ordination of the project has been taken over by LBS Co. Ltd from IBM Japan.

63 participants have taken part in the programme since the first study visit in early 1992, including candidates from Poland for the first time in 1996. Evaluation of each year's programme and individual appraisals of participants' experience show that:

- EMTP has been highly successful in assisting a small group of future business leaders from CEE, a number of whom have received promotions in their jobs after participating in the programme; and

- the programme is a good demonstration of global corporate citizenship by Japanese business leaders, which focuses on the application of business skills rather than philanthropy alone (although this has also played a role), and which builds long-term business relationships through the alumni network for EMTP 'graduates', which is administered by AOTS.

The Institute for Integrated Learning in Management (IILM)

IILM was established in October 1993 by the Charitable Trust founded by Group Usha, one of India's major conglomerates with investments in areas such as iron and steel, telecommunications, software, shipping, mining and real estate development. IILM's mission is to 'make knowledge work' through its five objectives:

- To provide students with an awareness of the broad range of knowledge required in modern management;
- To equip them with specialised knowledge required in particular professions;
- To develop the analytical and behavioural skills required to make effective use of this knowledge in employment;
- To groom and develop the confidence and overall personal skills of every individual; and
- To increase global understanding and facilitate further management studies in India and abroad.

The initiative offers full-time and part-time post-graduate programmes in business management and executive development programmes for working managers, through four campuses in India. It is developing links elsewhere in Asia and has recently entered into a partnership with the UK- based Bradford University to enable students in India to study for a British degree.

The Bank advocates a threefold approach to improving health. First, it is essential to foster an economic environment that enables households to improve health, by promoting economic growth and basic education. Second, governments need to increase the impact of their spending on health by redirecting spending toward the most cost-effective public health interventions and by improving the management of services. Third, governments need to encourage greater diversity and competition in the financing and delivery of health services.

Investing in People
The World Bank, 1995

(iv) HEALTH AND NUTRITION

There are strong moral and economic arguments for increased efficiency and effectiveness in the investment and delivery of health services, especially in developing countries, but also in OECD and transition economies. Numerous studies demonstrate direct links between health and nutrition levels, and the ability of children to benefit from schooling, and the productivity and length of people's working lives.

As far as the **developing world** is concerned, health and life expectancy have greatly improved over the past forty years, due to a combination of improved medical technology, expanded medical services, higher incomes and education levels, and public health measures, especially clean water and sanitation. Enormous challenges remain however. In its 1995 Annual Report, the World Bank points to the following statistics: three million children in developing countries die every year because of lack of clean water; 12 million children under the age of five die of various other diseases; more than a million people are blind because they do not get enough Vitamin A; another 50 million are seriously impaired, both mentally and physically, because their diets lack iodine; and malnourished mothers give birth to low-birthweight babies, who then become the most likely candidates to perpetuate poverty.

In these countries there is a strong need for health-care reform to improve the efficiency, effectiveness, and accessibility of health-care and to focus on preventative strategies. Areas which warrant particular attention, are:

* primary health-care and the associated linking of locally delivered and appropriate health services, provided through community clinics and schools, and focused on improving nutrition levels, immunisations, health education, family planning, and maternal and child-care;

* public programmes to improve access to clean water and sanitation and to tackle other environmental and social health hazards, associated with inadequate housing, high pollution levels and so on.

Enormous health-care challenges have also emerged in the **transition economies** of central and eastern Europe and the Former Soviet Union. Both UNDP's 1996 Human Development Report and The World Bank's 1996 World Development Report point to worsening health and mortality indicators and rising malnutrition and under-nutrition in these countries. The UNDP report estimates that more than 450,000 adult deaths in central and eastern Europe can be attributed to increased suicides, alcoholism and incidence of coronary disease and strokes. As massive state-owned enterprises are privatised and unbundled, the thousands of child-care facilities and clinics which they supported under the old regimes are threatened. This situation is exacerbated by the inadequacy of bureaucratic and poorly funded public structures to deal with the shortfalls.

Even in the world's **OECD economies** the future of state-supported health care and welfare systems is threatened, and the need to search for new solutions and to invest in health-care reform is paramount.

Finally, in countries throughout the world, the **spread of HIV/AIDS** has become a leading public health problem and a drain on economic progress. The 1996 UNDP Human Development report states that 18 million people worldwide have been infected with HIV and some 2.5 million people have died of AIDS. Although 90% of new infections are in developing countries, in both Europe and North America AIDS is now the leading cause of death for adults under the age of 45.

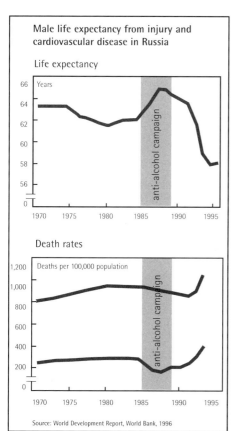

Male life expectancy from injury and cardiovascular disease in Russia

Life expectancy

Death rates

Source: World Development Report, World Bank, 1996

In almost every single one of these areas there is a potential role for the private sector to play – either through its core business activities, or through social investments and engagement in the policy dialogue. There is also a clear need for greater public-private partnership. In some cases there is potential for the private sector to get commercially involved in the direct provision of public health-care services, and a recent World Bank report, *Private and Public Initiatives: Working Together for Health and Education*, looks at a range of options in this area. Both health-care and non-health-care companies also play an important role in the way they deal with issues such as health care benefits for their employees and HIV/AIDS in the workplace. Companies can also invest in a wide range of projects, such as health education, immunisation programmes and nutrition improvements through their community investment or philanthropy budgets.

The following vignettes look at some examples of corporate action in these areas. They look at the leadership role being taken by Levi Strauss, and by The Commercial Farmers Union in Zimbabwe, on HIV/AIDS in the workplace; they profile the way in which SmithKline Beecham, IBM, Sakal Papers, Johnson and Johnson, Merck & Co., and Eli Lilly have made social investments in helping governments and international agencies to tackle disease and other health problems; they look at a nutrition project in South Africa run by a Unilever subsidiary; and they describe how the British water industry supports the work of WaterAid. These are a tiny sample of examples, but they give some indication of how companies can play an active and valuable role in improving health and nutrition standards. Several other health-related case studies are profiled in Section III.

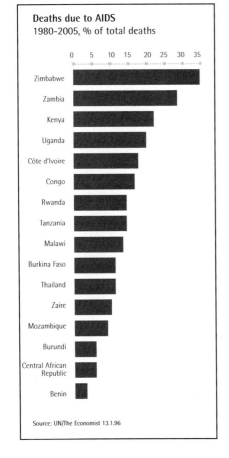

Deaths due to AIDS
1980-2005, % of total deaths

Source: UN/The Economist 13.1.96

- **Levi Strauss** is one of the companies which has made a clear corporate commitment to HIV/AIDS prevention and education. It has communicated its HIV/AIDS policies to all its employees, which include workplace prevention and care programmes, non-discrimination, employee assistance and community involvement. These policies have been implemented in many parts of the organisation around the world. For example, when it opened its business in South Africa last year, the company made a strong commitment to local HIV/AIDS prevention and education, and to being a corporate leader in this field in South Africa. It has also played a key role in the nationwide AIDS campaign launched by the Confederation of Indian Industries(CII).

- **The Commercial Farmers Union (CFU)** in Zimbabwe, which represents some 4,600 large-scale farmers and farming companies throughout the country, employing at least 270,000 regular workers and many thousands more casual or contract workers, is a good example, along with CII in India, of an industry association which is mobilising all of its members to tackle the issue of AIDS. The CFU recognises that AIDS is a threat not only to the productivity and prosperity of the country's commercial farming industry, but also to the survival and well-being of hundred of thousands of farm workers and their families, who live on these farms. It ran its first pilot scheme in 1986, spearheaded by one of its farming members, Peter Fraser-Mackenzie. Since that time the CFU, with support from organisations such as USAID and funding from its members, has developed a comprehensive education and support programme in farms throughout the country. This includes the supply of condoms; establishment of workers' AIDS committees; dissemination of information and education materials; consultations and discussions with farm workers about lifestyle decisions; and the establishment of support programmes for families. Industrial companies in Zimbabwe and their trade associations have followed the lead of the farming community in taking a pro-active approach to the problem of HIV/AIDS.

THE WORLDWIDE CHILD SURVIVAL PROGRAMME

This initiative was launched by Johnson & Johnson in 1987 in partnership with UNICEF, and is aimed at reducing the mortality rate of children under five years old in developing countries. Its strategy for achieving this goal is to provide funding and in-kind resources which are targeted at improving access to basic health services and educating people on the benefits of breast feeding, immunisation and necessary preventative methods for their children's health. The initiative is focused on developing countries where J&J is active, and the company and UNICEF decide jointly on the projects to be implemented.

Some of the projects which have been undertaken by the Worldwide Child Survival Programme are as follows:

- **In Guatemala**, a breast feeding programme and the development of growth monitoring methods have been introduced. In addition, thousands of rehydration packages have been distributed to children inflicted with chronic diarrhea;

- **In Kenya**, where some two thirds of all births take place in the home, the company devised and distributed special home delivery kits;

- **In Mexico**, funding has been used to establish immunisation and breastfeeding programmes in rural areas;

- **In Thailand**, the project has focused on reducing the preventable condition of iodine deficiency, present in nearly one in four people. J&J has distributed iodized salt around the country and is attempting to iodate the drinking water in public schools, and

- **In Zimbabwe**, the programme instructs parents about the importance of proper child care, immunisation and the importance of clean water.

- **SmithKline Beecham** has made a strong commitment to develop a community investment structure that is based on partnership and leveraging resources with other players; has a consistent global approach, but with local applicability and ownership; measurable results; and a focus on projects with clear health benefits. Its evolving community management strategy is described on page 88, and the company supports a wide range of community health projects around the world. It achieves this social investment through a range of activities such as supporting community consultations and education programmes on health issues; forming partnerships with health NGOs, such as Project Hope which is profiled on page 226; and donating medicines. During the Rwandan civil war, for example, the company donated US$1.2 million worth of antibiotics – 4.8 million doses of Amoxil^{TM} chewable tablets. This type of tablet offered a clear advantage over traditional tablets and capsules in a crisis where the water supply was severely limited. The company is also co-ordinating a programme, aimed at tackling worm infection which is linking together academic institutions, governments, NGOs and communities in countries such as Indonesia and Pakistan.

- **The IBM Foundation** has invested in a number of innovative health projects in Africa. It provided a grant of technology to The Health Foundation to expand its successful *Communications for Better Health* programme (formally INFO-MED) into Nigeria, Zambia, and Tanzania. CBH provides health professionals in developing countries with access to up-to-date health information, which can now also be accessed on the Internet. In Rwanda, IBM has also partnered with CARE International to establish a water systems project which has vastly improved the quality of life for the Byumba community.

- **Sakal Papers Ltd.** in India is a publishing company established in 1932 with the mission of "social change through education". It has established the Pariwar Mangal Trust, which is working on an innovative experimental effort to co-ordinate the working together of industry, regional government departments, banks, advertising agencies, institutions such as the Population Fund of India and even individuals towards a common goal of maternal and child health-care, involving the local community and utilising and adding value to the existing government infrastructure. The programme consists of several components, including: the establishment of community health posts in remote villages which have no medical facilities; training for local women to support these health posts; referral and free transportation for high risk pregnancy cases; communications packages ranging from street-plays and puppet shows to community consultations and sex and AIDS education; and income generation schemes to empower and motivate rural women to be able to take decisions on planned families. Sakal Paper has encouraged a number of other companies to support this initiative, and it offers a model of the role that companies can play in the field of community health care.

- **Johnson and Johnson** have worked with the Wharton Programme for Nurses in the USA to develop a Nurse Leadership programme, which they currently operate in the United Kingdom in partnership with the King's Fund, and hope to roll out to parts of central Europe. The company and its foundation see the training and empowerment of nurses, not only in medical skills, but in managerial and leadership skills as being critical to supporting the health-care reforms which are being undertaken throughout the region. J&J also run an extensive campaign in Russia, educating people about womens' health issues. J&J's innovative Worldwide Child Survival programme with UNICEF is described on this page.

THE MECTIZAN DONATION PROGRAMME
Helping to control riverblindness in Africa

In 1987, Merck & Co. announced an initiative to donate Mectizan, a drug the company had developed to combat riverblindness, free of charge to all those in endemic countries where it was needed, for as long as it was needed. In doing so, it launched one of the most impressive corporate citizenship initiatives on record, and became part of an international partnership of donors and NGOs who have been forging a coordinated global effort against riverblindness since the early 1970's. Riverblindness (Onchocerciasis) has been a serious public health problem and constraint on socioeconomic development in much of West Africa and elsewhere on the continent for many years.

An Onchocerciasis Control Programme (OCP) was launched in 1974 by a coalition of the World Bank, WHO, UNDP and FAO, with funding from more than 20 bilateral and multilateral donors. OCP was established to eliminate riverblindness in an 11-country subregion of West Africa and has been highly successful in its mission – reducing infection rates from 15% to less than 1% through a programme combining extensive aerial spraying, with the use of Mectizan treatments. In December 1995, the World Bank and other partners, including a coalition of 11 development NGOs, launched a new initiative, The African Programme for Onchocerciasis Control (APOC). This initiative will implement community-based drug treatment programmes in a further 16 countries, using the Mectizan drug donated by Merck & Co. The WHO estimates that 15 million people are infected with the disease in these countries, which include Angola, Burundi, Cameroon, Chad, Congo, Ethiopia, Gabon, Liberia, Malawi, Nigeria, Suda, Tanzania, Uganda and Zaire.

The decision to donate the drug free of charge was a complex one for the company. A wide range of issues needed to be addressed in finding the balance between commercial imperatives and global corporate citizenship. Once it had made the decision, Merck established an independent Mectizan Expert Committee (MEC) to develop and administer guidelines for distribution, monitoring and record keeping, whilst the company retained responsibility for manufacturing, marketing and education. The MEC and the donation programme are both housed at the Carter Centre in Atlanta. Since 1988, 60 million tablets have been donated and there have been treatment programmes in 32 countries in Africa, Latin America and the Middle East. By the end of 1995 some 13 million people were being treated with donated supplies of Mectizan, a number which will increase with the APOC initiative.

WATERAID

WaterAid is an independent charity which was created in 1981 by the people and organisations of the British water industry. From an initial income of UK£25,000, WaterAid's funds have risen to over UK£7 million per year. It helps over three million people in Africa and Asia to improve their drinking water supply and sanitation systems through low-cost, self-help projects using technologies that are easy to build and maintain. Water Aid currently funds projects in Bangladesh, Ethiopia, The Gambia, Ghana, India, Kenya, Mozambique, Nepal, Nigeria, Pakistan, South Africa, Sri Lanka, Tanzania, Uganda, Zambia and Zimbabwe. WaterAid has a unique relationship with the British water industry. People working in the water industry support WaterAid in a variety of ways ranging from being grass-roots fundraisers to members of the board of trustees. This support includes employee fundraising, payroll giving, community outreach and significant gifts in kind, of which the Customer Appeal is the largest. This is an appeal on behalf of WaterAid from the water industry and is sent out with water bills to approximately 20 million homes each year.

- **Eli Lilly and Company** is working with the American International Health Alliance (AIHA), which supports 23 health-care partnerships in 10 of the newly independent states of the former Soviet Union, through a co-operative agreement with USAID. In 1995, for example, it donated US$3.6 million worth of insulin, antibiotics and other medicines to the people of Ukraine, through AIHA, as part of an effort which has been on-going since 1990. The US Department of State made arrangements for providing free shipping of the Lilly medicines to Ukraine. In the ten years since the Chernobyl Nuclear Plant disaster, Eli Lilly has also donated some US$7 million in medical aid to the people of Chernobyl, working with the Counterpart Foundation Inc., a relief organisation sponsored by USAID and the US Department of State.

- **Unilever** subsidiary, **Vandenburgh Foods**, established the Rama Nutrition Education Project in Natal, South Africa in the mid-1980s. The initiative is an integrated community nutrition project which teaches school-children the basic requirements of a healthy diet and, most importantly, shows them how to plant tiny, highly-productive vegetable patches, using recycled household waste as compost. The company has worked closely with school authorities, teachers, research institutes and universities throughout the project – to maximise both its educational and research benefits. It has reached hundreds of schools, thousands of teachers and hundreds of thousands of schoolchildren and their families. Vandenburgh Foods provided all the initial funding for the initiative, managerial and logistical support and teaching and information materials. The project, described by Harvard's Centre for Population Studies as one of the best in the world, is an interesting model of a partnership which has provided educational and nutritional benefits and also supported wider community development.

MANGUEIRA/XEROX OLYMPIC PROJECT

It is impossible not to feel motivated and inspired by the bright pink and green uniforms, the gleaming sports facilities and the noise and energy generated by several hundred youngsters simultaneously playing soccer, basketball and volleyball. It is also difficult to imagine that the vast majority of them come from one of the poorest favelas in Rio de Janeiro. Despite this, they look remarkably fit and healthy, and every single one of them, in order to be here, has to demonstrate that they are regularly attending school. The project supporting these activities is making a valuable contribution to breaking the cycle of deprivation and poverty which limits the prospects for many of the world's youth. It is a model worth consideration by other countries and communities.

Started in 1987, by Xerox do Brasil, the Mangueira Olympic project has the goals of setting up alternatives to prevent children from being attracted to anti-social and illegal activities, and supporting the physical, psycho-social and recreational development of children living in the Mangueira favela. The key pre-requisite for children participating in the project is regular school attendance. Once they can demonstrate this, they are able to participate in a variety of sports such as athletics, soccer, volleyball, basketball and swimming. There is a strong emphasis on using sport to help these young people to develop team-building skills and a sense of purpose. Xerox sponsorship covers: sports equipment, uniforms, suitable meals, transportation, coaches and physical education instructors, masseurs, physiotherapists, psychologists, and sports federations. It invested US$300,000 a year in the project until 1994 and in 1995 increased this to US$500,000. The results have been encouraging. There has been a clear drop in the crime-rate in the neighbourhood, according to police statistics. Attendance at the 12 neighbourhood schools has increased from 40% to almost 100%. According to the Juvenile Court Judge of the Second Judicial District, there have been no reported youth crimes in the community for several consecutive years. The centre's teams have competed successfully in nationwide championships and a few youngsters have been invited to join professional clubs. Much harder to quantify, but impossible to ignore, is the vibrance and energy of several hundred young people as they build a better future.

(v) YOUTH DEVELOPMENT

By the turn of the century nearly half the world's population will be under the age of 20, many of them in developing countries. These are the citizens, workers and consumers of the near future and their ability to play an active and productive role will be crucial to social stability and economic progress, as well as to corporate success.

Youth development is intricately linked to the other issues already covered in this section: education; training and skills development; and health and nutrition. The following examples look at some programmes which offer integrated approaches, targeted specifically at youth between the ages of five to twenty. The first looks at an innovative initiative in Brazil to establish market-driven incentives for child-friendly companies; the second looks at the work of BankBoston in helping to mobilise youth volunteers for the benefit of both their personal development and their communities; and the third looks at The Prince's Youth Business Trust model for youth enterprise, which is being adapted around the world.

Empresa Amiga da Crinça
Promoting child-friendly companies in Brazil
• •

With support from the ILO, UNICEF and a number of Brazilian companies, the Abrinq Foundation has launched a campaign to promote Child-Friendly Companies. The Foundation certifies companies as being "child-friendly" if they do not use child labour and if they contribute to child development. Companies that meet the Foundation's standards can use the child-friendly seal on their products and company literature, in the same way that they certify other quality standards such as ISO 9000.

In order to qualify, companies must demonstrate a commitment to fostering education for children or vocational training for adolescents. They can, for example:

• build, maintain or support schools or day-care centres;

• develop apprenticeship programmes;

• provide funding for the Municipal Funds for Children's Rights; or

• invest in cultural, athletic or artistic programmes.

Over 40 multinational and domestic companies have earned the child-friendly seal and their projects are used as models to encourage other companies to take action. These model projects include Bradesco Bank's initiative supporting 94 schools throughout Brazil and the Mangueira Olympic project run by Xerox do Brasil in Rio de Janeiro, which is profiled opposite.

> We recognise the significant role that we can play in stimulating the interests of a new generation of young people in the areas of business education, entrepreneurship, and banking, as well as in the area of community development and revitalisation, by using the diverse talents and expertise of our employees and the resources of our Foundation, to work with youth.
>
> Ira Jackson, SVP, Bank of Boston

TRAVESSIA: Housing homeless youth in Brazil

Recognising the need for new approaches to deal with the epidemic of homeless youth in Sao Paulo, the employees' union of Banco de Boston Brazil pledged US$250,000 to establish an organisation to address this issue. Under the leadership of the then bank president Henrique Meirelles (now President and COO of BankBoston in the USA) the bank matched its employees' US$250,000 to launch Travessia. Travessia seeks to build capacity among human service providers and the homeless children they seek to serve. It has recently hired street workers who reach out to the children, identify their needs and connect them to appropriate service groups. The organisation has also forged positive relationships with the local media, public officials and businesses, to change the climate for working with these at-risk children. The partnership between the employees union and the bank has served as a national model, and is one with international applicability.

BankBoston

Banking on youth at home and abroad

Founded in 1784, BankBoston is the oldest chartered bank in the United States and was the second US bank to open an international branch in 1917. Today, the bank has over 650 US offices and more than 100 international offices in 23 countries in Latin America, Europe and Asia.

It has had a long-standing commitment to community investment, and youth issues are one of its areas of focus. Three of the main youth projects which it is involved with – City Year and YouthBuild in the USA and Travessia in Brazil – offer useful models for adaptation elsewhere.

City Year

In 1988, the co-founders of City Year, Alan Khazei and Michael Brown, both recent graduates from Harvard Law School visited BankBoston executives to share their vision of City Year. They wanted to establish an urban peace corps which would unite a diverse group of young people aged 17-23 for a year of full-time community service and personal development. BankBoston was so enthused with the idea that it made the first corporate gift of US$25,000 and has been one of a growing number of companies, most notably Timberland, which has supported City Year teams ever since. Collectively, these teams have cleaned up community parks, run after-school programmes, worked with the elderly and participated in environmental projects, providing hundreds of thousands of community service hours. The project has served as a national model for community service and a key prototype for the Americorps programme. It has been replicated in five other American cities and more than 160 delegations of people from other countries have visited the project in Boston. There are now efforts underway to assess its viability in some of these other countries.

BankBoston's contribution has extended far beyond cash contributions. Senior Vice President Ira Jackson served on City Year's first Board of Directors and was a strong advocate and mentor for the programme. A bank officer was seconded to the project for two years to help with its fundraising and thousands of BankBoston employees have raised several hundred thousand dollars through City Year's annual Serve-a-thon.

YouthBuild

YouthBuild Boston is a programme which involves unemployed and unskilled young people in renovating abandoned buildings in the inner city as affordable housing for the homeless. Even more important, the programme is structured to comprehensively address the underlying needs of young people who have dropped out of school, graduated with inadequate education or have been unable to keep a job because of lack of training in life skills.

BankBoston has provided an array of support to YouthBuild, including: construction financing for a housing rehabilitation project; a significant credit line through BankBoston's First Community Bank; direct grants and fundraising support; and the leveraging of a partnership with a major Boston law firm which has provided pro bono legal support and funding to YouthBuild.

TRANSFERRING GOOD PRACTICE TO INDIA AND SOUTH AFRICA

The Bharatiya Yuva Shakti Trust (BYST) was registered as an NGO in India in 1991 and officially launched by HRH The Prince of Wales in 1992. As with its British counterpart, it helps underprivileged youth, with a special focus on women, to start up their own businesses. It is supported by a growing number of Indian and multinational companies, and by the Confederation of Indian Industries. To date BYST has operations in Delhi, Madras, Haryana and more recently Pune. In Pune the programme has been established by a partnership between UK-based Grand Metropolitan, its subsidiary International Distillers India, and BYST. British ODA have also given support to the initiatives, which is now reaching more than 250 young entrepreneurs, employing about 1,000 people.

Nations Trust in South Africa was launched in March 1995, with Her Majesty The Queen and President Mandela as its patrons. Its goal is to assist disadvantaged young people to achieve things for themselves and for the communities in which they live. Although the initiative is still being established, its three focus areas will be:

- helping young people to start their own businesses

- developing programmes to support study outside the classroom

- institutional capacity-building for youth clubs and organisations which develop young people, and training for people who lead such organisations.

As at July 1996, a total of 45 young entrepreneurs had received loans to start their own businesses, in diverse areas such as: dressmaking, tailoring, brick-making, hair salons, mobile cinema, graphic design, welding and butchery. These young entrepreneurs will be supported in their first year by locally-based 'community mentors' and also by volunteer 'business mentors' who will provide technical assistance, business advice and personal counselling. Initial funding and in-kind support for the Nations Trust has come from both public and private sources, including the British ODA and UK-based Prince's Trust and some leading South African companies, most notably ABSA Bank, ESKOM, South African Breweries, Nampak and Liberty Life.

Established in the United Kingdom in 1986, The Prince's Youth Business Trust (PYBT) has helped more than 27,500 disadvantaged young people to start their own enterprises and in doing so has become one of the biggest wealth creators in the country, with a leverage ratio several times higher than many of the best venture capitalists. It has achieved this through a methodology which combines:

- assessment of the potential and viability of young peoples' business proposals by panels of local business people around the country;

- provision of flexible financial support, in the form of a loan or a grant; and

- an innovative and successful mentoring programme, which matches individual mentors – usually business people with a wide range of expertise – to young entrepreneurs in order to give them managerial support, business advice and personal encouragement.

PYBT is currently supporting about 4,000 young entrepreneurs a year – the majority of them long-term unemployed. Applications from ethnic minorities, people with disabilities and young ex-offenders are particularly encouraged. An independent audit has shown that over 60% of these businesses were continuing to trade after three years, a statistic of which any small-scale business programme would be proud.

PYBT has established a nationwide network of 37 business boards to assess proposals and more than 6,000 business volunteers. It has also established partnerships with the commercial banks, who will send young people they have had to turn down to PYBT and then match the PYBT loan, confident that these young entrepreneurs will have a better chance of success as part of the PYBT support network. Morgan Stanley has also entered into an innovative partnership with PYBT through which it has invested in 20 business for UK£2,500 each and then matches its own staff to these businesses as mentors. The British government has also established a partnership with the banks, through which it has made a UK£6 million grant to service write-offs and costs of borrowing, against which the banks have made a UK£6 million loan, at commercial rates, to PYBT. The government also offers matching funding to the young entrepreneurs after they have been in business for five months. These partnerships enable PYBT to achieve an 8:1 leverage on the government's funding.

In recent years PYBT has worked with Youth Enterprise Services International (YESI), profiled on the following page, to help adapt its model to other countries. Two key initiatives have been in India and South Africa, which are described opposite.

The Prince's Trust, of which PYBT is a part, also runs a nationwide youth volunteering programme, bringing together unemployed and employed young people to work on community projects. The programme is supported by government and the business sector, and parts of it have been adopted to other European countries, as the Polish profile on page 262 illustrates.

Youth Enterprise Services International

YESI is a network of youth development organisations from around the world, focused specifically on the important area of youth enterprise. Unemployed youth are one of the greatest sources of social unrest and yet many of them display great entrepreneurial talents, often applied to illegal activities. Helping them to set up their own businesses can make a great difference to them and their communities.

The YESI mission is to develop the creativity, ideals, courage and spirit of enterprise in the youth of the world working towards achieving sustainable development, alleviating poverty and ensuring a better future for all. YESI addresses the challenge of youth enterprise at three levels: youth motivation and enterprise education; business and management training; and start-up financial support and advice for business and community enterprises run by young people. It operates through a global network of partner organisations, such as:

- **The Prince's Youth Business Trust**, where YESI is head-quartered;

- **Junior Achievement International**, which offers an extensive range of curriculum based and ex-curricular economic and business training for young people worldwide, through a working relationship between business and schools;

- **The Trickle-Up Programme** based in New York, which has helped more than 30,000 micro-enterprises in 90 countries since 1979 with small grants;

- **The Commonwealth Youth Programme**, which provides technical support for Commonwealth governments on youth issues;

- **The Duke of Edinburgh's Award Scheme**, which operates in some 58 countries and runs personal development programmes for young people;

- **The Organisation for American States Caribbean Youth in Business Project**, which supports youth enterprise throughout the Caribbean; and

- **The Conference of Ministers of Youth and Sports of French Speaking Countries**, active especially in Francophone Africa.

The challenge of transferring "good" practice in youth development

The current leaders of the world community are in real danger of failing one of our greatest hopes for future social and economic sustainability; the world's youth, especially those that have entered their teen years with little education and little inclination to be responsible and active citizens in their communities and countries. From the angry disillusioned youth selling drugs and engaging in gang warfare in the inner cities of the USA and UK, to millions of homeless and hopeless youngsters living on the margins of society in places like Rio de Janeiro, Manila and Johannesburg, this is a source of social instability and wasted economic contributions which the world cannot afford.

There are now numerous innovative and successful initiatives around the world, targeted at harnessing the potential of these young people and giving them not only hope in their own futures, but also a stake in the future of their societies. The problem is that these initiatives, while often very successful, are too small and too limited to reach the millions of young people that would benefit from them. The international community, working with national governments and local business and community leaders, has a major responsibility and opportunity to scale-up the positive impact that these initiatives have demonstrated.

NGOs and multinational companies working in the field of youth development, have a critical role to play in this process of global replication and scaling-up. Some of them are already taking a lead. One of the leading NGOs is the International Youth Foundation, which is profiled on page 228. Another is the UK-based Youth Enterprise Services International.

Multinational companies can also play a valuable role in transferring good practice through their global networks. One that has been especially effective in the area of youth enterprise is **Shell International**. For a number of years, Shell UK has run an innovative scheme giving awards, in the form of start-up funding and advice, to young entrepreneurs. This programme, called LiveWire, has now been adapted to Hungary, as a locally owned Hungarian programme called Eletpalya. The process has been assisted with financial and managerial support from Shell International and its Hungarian subsidiary. Shell in South Africa has also adapted the LiveWire model to local circumstances and needs in that country. The programme in South Africa offers advice, technical support, cash awards and media recognition for young people between the ages of 16 and 26 who want to create their own work – to become "job creators rather than job-seekers" in the words of a Shell manager.

Other multinational companies such as BP, American Express, Grand Metropolitan and the Kellogg company are also operating programmes for young people that are being adapted internationally through the company's network of subsidiaries. These examples demonstrate that:

- world class companies are beginning to look at internationalising their community investment activities in the same strategic manner as their marketing, production and other core business functions; and

- these companies see the critical importance of programmes targeted at supporting the world's youth.

Such programmes offer great potential for increased co-operation between international agencies, national governments and these multinational companies.

> The reality is that there are more telephone lines in Manhattan than in sub-Saharan Africa.
>
> South African Deputy President,
> Thabo Mbeki

> Our dream today is not fundamentally about technology. Technology is a means to an end. Our dream is about communication – the most basic human strategy we use to raise our children, to educate, to heal, to empower and to liberate.
>
> US Vice President,
> Al Gore

> In a profound sense, our mission is to set the world free through communications.
>
> Robert E Allen,
> Chairman and CEO,
> AT&T

Supporting human development through information technology

The emerging Global Information Infrastructure (GII), born from the explosive growth in and gradual convergence of telecommunications and computer technology, promises to revolutionise the way society lives, works and learns. By connecting people-to-people and people-to-information, the GII promises to create a Global Information Society offering new opportunities for economic prosperity, education, health-care, environmental protection, democracy and empowerment; all essential elements of sustainable development.

The promise of the Global Information Society however is tempered by the reality that four billion of the world's five billion people lack access to basic telecommunications and information services. The growing disparity between those with access to information and those without promises to stifle development efforts and exacerbate pressing social, environmental and economic challenges. A growing consensus has emerged across government, business, NGOs and development agencies that the full potential of the Information Revolution will only be realised as more people and communities have access to its benefits.

The private sector – both information technology and non-information technology companies – is well-placed to help realise this potential by working in partnership with other sectors such as development agencies, NGOs and community institutions such as schools, libraries and clinics to increase local access to information technology.

- **The World Bank's InfoDev programme** is working with the private sector on a number of demonstration projects to leverage information technology for education purposes, for example in South Africa and Jamaica (see page 234).

- In western and eastern Europe, **Microsoft** has launched The Road Ahead programme, to help unemployed people to develop the skills and knowledge they need to find employment in the rapidly changing and growing information technology industry. The initiative falls under three main themes: life-long learning, employability and the innovative use of new technology to the benefit of society.

- **IBM** is working with the University of Chile and a group of researchers to develop an environmental information and monitoring system to control the loss of productive lands in Chile's arid sub-tropics. It is supporting similar environmental monitoring programmes elsewhere, and mobilising information technology for education in poor communities, for example via its "Reach and Teach" programme in South Africa.

- In partnership with **AT&T** and the government of Costa Rica, the Caribbean/Latin American Action task force has developed a pilot project linking rural health clinics with regional and national medical centres, enabling health practitioners in remote areas to consult with regional and national practitioners and experts.

- It is not only the telecommunications companies that are harnessing the power of technology for education and social goals, **BP Science Across the World** uses information technology to broaden student's understanding of global scientific and environmental issues and encourage global links between schools and industry.

- In Bangladesh, Grameen Bank has recently been granted a license to launch, **Grameen Telecom**, in partnership with some of the world's leading telecomms companies. It is envisaged that this initiative could create 60,000 micro-enterprise jobs for the rural poor.

GLOBE

● ●

GLOBE – Global Learning and Observation to Benefit the Environment – is a hands-on environmental and education programme originally envisioned by US Vice President Al Gore that joins students, educators and scientists from around the world to study the global environment via the Internet.

The objectives of GLOBE are:

• to enhance the environmental awareness of individuals worldwide,

• to increase scientific understanding of the earth, and

• to help all students reach higher standards in science and mathematics.

Over 1900 US schools are participating in GLOBE. In addition, over 110 countries have expressed interest in GLOBE and over 21 countries – including Australia, Benin, China, Egypt, Israel, Russia and South Africa – have joined GLOBE.

GLOBE students conduct an array of observations ranging from basic weather parameters such as temperature, atmospheric pressure and precipitation, to more sophisticated measurements such as water chemistry, bio-diversity and biomass assessment. Students take progressively more sophisticated measurements as they advance through school, and improve their mathematics and science capabilities while learning more about the environment.

The business community actively supports GLOBE worldwide. For example, in Benin, the Association of Black Telecommunications Workers of AT&T provided the programme with information technology. Working with the Beninese Ministry of Education, the equipment was distributed to GLOBE schools throughout the country. The US Agency for International Development (USAID) enhanced the initial business involvement by sending eight Beninese teachers plus the programme's country co-ordinator to one of GLOBE's international training and development workshops. In addition, USAID supported the participants' computer skills training upon their return. Enthusiasm for GLOBE in local schools and communities has resulted in the Ministry of Education integrating GLOBE into its mainstream education programmes and budget.

In China, Ameritech is working with the Chinese National Environment Agency (NEPA) to develop the programme nationwide. Under an initial five year partnership, NEPA will expand the programme to all provinces and major cities in China. Ameritech is ensuring that all GLOBE schools have the required information technology and Internet connection and service, environmental measurement and science equipment and teacher training. While assisting China in developing the use of information technology in education, Ameritech sees its partnership as providing strategic commercial benefits through market penetration and improved relations with key stakeholders.

> One ambitious plan for students using computers is GLOBE... a fine way for large numbers of children from many nations to learn about global co-operation, communication and environmental issues.
>
> Bill Gates, CEO, Microsoft
> in The Road Ahead

2.4 Environmental Sustainability

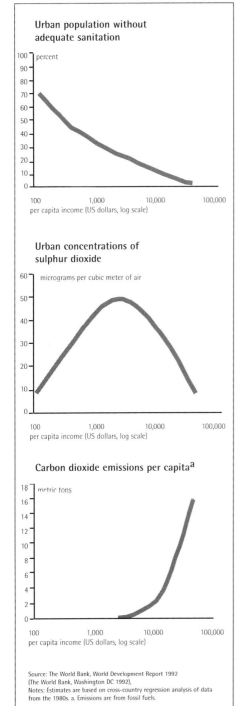

Urban population without adequate sanitation

percent

100
90
80
70
60
50
40
30
20
10
0

100   1,000   10,000   100,000
per capita income (US dollars, log scale)

Urban concentrations of sulphur dioxide

micrograms per cubic meter of air

60
50
40
30
20
10
0

100   1,000   10,000   100,000
per capita income (US dollars, log scale)

Carbon dioxide emissions per capita[a]

metric tons

18
16
14
12
10
8
6
4
2
0

100   1,000   10,000   100,000
per capita income (US dollars, log scale)

Source: The World Bank, World Development Report 1992
(The World Bank, Washington DC 1992).
Notes: Estimates are based on cross-country regression analysis of data
from the 1980s. a. Emissions are from fossil fuels.

I t is more than 30 years since Rachel Carson wrote her seminal book *Silent Spring*, passionately exposing the human and ecological dangers of indiscriminate chemical use and launching a movement which started asking serious questions about the link between economic growth and the natural environment. For much of the intervening period, business was viewed as the problem; the enemy to be confronted. In 1987, two British environmentalists, John Elkington and Tom Burke, wrote what in retrospect was also a seminal book, *The Green Capitalists*. Whilst certainly accepting that business was part of the problem, they argued that it could also be a major part of the solution, and that there would be real business opportunities in creating this solution.

The last ten years have witnessed a growing realisation of their early vision. From the first World Industry Conference on Environmental Management (WICEM) in 1984, to the prominent role played by the World Business Council for Sustainable Development (WBCSD) at the Rio Earth Summit, and its own seminal report *Changing Course*, to the environmental leadership of hundreds of companies and business associations today, there has probably been greater and more fundamental change in the approach of the business sector to environmental issues than in any other sector. While there are still far too many companies – major players as well as millions of small-scale enterprises – which are adding to the planet's environmental problems with little thought of their consequences, a growing number of corporations have made a genuine and substantive commitment to managing and improving their environmental impacts. For many of them it is a commitment which recognises not only the responsibilities, but also the competitive advantages of environmental leadership.

The private sector has a critical role to play in the drive towards environmental sustainability. It is a role which is twofold. The two greatest sources of environmental problems are poverty and unsustainable production and consumption patterns, and the private sector has a major contribution to make in tackling both of these issues. As the graphs on these two pages illustrate, environmental degradation does not necessarily disappear with industrialisation and growth in GDP, it simply changes in nature. The environmental problems and human health hazards associated with extreme poverty, lack of water, sanitation and other basic services, are replaced by increases in waste, and dramatic increases in carbon dioxide emissions as per capita incomes grow, and as nations and their populations produce and consume more. The private sector can therefore play a dual role in promoting environmental sustainability by:

• helping to tackle poverty through its contributions to economic and human development as already covered, and by

• investing in cleaner production and promoting more sustainable consumption patterns.

There have been an enormous number of initiatives undertaken by individual companies and by groups of companies in these areas. There

AGENDA 21: The role of business and industry

Agenda 21 listed a number of ways in which business and industry can play a role under the headings of cleaner production and responsible entrepreneurship.

Under cleaner production it called for the private sector to:

- strengthen relationships with government
- report on environmental records, use of energy and raw materials
- adopt and report on voluntary codes of conduct such as the ICC Charter and Responsible Care
- implement cleaner production policies, taking into account suppliers and consumers
- internalise environmental costs

- improve environmental awareness and responsibility
- co-operate with workers and trade unions
- collaborate with international organisations on cleaner production education, training and awareness activities
- strengthen cleaner production information dissemination.

Under responsible entrepreneurship it called on business to:

- co-operate with government in establishing venture capital funds
- support environmental training
- encourage global standards, practices and technology transfer
- develop partnerships with SMEs
- establish national councils for sustainable development
- increase research and development

has been a plethora of conferences, case studies and consultations on almost every aspect of environmental management and in almost every sector around the world. There have been encouraging examples of useful policy dialogue and practical action – at the level of both core business activities and community investment activities. There has also been constant and valid reminders that business is still not doing enough. It is not within the remit of this publication to look at these issues in detail. The following profiles are included merely as a small sample of initiatives that are being undertaken by groups of companies and by individual companies, in the drive towards sustainable development.

The first profile looks briefly at the work of the World Business Council for Sustainable Development (WBCSD), which played a critical role in setting a new vision for business with its report to the Rio Earth Summit *Changing Course*, and which continues to mobilise business leaders around the world. There are other active cross-border and cross-sector initiatives such as European Partners for the Environment, the International Chamber of Commerce, the International Network for Environmental Management (INEM) and the Global Environmental Management Initiative (GEMI) which are not covered here, but which are also good examples of the approaches that business is taking at the international level.

The second profile looks at one of the most outstanding examples of a national business network, the Industrial Environmental Forum in South Africa. There are a number of other impressive national business organisations such as Business in the Environment in the UK, Philippine Business for the Environment, the Hong Kong Private Sector Committee for the Environment, the Environmental Forum of Zimbabwe, the national affiliates of the WBCSD throughout Latin America and parts of Asia and so on. There are also industry associations such as the Keidanren, the Confederations of Indian Industry and British Industry, which have established active environmental units and charters for action.

The third profile looks at an industry sector initiative – The International Hotels Environment Initiative. Whilst the chemical industry's Responsible Care programme (profiled on page 77) is probably the best known of all the sector initiatives, others such as IPIECA (The International Petroleum Industry Environmental Conservation Association); ICME (The International Council on Metals and the Environment) and The World Travel and Tourism Council (WTTC) are also active in mobilising their members to take action on environmental issues.

The fourth profile offers "snap-shots" of a few individual companies which are members of the PWBLF: 3M ABB, Johnson Matthey, Wheelock and Abercrombie & Kent.

Finally, this section looks at probably one of the most important industry sectors of all in terms of achieving environmental sustainability: the financial sector.

Population without safe water

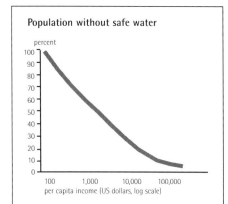

percent

per capita income (US dollars, log scale)

Urban concentrations of particulate matter

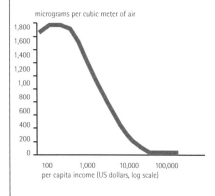

micrograms per cubic meter of air

per capita income (US dollars, log scale)

Municipal wastes per capita

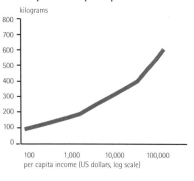

kilograms

per capita income (US dollars, log scale)

Source: The World Bank, World Development Report 1992 (The World Bank, Washington DC 1992).
Notes: Estimates are based on cross-country regression analysis of data from the 1980s. a. Emissions are from fossil fuels.

The World Business Council for Sustainable Development

In 1990, at the invitation of Maurice Strong, Secretary General of the UN Conference on Environment and Development, Swiss industrialist Stephan Schmidheiny brought together a unique and unprecedented group of 48 business leaders from 25 countries throughout the world and from a wide range of industry sectors, to present a global business perspective to the UNCED Conference in Rio de Janeiro. Their final report, *Changing Course* was publicly endorsed by every single member and helped to set a new vision for the role that business can play in promoting eco-efficiency and sustainable development. At the same time, the ICC was launching its Charter for Sustainable Development, and after the Rio Conference it established the World Industry Council for the Environment to tackle the practical and managerial aspects of putting the vision of environmental leadership into practice.

In January 1995 these two organisations merged to create the World Business Council for Sustainable Development (WBCSD); a coalition of more than 120 business leaders drawn from some 34 countries and more than 20 major industrial sectors. In addition, the WBCSD's network of national and regional business councils and partner organisations brings in a further 600 companies, many of them the leading players in their countries.

In broad terms, the WBCSD aims to develop closer co-operation between business, government and all other organisations concerned with the environment and sustainable development. It also seeks to encourage high standards of environmental management in business itself. More specifically, its objectives are:

- **Business Leadership** – to be the leading business advocate on issues connected with the environment and sustainable development;

- **Policy Development** – to participate in policy development in order to create a framework that allows business to contribute effectively to sustainable development;

- **Best Practice** – to demonstrate progress in environmental and resource management in business and to share leading-edge practices among its members; and

- **Global Outreach** – to contribute to a sustainable future for developing nations and nations in transition.

During the past year the WBCSD has undertaken a number of major policy and research activities, which will help to set a new agenda in several industry sectors. The first of these was a study on the role of the financial sector in promoting sustainable development entitled Financing Change. One of the key conclusions of this report was that methods need to be developed to value and price eco-efficiency in order for the financial markets to start rewarding it. In response to this, the WBCSD has now established a working group to look at environmental shareholder value. Policy work has also been undertaken on trade and the environment, sustainable production and consumption, and climate and energy issues.

In the best practice area, the WBCSD has concentrated on putting into practice the concept of eco-efficiency which was coined by the original BCSD's report *Changing Course*. It is also developing guidelines and case studies to help companies to integrate environmental assessments into their business decision-making process.

THE PAPER CYCLE STUDY

A ground-breaking project, spearheaded by Erling Lorentzen of Aracruz Celulose, a member of both the WBCSD and the PWBLF, has been a study of the entire paper cycle – forestry, pulp and paper making, paper use, recycling, disposal and energy recovery. The study is global in perspective and looks ahead to the year 2020. The WBCSD task force that put the project together commissioned the International Institute of Environment and Development (IIED), an independent, not-for-profit organisation with more than 50 specialists in the natural, social and economic sciences, to carry out the study. This has ensured its independence from vested interests. The final report has been based on consultations with a wide range of stakeholders around the world. It covers two main areas: costs and benefits, and policy recommendations, and will now form the basis for a series of follow-up meetings in places such as Brussels, Bangkok and Rio, aimed at taking the proposals for action forward.

The WBCSD is also helping to build capacity in developing and transition economies. In 1995 it produced a report, in co-operation with the PWBLF, on Multiplying Managerial Skills in Central and Eastern Europe and the Former Soviet Union. This led to a proposal to establish a leadership development programme in Russia which has now been implemented by an unprecedented partnership between a group of Scandinavian companies and donor agencies and is profiled on page 244. In a partnership with UNEP, Green Cross International and CEFIC, the WBCSD is working on a programme to transfer expertise on environmental emergency response to central and eastern Europe. It is also looking at the issue of environmental liabilities in central and eastern Europe, and supporting education and training activities in Latin America.

The Industrial Environmental Forum of Southern Africa

The Industrial Environmental Forum of Southern Africa (IEF) was established in 1989 by a small group of corporate chief executives, who recognised a growing need to reconcile developmental imperatives and increasing pressures for environmental protection. As South Africa moved into a new democratic era, environmental and developmental challenges escalated. So too did the need for an influential, cross-industry business voice on such matters. South African companies re-entering international markets discovered that environmental criteria had become pre-conditions of trade, and the new government started to look seriously at environmental regulation. The achievement of democracy also meant increased transparency and scrutiny of business by NGOs, which now have an unprecedented influence on environmental policy and legislation formulation.

The IEF has grown to a membership of 50 large companies. Diverse sectors are represented – mining, energy, chemicals, forestry, paper and pulp, food production, water provision, retail, beverages. financial institutions, automatives and airlines. The members represent a mixture of major South African companies, such as Eskom, Anglo American, Gencor, and Barlow Rand and multinationals such as BP, Afrox, Johnson Matthey, Shell, the Kellogg company and Volkswagen. An associate membership capacity exists for research institutions, consultants, academia, and other business associations.

In signing up to IEF membership, companies are expected to ensure a senior representative actively participates in IEF activities. A 10 point code of conduct gives members a public yardstick against which their commitment can be evaluated. This includes a commitment beyond legislative compliance and implicitly to continuous improvement. The members are also signatories to the International Chamber of Commerce Business Charter for Sustainable Development. However, probably the most binding

commitment amongst members is to ensure the efficacy of self-regulatory approaches to environmental management and negotiated definitions of what is actually meant by this concept in African terms.

The wide-ranging membership of the IEF provides a considerable resource of environmental experience and expertise. Internally this offers review and benchmarking opportunities. Externally the IEF has been able to play a valuable role:

- nationally, advising the new South African government as it develops environmental regulations;

- regionally, supporting business-led initiatives being established elsewhere, such as the Environmental Forum of Zimbabwe and the Namibia Business Forum for the Environment, plus initiatives in Mozambique, Tanzania, Kenya and Ghana; and

- internationally, IEF delegations have performed an advocacy role in the formulation of environmental management systems, standards and conventions, often bringing an important developing country perspective to the table. The IEF also promotes investment opportunities in sustainable development projects in the region, such as the Cleaner Production Centre in Zimbabwe, supported by UNIDO and UNEP.

Importantly, the IEF provides a viewpoint that is relevant to Africa and born out of the experience of doing business there. The success of the IEF itself has been largely attributable to the commitment of a small group of major corporations. Principal among these has been the electricity utility Eskom. A member of the WBCSD, Eskom underwrote initial risks, seconded its Corporate Policy Advisor as Director of the IEF, provided office and logistical support and encouraged other leading companies and their chief executives to join, what in 1989, was a pioneering initiative.

THE IEF'S OBJECTIVES AND ACTIVITIES

The principal objective of the IEF is to mobilise a greater commitment by South African business to environmental responsibility and accountability, and ultimately to take a leadership position in these matters, both nationally and regionally, from a business perspective. It achieves this in a number of different ways:

- Unlike similar organisations in the OECD countries, the focus of attention is primarily on sustainable development issues as opposed to "pure" environmental concerns;
- Initially IEF dialogue focused on environmental management issues within companies, but has slowly progressed to all relevant stakeholders;
- Debate is encouraged at a strategic level – tracking significant domestic

and international trends and recommending appropriate responses to members, while day-to-day operational issues tend to be handled on an *ad hoc* basis, usually by the companies working with other environmental consultants and advisers outside the forum itself;

- Assisting companies with environmental management capacity enhancement is an important function. For example, advice on (and review of) training courses, policy formulation, compliance issues, performance monitoring and measurement systems is provided to members on request;
- Management tools have been adapted from existing international initiatives to make them more relevant to business in Africa;
- Technical assistance and support is also offered to environmental business organisations elsewhere in Africa.

The International Hotels Environment Initiative

Travel and tourism, the world's largest industry, is forecast to double in size over the next decade or so, directly and indirectly stimulating 144 million new jobs worldwide by the year 2005. It is a sector which is of growing importance to many developing and transition economies, as well as OECD economies, and the hotel industry is an important component of this sector. The International Hotels Environment Initiative (IHEI), a sector-specific programme of The Prince of Wales Business Leaders Forum, is an international network of hotel executives pooling effort, expertise and experience to promote environmental good practice across the global hotel industry.

The mission of the IHEI is to encourage the continual improvement of environmental performance by the hotel industry and its suppliers. The IHEI also positions the hotel industry in a leadership role in a world increasingly aware of the environmental performance of business. The IHEI International Council, consisting of 12 of the world's major hotel chains, provides core funding for the London team which is used to leverage project funding from government agencies and other private sponsors. The programme also has an Asia-Pacific Council, comprising 18 Asia-based companies, which steers and funds activities in this region.

IHEI delivers its mission via three strands of activity:

1 Raising awareness
Promoting the ideas, experiences and business benefits of sound environmental action through a high profile media campaign and platforms at international conferences and exhibitions.

2 Providing 'Tools for Action'
The IHEI produces a range of hotel-specific environmental management tools which, thanks to the financial support of partners, can be offered to the industry at subsidised rates. These include:

- *Environmental Action Pack for Hotels* – a practical, step-by-step guide for all hotel staff, produced as a partnership between by the IHEI, the United Nations Environment Programme and the International Hotel Association, sponsored by Diversey Corporation.

- *Going Green Makes Cents* – video for hotel managers, show-casing the most simple and effective environmental measures hotels can take.

- *Green Innovations* – an environmental resource directory for hotels.

- *Environmental Management For Hotels*: the industry guide to best practice, both as a reference manual and as a student textbook.

3 Collaborating with partners.
On the ground, currently in nineteen countries, the IHEI forms partnerships with influential national organisations. Their ownership of the programme and their networks and links enable the IHEI to maximise its impact with minimal resource. An example is the Environmental Hotels of Auckland programme, catalysed by the IHEI, but set up by the local industry together with Regional and City Councils and the Ministry of the Environment.

Internationally the IHEI is supported by government agencies such as the European Commission and the United Nations Environment Programme.

Working with several international organisations, the IHEI is currently developing a programme which will expand the network's focus from environmental management issues in existing hotels, to the environmental responsibilities associated with siting, designing and constructing new hotels.

The diverse and geographically widespread contacts in the IHEI global network are kept in touch through *Green Hotelier* – a quarterly subscription magazine showcasing hotel environmental trends and good practice from around the world.

The IHEI International Council:

Accor • Forte Hotels • Hilton International • Holiday Inn Worldwide • Inter-Continental Hotels and Resorts • Mandarin Oriental Hotel Group • Marriott Corporation • Marco-Polo Hotels • Radisson SAS • Renaissance International Hotels • ITT Sheraton • The Taj Group of Hotels.

The IHEI Asia Pacific Council:

Banyan Hotels and Resorts • Century International Hotels • Conrad Hotels • Dusit Hotels and Resorts • East India Hotels • Holiday Inn Asia Pacific • Hong Kong and Shanghai Hotels • Inter-Continental Hotels and Resorts • ITC Welcome Group • ITT Sheraton • Mandarin Oriental • Marco Polo Hotels • Renaissance Hotels International • Sedona Hotels International • Shangri-La International • Shilla Hotels • SMI Hotels and Resorts.

3M: Pollution Prevention Pays

3M has been one of the pioneers in bringing environmental issues onto the mainstream business agenda. Almost fifty years ago, 3M's CEO William McKnight stated: "In industry, almost any saving of materials is at least an indirect saving of natural resources, and manufacturers who realise this are probably operating at a much higher level of efficiency than those who do not. That efficiency means a more economical product." McKnight went on to note that this translated into more jobs and more prosperity.

In 1975, 3M was one of the pioneers in adopting a corporate Environmental Policy, which states (among other provisions) that the company will solve its own environmental problems, prevent pollution at source, and develop products that have a minimum effect on the environment. An important element of this is the company's commitment to applying the same environmental standards and goals around the world, even when local standards are less demanding.

Also in 1975, 3M initiated its Pollution Prevention Pays – or 3P – programme. Since then employees have developed more than 4,400 pollution prevention projects worldwide, eliminating 1.4 billion pounds of pollutants and saving more than US$750 million.

Investing for continuous improvement

The company's commitment to meeting its environmental targets, and to continuously improving its environmental performance on a world-wide basis, is underpinned by sizable investments in technologies and products, as well as in the establishment of comprehensive management systems and the training and motivation of its employees. Each year, for example, the company spends about US$150 million on R&D specifically directed at achieving its environmental goals. The majority of this investment is related to new and modified products; the rest is directed at improving processes.

A keystone of 3M's investment is the company's new Environmental Management System (EMS), which emphasises sustainable development and continuous improvement of the environmental performance of 3M's products and processes. The EMS includes audits to verify performance and identify improvement opportunities, and requires the incorporation of environmental challenges and opportunities measures into the strategic plans of every business unit.

One of the most important investments continues to be in training and motivating employees. The company undertakes extensive training around the world to create a culture of problem-solving and innovation and has a recognition system for employees who have innovative ideas that help to meet its environmental goals.

Environmental responsibility as competitive advantage

As 3M's environmental thinking has evolved, the company has come to appreciate that its ability to apply technologies to environmental problems – and bring the solutions to the market quickly – constitute an important competitive advantage. In the past few years the company has been able to open new markets with technologies and products that leap-frog the competition and at the same time reduce environmental impact – these include solvent-free adhesives, water-based printing products and many consumer and office products made from recycled components. What is especially important is that these products are sold world-wide, not only in the OECD markets.

The company's recognised leadership in the environmental field also has positive implications for its overall corporate reputation and brand recognition. In 1996, 3M received the Presidential Award for Sustainable Development in the United States; was ranked third in eco-performance among the 50 largest chemical-using companies in the world, by the respected Hamburger Umwelt Institute in Germany; and ranked the third "most Admired" in the "Community and Environment" category of Fortune Magazine's global poll of business leaders.

SETTING CLEAR GOALS and ACHIEVING MEASURABLE RESULTS

3M continues to set aggressive goals for the reduction of pollutants. As of year-end 1995, results include: worldwide waste generation rates were cut by 25% versus 1990; all releases have been reduced by 40% in the United States; and global air emissions of point-source VOCs are down over 70% versus 1987. This was accomplished through the use of innovative technologies – such as solvent-free manufacturing – and the installation of emissions control equipment. Since 1973, 3M has also reduced energy use per unit of production by over 60% saving a cumulative 320 trillion BTLs and reducing carbon emissions by 5.4 billion pounds per year.

3M's current environmental goals include the following: 3M is working to cut all releases to air, water and land by 90% at 3M facilities worldwide (using 1990 as a base) by the year 2000. Ultimately the company intends to bring all releases to the environment as close to zero as possible.
By the year 2000, 3M also expects to cut waste 50% (from 1990 levels) and to improve energy efficiency by 3% per year. The company is also placing more emphasis on life-cycle management, which takes into consideration a product's impact on the environment and human health and safety at all stages of the product's life cycle, from development, through manufacture, shipping, customer use and disposal.

The practical problems of bringing these modern, environmentally friendly technologies to places like China, India, Russia, Ukraine etc. are of course big. Western and Japanese exports of products, plants and processes will only play a marginal role. The vast majority of investment must come from within these countries. Licensing is one route, but it will not be enough and it often does not penetrate deep enough. We will need to share technology by creating partnerships or joint ventures and by tying these emerging countries into global networks.

Percy Barnevik
President and CEO, ABB
IMF/World Bank Annual Meeting,
1996

Asea Brown Boveri: Transferring eco-efficient technologies

● ●

The enormous growth in energy demand and infrastructure development in many of the world's rapidly emerging and industrialising economies is well-known, especially in China and India. If these demands are not met by cleaner technologies, there will be no chance of achieving sustainable development. Whilst governments and industrialists in OECD countries continue to fine-tune the environmental impacts of their own industries, it is in the industrial plants of the emerging economies that greater environmental investment and innovation is critically needed. ABB is a world leader in developing eco-efficient technologies in a wide range of industry areas from electricity transmission to transportation, and is building a global network of joint ventures and strategic alliances to install these technologies in many developing and transition economies. The following vignettes illustrate the impact that some of these have had:

- ABB is installing an advanced wet flue-gas desulphurisation system in one of Poland's largest coal-fired power plants. The system will cut sulphur emissions by 95% and provide commercial grade gypsum for the building industry. In an aluminium plant in Bahrain, ABB pollution control equipment will recover 26,000 tons of flouride per annum.

- ABB high-voltage direct current (HVDC) electricity transmission systems carry up to five times as much power as conventional systems with 20-30% less energy loss. These HVDC systems are being installed on all five continents.

- ABB process automation systems in the textile industry have been shown to increase productivity by up to 15%, and lower energy consumption by 20% and chemical use by 15%.

- ABB has delivered more than 3,500 wind generators around the globe.

One of the key factors underpinning the company's success in technology cooperation has been its strong commitment to training and building the capacity of local people in all the markets where it operates. It currently has orders of US$10 billion and 70,000 employees in 95 emerging and transition economies. Every year ABB spends tens of millions of dollars, drawing on the expertise of internationally renowned academic and vocational institutions, to train these people in eco-efficient technologies and modern management methods.

Johnson Matthey: Cutting emissions through catalytic systems

● ●

Johnson Matthey is another company which is building commercial reputation and success through the development of eco-efficient and clean technologies. Vehicle emissions are the source of major environmental problems. In the early 1970s the company pioneered the technology for autocatalysts and today has over one third of the world market, making a vital contribution to cutting emissions.

It recently launched the first catalyst to work effectively on heavy-duty diesel vehicles, called the 'Continuously Regenerating Trap' or CRT. Trials in the UK and Sweden have demonstrated that the CRT technology, which can be retrofitted to existing heavy-duty vehicles, has the ability to remove over 90% of particulate, carbon monoxide and hydrocarbon emissions giving an exhaust free of smoke and smell.

The Woo Wheelock Green Fund

In the past few years, The Woo Wheelock Green Fund has funded, either jointly with the Hong Kong Government or on its own, six environmental projects for a total of more than HK$3.5 million. These range from high-tech scientific research with implications not only for HK but for cities worldwide, to community activities such as Earth Day celebrations and environmental resource centres. They include the following:

- A pilot housing estate scheme which is employing a multi-disciplinary approach to work with 40 families on one of HK's major housing estates to develop green household technologies, with an emphasis on water and energy. If successful, the pilot will be used as a blueprint for government in other high density housing areas and has potential applicability in many rapidly growing mega-cities, not least in China and other parts of Asia.

- A scientific study to explore the potential contribution of solar energy as a renewable energy source in HK by studying energy generated from photovoltaic panels through a full 12-month period of Hong Kong weather from a series of panels of different orientation and tilt.

- A research study on resources and recycling in the Hong Kong construction industry

- Environmental Resource Centres designed to serve the public, community groups and educational establishments as part of an effort to increase environmental awareness. The first resource centre had more than 18,000 visitors in its first year of operation.

Abercrombie & Kent: Friends of Conservation Foundation

Successful and sensitive ecotourism provides economic benefits for the 'host countries,' both from direct revenue and direct employment, and by encouraging the development of tourist infrastructures. It can also generate much-needed funds for conservation and management of protected areas. Abercrombie & Kent is one of the world's premier travel companies operating tours to developing economies. Through a combination of its core business activities and its community investment budget, the company helps to channel donations to sustainable development projects in areas where the it is operating tours and tourist facilities.

In the early 1980s, A&K established the Friends of Conservation (FOC) Foundation to assist areas in most urgent need. Today the company donates $10 for each traveller to Africa to the work of FOC. In addition, it absorbs the foundation's overhead costs. FOC works with local people in East Africa to preserve wildlife habitats a as renewable resource. FOC operates through five long-term programmes:

- wildlife monitoring programmes which provide the foundation for ecosystem management;
- anti-poaching support including supply of communications equipment, patrol vehicles, and air support;
- re-creation of habitat. FOC provides infrastructure services to support the restocking of the Mkomazi Game Reserve;
- rhino translocation and veterinarian programme;
- and education – production of conservation information materials for visitors, tour drivers and FOC rangers and conservation education for local people and schoolchildren.

Mobilising the Financial Markets

The environmental record of the financial sector todate has not been impressive. The developed capital markets have no problem in mobilising large amounts of capital, but their focus on quarterly dividends, daily stock prices, hourly exchange rates and short-term profit maximisation, all too often result in the allocation of capital to short-term consumptive uses rather than long-term investment. In developing countries, inadequate legal, fiscal and institutional infrastructures, often coupled with government interference and bureaucracy, result in capital markets that at best operate inefficiently, unable to mobilise even domestic savings let alone international capital, towards more sustainable investment, production and consumption activities.

In the last few years there have been encouraging signs from different parts of the financial sector that this situation is starting to change. While environmental liability and risk management remain the most important concern for most financial institutions, some of the world's more visionary banks, fund managers and insurance companies are beginning to look at the opportunities offered by the environmental movement. For example:

- Some banks are establishing specialised environmental lending units and risk management rating systems and a number of leading players such as National Westminster Bank, Union Bank of Switzerland, Deutsche Bank and Swiss Bank Corporation have signed the *UNEP Banking Charter* and started to produce environmental reports;

- Insurance companies are launching environmental risk management and investment products and have recently mobilised as an industry sector around the issue of global warming. A group of leading players spearheaded by NPI in the UK; Sumitomo Marine and Fire in Japan; Uni Storebrand in Norway; General Accident in the UK; Gerling-Konzern Globale in Germany; Swiss Re in Zurich, and UNEP's Industry and Environment office, have recently launched a *Statement of Environmental Commitment by the Insurance Industry*, which has been signed by more than 50 insurance companies worldwide;

- Green or ethical investment funds are growing in number, size and influence, especially in the USA and the UK, but also elsewhere in Europe. In the UK the Social Investment Forum has been established to mobilise the ethical and mainstream investment sector;

- Multilateral and bilateral donor agencies are integrating environmental criteria into their lending and grant programmes and the World Bank's Vice Presidency for Environmentally Sustainable Development is undertaking research on finding new ways to measure different types of capital, as profiled on page 29;

- The accounting sector is also developing expertise in environmental auditing and reporting and organisations such as the Centre for Environmental and Social Accountancy Research are working on developing systems of measurement and full-cost accounting;

- The World Business Council for Sustainable Development has produced a book *Financing Change*, which for the first time provides a comprehensive overview of the challenges and opportunities associated with the "greening of the financial markets"; and

- In both the USA and the UK business-led organisations, such as the Business in the Environment in the UK, the City of London's

The capital markets are one of the single most important determinants of business behaviour. The availability and cost of capital on the one hand, and its potential returns on the other, influences the nature of almost every production, consumption and investment decision. The nature of these decisions is in turn a crucial determinant of the environmental soundness and long term sustainability of business activities. The financial markets and the institutions that operate in them therefore have a vital role to play in achieving sustainable development. Their ability to mobilise savings, both domestically and internationally, and the way in which they allocate them, can either promote or undermine the efforts of all other sectors.

Environmental Forum jointly launched by the Bank of England and the Corporation of London, and the Environmental Bankers Association in the USA, are undertaking research, surveys, campaigns and consultations with key players in the financial sector to further the debate.

In most countries, however, these initiatives remain the exception rather than the norm. The majority of financial institutions continue to take an *ad hoc* and piecemeal approach to the environmental challenge, viewing it all too often as a cost and annoyance, rather than an opportunity. This situation is unlikely to change fundamentally until methodologies for assigning values and prices to eco-efficiency and environmental externalities are better developed. On-going efforts by visionary fund managers, insurers, bankers, accountants, business leaders and government officials, to develop mindsets and methodologies which can accommodate the concept of environmental shareholder value will be absolutely critical to this process. So too will on-going efforts by governments to develop tax reforms and incentives to reward environmentally responsible business.

The following vignettes, briefly describe the activities of a few industry leaders: the National Westminster Bank; Uni Storebrand and NPI's Global Care Funds. The following page looks at some of the responses by the financial sector to the critical issue of global warming, overviewing an innovative partnership which is being undertaken between Greenpeace and the financial sector, and profiling some of the activities of the insurance group, Sedgwick.

a) The commercial banking sector

The need to manage environmental risks in the face of increasing lender liability, both direct and indirect, is forcing many banks to reassess their lending policies and procedures. Some are also responding to the growing profit opportunities of financing the production of environmental goods and services and clean-up operations, as well as producing environmental information services for customers. A few retail banks are taking advantage of "green consumerism", to establish environment linked savings accounts, loans and credit cards – which serve to mobilise funds for environmental groups and at the same time, are aimed at increasing the bank's customer base and/or profits. A number of commercial banks are also impacting environmental issues through their debt reduction and conversion programmes. And, a few are developing comprehensive environmental management policies and systems, with auditing and reporting procedures for measuring their internal environmental housekeeping and the quality of environmental risk management in their lending and investment decisions.

The UK-based **National Westminster Bank** has been one of the leaders in many of the above areas. The NatWest Group consists of an international portfolio of businesses which provide a broad spectrum of financial services to customers ranging from individuals and small businesses to multinational companies. In the UK alone, the bank services around 6 million personal customers and 900,000 small businesses. In 1990 it established an environmental management team and formulated an environmental policy, which outlines the bank's commitment to address not only environmental risk factors, but also the development of banking products and services that promote environmental protection, where there is a sound business rationale. The policy, which is outlined opposite, gives a clear indication of the integrated approach which the bank has taken to environmental management. This approach encompasses the three-areas of corporate citizenship outlined throughout this publicatio; core business activities,

NATWEST GROUP'S ENVIRONMENTAL POLICY

The NatWest Group is committed to achieving environmental best practice throughout its business activities, wherever this is practicable. We recognise that the pursuit of economic growth and a healthy environmental must be closely linked and that ecological protection and sustainable development are collective responsibilities in which governments, businesses, individuals and communities all have a role to play.

Our environmental responsibility programme is based upon continuous improvement, consistent with current knowledge. Environmental management continues to be a corporate priority, fully integrated into our business. We believe sound environmental practice is a key factor demonstrating effective corporate management. We will seek to educate and train our staff to act in an environmentally responsible manner.

We will conduct internal environmental reviews and will publish the results. The reviews will measure our performance and ensure that we are meeting our policy goals as well as compliance requirements.

We will seek to develop suitable banking products and services which promote environmental protection, where there is a sound business rationale.

We will encourage our customers to consider fully the environmental implications of their businesses and the impact of them on environmental issues. We will share information with customers as appropriate.

We recognise that environmental risks should be part of the normal checklist of risk assessment and management. As part of our credit risk assessment, where appropriate, environmental impact assessments may be requested.

We will encourage our suppliers to pursue best practice. Our procurement policy will take account of this.

Through our community relations programmes we will continue to support groups which help to protect the environment and inform wider audiences of the issues involved.

community investments and policy dialogue. The bank has also made a clear commitment to influence key stakeholder groups such as customers, suppliers, community partners and policy-makers. In the latter case the bank has played a lead role in influencing British environmental policy through its chairing of the Advisory Committee on Business and the Environment which was profiled on page 74.

The bank's Environmental Responsibility Programme has four main components:

- Management of business risks;

- Identification of business opportunities;

- Management of internal housekeeping to reduce NatWest's environmental footprint; and

- Participation in the environmental debate and policy development in matters important to the Group and its customers.

Although the fourth item is managed centrally, the bank has attempted to push responsibility for the other items down to individual business units.

Two key elements of the Environmental Responsibility Programme are an externally verified audit process and integration of environmental issues into the bank's Balanced Business Scorecard (BBS). The latter is an innovative management tool which NatWest has used since 1992, and which requires the bank to assess the relationship between all the stakeholders within the organisation and the trade-offs which exist between these various groups. The 1995 audit, which was undertaken by Co-opers & Lybrand, reviewed four main factors in the bank's Environmental Responsibility programme: commitment, co-ordination, communication and control.

b) The investor community

Investors, especially institutional investors, who manage some US$8 trillion of assets globally, are also responding to the environmental challenge. Some of them are establishing specialised environmental investment or "green" funds, with both ethical and/or profit criteria as motivating factors. Many of them are also starting to incorporate environmental research into their normal investment activities, on the basis that bad environmental practice is bad business and could potentially undermine the value of their portfolio – as the holders of Exxon shares discovered after the Valdez oil spill. A few investors are taking a more activist role in company management, by encouraging the adoption of environmental management codes (such as the CERE's Principles profiled on page 79) and in some cases, even using their proxy rights to influence management on environmental matters. The institutional investor community is growing in size and power. It is likely to be an increasingly powerful force for change if its strength can be harnessed to the environmental cause.

One of the institutional investors which has a long tradition in providing life assurance services and benefits to the public and is now playing a leading role in developing investment funds to promote sustainable development, is the UK-based **National Provident Institution**. Established in 1835, NPI is a mutual company owned 100% by its members and is currently the eight largest mutual office in the United Kingdom. It manages money on behalf of more than 500,000 policyholders, and has total assets of over UK£9 billion. In August 1991 it launched its first Global Care Unit

Trust. This trust, and other funds managed by NPI's Global Care team, aims to generate satisfactory financial returns from companies which make a positive impact upon the world. In doing so, their ultimate aim is to enable people to achieve long-term financial security through growth in the value of their savings and pensions, whilst at the same time investing in a better world, both environmentally and socially.

To meet these goals, NPI's Global Care investment team take a proactive stance, seeking to invest in industry sectors and individual companies which the managers believe have prospects for substantial growth in the future through producing goods and services that offer solutions to environmental and social problems. These industries include, health care, education, telecommunications, pollution prevention, renewable energy, recycling and community banking. The investment team not only makes investments where it sees prospects for financial growth, but also where its sees prospects for continuous improvement in social and environmental practices and where it can encourage corporate managers to achieve this through on-going dialogue. The team have pioneered sector research, providing comparative environmental analysis of companies with similar activities. The Global Care team also engages actively in the public policy arena, working in co-operation with other financial sector institutions to advance the debate on issues such as corporate governance, and environmental and social standards and practices. The Global Funds have performed well, often outperforming their sector average.

c) The insurance sector

Insurance companies are also starting to influence company behaviour on environmental issues, both in their capacity as a major source of institutional investment funds and as insurers, which can no longer afford to ignore environmental costs and risks in their policy valuations.

Uni Storebrand is Norway's leading private sector supplier of financial and insurance services to companies and individuals. Founded in 1767, the company serves more than 1 million customers. Its core product areas are property and casualty insurance, life insurance, pensions and savings. It has built a strong reputation for its contributions to enhancing quality of life and environmental performance through the provision of pro-active loss prevention programmes, helping its customers to reduce the risks of accidents, hazards and catastrophes. In 1994, the company built on this platform to formulate an Environmental Policy and Plan, which consists of ten areas of activity. These include:

- price differentiation in underwriting decisions, which reflect environmental risk;

- the implementation of environmental purchasing standards;

- asset management, including environmental standards for its real estate portfolio;

- development of environmental funds; and

- international co-operation with other environmentally pro-active insurance companies.

Senior insurers, bankers and financial analysts have recently summarised the financial sector's emerging concerns in the world's first book on the subject, entitled: *Climate Change and the Financial Institutions: the emerging threat, the solar solution.* The book was published by an affiliate of the Gerling Group of insurance companies and edited by Dr Jeremy Leggett from Greenpeace and Oxford University. Greenpeace is now working on a three year programme which is aimed at achieving global-warming risk abatement for financial institutions, via collaborative building of new markets in solar energy. The programme, called **The Oxford Solar Investment Summit (OSIS) Process** – will consist of several major summits, supported by extensive consultations and research on both the policy and legislative framework, and practical market solutions. To implement this initiative, Greenpeace is working in partnership with a group of: financial institutions (including the World Bank and some of the world's major insurance companies and banks); and solar suppliers and consumers (ranging from architects, developers and builders, to cities, development agencies, energy companies, the hotel and tourism industry, Olympic Games committees, the information technology industry, electrical utilities, environmental groups and academic institutions). An advisory board has also been established for the OSIS initiative and comprises top strategists from around the world in the financial sector, the energy industry, the environmental movement and the policymaking community. OSIS is an excellent example of different sectors and organisations – who have either totally ignored each other, if not been in direct confrontation in the past – coming together to find visionary and practical solutions to a major global problem.

The company chairs the WBCSD's working group on Shareholder Value and the Environment, in partnership with Swiss Bank Corporation and DuPont, and played a lead role in establishing the Statement of Environmental Commitment by the Insurance Industry. In partnership with US-based Scudder, Stevens and Clark, one of America's oldest and largest investment management firms, Uni Storebrand has launched the Environmental Value Fund (EVF). The goal of the fund is to provide competitive long-term returns measured against the MSCI World Index by actively investing in securities on a global basis. One of the unique features of EVF is its ability to demonstrate the eco-efficiency of the portfolio and to measure this as the fund's Environmental Dividend.

d) Climate change and the financial sector

The environmental risk arising from Global Warming and Climate Change is an issue with which the financial sector, especially the insurance industry, is increasingly concerned. Risks to the financial sector include potentially unmanageable property and catastrophic insurance losses, and the physical and legislative erosion of the value of many debt and equity instruments.

The insurance sector however recognises the opportunities as well as threats in this area and a growing number of insurance companies – both underwriters and brokers – are establishing environmental risk management units; contributing to national and international governmental bodies on the subject of Global Warming and Climate Change; and entering into new and innovative initiatives with academic institutions and environmental NGOs such as Greenpeace, to promote and profit from markets that defuse the global-warming threat, such as solar energy. In short, they are looking at the growing needs in environmental risk management, but at the same time, the growing opportunities and importance of risk abatement.

The Sedgwick Group operates in 68 countries in risk consultancy, insurance and re-insurance broking, employee benefits and financial services. It has been a leader in the broking sector in establishing a dedicated service to address the issue of global warming and climate change, and the importance of risk management in this area. As with the now more familiar problem of general environmental risk, Sedgwick recognises that the subject is highly technical and that assessments are, by necessity, subjective. It is, however, convinced that this does not stop valid judgements being made and the information being used to protect client companies, their third party "stakeholders" and the environment. By assisting its clients actively to manage these types of risk, Sedgwick believes it will obtain a commercial advantage. It has executed case studies and consultative projects for multinational clients, including major telecommunications carriers; contributed on a consultative basis to the UK Government and the Chartered Insurance Institute on the subject of Global Warming and Environmental Change; and to the UK's input to the International Decade for Natural Disaster Reduction; and is currently negotiating a joint venture to produce a world atlas of Natural Perils, which will incorporate information about the risks associated with Global Climate Change.

2.5 Social Cohesion

> Today, having abandoned the promise of social engineering, virtually all serious observers understand that liberal political and economic institutions depend on healthy and dynamic civil society for their vitality. "Civil society" – a complex welter of intermediate institutions, including businesses, voluntary associations, educational institutions, clubs, unions, media, charities, and churches – builds, in turn, on the family, the primary instrument by which people are socialised into their culture and given the skills that allow them to live in broader society and through which the values and knowledge of that society are transmitted across the generations.
>
> Francis Fukuyama
> Trust: The Social Virtues and the Creation of Prosperity, 1995

One of the greatest threats to the long-term stability and prosperity of communities around the world is the break down in social organisation and cohesion; in the networks, societal norms and bonds of mutual trust and cultural understanding that enable disparate individuals, ethnic groups and organisations to work together and live together for mutual benefit.

There is much talk in political circles today, especially in the USA and UK, about the need to build a stakeholder society in which all members feel that they have an economic and personal stake in helping to achieve the "common good". This need is strong everywhere, not least in the transition economies of central and eastern Europe and the former Soviet Union, where people are struggling to come to terms with a new social order that lacks the authoritarianism of the past, but also the security of lifetime employment and inexpensive, albeit inefficient, social services. In many developing countries there is concern about the impact of rapid economic growth and outside cultural influences on indigenous communities. In mega-cities the world over, there are growing problems of crime, drugs, gang warfare, family breakdown, declining support for traditional social structures such as the church, and a strong sense of alienation and marginalisation for large groups of the population.

In an increasingly complex, confusing and uncertain world, the need for trust and strong social networks has never been greater, nor more threatened by the very same factors which are making it necessary. Companies, as social organisations and as key stakeholders in a stable and prosperous society, have a critical role to play in minimising the negative impacts that the drive for economic competitiveness has on social cohesion and trust and by making proactive investments in helping to build civil society, strong communities and cultural respect and understanding.

There are a number of issues in particular that large companies can play a role in tackling. These are:

- **The fight against social exclusion**, resulting from unemployment, poverty and lack of access to housing and basic social services;

- **The fight against corruption**, both within the business sector and in society at large;

- **The fight against crime**, both white-collar commercial crime, and crime in society;

- **Building the capacity of NGOs and community-based organisations** in order to strengthen civil society;

- **Building ethnic and cultural understanding**, both within communities and countries and between them;

- **Building community-based enterprise** and supporting the emergence of a new type of entrepreneur – "the social entrepreneur".

Many of the examples profiled in this publication support the above objectives. The following profiles focus on some initiatives specifically established to: tackle social exclusion, corruption and crime; build capacity for cross-sector partnerships and social entrepreneurship; and invest in the arts and cultural diversity.

The European Business Network for Social Cohesion

Companies and business associations participating in the network include:

ACCOR • Bayer • British Petroleum • British Telecommunications • Groupe Glaverbel • Ini-Teneo • Levi Strauss Europe • Philips International • Societe Generale de Belgique• London Enterprise Agency • The King Baudouin Foundation • Manifest des Enterprises contre l'Exclusion • International Christian Union of Business Executives • Formidlings Aarhus Centre • Sodalitas • Swedish Jobs and Society • The Confederation of Netherlands Industry and Employers.

"More than 18,000,000 people unemployed; 53,000,000 living below the poverty line; approximately 5,000,000 living in inadequate housing" ...these figures, issued by various European organisations, illustrate the extent of social exclusion and poverty within the European Union. Many businesses are involved in the fight against social exclusion as an expression of good corporate citizenship. They recognise that exclusion is a waste of human resources and a threat to social cohesion as well as a contributory factor to the rise of collective costs and financial burdens for business.

It is within this context that a group of business leaders decided to formulate a **European Declaration of Business Against Exclusion**. The Declaration is not a binding commitment, but it is a message from businesses to businesses designed to heighten awareness of, and involvement in, areas which can effect greater social cohesion. The Declaration was presented in Brussels in January 1995, at a meeting attended by twenty business leaders, the former President of the European Commission, Jacques Delors and the present Commissioner for Employment, Industrial Relations and Social Affairs. The initiating companies were encouraged to use the Declaration as a practical instrument for project development and exchange. In follow-up to the Declaration and to the results of a conference attended by 200 business leaders from different parts of Europe, a decision was made to create the European Business Network for Social Cohesion.

The objectives of the network are threefold:

- to inform companies and financial institutions of the dimensions, causes and effects of social exclusion;

- to encourage business contributions in a joint effort to promote social and economic cohesion;

- to make businesses and their activities and requirements in this field more visible to the policy-makers and other social actors.

To achieve these long-term objectives the network is focusing on identifying, analysing and sharing best practice, and developing partnerships with other social actors, companies and institutions which seek to promote social cohesion programmes. It is currently active in eight countries in the European Community.

European Declaration of Business Against Exclusion

The Declaration recommends five areas of action which can be taken by its signatories and other businesses, each of which is backed up by detailed guidelines and examples. The five areas are:

1. Promoting integration on the labour market;

2. Helping to improve vocational training;

3. Avoiding exclusion within the business and minimising redundancies or providing for appropriate measures where they are inevitable;

4. Promoting the creation of new jobs and businesses; and

5. Contributing to social integration in particularly deprived areas and of particularly marginalised groups.

Transparency International (TI)
Building a global coalition against corruption

Corruption is always and everywhere an impediment to business as well as to morality. Corruption wastes resources, discourages investment, cuts productivity, and nurtures enterprises whose success can only be temporary – exactly what a developing country can least afford. Transnationals can – and, I would argue, must – play a central role in transferring sound commercial ethics to the developing countries where they work and trade.

Julius Tahija

Chairman, Caltex Pacific Indonesia

Harvard Business Review,

Sept-October 1993

Corruption, involving public officials in large-scale business transactions, is devastating the lives of tens of millions of people and destabilising dozens of countries. Corruption today is an important cause of poverty and a critical factor in constraining economic growth.

Accountability and Transparency in

International Economic Development

A conference to launch TI in

Germany, May 1993

Transparency International (TI) is a not-for-profit, non-governmental organisation which was launched in May 1993 to counter corruption both in international business transactions and at national levels, through its National Chapters. It offers one of the most encouraging examples in the world of how an NGO can mobilise governments, companies and international agencies to take action on a difficult and sensitive issue. It is also a good example of an NGO which is establishing an international profile and ability to advocate at the international level, whilst at the same time supporting a network of locally focused and locally-led national chapters.

Transparency International's mission is:

- To curb corruption through international and national coalitions encouraging governments to establish and implement effective laws, policies and anti-corruption programmes;
- To strengthen public support and understanding for anti-corruption programmes and enhance public transparency and accountability in international business transactions and in the administration of public procurement;
- To encourage all parties to international business transactions to operate at the highest levels of integrity, guided in particular by TI's Standards of Conduct.

Transparency International's strategy for achieving this vision is threefold: it establishes coalitions of like-minded organisations and individuals to work with governments (wherever possible) to assist in developing and implementing national anti-corruption programmes; it has initiated an information centre and conducts practically-oriented research into ways of containing corruption; it participates in public fora; and uses publicity campaigns to broaden public awareness of the damage caused by corruption, the need to counter it, and the means to reduce it; and it builds National Chapters of TI that foster anti-corruption programmes in their own countries.

The organisation is active on numerous fronts both internationally and nationally through the local chapters which have taken, or are taking root in more than 65 countries. Some of its key initiatives in 1995-1996 include the following:

- The *Islands of Integrity* approach, which aims at progressive elimination of corruption through anti-bribery pacts of all competitors in distinct markets, has attracted the interest of governments in countries such as Jordan, Nepal, South Africa, Argentina, Tanzania and Uganda;
- Publication of a unique *TI Sourcebook on National Integrity Systems*, in August 1996 which offers a potent tool for analysing and strengthening national integrity systems and reducing corruption levels. The book is already being translated into six languages and has a companion volume of over 1,000 pages of documentation of best practice in individual countries;
- The *Corruption Ranking*, which is prepared in association with the University of Gottingen and has attracted extensive international media attention and government responses; and
- a partnership with the World Bank which is operating at the local level, where TI staff have worked with the Bank's Economic Development Institute (EDI) to facilitate the formation of national integrity committees and the staging of workshops and courses on investigative journalism, and at the policy level, through on-going dialogue with the bank's senior management.

South Africa's Business against Crime initiative

The presence of crime and the fear of crime affects the whole of society, on both individual and communal levels. It is an issue that can threaten the stability and development of communities, undermine the authority of the state; and adversely affect the development of the economy and inward investment. Crime also imposes a cost to the individual, in terms of personal injury, increased fear of crime, loss of self-confidence and a lack of faith in society's ability to prevent its members becoming victims.

The rising level of violent crime and commercial, "white-collar" crime and corruption is one of the most serious threats to the stability, prosperity and international reputation of the newly democratic South Africa. The country has one of the highest crime and murder rates in the world and concern about the crime level is one of the main issues raised by trade delegations visiting South Africa. Government ministers and business leaders accept that it is contributing to the fact that foreign capital investment has only increased modestly since the 1994 elections.

In response to this problem, Business South Africa, the umbrella organisation for all the country's chambers of commerce, has launched a *Business Against Crime* programme, which is managed on a nationwide basis by the National Business Initiative (see profile on page 246). The BAC programme is based on the belief that while many individual companies are applying substantial resources to combat and prevent crime and corruption, the collective application and/or co-ordination of these efforts will be more effective and efficient than individual action. It also draws on international experience which clearly demonstrates that effective and sustainable crime prevention is only possible through coherent and integrated strategies supported by all sectors of society. Since its launch last year some of BAC's initial activities have been as follows:

Information management
One of the biggest problems the government faces in tackling crime is the fragmentation of individual departmental efforts and lack of an integrated criminal justice information management system. BAC is therefore utilising international best practice to develop a master plan outlining the architecture of an efficient criminal justice information system and how such a system could streamline and enhance the efforts of the South African Police Service, the courts and other components of the country's justice system.

Commercial crime
The increasing level of this type of crime has high financial and credibility costs for the government, companies and households. BAC aims to help enhance the capacity of official investigation bodies through improved use of available resources and the acquisition of additional resources and training. It also aims to help companies and industry bodies put in place mechanisms that will reduce the opportunities for commercial crime. This will include campaigning for a return to ethical business practices; providing and promoting a model prevention and response plan; and helping to establish industry specific initiatives in areas such as banking, electronics, textiles and retailing.

Highway patrol
Car hijackings have become an increasingly common and violent form of crime – especially in Johannesburg. One of the obstacles that the provincial government has had in combatting this problem has been its lack of equipment – in terms of both vehicles and radio equipment. BAC has worked with BMW, which has one of its largest production plants outside Germany in the region, on a programme to help combat this problem. After extensive consultations on the needs and capabilities of the highway patrol unit, BMW agreed to make available 100 BMW cars which would have both the speed and all the necessary electronic equipment, to maximise the chances of catching hijackers before they reach the country's borders.

Management training at police stations
BAC has also worked with the South African Police Service to identify 100 priority stations throughout the country and then to work with each of these to improve management systems and performance at the local level and to help train all station commanders through university-based modular training courses. The use of information technology has played a key role in this process and ABSA Bank and others have helped to develop and provide information mechanisms to enable the process to occur.

Along with these practical initiatives, BAC is also developing a communications campaign to increase awareness and business support for its efforts. BAC has focused on reviewing international best practice and has organised visits to the UK and the USA to look at public-private crime prevention efforts in these countries. In 1995, working with The Prince of Wales Business Leaders Forum, BAC also held a workshop on crime prevention in which several international experts participated as part of the PWBLF's INSIGHT programme.

Capacity and institution-building for civil society

Since my involvement with the Learning from Experience programme I feel a completely different person. It would never have occurred to me to work with business in my community development role. Now I cannot imagine not working with business in some way or another. Of course it is hard and I have had to learn for myself what works and how to deal with things that don't always work smoothly. But the difference is that now I have the confidence to try!

Judit Solymosi

Association for Community

Development, Hungary

THE SYNERGOS INSTITUTE

Founded in 1986, The Synergos Institute is dedicated to alleviating poverty by bringing together rich and poor to develop collaborative approaches that address the underlying causes and conditions of poverty. Synergos, which means "working together" in Greek, was founded on the belief that the people directly affected by poverty have great resources, energy and local knowledge to contribute to their own solutions and should play a central participatory role in problem-solving. It therefore works through local partner organisations and maintains close ties with voluntary organisations and grassroots communities around the world. At the same time, Synergos interacts regularly with policy makers, donors and business leaders in some 20 countries, encouraging them to get involved. Its main programmes include: on-the-ground partnership efforts in the Chimalapas rainforest of Mexico and Roda Vida in Rio de Janeiro; efforts to develop innovative financing mechanisms and strengthen sources of financing for local voluntary organisations; research and documentation on good practice in business-community partnerships and the role of private foundations; and policy development and public-sector dialogue.

Partnership between different sectors and organisations is the thread which creates the tapestry of formal and informal networks underpinning a healthy and vibrant civil society. Without trust, mutual commitment, regular contact, shared information and joint participation, there is little chance of building the social capital so critical to sustainable development. As many of the case studies in this publication illustrate, partnership between different social actors is a relatively new approach to problem solving; and one in which participants are still finding their way. Most of the companies and NGOs profiled in this publication are large, well-established organisations with the necessary managerial skills and resources to cooperate on a relatively equal basis. If these organisations are still finding their way, the situation is even more challenging for the hundreds of thousands of NGOs and CBOs and small-scale businesses operating at the grassroots level where the skills, resources, mutual awareness and confidence to experiment with new relationships is often lacking. Yet it is at this local level that partnerships need to be forged and civil society needs to be strengthened, if there is to be any hope of alleviating poverty and achieving sustainable development.

The Prince of Wales Business Leaders Forum (PWBLF), the Synergos Institute and PACT (Private Agencies Collaborating Together) are three of a growing number of international NGOs dedicated to building partnership capacity and appropriate institutional structures at the local level. In the case of the PWBLF, its main focus has been on how to bring business into the circle of NGO-CBO and government relationships, and it has developed a partnership methodology which has been tested and adapted to different situations around the world. In this process it has created an International Partnership Network (IPN) consisting of over 1,000 individual partnership practitioners drawn from all sectors and more than 40 countries. Both PACT and Synergos are members of the IPN's partnership advisory group and have collaborated with the PWBLF on specific workshop and research projects. They also run extensive capacity building programmes themselves, which are briefly profiled below.

PACT

Established over 25 years ago, PACT's mission is to contribute to the growth of civil societies around the world by strengthening the community-based non-profit sector as a whole and directly helping to build the capacity of individual NGOs to identify and implement participatory approaches that promote social, economic, political and environmental justice. Working closely with USAID and other donors, it has contributed to strengthening efforts involving more than a thousand local NGOs and literally millions of individuals in over 30 countries. PACT's projects are aimed at: instilling and nurturing leadership and management skills in local NGOs; forging coalitions and strategic alliances between local NGOs and donor agencies, research institutes, foundations and, increasingly, companies; offering expertise on conflict prevention and resolution; training and technical assistance in areas such as project and financial management; and advocacy work and publications.

In 1995, PACT's portfolio comprised 20 projects in 12 countries in Africa, Asia and Latin America. These include projects in Botswana to strengthen institutional support for community development; South Africa to strengthen NGO capacity and support black entrepreneurship; Madagascar to team

LEARNING FROM EXPERIENCE

The Learning from Experience programme was an 18-month capacity and institution-building initiative with 90 people from the business, community and government sectors in Bulgaria, the Czech Republic, Hungary, Latvia, Poland, Russia and Slovakia. The objectives of the programme were: to build the confidence and capacity of key individuals who would be in a position to pioneer partnership approaches in their own sectors and countries; to demonstrate the potential effectiveness of partnership approaches by giving them direct experience of successful projects and programmes; and to create a network of partnership practitioners in the region who would be able to exchange experience and support each other over the longer-term.

The programme was based on the belief that people never really learn from being told, but from seeing, feeling, touching and experiencing. Each of the 90 individuals participated in a study visit to the United Kingdom, consisting of a retreat in Wales for reflection and partnership building, followed by placements with partner organisations in relevant sectors around the country and a two day assessment and feedback session. The initial stage of the programme culminated in a comprehensive evaluation and attitude survey of the participants, collection of case studies on their projects, and a three day workshop and high-profile meeting in Hungary at which they received certification for the capacity building programme. Efforts are now underway to strengthen and expand regional networks established around specific issues, such as environment and education. Some of the British partner organisations which participated in the programme included: The Groundwork Foundation; Business in the Community; British Airways; British Petroleum; United Biscuits; National Westminster Bank; British Telecom; Thames Water; Manchester and Mid-Yorkshire Chambers of Commerce; the Confederation of British Industry; and a number of local government authorities.

The first 43 participants, of the final total of 90, estimate that they have reached 7,400 others back in their local communities – seeding ideas of a partnership approach; and in some cases establishing new partnership activities ranging from local neighbourhood to national initiatives.

international conservation organisations such as WWF, CARE and Conservation International with local NGOs; a women's literacy programme in Nepal; a community outreach project in Cambodia; NGO support in Peru; a programme with street children in Indonesia; and a private rural initiatives project (PRIP) in Bangladesh. PACT has recently launched the Corporate Community Investment Network (CorCom), a programme to analyse, promote and build capacity for stronger linkages between business and the nonprofit sector in advancing their mutual interests in sustainable economic and social development.

The PWBLF's Partnership Programme

The PWBLF's partnership capacity-building programme is targeted at individuals within every sector, who have the potential of playing a catalytic and nurturing role in building cross-sector partnerships in their own communities and countries. The programme is structured around:

- cross-sector workshops which are designed and managed in collaboration with local partner organisations, and are aimed at bringing together, often for the first time, people from business, government and the voluntary sector;

- research, production and dissemination of case studies and practical manuals covering different tools and aspects of partnership-building; and

- INSIGHT activities consisting of local, regional and international study tours and project visits, and short-term internships with organisations actively engaged in partnership initiatives.

Since 1992 the PWBLF, working with local partners, has designed and run nearly 50 partnership capacity-building workshops and events, involving more than 2,500 people from the three main sectors: business (approx. 40%); community (approx. 40%) and government (approx. 20%). By the end of 1996, 38 capacity-building workshops will have been completed in central and eastern Europe (in Bulgaria, the Czech Republic, Hungary, Poland, Russia and Slovakia) and 16 will have taken place in Mexico, Brazil, South Africa, Zimbabwe, India, Bangladesh and Egypt.

The structure and subject matter of each workshop has varied according to local needs and capacities, as have the outcomes. In some cases the outcomes have been at the level of individual action, in others the workshops have resulted in the formation of cross-sector partnerships at both a local city-wide level and at a national level. The Krakow Development Forum, for example, which was profiled on page 190, resulted from one of these workshops, as did a national network of environmental initiatives in Bulgaria. Examples of recent workshops have been a one day seminar in Gyor, Hungary, focused on partnership between the education and business sectors; a workshop on cross-sector approaches to development, focusing on tourism, in Poprad, Slovakia; and a week-long series of activities in Kazimierz, Poland aimed at supporting community-based urban renewal.

As part of the process of building local skills and capacities, the Forum has run train-the-trainer workshops in India and central and eastern Europe. It has also organised regional and international INSIGHT visits for more than 140 partnership practitioners from different sectors and countries to look at partnerships in the USA, Brazil, South Africa, United Kingdom and Egypt, aimed at tackling issues such as urban renewal, community development, education, environmental management and crime prevention. The Learning from Experience Programme described opposite was a combined train-the-trainers and INSIGHT initiative.

The PWBLF Partnership Programme publishes a regular newsletter, *Partnership Action*, and has produced three publications in its Partnership Handbook series, one of which has been translated into 8 languages. Research is currently being undertaken on the role of the intermediary, both individuals and organisations, in the process of cross-sector interaction.

Social Entrepreneurship

Building links between economic, natural, human and social capital

Societies progress or stagnate depending chiefly on whether or not their people see and seize opportunities: the farmer who tries a new seed; the teacher who tries a new text; the merchant who goes after a new market. A dynamic society sees millions of changes each year. The faster a society changes, the greater the need for more adaptation and change. These small changes are triggered by major pattern shifts. The railroad and the personal computer redefined their fields, launching cascading waves of follow-on adjustments and improvements. This is just as true in the social arena. Florence Nightingale redefined her field every bit as much as Andrew Carnegie did his. Whether or not a society generates a vigorous flow of these critical major innovations depends on its entrepreneurs. Their central importance to the economy has long been understood. However, no language even has a word that describes the public entrepreneur. Nor is society organised to support and reward them. That is a tremendously expensive mistake.

William Drayton

Founder of Ashoka

All over the world there is growing recognition of the need to radically change the way society perceives, defines and encourages entrepreneurship. In particular, there is growing recognition that entrepreneurship applies not only to making financial profits, but also to creating social change. There is also growing recognition that the personal characteristics which define business entrepreneurs also define millions of individuals working in their communities to tackle the challenges of education and training, human rights, health, culture and heritage, disability, discrimination, legal injustice, environmental sustainability, women's issues, appropriate technology and community development. These personal characteristics include: a driving vision and sense of mission; the readiness to take risks; the ability to recognise and seize opportunities and to develop under-utilised resources; and the capacity to innovate and motivate.

Whether we call these people social entrepreneurs, public entrepreneurs, or community entrepreneurs, there can be no doubt that together with their profit-driven counterparts in the private sector, these individuals have a crucial role to play in the achievement of sustainable development, especially in a world where governance and responsibility is increasingly shared between the public, private and voluntary sectors.

In many countries, however, there is still insufficient support even for business entrepreneurs – especially those in the informal sector which accounts for such a large percentage of wealth and employment creation in most developing countries – let alone support for and recognition of social entrepreneurs. There is an urgent need to change this situation. There is also a need to break down the perceptual barriers which suggest that profit-driven entrepreneurs have no social conscience and socially-driven entrepreneurs have no business sense. This is often not the case and there is a great deal that both can learn from each other, and much that they can share with public officials in government, who also need to be increasingly entrepreneurial in the way they carry out their work. To many people the concept 'social entrepreneurship' may sound like an oxymoron, but the experience of millions of private sector business leaders and voluntary sector community leaders from all over the world demonstrates that this is no longer the case – if it ever was.

It is not too far-fetched to suggest that the promotion of greater levels of entrepreneurship in society, and the support of individual entrepreneurs who are socially responsible and economically literate, are two of the most critical challenges facing governments, educators, business leaders and other decision-makers in today's world. This is the case regardless of whether the country is Germany or Ghana; or the city is Birmingham or Bangkok. Obviously entrepreneurship is not something that can achieved with "top-down" approaches. But it can be encouraged and enhanced by creating an enabling environment of appropriate incentive structures, experiential learning, greater societal recognition, and support systems and networks. Despite the growing evidence of both the existence and the critical importance of social entrepreneurship, it is a field which requires much greater understanding, research and analysis. The recent decision by Harvard Business School to establish a 'Social Enterprise Initiative', profiled on page 92, is an encouraging move in this direction.

ASHOKA'S FELLOWS

Ashoka's 700 Fellows are engaged in a diverse and rich variety of activities in some 30 countries ranging from: literacy and learning, to housing and health; from efforts to reform unjust legal systems, to efforts to reform unsustainable patterns of economic growth; from rainforests to cities; and from local level initiatives to influencing national change. Gloria de Souza, a 1982 Ashoka Fellow, has developed a system of teaching which is now officially mandated for the Indian primary school system, affecting the lives of millions of schoolchildren. Antonio Paz, organised thousands of residents to rebuild their homes after the 1985 Mexican earthquake. Mary Allegretti in Brazil has so far saved more than seven million hectares of rainforest through her idea of developing extractive reserves, and working with local communities and rubber tappers to achieve it. She is now working in state government continuing her enlightened policies. Nelson Agyemang is running youth rehabilitation and empowerment activities in Ghana. In South Africa, Gcina Mhlophe has launched a storytelling programme to preserve traditional cultures and spur education. And in Thailand, Thongbai Thongpao is providing legal assistance to tackle human rights issues, seeking especially to ensure children's rights and freedom of the press. Just a few of the hundreds of visionaries supported by the Ashoka programme.

ASHOKA
Mobilising venture capital for society's changemakers

Ashoka is a pioneering global initiative, which has particular relevance for developing and transition economies. Established in 1981, Ashoka is an international development NGO which can claim to be one of the world's first non-profit venture capital groups. Simply stated, it provides both seed money and recognition to outstanding social entrepreneurs throughout Asia, Africa, Latin America and Central and Eastern Europe, to give them time and encouragement to develop and root their ideas. Ashoka's investment in these social entrepreneurs – called Ashoka Fellows – is very similar in approach to venture capital for the profit-oriented entrepreneur:

- It is invested in an innovator with a new idea, and who has the drive and vision to make it succeed; and

- Ashoka's support is given at that crucial point between the launch of an idea and its proven success.

Ashoka not only provides individuals with seed funding, but also enables them to become part of national, international and issue-based networks with fellow entrepreneurs. Apart from lack of financial support, the loneliness of being a social changemaker is another major obstacle to success. For a woman trying to improve the opportunities for street children in Rio de Janeiro, the ability to share her hopes and frustrations with a fellow Brazilian working on youth issues, or with someone from Bangkok also working with street children, can help to overcome this problem of isolation. Ashoka also helps to raise the profile of these social entrepreneurs, often at a national level, which makes it easier for them to raise funds and support in their own countries and communities.

The leverage potential of an initiative like this – which invests in outstanding individuals who have the potential to create societal change – is enormous. For an average annual cost of US$3,000 in India, US$12,000 in Brazil and US$3,000 in Indonesia, for example, Ashoka Fellows in these countries have a better chance of developing their ideas and in some cases affecting the lives of thousands and even millions of people. Approximately a quarter of Ashoka's Fellows are already influencing national-level change in their fields. Many others have left their mark at the state level – and in a country like India that can mean impacting as many as 160 million people. Even those that remain operating at the level of their local community will usually impact the lives of several hundred people.

To date Ashoka has been funded mainly by private sector, philanthropic donations from individuals, companies and foundations. However it is now developing innovative mechanisms to work more strategically with the private sector. An initiative which illustrates this approach is the Entrepreneur-to-Entrepreneur (E2) programme which pairs social entrepreneurs with their commercial counterparts, and is currently being developed in 15 Latin American countries. Multinational companies with interests in specific geographic areas or issues such as education and health, can also develop relationships with individual entrepreneurs or networks of entrepreneurs who are working in these geographies or issues, and provide not only financial support, but also managerial and technical advice, in return for access to carefully selected community leaders and their projects. A major insurance company in South Africa, for example, is currently working on such an approach with Ashoka South Africa.

THE LITTLE LIBRARY PROJECT IN SOUTH AFRICA

This is an early childhood development programme which designs and produces children's books aimed at educating young South Africans about their country's rich ethnic, cultural and religious diversity. Initially established as a project of the READ educational trust, which is supported by a wide range of companies, the Little Library has become an independent not-for-profit company, with financial and managerial support from the Liberty Life Foundation. It works with community-based creative teams, which are mixed in terms of age, race, sex, language, culture and background, to develop and test children's books. After piloting in local schools, the best stories are translated into the country's nine languages and distributed nationwide with laminated posters, audio-tapes, puppet templates and teaching guides.

Celebrating cultural diversity

The ability of people to respect and celebrate cultural and racial diversity is deeply embedded in the concept of social cohesion. The social instability that stems from cultural or racial intolerance not only results in fractured communities, civil strife and human tragedy, but also undermines economic competitiveness in an increasingly global and multicultural world economy. Despite great strides that have been taken in many countries to remove racial discrimination and to increase multicultural understanding, there is much that remains to be tackled. It is an area in which government has a critical facilitating role to play, but in which the voluntary and private sector also need to take a lead.

Timberland's Anti-Racism Campaign

In 1992, the US-based footwear company Timberland initiated a series of advertisements in the German media to address the wave of racial intolerance and hatred that was sweeping the country. Its Stamp Out Hatred campaign was an interesting example of social marketing which targeted and mobilised not only opinion leaders, but also reached out to groups such as skinheads who were both buyers of the company's boots and key instigators of racially motivated strife. The campaign encouraged other German companies to tackle the issue of racism through the marketplace and media. Timberland subsequently ran versions of this advertisement in other countries, including the USA, France and England. In the USA its advertisement ran with the headline Give Racism the Boot and encouraged people to get involved with City Year, a Boston-based urban youth corps, which brings together young people from different backgrounds and ethnic groups to work in the community.

The St Petersburg Museums Programme in Russia

The preservation of Russia's artistic and cultural heritage is important not just as an end in itself but also for the impact it has as a tool for tourism, employment, urban regeneration and social stability in the country. For the past three years, The Prince of Wales Business Leaders Forum has been working with a group of museums in St Petersburg and a coalition of private sector partners, to help build capacity in the culture and heritage sector. To date the programme has mobilised over US$1 million for partnership capacity-building and other projects from donor agencies such as the British Know-How Fund, foundations such as the Soros Foundation and individual companies. Issues being tackled include:

- Advocacy;
- Finance;
- Marketing;
- Customer care; and
- Business and community participation and partnership building.

Investing in the arts and cultural heritage

There is also a need for different sectors to work together in preserving, sharing and enriching the arts and cultural heritage that helps to shape societal values and norms; and at the same time serves as a spur to future creativity and innovation. In his book, *The End of History*, Francis Fukuyama describes "a very sad time" when "economic calculation, technological problems, environmental concerns and the satisfaction of sophisticated consumer demands" will replace art and philosophy and "the worldwide ideological struggle that called for daring, courage, imagination and idealism." A society without arts, philosophy and idealism will not only be spiritually poorer, but ultimately economically poorer. As governments the world over struggle to fund arts and heritage budgets, the private and voluntary sectors again have an increasingly important role to play - not only in funding, but in developing other partnerships which support the arts and increase their access to as wide a group of people as possible

The Association for Business Sponsorship of the Arts in the UK

This 20-year old organisation encourages business to support live culture and organises relevant training programmes which aim to bring artists into the workplace. Faced with declining corporate sponsorship budgets for the arts, ABSA is emphasising the need for new models of business-NGO partnership. An area of growing interest in today's highly competitive and knowledge-based economy, is the potential role that the arts can play in unlocking creativity for businesses. For example, ABSA has worked with the management consultants, McKinsey and Co. on developing creativity classes for its staff; and with the retailing chain Marks & Spencer on an 'Arts at Work' programme, which brings innovative combinations of arts and science practitioners into the workplace.

Funding civil society organisations and community-based initiatives

The importance of mobilising the financial markets for environmental sustainability has already been briefly reviewed. Access to finance is also crucial to the establishment and strengthening of civil society initiatives. Mobilising sustainable and appropriate sources of funding to: a) capitalise and fund the operations of non-profit, non-governmental (NGO) and community-based (CBO) organisations, and b) project finance specific community projects which are unlikely to generate commercial, market-rates of return, is one of the greatest challenges faced by many civil society organisations. Those that have traditionally been supported by government grants and funds from donor agencies are facing the consequences of declining public sector budgets and are having to develop new, innovative ways of raising funds.

The business sector is an obvious source of such funds, but here as well budgets are limited, and increasingly companies are looking for mutual benefit rather than one-way charitable hand-outs to civil society organisations. For certain NGOs and CBOs there is also the issue of reconciling their campaigning activities, which are sometimes targeted against big business and the private sector, with their need for core and/or project funding from the private sector. Whilst some companies may be acceptable sources of finance, others are not. Equally, more and more civil society organisations are conscious of the need to search for local, rather than external funding sources, which have a greater chance of being more sustainable over the longer-term. Linked to this is the challenge of balancing grants, with other types of funds which can be recycled (i.e. loans) and/or earned on an on-going basis (i.e. community payment for services and products).

In short, NGOs and CBOs are having to become more financially sophisticated and innovative than ever before. Whilst money is only part of the equation in mobilising resources and partnerships for civil society activities, it is an important part. Companies can play a vital role in sharing their own financial management expertise with NGOs and CBOs and in helping them to access and leverage private sector funding and create new types of funding sources and mechanisms. In recent years some of the mechanisms which have started to gain increased attention are as follows:

- **Community development banks** – which may be established specifically as community banks (such as Shorebank in Chicago, an outstanding model of community banking which has been adapted elsewhere in the USA and in countries such as Poland and South Africa); or established as subsidiaries of existing commercial banks (such as BankBoston's First Community Bank created in 1989 as a "bank within a bank" with the goal of reaching out to the minority, low-income communities of Boston). The USA has been a leader in this field, in large part as a result of the Community Reinvestment Act which requires US banks to reinvest in low-income communities.

- **Community development funds** – which may be loan funds or venture capital funds and operated on a for-profit or not-for-profit basis. A growing number of examples of these exist, capitalised either by individual companies, or groups of companies, or a combination of public-private finance;

- **Microfinance intermediaries (MFIs)** – aimed specifically at funding micro-enterprise activities and which can have the same range of characteristics as community development funds. A growing number of inspiring examples exist in this field, from the well-known Grameen Bank in Bangladesh to BancoSol in Bolivia. Equally important, is the increased activity in this field on the part of organisations such as Citicorp, through its Banking on Enterprise initiative profiled on page 119 the World Bank, through its CGAP programme profiled on page 232, and UNDP through the recent launch of its MicroStart initiative, which will support MFIs in up to 25 developing countries, with funding and technical assistance.

- **Social funds** – which are often created on a nationwide or sectoral basis with government and donor agency backing, and with the goal of supporting development in the social sectors and poverty alleviation. This type of fund has grown rapidly in developing countries since the 1987 launch of the Bolivia Emergency Social Fund to mitigate against the social costs of structural adjustment.

- **Community cooperatives and credit unions** – these have played a longstanding role in community financing and can provide useful vehicles for other funding activities.

- **Debt-swaps** – which have gained attention especially in the field of debt-for-nature swaps, but are also being used as funding mechanisms for other activities, such as the International Youth Foundation's debt swap with JP Morgan profiled on page 229.

- **Ethical investment and banking organisations** – again these have been active mainly in the environmental field aiming to achieve positive financial returns through investing in environmentally sound activities, However a number are looking at investing in projects in the wider social sphere, including in community enterprise. They include examples such as the NPI Global Care Fund profiled on page 167, the Calvert Fund in the USA, and the Co-operative Bank and Triodos Bank in Europe.

Apart from the examples elsewhere in the publication, one of the most interesting cases of an individual company establishing its own venture capital fund for social and environmental projects is provided by Ciba, the Swiss pharmaceutical corporation. This initiative is described on the following pages.

CIBA'S Risk Fund
Linking social good and commercial potential

•••

We aim not only at the highest possible efficiency and effectiveness through our work – and a candid accounting of it – we also wish to make a contribution to upgrading the quality of development cooperation. Keeping in mind that public and private resources for development cooperation are more likely to shrink than expand, we believe this to be the most important aspect of our work.

Dr. Rudolf Schneiter
President, Ciba Foundation

Ciba, the Swiss pharmaceutical company which has recently merged with Sandoz, has operations in developing countries around the globe. Two of the main vehicles it has developed to support its social responsibility activities in developing countries are the Ciba-Geigy Foundation and the Ciba Risk Fund. The foundation, established in 1979 and fully endowed by the company, like many other major corporate foundations was established to consolidate and reinforce the company's contributions in the field of humanitarian assistance, made independently of business activities.

The Risk Fund, on the other hand, is one of the most innovative and unique approaches to corporate social investment in the world and offers enormous potential for replication and scaling-up.

The Risk Fund was established in 1988 as one of Ciba's instruments to put into practice what the company committed itself to in its Vision 2000: 'to strike a balance between our economic, social and environmental responsbilities."

Endowed with an annual budget of SFr. 5 – 10 million, the fund is intended to encourage the company's business units in developing countries to take up innovative projects with novel commercial aspects and social or environmental benefits, even if they entail long start-up periods, high pre-investments and costly project supervision and servicing.

The company requires applications for Risk Fund projects to meet the following criteria:

- The projects must have the potential of being profitable in the long-term and must solve specific problems in developing countries.

- The projects must not replace regular business activities. The fund will not support projects that could be financed by the divisions as part of normal business.

- The applicant division must participate in the costs or investments involved; and after the start-up phase (five years at most) the project must be self-supporting.

Some twelve projects have been started since the Risk Fund was launched . Of these six have been successfully completed and two have been withdrawn or discontinued as unfeasible. The company is almost unique in publicly reporting on one of the projects that failed – a project to encourage export promotion of SenegaleseTextiles – in its 1996/97 corporate responsibility report. This sends a strong message not only about its willingness to be transparent and to learn from failures as well as successes, but also its willingness to share these lessons with others.

Two of the main projects which have been supported by the Risk Fund are a multi-country project to improve the safety and effectiveness of plant protection agents in developing countries; and another multi-country project in social marketing for epilepsy. These are briefly described opposite.

BASIC PRINCIPLES FOR CIBA'S ACTIVITIES IN DEVELOPING COUNTRIES

Ciba has set forth its own principles in its policy for business activities in developing countries

1) Ciba acts in partnership with developing countries to advance their economic potential in the interest of both partners. It fully observes the rights and duties arising out of such a partnership.

2) In making business decisions (for example about products, services, technologies, and investments), Ciba considers the impact on the development of the host country in addition to economic criteria. Ciba is prepared to take a long-term view of profit in developing countries.

3) If a developing country adopts measures to protect its economy (for example, import restrictions, export obligations, or conditions for ownership) Ciba cooperates as long as partnership and adequate returns are not jeopardised in the long-term.

4) Ciba considers it a duty to advise its partners against undertakings of doubtful benefit (for example prestige projects) even if such a move proves detrimental to our economic interest.

5) Ciba has progressive social and personnel policies in developing countries, adapted to local conditions. In particular, Ciba trains employees locally if possible, and abroad if necessary; allows capable staff to gain international experience in the company; and considers nationals for executive positions.

6) The quality of Ciba's products is the same in all countries.

7) In environmental protection and safety, Ciba pursues the same objectives in all countries. Through the transfer of technology, Ciba helps to make chemicals more environmentally sound and safer.

8) Information and advice are based on the same scientific knowledge in all countries. Ciba thus pursues safe and proper use of its products.

9) The prices of Ciba products are determined by the particular national market and competitive conditions.

Improving safety and effectiveness of plant protection products

There has been much controversy about the use of chemical plant protection agents in developing countries. This relates to: their safety and proper use in prevailing conditions of illiteracy and poor information; the environmental and health costs of improper usage; and the aggressive marketing tactics of the multinational chemical companies. Ciba's Risk Fund project was launched to clarify the following questions:

1. What factors hinder the safe and effective use of these products?

2. What can the manufacturer do, in collaboration with other institutions and extension services, to eliminate these factors?

3. In a given sociocultural context, what communication methods are suited to furthering rational and safe use of these products?

4. What is the objective cost/benefit ratio of a rational, safe and effective use of these products?

Launched in 1991 in Zimbabwe, Mexico and India, with a budget of SFr 4 million borne by the Risk Fund and additional resources contributed by the Plant Protection Division in Basel and collaborating Group companies, the initiative has had several stages. The first was a KAP Study – researching knowledge, attitudes and practices – in selected "intervention regions" in each of the three pilot countries. Initial findings from this were then used to develop information and education programmes, followed by further KAP studies to assess their impact. The project will conclude in 1997 with an independent evaluation and publication of the results.

The social marketing programme for epilepsy (SMPE)

This initiative was launched in 1990, with the aim of: reducing the treatment gap in epilepsy; improving clinical management of the problem; dispelling misconceptions about the condition; and developing the anti-epileptic drug market and increasing or maintaining market share.

The programme was launched in 1990/91 in four pilot countries: Indonesia, Egypt, Ecuador and Kenya, and has had encouraging results in a number of ways. In Indonesia, for example, about a third of all doctors attended SMPE events between 1990 and 1993; in Egypt the number of people treated for epilepsy increased from 170,000 in 1989 to more than 300,000 at present; and in Ecuador 20,000 teachers were advised how to help children with epilepsy, with the result that today some 73% of teachers are willing to accept a child suffering from epilepsy in their classes compared to only 55% in 1990. These positive social benefits were matched, at least in Indonesia and Egypt, to a substantial increase in sales of anti-epileptic products, including the company's brand. The success of the pilot programmes has encouraged the company to introduce SMPE in South Africa, Mexico and the Philippines.

2.6 Integrated Community Development

When properly designed, community based programmes can be highly effective in managing natural resources, providing basic infrastructure or ensuring primary social services. Participation in community based development (CBD) depends on reversing control and accountability from central authorities to community organisations. Successful design requires tapping into local needs, understanding and building on the strengths of existing institutions, and defined the changes needed in intermediary implementing agencies to support community action.

Designing Community Based Development
World Bank Dissemination Notes, 1995

Local Economic Development (LED) is about local people deciding to take charge of the economic and employment future of their community. It is about seeking consensus around development issues at the local level. It is a process of identifying and harnessing community energy, resources and opportunities to stimulate sustainable economic and employment activity.

Taking the LEAD,
The National Business Initiative of
South Africa, 1996

Over the past ten years, the single greatest shift in the thinking and practice of development projects has been the recognition that development is about people living at the local level, and not about externally imposed plans developed at the macro level. The latter are merely tools. If they are not designed in an integrated manner and in genuine consultation with the people most directly affected by them, they have little chance of creating sustainable benefits after their initial implementation. Three fundamental principles lie at the heart of a more people-centred, community-based approach to development – be it in developing, transition or OECD economies. These principles are: community participation; integrated, local solutions; and partnership.

COMMUNITY PARTICIPATION

Participatory approaches to development reflect the belief that local empowerment and self-help are the most effective ways of finding and sustaining solutions to rural and urban development challenges. Such approaches have been pioneered and practised for many years, especially by community workers and non-governmental organisations, such as PACT and the Synergos Institute profiled on page 174. What is new is the growing efforts to mainstream this approach into the operations of government departments, the major bilateral and multilateral development agencies and corporate activities. The World Bank's recently produced *Participation Sourcebook*, which is profiled opposite, offers an example of how one major development agency is attempting to achieve this. The evolving approach of companies to their community investment activities, outlined on pages 65 to 67, also reflects a fundamental shift from paternalistic philanthropy to more participative partnership.

INTEGRATED, LOCAL SOLUTIONS

As already discussed, this theme lies at the heart of sustainable development. It recognises the need to tackle development in a more holistic way; taking local economic, social, political, cultural and environmental conditions into account, and searching for solutions that address the linkages between these local conditions. For example, drugs education and prevention programmes will have minimal effect unless simultaneous efforts are made to address the underlying causes of poverty; family breakdown, unemployment, low educational attainment, lack of community role models and social marginalisation. Likewise, projects to conserve wildlife and natural habitats in parts of Africa, Asia and Latin America are doomed to failure unless they can be made economically viable and the economic benefits shared with the communities living in or close to these habitats.

Today, this approach is treated as "common sense" by most people working in development projects, especially at the local level. Yet it was less than ten years ago when the logic and effectiveness of such an approach was less obvious to project managers and policy-makers. Even today, most

> The *Participatory Sourcebook* presents the new direction the World Bank is taking in its support of participation, by recognising that there is a diversity of stakeholders for every activity we undertake, and that those people affected by development interventions must be included in the decision-making process
>
> James D. Wolfensohn
> President, The World Bank

departments of national government are still organised along sectoral divisions: education, labour, health, housing and urban development etc. with insufficient linkages between them. This often leaves local authorities, companies and community-based organisations struggling to piece together different government policies and funding programmes, in order to achieve a more integrated approach to development at the local level. The US Government's Empowerment Zone and Enterprise Communities initiative, described on page 186, offers a good example of a national initiative aimed at overcoming this challenge and supporting more integrated local initiatives.

PARTNERSHIP

As has been emphasised throughout this publication, integrated community development requires an increased emphasis on the role of cross-sector partnerships between the public and private sector, between local and national government, and between corporations and the communities in which they operate.

THE WORLD BANK PARTICIPATORY SOURCE BOOK

Published in early 1996, the **World Bank Participatory Sourcebook** was prepared with support from the Bank's vice presidencies for Environmentally Sustainable Development and Human Capital Development and Operations Policy. The preparation process involved discussions and consultations with over 200 Bank staff and consultants, production of 18 working papers covering a range of sector-specific and cross-cutting themes, and feedback from several hundred reviewers both inside and outside the Bank. Aimed at bank staff and other professionals in the development field, its goal is to share concepts, case studies, experiences, guidelines and tools, on how to implement more participatory approaches in economic and social development.

The sourcebook defines participation as: "a process through which stakeholders influence and share control over development initiatives and the decisions and resources which affect them". It describes the Bank's traditional

approach to projects as the "external expert stance" in which project sponsors and designers placed themselves outside the local system they were focusing on and viewed other stakeholders only as sources of information and opinions, rather than partners in project design and implementation. In contrast, the "participatory stance" requires an approach founded not only on listening and consultation, but also on social learning and invention; one that involves stakeholders from the beginning and views them, rather than the external experts, as the starting point for project planning and decision-making. Drawing on 16 case studies from around the world, the sourcebook provides detailed examples of the successes and challenges of participatory development. It draws out lessons of successful community organisations and sets out a series of "practice pointers" on how to achieve participatory planning and decision-making, and how to enable the poor to participate.

One of the key messages of the sourcebook is the importance of local capacity building in the process of community-based development. It

argues that: "getting the participation of the poor involves a lot more than finding the right technique. It requires strengthening the organisational and financial capacities of the poor, so that they can act for themselves. In searching for ways to build local capacity, we found it useful to think in terms of a continuum along which the poor are progressively empowered." This continuum is illustrated below.

The sourcebook concludes with a summary of participatory methods and tools, including:

- Workshop-based methods for collaborative decision-making;

- Community-based methods for collaborative decision-making, such as participatory rural appraisal (PRA);

- Methods for stakeholder consultation, such as beneficiary assessment and systematic client consultation; and

- Methods for social analysis, such as social assessment and gender analysis.

Poor viewed as beneficiaries-recipients of services, resources and development interventions.	**Poor viewed as clients capable of demanding goods and services from govts. and private agencies**	**Poor viewed as owners and managers of their assets and activities**
Support in the form of community organising, training and one-way flow of resources through grant mechanisms	**Move from welfare-orientated approaches to building sustainable, market-based financial systems; decentralising authority and resources; and strengthening local institutions**	**High level of intensity in participation**

WHAT ROLE FOR THE PRIVATE SECTOR IN INTEGRATED COMMUNITY DEVELOPMENT?

Firstly, and most importantly, through core business activities. For example, through decisions on location and investment; through the responsible production of goods and services which minimise negative environmental and social impacts on local communities and widen economic opportunities; through procurement and purchasing policies targeted at building relationships with local producers and suppliers; through innovative financing techniques; and through employment and training programmes.

Secondly, through social investment – not just giving philanthropic grants to local charities, but also through sharing managerial and technical expertise with local government, local NGOs and community entrepreneurs, for example by offering training and advisory programmes; running employee volunteering schemes; undertaking social marketing initiatives; engaging in business-education partnerships; supporting community development trusts and venture capital funds; encouraging business associations to get more involved with community-based problem-solving; supporting universities and academic institutions to undertake appropriate research and training programmes; and where necessary helping to establish business partnerships for community-level action, such as The Atlanta Project, Cleveland Tomorrow, Bombay First, The Central Johannesburg Partnership and many others around the world.

Thirdly, business can also play a valuable role in contributing to the policy debate on rural and urban development, either directly as individual companies, or even more effectively, as groups of companies working through business associations or partnerships such as those described above. They can encourage local and national governments to streamline funding support for urban and rural local communities, to undertake a more holistic approach to local development, to develop creative tax incentives and so on.

(i) INTEGRATED URBAN DEVELOPMENT

Through the ages, our cities have reflected both the best and the worst of the human condition. At their best they have served as crucibles for many of the greatest social, political, architectural, artistic, scientific and technological advances in human history. At the same time they have often been repositories of poverty and disease, crime and environmental decay. The scale and intensity of these positive and negative impacts of urban life are accelerating dramatically as we approach the 21st century. Cities in both developed and developing countries are undergoing fundamental demographic changes and, by the turn of the century, over the half the world's population will be urban dwellers. Our ability to understand these changes, and to manage their socio-economic and environmental impacts, will play a key role in determining the long-term prosperity and sustainability of our diverse, yet interdependent societies.

The 1996 HABITAT II Conference, or City Summit, in Istanbul marked the culmination of a series of seven UN Conferences held since 1990 to draw up a common agenda of action for a more safe, healthy, just and sustainable world. It was fitting that the focus of this last summit was urban living and the future of our cities. It was also fitting that the summit focused on solutions as well as problems, and that following the precedent set at the Rio Earth Summit, it was attended by a rich diversity of people from different cultures and sectors. Two of the major fora held alongside the official summit were the World Assembly of Cities, attended by more than 500 Mayors and representatives of local authorities, and the World Business Forum, attended by some 400 business people and business students. The issues discussed by both of these fora and reflected in many other meetings and in the official summit, reflected a strong consensus on both the problems and solutions facing the world's urban centres and confirmed the growing level of global and cross-sectoral co-operation that has emerged since UNCED.

In a survey of mayors from 135 cities in OECD, developing and transition economies, carried out by UNDP a few years before the City Summit, the following urban problems were rated as the "most severe": unemployment; inadequate housing; garbage disposal; crime; poverty; poor sanitation and sewerage; air pollution; transportation; inadequate access to clean water; inadequate social services; civil apathy; and discrimination.

These problems call for a set of inter-related policies, programmes and projects. In the World Bank's publication *Liveable Cities for the 21st Century*, produced for HABITAT II, it focuses on three main priorities for action:

1   Bringing basic services to the slums, such as clean water, sanitation, basic roadways and footpaths and drainage, the lack of which has severe impacts on human health and economic productivity;

2   A healthier urban environment, by making investments to reduce emissions of dust, soot, and smoke from industry and power plants, cut lead in gasoline, and control microbial diseases, which are the three main environmental problems affecting human health; and

3   Finance for people in cities, by improving the efficiency, effectiveness and transparency of urban financing; developing public-private partnerships for financing urban infrastructure; strengthening the role and managerial capacities of local government; and ensuring that finances and the services that they fund are accessible to local communities and people.

The private sector can play an important role in all three of these areas.

The following profiles look at a range of city-wide partnerships rather than the activities of individual companies, although thousands of individual companies are making business and social investments which promote sustainable urban development. The first part highlights some of the developments in urban partnerships in the USA, which have applicability in other countries and are being supported by national and local governments, business and NGOs. It then profiles Groundwork, a nationwide urban partnership initiative in the United Kingdom aimed at linking community participation, economic development and environmental sustainability. This is followed by brief profiles on FORECOM in Rio de Janeiro, The Central Johannesburg Partnership, the Krakow Development Forum, Bombay First, The St Petersburg Partnership Initiative, and the work of Environmental Quality International, an innovative for-profit company supporting community development in Cairo, before closing on the challenge of replication and a profile on the global MegaCities Project. There are many other outstanding public-private urban partnerships around the world in cities such as Manchester in the United Kingdom, Curitiba in Brazil, Seattle in the USA, and Ahmedabad in India to name just a few, which are not profiled here. Details on these and others can be obtained from the HABITAT "Best Practices" project which was prepared for the Istanbul City Summit.

By the end of the 20th century, a permanent and far-reaching demographic shift will have taken place, fundamentally changing the world's social and economic landscape. For the first time in history about half the world's population will be living in urban areas – ranging from towns to mega-cities with populations of over 10 million people.

The fate of urban areas could go either way: they could become human and environmental disaster areas, or they could become centres of global creativity, prosperity and growth of the human spirit. In many ways, how we approach urban development is central to the broader challenge of development, because cities concentrate all problems and all opportunities. Working in partnership, I am convinced that we can ensure that cities of the 21st century become arenas of opportunity and hope for mankind.

James D. Wolfensohn,
President, The World Bank
UNEP's Planet Magazine, June 199

The Local Initiatives Support Corporation (LISC)

LISC is the country's largest nationwide, community development intermediary. It plays a vital role, and offers a useful model, as a link between corporations, public funding agencies and community projects, mobilising and leveraging both funds and managerial and technical expertise. Created in 1979 by the Ford Foundation and a group of six companies, LISC has focused its attentions on physical redevelopment, especially housing, in inner cities. In recent years it has diversified its activities with the launch of initiatives such as: the *National Equity Fund*, established in 1987 as a vehicle to pass federal low-income housing tax credits through to corporate investors and which has become one of the nation's largest non-profit syndicators of low-income housing; the *Retail Initiative*, which is aimed at facilitating supermarket investment and the creation of neighbourhood retailing centres in inner city areas, thereby creating local jobs, enhancing physical improvements and making goods and services more accessible to local residents; and the *Community-Building Initiative*, which is a nationwide campaign aimed at raising awareness about community development initiatives and encouraging both corporations and private foundations to make such initiatives a core part of their own business activities and/or social investment and philanthropic programmes.

One of the core features of all LISC's activities is the involvement of the private sector. Participation and commitment from business must be an element of any community development project in which LISC gets involved. It assesses a particular project and then helps the companies involved to contribute what adds the most value, both to the project and to the company. This could be financing, business and technical advice, or influence and contacts. Two of the key benefits of the LISC approach are its ability to give a "stamp of assurance" to companies on specific projects which they may be interested in but do not have the time or expertise to assess themselves and its ability to pool corporate funding. This enables it not only to mobilise funds which may not be forthcoming otherwise, but also to leverage these funds.

Public-private urban partnerships in the USA

The growing levels of poverty, homelessness, crime, unemployment, drugs, despair, marginalisation and alienation in America's inner cities are well-known. In the past five years increasing attention has been paid to the role of the private sector and market forces in tackling these problems, as opposed to heavy social investment programmes controlled by government. There is now growing consensus throughout the country that the role of national government is to provide a facilitative framework in which local governments, community organisations and business can develop partnerships to find appropriate solutions at the local level.

This new way of thinking is reflected in a number of nationwide and city-level initiatives, including the following:

- The Empowerment Zone and Enterprise Communities (EZ/EC) initiative is a key element of President Clinton's job creation strategy for America. At its core is the combination of tax incentives for business development, with a comprehensive and integrated approach to community revitalisation through performance-oriented block grants. What sets it aside from previous urban revitalisation efforts is that the community drives the decision-making. Residents decide what happens in their neighbourhoods, not federal officials in Washington. It is also performance driven – each EZ/EC community has written "benchmarks" or quantifiable goals that determine how the money will be spent and what the results of the activity will be. The programme has been structured as a ten year initiative, but aimed at achieving "early-wins" – visible changes in neighbourhoods in the form of business start-ups, commercial and housing development and improved services. The programme provides tax incentives and performance grants or loans to create jobs and business opportunities in the most economically-distressed areas of inner cities. It also focuses on activities to support people looking for work, such as job training, child care and transportation. In December 1994, President Clinton and Vice President Gore designated 72 urban areas and 33 rural communities as Empowerment Zones or Enterprise Communities. They are receiving more than US$1.5 billion in performance grants and more than US$2.5 billion in tax incentives. One of the overriding objectives is to use this funding to leverage private sector financing and engagement, and already private sector investments amount to about US$1.5 billion, with a further US$1.2 billion committed. The urban Empowerment Zones are: Atlanta, Baltimore, Chicago, New York, Detroit, Philadelphia/Camden, Cleveland, Los Angeles. Boston, Houston, Kansas City and Oakland have been designated as enhanced Enterprise Communities.

- Many cities have also established their own public-private and corporate-community partnerships over the past five to ten years. Some of the best known are: The Atlanta Project, which is profiled opposite; the New York City Partnership, which was spearheaded by David Rockefeller; Cleveland Tomorrow, which has received support from the CEOs of major companies such as Joseph Gorman of TRW; and Rebuild LA, which was established after the LA Riots of 1992. Many cities are also establishing neighbourhood Business Improvement Districts, where local companies and communities have joined forces to tackle crime, environmental degradation, and joblessness. New York now has almost 40 BIDs and the idea is gaining popularity in other cities.

> If TAP creates anything, it is conversations and institutional partnerships between corporations and communities, between universities and neighbourhood volunteers, between city, state and federal agencies, between rival non-profit intermediaries, between the military and schools, businesses and governments, churches and health centres, synagogues and mosques, banks and public housing projects.

THE ATLANTA PROJECT (TAP)

The mission of The Atlanta Project (TAP) – an initiative of The Carter Center, established by former US President Jimmy Carter – is to unite Atlanta as a community to work together to improve the quality of life in its neighbour-hoods. It seeks to empower citizens to develop solutions to the problems they identify in their neighbourhoods, and to foster collaboration among government agencies, business, other service providers and people who want to help.

TAP links neighbourhoods, The Carter Center and volunteers in a partnership for progress. Twenty neighbourhoods, called "clusters", form the target area for TAP initiatives. To encourage community problem-solving, each cluster was identified as an area surrounding one high school, and includes the elementary and middle schools that feed into it. A high proportion of people in the cluster neighbourhoods are on welfare, live in sub-standard housing and suffer from long-term unemployment. Each cluster is assisted by cluster co-ordinators who live in the neighbourhood they represent. These co-ordinators work with steering committees comprising residents, service providers, school, religious and business leaders. Cluster co-ordinators listen to residents' concerns and motivate them to solve their problems; help residents identify resources; and share information between the cluster residents and The Atlanta Project Secretariat, based at the Carter Center. The key issue areas addressed by each cluster are community development; economic development; criminal justice; health; education; and housing.

The Atlanta business community has played a critical role in the project's development, ranging from mobilising funding, to the contribution of managerial advice, secondments of senior managers, provision of goods and services, and establishment of core business linkages with local communities. Some companies support the project on a city-wide basis, others have formed comprehensive partnerships with specific clusters. Some of the key companies involved with the project include: Arthur Andersen, Atlanta Gas Light Co., AT&T, Coca-Cola, Deloitte and Touche, Delta Airlines, Georgia Pacific, Home Dept, IBM, Marriott, NationsBank, Northern Telecom, Sprint, Trust Company Bank, Turner Broadcasting and UPS. Home Depot, for example, donated materials for building the Collaboration Centre and provided store credits for individual clusters, IBM contributed hardware and software, the radio and print media have assigned journalists to different clusters, many of the banks have established banking services to clusters, in part as their fulfilment of the USA's Community Reinvestment Act, other companies have seconded senior level advisors to the project, and some are investing in adult literacy and other education programmes.

> The distress of inner cities is as much an economic as a social problem. Unless viable jobs can be created, social investments by themselves will be inadequate.
>
> Professor Michael Porter

- Leading universities and national NGOs, such as the Ford Foundation and the Conference Board, have undertaken research in the last few years to analyse corporate involvement in urban and community development, and to draw out key lessons for replication and scaling-up. Although focused on the USA many of these lessons have relevance anywhere in the world. Their reports include the Conference Board's research paper entitled *Corporations as Partners in Strengthening Urban Communities*, and the Ford Foundation's *Exploration of Corporate Involvement in Community & Economic Development*.

- Another relevant development has been the establishment of the Initiative for a Competitive Inner City (ICIC) by Professor Michael Porter from Harvard, with support from corporations such as Lotus, Textron, Pacific Gas and Electric, and Boston's Co-ordinating Committee, which consists of large companies. The ICIC's aim is to mobilise the private sector in supporting existing and start-up projects in inner cities. It does this through offering direct management advice and training, developing linkages between companies and communities, and liaison with local governments on economic planning.

GROUNDWORK in the United Kingdom

A wide range of stakeholder partnerships lie at the heart of the structure and activities of Groundwork. It is a national organisation, delivering solutions at the local level through a network of registered Groundwork Trusts, which number 42 throughout the United Kingdom. Established in 1982, it grew out of experimental work in the late 1970s by a British government agency called the Countryside Commission, which was focused on trying to restore the damaged natural environment in and around industrial sites, cities and towns. Over the past 14 years Groundwork has evolved into an organisation dedicated to promoting and demonstrating an integrated approach to urban regeneration and community development. Its focus has been especially strong in areas which have a history of industrial and economic decline, often with high unemployment, degraded landscapes and a relatively poor quality of life.

THE GROUNDWORK MISSION IS:

To bring about sustainable improvements, through partnerships, to the local environment and contribute to economic and social regeneration.

In 1995 the organisation worked with 3,775 partner organisations – drawn from the public, private and voluntary sectors – and mobilised 140,000 adult and 96,000 youth volunteers to participate in nearly 5,000 projects, ranging from business initiatives to education and physical improvements in urban areas. Three out of every ten people in England now live in an area served by Groundwork and the organisation assists with around 10% of all derelict land reclamation in England and Wales, plants over 1 million trees and creates some 100 hectares of new parks and recreation space on an annual basis. Its current turnover is close to US$50 million, which represents a leverage factor of 1: 4 on the core funding it gets from the British government's Department of the Environment.

Structure and Strategy

Groundwork is organised as a national network of local Trusts, supported by the Groundwork National Office which is a registered company and charity, providing a wide range of support services to the Trusts. These services include acting as a critical intermediary function as the main point of contact with the national government and other major public funders such as the European Union, and raising sponsorship from national and multinational companies for campaigns and local projects. The national office also spearheads

Groundwork's consultancy services to business and government, for which it is paid a fee and which represents another important source of funding.

Although the Groundwork National Office helps to develop nationwide campaigns, the responsibility for implementing these rests with the local Trusts which are governed by representatives from local government, business and the voluntary sector, managed by local staff and resourced, in part, by local sources. Each Trust is therefore different, depending on where it is located and the needs and capacities of that community. However the common goal is to work alongside existing groups, to 'add-value' and avoid duplication of effort, and to involve and 'empower' people and organisations who have not traditionally taken part in environmental activities.

All the Trusts in the Groundwork network focus, to a lesser or greater extent, on three main activity areas, and in so doing make a contribution to sustainable development and the conservation of the earth's resources. One of the keys to Groundwork's success is in working in the overlaps and making links between the different programme areas:

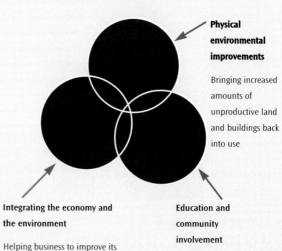

Physical environmental improvements

Bringing increased amounts of unproductive land and buildings back into use

Integrating the economy and the environment

Helping business to improve its environmental performance and competitiveness and create opportunities for employment generation and business involvement in community regeneration

Education and community involvement

Ensuring that results are locally "owned", relevant and long-lasting

Mobilising the business sector for community partnerships

Almost all of Groundwork's activities involve a combination of partners and objectives and offer a rich diversity of the many ways in which companies, community groups, schools and local government can work together. The national office has been especially effective at engaging the business sector in its activities at both a national and local level, and in leveraging public sector funds with private sector financing.

Groundwork engages the private sector in two main ways:

- **Firstly** it mobilises private sector resources – both financial and in-kind – to support nationwide campaigns for local Trusts and their projects. National level support comes mainly from large companies, but at a local level hundreds of smaller companies and business executives are engaged in supporting projects and serving as Trustees and advisors. In many cases these resources come out of corporate community investment budgets, or are offered *pro bono*, but equally important is the role that Groundwork plays in contracting local enterprises to carry out work on a fee basis.

- **Secondly** Groundwork works directly with local business associations and individual companies, mainly small and medium-size enterprises (SMEs), to improve their environmental performance and competitiveness. It therefore offers an excellent example of an organisation which builds corporate relationships by directly meeting core business needs, as well as by tapping into the community investment budgets of companies.

Some of the nationwide campaigns which Groundwork funds through a combination of public and private funding include: an education programme, *Greenlink,* which links companies to schools and is supported by Esso, and another called *Green-It,* enabling children to make designs using a computer-aided package which is supported by RTZ; a community programme called *Barclay Site Savers* which will assist local people in transforming pockets of derelict land into playgrounds and gardens and is jointly supported by Barclays Bank and the government; the *Young Leaders* project which Royal Bank of Scotland funds; another youth project called *ReBuild* supported by Arco; and *YouthWorks*, a programme supported by Marks and Spencer in partnership with Crime Concern, to work with young people on run-down housing estates; the Post Office and the DoE supporting the *Brightsite* programme to encourage small and medium-sized enterprises to improve their business environments; Royal Insurance supporting *Investors in the Environment* which seeks to define benchmark standards for environmental management in SMEs; UK Waste supporting a programme called *UK Waste Aware* which is designed to promote the benefits of waste reduction to SMEs; and the Department of Trade and Industry working with Shell to support a network of local *Business Environment Associations*, aimed at ensuring that local companies are up-to-date with, and capable of responding to, environmental developments and legal requirements of commercial importance.

Some of the direct services that Groundwork offers to companies include: an environmental review service; environmental training; cost-effective design and management advice to improve commercial site management; links into Business Environment Associations; advice and proposals for developing local school links and good community relations. On an annual basis the Groundwork network provides around 500 local companies with advice on site and design management; completes more than 200 environmental reviews for SMEs (which may struggle to afford such reviews otherwise); works with some 20 major companies to develop national campaigns and to publicise their environmental achievements; involves over 20,000 children with business; and trains some 20 young graduates in corporate environmental management.

Key success factors

The activities of Groundwork have not only grown in the United Kingdom, but have been adapted in Japan and the organisation is currently involved with capacity building activities in central and eastern Europe, most notably in Bulgaria. The Groundwork approach is an excellent model of: local action for achieving Agenda 21 within a national framework and support structure; a stakeholder-driven approach to tackling integrated economic, social and environmental problems; the value-added that can be achieved by different sectors working together; and the leverage impact that can be achieved by an intermediary organisation helping to mobilise public-private financing for local organisations, which are developing their own approaches and delivering their own solutions at the local level.

People themselves have the skills and the imagination to repair the damage of the past, to green the city, to create economic opportunities and to make places more liveable. But they need practical help and that's where Groundwork comes in. A case of professionals "on tap", not on top.

John Davidson, Founder of Groundwork

The Krakow Development Forum

The Krakow Development Forum (KDF) was created following a visit to Krakow by The Prince of Wales in May 1993, with 150 business leaders from Poland and other countries, and a cross-sector partnership building workshop held by the PWBLF,

The KDF's mission is "to build partnerships between business, local and national government, academic and non-governmental sectors for sustainable development through partnership projects designed to bring social, economic, environmental and cultural benefit to the Krakow community and its regional, national and international context."

The initiative has inspired a range of activities and projects aimed at building partnerships between different sectors. The intention is to promote projects that address problems beyond the remit or resources of any single individual, group or institution. The idea is also to provide models or case study examples for similar projects beyond the Krakow region in Poland and internationally. Two of the initiatives and projects developed by KDF include:

- **Revitalisation of Krakow's Kazimierz District** – an integrated urban renewal plan for the old Jewish quarter has been prepared by specialists from three cities: Edinburgh, Berlin and Krakow under the auspices of the ECOS programme of the European Union. The Krakow Development Forum, in partnership with PWBLF, has supported local action and involvement in Kazimierz through opening a field office which aims to serve local residents in Kazimierz, as well as visitors and potential investors.

- **Industrial Restructuring in Nowa Huta** – The Sendzimir Steel Works is implementing a restructuring programme to improve the factory's economic viability and to address the issue of the 250,000 Nowa Huta district residents who are dependent on the steel industry. This has been in undertaken in consultation with a wide range of partner organisations, both local and international, partly facilitated by KDF.

FORECOM in Rio de Janeiro

FORECOM was established in 1993 as a business-led initiative to support and replicate the activities of an existing community development organisation called Ação Comunitária do Brasil (ACB), which was set up in 1966. ACB aims to promote social and economic development in poor communities in Rio de Janeiro, by means of educational processes, self-help and community-led action. Consisting of more than 30 Chief Executives of major Brazilian and multinational companies, FORECOM focuses on: promoting practical partnerships between business and community leaders to increase the effectiveness and scope of existing projects in Rio de Janeiro; and establishing new programmes and projects in other parts of Brazil, for example in the state of Espirito Santo.

ACB's operational strategy is focused on the concept of self-help and it relies heavily on community involvement in implementing its programmes. It also places a strong emphasis on bringing the efficiency and practical approach of private enterprise to the social field. Under the FORECOM structure, efforts are being made to twin specific companies to specific communities and/or projects:

- **Job Training Centres** – ACB places a heavy emphasis on preparing people for better jobs in the formal sector, or self-employment opportunities in the informal sector. It currently operates three training centres in some of the poorest sections of Rio. These offer a wide variety of vocational training and managerial skills development. In the last 20 years of operation these centres have trained over 50,000 people for different professional occupations or crafts.

- **General Community Development** – ACB's field workers work and often live in specific communities and act as promoters of change, by: providing the initial drive towards better community organisation and self-help; and building local confidence and project management skills. Projects are selected in consultation with each community and cover a variety of areas, ranging from housing and urban infrastructure, to environmental improvement, education, health and issues of organisation and management.

The St Petersburg Partnership Initiative

The St Petersburg Partnership Initiative (StPPI) was established by The Prince of Wales Business Leaders Forum in 1993, as a result of contact between the former Mayor of St Petersburg, Anatoly Sobchak, and The Prince of Wales. The mission of the initiative has been to identify how international experience and expertise may be mobilised to support the regeneration of this historic city.

The programme has been supported by a wide range of companies with investment interests in St Petersburg. It has covered activities such as: tourism development supported by the World Tourism and Travel Academy, American Express, British Airways, Thomas Cook and Boeing; museums management supported by the Know-How Fund; the reproduction of the valued Pushkin manuscripts supported by a number of companies; professional training in real estate development and management supported by Grand Metropolitan and the Royal Institute of Chartered Surveyors; exchanges between hospital managers in the United Kingdom and St Petersburg; and a series of partnership-building initiatives such as workshops and the inclusion of local government, community and business leaders from St Petersburg on the PWBLF's international INSIGHT programme.

The Central Johannesburg Partnership

Officially launched in 1992, the Central Johannesburg Partnership (CJP) is a private-sector organisation committed to involving key stakeholders in Central Johannesburg in a co-operative effort to rejuvenate the central city area. Its mission is to promote: a sound economy; an attractive, clean, safe and vibrant city centre; affordable residential accommodation; employment opportunities; and a focus for the community. During its initial years the CJP was a tripartite partnership between business, local government and local community organisations. Although its structure has altered, following the country's first democratic elections for local government in 1995, the organisation continues to play a co-ordinating role between these three sectors.

CJP has established task forces and focus groups to mobilise business involvement on issues such as: transportation; public safety; retail; informal trading; inner city housing, especially addressing the issue of homelessness; and urban planning and development.

The organisation has also undertaken research to assess the applicability to South Africa of the American model of Business Improvement Districts and is engaged in an intensive process of reviewing other international best practice and adapting relevant models and lessons to South Africa, instead of trying to "reinvent the wheel". One of its recent undertakings has been to work with local and regional government and community-based organisations to undertake a visioning process for the city of Johannesburg. This has involved a series of extensive consultations between different sectors, and a cross-sector visit of over 20 local government, business and community leaders to the United Kingdom and the United States, to look at urban partnership initiatives in these two countries.

Bombay First

Launched in January 1995, and modelled largely on the innovative London First initiative, Bombay First is a private sector initiative aimed at providing information and resources to promote the interests of Bombay and those who live and work there. Its main objectives are to:

- sponsor, promote, finance and support policy initiatives and programmes for the improvement of Bombay's infrastructure and management, and for other activities aimed at improving the economic, environmental and social viability of the city. These could include transport and telecommunications improvements, housing and land policy, education and training, urban management and governance, and urban finance;

- bring to bear the best minds and intellectual resources, both domestic and international, on the problems and prospects for Bombay and its environs;

- conduct research towards both the macro and micro planning of the city;

- work closely with central, state and local government.

It is a catalytic organisation providing ideas, information and debate aimed at encouraging public-private partnership and innovative funding mechanisms, rather than being an implementing body.

The initiative has been funded by the business sector, with support from organisations such as The British Council, London First and the Bombay Chamber of Commerce and Industry, which was established in 1836 and has some 1300 members, including large and medium size corporations, trade organisations, banks, professionals and individuals.

Environmental Quality International in Cairo

Environmental Quality International, a private urban development consulting firm, exemplifies the role of business as partners in development by applying its core business operations and expertise in tackling key social, environmental and economic challenges facing local communities.

EQI is perhaps best known for its involvement in the Mokattam Zabaleen (garbage collectors) community in Cairo. In 1980, EQI was hired by the Governorate of Cairo to carry out a World Bank sponsored solid waste management programme for the city. EQI selected Mokattam, the largest zabaleen settlement, as the pilot area for the programme. EQI's commercial involvement in Mokattam was soon expanded to address key social challenges. The objectives of EQI's "massive up-grading project" were:

- to enhance the quality of life in the garbage collectors' settlement, and

- to up-grade the ability of the Zabaleen to meet the rapidly growing demands for their services resulting from Cairo's expansion and growth.

> We observed, we listened, we synthesised, and we came up with programmes that really worked. The solutions were incubated in the settlement, while our role was to discover and unleash this potential.
>
> Dr Mounir Neamatalla, founder, Environmental Quality International

EQI worked in partnership with the local Zabaleen association, El Gami'eya, to design and implement various projects. In addition, EQI applied its core management expertise to develop El Gami'eya's organisation and management structure. Two of the most successful projects undertaken by EQI in partnership with El Gami'eya were the Small Industries Project and the Income Generating Project for Female Heads of Households.

Small Industries Project

With support from Oxfam, the Small Industries Project aims to increase the income of garbage collectors by providing credit and technical assistance for the establishment of small scale waste recycling industries. In addition to generating local employment, the project also sought to increase the value of materials recovered from household waste. Project participants were able to sell their recycled materials for higher prices than before.

Income Generating Project for Female-Headed Households

With support from Oxfam and the Ford Foundation, EQI established a micro-credit and income generation programme for female heads of households. The programme was based on the realisation that women were by-in-large excluded from all community initiatives while there existed a large number of female heads of household who represented one of the poorest and most vulnerable groups within the settlement.

The project encouraged women to venture into non-traditional areas such as the assembly of table lamps and developing a system for insurance against illness and death of goats, thus increasing the security of goat raising which is a traditional activity. Together with loans, technical training and informal support between beneficiaries, extension workers, technical assistants and consultants was also provided to facilitate the exchange of information and development of required skills.

The MEGA-CITIES Project
Meeting the challenge of replicating good practice

All over the world people are developing innovative and inspirational approaches to urban problem-solving. In an era where resources are tight and the challenges are urgent, increased attention must be placed on identifying, transferring and adapting examples of these approaches both within cities and between cities. This requires the establishment of dialogue and conduits for knowledge transfer between different sectors, cities and countries. This transfer of knowledge should include not only information on different projects, but also the sharing of different methodologies, techniques and institutional structures to implement and sustain them. The "Best Practices Project" undertaken by UNCHS, in partnership with local authorities from around the world in preparation for the HABITAT conference, offers a useful framework of the potential for such an approach.

International NGOs can also play a vital role in this process and a good example is provided by the MEGA-CITIES project. Established in 1987, this global network is based on the premise that megacities around the globe often have more in common with each other than with smaller urban centres in their own countries and regions and there is great potential for transferring innovations from one city to another through a global network of co-ordinators from the different cities.

The organisation's mission is to reduce the time lag between urban innovations and their implementation. To achieve this mission MEGA-CITIES operates at two levels: on one level it shares workable solutions among the cities and puts the lessons of experience in the hands of policy makers and the public; and on another level it seeks to gain a deeper understanding of the process of innovation and the consequences for deliberate social change in cities.

This approach combines theory and practice and is based on collaborative efforts among the various sectors to increase the efficiency in finding urban innovations and then multiplying them for the greatest impact. The process of finding, evaluating, documenting and disseminating these innovations lies at the core of MEGA-CITIES activities. Projects are evaluated according to:

- their values – is the innovation socially equitable, economically viable, politically participatory,

ecologically sustainable and culturally acceptable?

- their impact – does the innovation have significance, novelty, quality, scope and proven merit?

- their practicality and replicability.

Innovations are transferred via a network of co-ordinators and teams of people drawn from academia, business, government, grassroots groups, non-governmental organisations and the mass media. Groups of these people meet on a regular basis to share their experiences face-to-face and the MEGA-CITIES project also produces publications detailing case studies of urban innovations.

The cities that are involved in the network include Accra, Bangkok, Beijing, Bombay, Buenos Aires, Cairo, Calcutta, Dehli, Karachi, Jakarta, Istanbul, London, Los Angeles, Manila, Mexico City, Moscow, Nairobi, New York, Rio de Janeiro, Sao Paulo and Tokyo.

MEGA-CITIES concentrates its efforts in the following four areas:

1. Environmental Regeneration – toward circular systems for water, sanitation, garbage, food and energy.

2. Poverty and Income Generation – toward alleviating poverty and strengthening the informal sector.

3. Decentralisation and Democratisation – toward greater local participation in planning, service delivery, resource allocation and urban management.

4. Women's Empowerment and Well-being – toward greater choice, access and voice.

The innovations that MEGA-CITIES has helped to transfer between cities range from the Zabaleen garbage recycling and income generation programme in Cairo, which was transferred to Manila, to the transfer of Bangkok's highly successful Magic Eyes Campaign, which mobilised children, through a massive private-sector supported media campaign to alter littering habits and clean up the city, resulting in a decrease of some 80% in litter, and Sao Paulo's pollution ALERT initiative, which alerts the general public, drivers and local authorities to levels of pollution in the city.

If you look around the world you will find that in every so-called first world city of high finance, high tech and high consumption, there is a third world city of joblessness, homelessness and hopelessness. And vice versa. Janice Perlman, Executive Director, MegaCities Project

(ii) INTEGRATED RURAL DEVELOPMENT

Despite the dramatic increase in urbanisation around the world, agriculture remains the backbone of the national economy in a number of countries. In these countries it accounts for a significant percentage of national employment, GDP and exports; produces inputs for manufacturing; provides markets for finished products; and in many cases serves as the basis for national food security. The need to increase agricultural productivity, without destroying the natural environment and the social fabric of rural communities, is one of the greatest challenges in the drive towards sustainable development. There is also the need to increase rural income and employment opportunities, both on and off farms, in order to to slow the rate of rural-urban migration which is causing its own social and environmental problems in many developing countries.

Despite its importance, in many of these countries the rural sector is characterised by:

- low productivity;

- high levels of rural poverty, with few "off-farm" livelihood opportunities;

- under-investment by governments, which are focused on meeting needs in the more politically important urban areas;

- unequal and limited access to credit, appropriate technologies, land, markets and information;

- polarisation between large scale, energy intensive, high input/output commercial farming (often heavily subsidised and focused on cash crops for export) and small scale, low-input/output peasant farming; and

- increasing environmental degradation including soil erosion, desertification, declining soil fertility and salinisation, deforestation, habitat and species loss, water contamination, and health hazards from agrochemicals.

A combination of rapid population growth, fragile ecosystems, poor weather conditions and inappropriate government policies, are key causes of this situation. Reversing it, in order to simultaneously increase rural-based livelihood opportunities, agricultural productivity and environmental protection, requires:

- an enabling policy environment: flexible, full-cost producer prices, secure tenure, fewer subsidies, open markets etc.;

- more integrated and participatory approaches to rural development, looking at rural systems in a more holistic manner and developing a range of on-farm and off-farm income opportunities;

- capacity-building and empowerment in the rural sector, including training, institution-building, extension services and improved access to financial and technical inputs, especially for women;

- support for effective governance at the local level;

- research and investment in labour intensive, environmentally sound technologies and farming practices i.e. integrated pest management, minimum tillage, agroforestry, intercropping, crop rotation, aquaculture, small-scale agro-industries etc.;

- increased investment in rural infrastructure i.e. dams, roads, marketing depots, schools and hospitals;

The success of sustainable agriculture and rural development will depend largely on the support and participation of rural people, national governments, the private sector and international co-operation.

Chapter 14, Agenda 21

THE FARMERS DEVELOPMENT TRUST IN ZIMBABWE

The Farmers Development Trust (FDT) was established in 1993 and offers an excellent example of cross-sector partnership between the Government of Zimbabwe, the private sector, the Commercial Farmers Union (which represents the interests of the country's large, mostly white, commercial farmers), the Indigenous Commercial Farmers Union, international organisations, non-governmental organisations (NGOs), community-based organisations (CBOs) and a large number of small-scale farmers who are participating in the FDT's training programme, and individual commercial farmers who are sharing their time and expertise.

The FDT's mission is to train and support small-scale farmers to enable them to play a full part in Zimbabwe's formal economy. Its development goals are as follows: broadening the country's agricultural production base; improving the rural economy by bringing indigenous farmers into the mainstream of commercial farming; implementing natural resources management; improving farm health and occupational safety; and increasing farm literacy.

Each partner in the initiative plays a key role. The Government, for example, is responsible for providing the land and physical resources for training and the establishment of model resettlement farms. Funding support for this is provided by a number of bilateral and multilateral donors agencies. Training – both formal and informal – is the responsibility of the FDT, which works closely with the management committees of model resettlement farms to assess training needs, and with the Commercial Farmers Union and experienced commercial farmers to provide technical and managerial advice.

The FDT runs ten month training courses for small-scale farmers and these courses are supplemented to reach a wider group of people by field days, demonstrations, farmers meetings, consultations and regular monitoring by experienced commercial farmers. The Trust ultimately hopes to be reaching some 850,000 small-scale farmers throughout the country, an enormous undertaking that is crucial to the development of Zimbabwe's agricultural-based economy.

- greater co-operation between large-scale agribusiness and small-scale farmers, and between rural communities and other primary resource producers operating in remote rural areas such as oil and gas companies, mines and forestry projects. In particular, mutually beneficial rural co-operation should be investigated, such as agricultural outgrower schemes between smallholders and agroprocessing companies, and industrial subcontracting and supplier partnerships between small-scale rural enterprises and neighbouring companies.

Governments have to play a lead role in providing the necessary policy and infrastructural framework for more integrated and sustainable approaches to rural development, but within such a framework the role for companies to work in partnership with rural communities is enormous.

The following pages look at a range of rural development initiatives managed by multi-stakeholder partnerships and by individual companies from the agribusiness, oil and gas, mining, forestry and manufacturing sectors. The four vignettes on this page look at nationwide partnership initiatives in Mexico, Thailand, Chile and Zimbabwe, followed by a longer profile on Landcare, an outstanding nationwide programme in Australia. These are followed by profiles of the rural development work being undertaken by the Tata Group and Hindustan Lever in India; BP in Colombia; Aracruz Celulose in Brazil; the Mumias Sugar Company and Bamburi Portland Cement in Kenya; Rio Tinto in Zimbabwe; Golden Hope Plantations in Malysia; B&Q in Papua New Guinea; and the Odebrecht Corporation in Latin America.

- **The Fundacion Mexicana para el Desarrollo Rural (FMDR)** operates all over Mexico, through more than 40 Development Centres. Its objective is: to promote an increase in the productivity of rural people and rural groups, and integrated human development, through the subsidiary support of the foundation and its development centres." Several hundred Mexican and multinational companies help to finance FMDR's activities and also offer technical assistance and business linkages to rural development projects. The key philosophy of the programme is to build local capacities and incentives for rural development.

- **The Thai Business Initiative for Rural Development (TBIRD)** has mobilised over 100 companies to work in partnership with rural villages, especially in the poor northern area of the country, to support a range of agricultural and other rural income activities. It is profiled in detail on page 258.

- **Chile's Corporation for Rural Development (CODESSER)** operates fifteen agricultural and two industrial training schools in various parts of the country and works closely with the local private sector on developing appropriate training programmes which reflect the needs of the workplace, offering work experiences for trainees, and securing future jobs for trainees when they have finished their courses. For each of the schools a support group of about seven prominent local farmers or industrialists is established and this group plays a key role in the school's activities. The school has also signed agreements with the National Society of Farmers and The National Service for Employment and Workers' Training to ensure that the programmes it offers meet national standards in terms of both content and quality.

LANDCARE in Australia

Co-operation between all stakeholders including Federal, State and local governments, industry and the community has been essential to achieving effective results. In the final event decisions regarding land management should primarily be the responsibility of the land managers themselves, because of their links with the land and because of the need for their long term commitment to sustainable use of their natural resources.

Jesse Blackadder

Landcare, Australia

Landcare Australia's family of caring corporates:
Alcoa Australia • Adelaide Brighton • Amway • Ansett Australia • Apple Computer • Auseon • Australian Broadcasting Corporation • Australian Co-operative Foods • Australian Nature Conservation Agency • Australian Property Group • Australian Solid Fuel • Banrock Station • BHP • British Petroleum • British Aerospace Australia • Burk Associates • Cadbury • Chinese Chamber of Commerce • Clipsal • CRT • Coca-Cola • Countrylink • Conservation and Natural Resources • NSW Government • Primary Industries • Du Pont • E.S.R. • FIFA • Flag • Ford Motor Company • Freehill Hollingdale & Page • Fuji Xerox • Gallagher • Gowings • Hanimex • Incitec • Johnson & Johnson • Kleenex • Kraft • McDonald's • Monsanto • MSD Agent • Nabalco • National Landcare Programme • Neway • Nippys • North Limited • Pioneer • Olacer Pacific Ltd. • PWCS • Ricegrowers Association • Sunrice • Telstra • TNT Logistics • Uncle Toby's • Wattyl • Westpac

During the mid-1980s farming communities all over Australia were struggling to cope with the dual problems of:

- **declining rural incomes and livelihoods** – in the face of increasing international competition, national economic restructuring and low prices; and

- **severe land degradation** – driven by a combination of drought and the legacy of many years of inappropriate land management.

In 1988, two organisations normally considered to be on different and usually confrontational sides of the development/environment spectrum, joined forces to tackle these inter-dependent challenges. The National Farmers Federation and the Australian Conservation Foundation worked together on a joint proposal to the Australian government. Recognising that government-directed programmes were not always effective, often tackling symptoms rather than causes, the two organisations proposed a community-led alternative which would have both public and private sector support. In 1989 the National Landcare Programme was launched.

The programme is a national framework for partnership between the community, industry and government, aimed at achieving more sustainable systems of land use and management at local and regional levels. A vital intermediary role is played by Landcare Australia Ltd. a non-profit company established in October 1989. Each group of partners plays a unique, but critical role:

- The Federal Government of Australia provides funding and other forms of support for all levels of landcare activity – ranging from financial support to individual community-level landcare groups and regional committees, to the sponsorship of a high-profile national award for the individual Australian who is deemed to have made the greatest contribution to the Landcare programme each year, to support for Landcare Australia's administration costs on a fee for service basis and the provision of government secondees as staff members.

- Landcare Australia plays a crucial role in promoting the landcare ethic on a national basis; encouraging and facilitating public awareness and participation; disseminating educational materials and information to schools and the public; publicising landcare activities through the media; running national campaigns to raise both funds and awareness; co-ordinating a high-profile national award scheme with ten awards sponsored by business, government and environmental groups; working with the corporate sector to ensure their active participation; distributing funds to appropriate projects; and extending tax deductibility to funding received by individual community groups so that they do not have to invest in all the legal work to achieve this status on their own. In February 1994 the organisation established the Landcare Foundation, which focuses on raising tax-deductible funds from the corporate sector.

- Regional councils and committees play a valuable co-ordination and leadership role at the state level, with public and private sector support being provided for a network of state landcare specialists and co-ordinators, with a range of technical skills in both the environmental and agricultural field.

REPLICATING GOOD PRACTICE
"From Landcare to Officecare and Coastcare"

The Landcare model has been so successful in mobilising support and practical action at both a national and local level that Landcare Australia has recently launched two new campaigns aimed at applying the same principles to different challenges:

- **Officecare** was launched in 1995 by a partnership between Landcare Australia and the company Fuji Xerox, with the goal of encouraging office workers to form groups (along the lines of landcare groups) to look at ways to save resources in the office through the practice of "Reduce waste, Re-use materials and Re-cycle ...virtually anything". Given that most Australians work in offices, the potential for achieving a similar multiplier effect to the Landcare programme is enormous. The initiative has been launched with the distribution of more than 40,000 free Officecare kits and a national paper recycling campaign supported by Fuji Xerox and Australian Paper Recycling called "The Australian Paper Chase".

- **Coastcare** has been launched by a partnership between Landcare Australia and the Government's Department of Environment, Sport and Territories, to apply the principle of community mobilisation to improving environmental management of the country's coastline. As with landcare, the initiative will involve government funding and technical assistance, an intermediary role for Landcare as the facilitating, marketing and promotional driver, corporate support and community action.

- Landcare Australia is also in contact with groups in the Netherlands, Nepal, India, Canada and South Africa to share its experiences and support similar activities in these countries. In 1992/93 the organisation acted as a consultant for the establishment of Landcare New Zealand, which now has about 60 landcare groups.

- More than 80 Australian and multinational companies and business associations support Landcare on a national basis through financial, managerial, technical and in-kind support for the Landcare Foundation and national campaigns, with hundreds of companies supporting individual Landcare groups and helping to run local landcare initiatives in their own communities. In the two years since it was launched the foundation has raised some A$5 million and funded over 120 Landcare group projects tackling land and water degradation. Many millions of dollars in cash and in kind are also raised from the business sector for various national campaigns and local activities.

- The media plays a key role in partnership with Landcare Australia to raise awareness and publicise Landcare activities, often at little or no cost to the organisation. During the 1996 National Landcare Month, for example, the newspapers published 192 articles reaching 8.5 million people. A series of 30-second commercials highlighting the theme *"Landcare is good business"* were aired by one of the national TV stations, reaching some 50% of their target audience of corporate decision-makers and opinion leaders. Another recent media campaign, supported by Channel 9 and fronted by a well-known Australian celebrity, challenged Australians to plant a million trees in just seven days in the Murray River area. Some A$850,000 was raised in sponsorship, more than 10,000 volunteers planted 2 million trees, schools and Landcare groups pledged to plant a further 3.5 million trees at a later date, and close to 2 million people watched the initiative on television. This ongoing media support has ensured that national awareness levels of the Landcare programme have risen from 22% in July 1991 to 69% in September 1995, with awareness levels being over 80% in rural communities.

- The Landcare network of more than 3,000 autonomous Landcare groups all over the country, ultimately plays the most crucial role of all. Although these may receive technical and financial support from the other partners, they are formed and run entirely by the local community and normally consist of a mixture of farmers, community groups, local government, local companies and schools. Thousands of Australians are joining in. More than 30% of all farmers are members of a Landcare group and the number of community groups continues to grow in both rural and urban areas.

Six years after its launch, the Landcare programme has evolved into a partnership model which has lessons to share world-wide – in OECD, developing and transition economies. It is a model for an integrated, community-led and government-supported approach to sustainable rural development. It is also an example of how a strong spirit of volunteerism and responsibility – both corporate and individual – can be mobilised on a national and local scale. Landcare Australia employs a full-time staff of only six people and its enormous multiplier effect is due entirely to the partnership of government, business, the media and community groups. Obviously its wide acceptance is also a reflection of the social, economic and cultural background of the Australian population, but many of its attributes could have relevance elsewhere.

Tata Iron and Steel
Rural Development Society in India

The Tata Group, India's largest business house, owns some 80 highly diversified companies ranging from watches and tea, to hotels and steel, and has a turnover in the region of US$5 billion a year. The group is one of the developing world's emerging champions – not only in terms of its business strength, but also in terms of its social commitment.

From the outset, the Tata family have pioneered the trusteeship idea of management, with the result that not only is 80% of the parent company, Tata Sons Ltd., held in philanthropic trusts (which have been responsible for establishing a number of India's most respected public institutions in the fields of science, technology, medicine, energy, social services and the performing arts), but the philosophy of social conscience still pervades the company's manifold business activities today. It is a philosophy that has not only enabled the Tata Group to enjoy an excellent relationship with its thousands of workers, who have not engaged in a strike for over 70 years, but one which also underpins the company's unparalleled reputation for commercial integrity which, combined with its diversified industrial strength, makes it a first stop for many foreign investors entering the Indian market.

The group's flagship company Tata Iron and Steel Company (TISCO) is based in Jamshedpur and employs 72,000 people. It offers one of the best examples in the world of how a company's approach to social responsibility outside its factory gate, has evolved from paternalism to partnership.

> The private sector should realise that they have to play their part in the spirit of trusteeship advocated by Mahatma Gandhi. No business success is worthwhile unless it serves the needs or interests of the country and its people, and it is worthless if it is not achieved by fair and honest means.
>
> JRD Tata

TISCO first established a social welfare scheme in 1916 to provide assistance in the rural areas surrounding the steel town of Jamshedpur. The scheme is now supported by some US$2.5 million a year from TISCO and encompasses a community development programme, a trust for family health and the Tata Steel Rural Development Society (TSRDS). Established in the late 1970s, TSRDS was set up as an independent society, which receives an annual grant from the company but is independent to forge other partnerships and funding relationships. In essence it is an NGO, with a strong business ethos, focusing on: education and literacy; health and medical activities; agriculture and irrigation; drinking water; vocational training; and income generation.

After 10 years of operation TSRDS's managers felt that the society wasn't delivering the type of rural development support that was needed and undertook a major reassessment. They drew up a set of lessons which have fundamentally reshaped TSRDS's approach and effectiveness. They include:

- **Participatory development** – TSRDS realised that this was not happening as much as it should. Today they acknowledge that even building a simple well can, and must, be done as an exercise in local participation, and that every single input can play a role in empowering people. Over the years they have built more than 2,000 wells – in addition to schools, community centres and other types of infrastructure – and are now appreciating the important cumulative effect that these efforts can have on getting people involved in determining their own development.

- **Professional and local staff** – they realised that in many cases community development managers in their company were often the wrong people, with the wrong reporting lines and working within the wrong structure – normally in public or industrial relations. Although they recognise the critical importance of keeping corporate staff aware and if possible involved in the company's social activities, they have seen the need to create a professional team of development experts. As a result TSRDS is now structured as a separate group to the company, operating like a large development NGO (albeit with corporate support and strategic direction). Its 800 staff are trained and developed as part of a permanent, professional organisation, and receive salaries and benefits in accordance with company practice. Equally important, 50% of the staff are from the different communities and ethnic groups which TSRDS serves, and although women are still under-represented on the staff team there is an effort to change this. Viraf Mehta, the visionary director of TSRDS, dedicates time and energy to keeping his own awareness levels high. Every year he spends at least 30 days sleeping, eating and living in different villages.

- **Top management support** – this is deemed to be crucial and has long played a key role in Tata's successful and adaptable community development ethos. Today TISCO has six managing directors – personnel, marketing, production etc. ...and the sixth is social development.

- **More money isn't always the answer** – TSRDS realised that vast budgets can sometimes be a hindrance to sustainable rural development. They can make it less necessary to consult and co-operate with others and can result in pampering beneficiaries and actually making them more, rather than less, dependent on hand-outs from external sources. A few years ago TSRDS voluntarily froze its budget and has spent the last three years focusing on developing consultative, partnership-driven solutions, including an emphasis on the contribution of beneficiaries to the process – such as their time and labour. Today TSRDS is collaborating with over 400 organisations – both NGOs and many smaller community-based organisation (CBOs).

- **Accountability** – the organisation regularly undergoes a comprehensive process of analysis, accountability and audit – including social audit. It has always invited external auditors to come in and do its social audits – of which there have been several. Six years ago it also started to do a few other things: it is putting mechanisms in place to make itself more accountable to the entire community; its partner organisations are encouraged to make inputs to the process; and expert NGOs from around the country and the rest of the world are invited to spend 4-5 months with TSRDS – both advising on, and learning from their approach. As Viraf Mehta explains, "I am chasing quality rural development, and I benchmark against other NGOs – the best I can find."

- **Changed terminology** – an emphasis has been placed on moving away from paternalist terms such as "adopting" a village. TSRDS is training its staff to stop calling projects "our" projects, and to encourage a village-by-village approach to needs-assessment and local ownership of development solutions. In this way TSRDS sees itself increasingly as a facilitator which can leverage financial, technical, organisational and managerial resources for the beneficiaries to make use of themselves, rather than an organisation which is "doing development".

- **Encouraging local CBOs** – increased effort has been put into helping small, community based organisations to register and develop themselves. TSRDS helps them with institution and capacity building, shares its training programmes with them, and has established a forum through which they can exchange ideas and experiences and access an on-going support network of like-minded organisations dealing with similar problems.

- **Mainstreaming back to the company** – despite its growing focus on evolving as a professional development NGO, TSRDS still places great importance on keeping the business units in the Tata Group informed and aware of the important linkages between the group's commercial and social activities. The Group derives some clear commercial benefits from the successful TSRDS approach, including: good industrial relations; rapport from local communities and good relations with local government; international exposure; and enhanced reputation. Equally important is the fact that TSRDS /TISCO serves as an internal consultant for Tata's other 78-80 companies, and is currently helping them all to establish their own company-based community programmes in partnership with the best NGOs in their areas, building on the lessons TSRDS has learnt. By 1997 some 50 out of the 80 Tata companies will have these programmes established.

British Petroleum in Colombia

In BP. we have attached great importance towards holding joint programmes with customers, suppliers and partners in order to discover more effective ways of doing business together, and of benefiting from each other's experience in the business, social and environmental dimension and in technology transfer. 'Benchmarking' plays a prominent part here, and certainly helps BP to promote continuous improvement by focusing on best practice outside the organisation.

Sir David Simon
Chairman, BP
IMF/World Bank Annual Meeting,
1996

In 1986 British Petroleum began a major oil and gas exploration programme in Colombia which has resulted in the largest oil discovery in the western hemisphere in the last 20 years. Oil production began on the Cusiana field in 1994 and the project's total cost is estimated at US$6 billion. In terms of investment and scope, it is among the largest projects ever designed, procured and constructed in Colombia.

The project is located in a politically, socially and environmentally sensitive area, which poses a major management challenge to BP and its joint venture partners Ecopetrol, Total and Triton and the activities have not escaped controversy. This has focussed in particular on the operations and reputation of local security forces in the region and the government requirement of oil exploration companies to pay a "security tax" and record public consultations.

Operations are in the Casanare province of Colombia, as well as in six other Departments of the country, which are crossed by the pipelines routes. The Casanare region has a relatively poor agrarian-based population of 220,000 people. GDP per head is about half the national average, and the local workforce is unskilled and suffers from high levels of unemployment. Various guerrilla groups are operating in the region, and the oil companies represent an obvious target for local discontent. This sensitive security situation is exacerbated by high expectations that the arrival of international oil companies will guarantee better employment prospects, heavy investment in social and economic infrastructure, and direct benefits from royalties and tax revenues. Responding to local community needs without fuelling unrealistic expectations is therefore a delicate balancing act which BP is aiming to achieve by working in partnership with both the local community and with local and central government agencies. This is obviously easier said than done in such politically sensitive circumstances, and with such a wide range of often conflicting stakeholder interests to be consulted. The BP consortium however sees such an approach as the best way to proceed and is mindful of the need to integrate its community investment into its core business strategy for the region.

The area is also the source of several rivers which form the headwaters of the Orinoco River. This is of great importance as a source of water for domestic, agricultural and industrial use, and for its unique ecology, which has resulted in a proposal to make the Orinoco delta a World Heritage site. When BP arrived in the area local knowledge of the river systems was extremely limited and there was no proven methodology for assessing impacts of oil and gas operations on these systems. BP's Colombia management claim to have drawn lessons from earlier environmental problems and approaches and over the past few years they have developed a comprehensive community and environmental management programme to address these issues.

On the **environmental** front, working with local staff and consultants, BP has carried out a major study of the physical, chemical and biological characteristics of the local river systems, and has developed a methodology for monitoring the oil project's impact. The study has not only established new standards for baseline environmental monitoring in Colombia (which

WORKING with NGOS, LOCAL and NATIONAL GOVERNMENT and THE WORLD BANK

The Prince of Wales Business Leaders Forum and the World Bank co-chair a series of informal meetings between business leaders and development professionals called *The Washington Forum*. At a meeting of this Forum in November 1994, BP Colombia presented their work to the World Bank via teleconference. A World Bank delegation then visited the project in 1995. An innovative multi-stakeholder partnership has been launched to establish an Integrated Childhood and Youth Centre. The partners involved include the BP Foundation, the World Bank, the Colombian government, the Mayor of Tauramena, and two local NGOs – Minuto de Dios and Fundacion Amanecer. The Centre is designed to provide the region's pre-school population, mothers and youth with a comprehensive health care and community facility offering education and health services, nutrition and lifestyle counselling, recreation and sport activities, and awareness about income opportunities. The programme commenced in September 1996, with a budget of about US$400,000. It will initially reach about 365 people. If successful, it will offer a valuable example of how the resources of business, especially its managerial and delivery skills, and the community consultation skills of the NGO sector, can be combined with the financing and infrastructural resources of government and international funding agencies to meet community needs.

are currently being integrated into national environmental monitoring procedures) but has also:

- built the capacity of local technical experts;

- established a large reference collection of local flora and fauna, (which is being used by Colombian scientists for various research studies);

- provided the basis for an extensive community environment education programme; and

- developed a methodology which can be adapted for use and comparative studies anywhere in the tropics.

BP's **community investment strategy** has been to: identify essential needs; complement (rather than replace) government responsibilities; encourage community self-help; avoid any accusations of paternalism, and establish a delivery structure that is cost-effective and sustainable. To implement this strategy BP has pooled resources with its joint venture partners to support separate independent community foundations to deliver community projects. This joint approach has not only substantially reduced costs, minimised replication and increased bargaining power with the government and suppliers, but has also created a funding and management structure which can continue after the oil companies have left. Visiting specialists have seen this as a potential model for similar operations elsewhere.

In 1994-96, BP's total community investment in the region was more than US$2.9 million of the total $6.47 million expenditure of the consortium. This money was allocated mainly to infrastructure support, education, income-improvement activities and institutional strengthening programmes, including management training for local government officials. The impact of these activities has been encouraging:

- 500 community infrastructure projects have been undertaken since 1994, each with active involvement and in-kind contributions from the communities themselves. These projects have covered 514 villages and directly benefited over 180,000 people;

- 5,223 students have passed through the technical training programme;

- 6,000 jobs have been created in villages close to the oil project;

- 7,975 families have received consulting services as part of BP's support for social housing;

- 684 institutions and 1,000 teachers have benefited from the company's environmental education programme since 1993; and

- loans valued at US$1 million have been made to micro-enterprises.

BP's strategy to support this foundation is an example of a partnership approach which brings leverage of other resources, and involvement from the oil consortium, business and public authorities, beyond cash.

Aracruz Celulose in Brazil

In Portuguese we translate sustainable development as 'desenvolvimento sustentavel' which I think expresses Brazil's needs better than the English translation as it puts development first. You cannot have environmental quality when people are too poor to eat. In countries like Brazil the best way to relieve pressure on forests and on other natural resources is to alleviate poverty, give people jobs and give them a stake in preserving their natural environment.

Erling Lorentzen, Chairman, Aracruz Celulose

Aracruz Celulose was founded in 1967, and began construction on a pulp mill in 1975, with the first pulp being produced in 1978. Today the company is the world's largest producer of eucalyptus market pulp and is one of Brazil's leading exporters. It accounts for one in every four bales of bleached eucalyptus pulp marketed internationally and exports to over 20 countries.

Since its establishment, the company has earned a positive reputation both nationally and internationally for its efforts to incorporate social and environmental factors into its corporate vision. It has achieved this through both its core business operations and its broader community involvement activities.

When the first trees were planted in 1967 the area was severely degraded. Farmers, charcoal makers and loggers had stripped vast tracts of woodlands. Almost no reforestation had taken place, and many attempts to plant crops had failed. The area was not only facing soil erosion and depletion problems, but also increasing poverty and unemployment, leading to a flow of people to the burgeoning shanty towns of the cities.

Since that time the 132,000 ha of eucalyptus plantations established by Aracruz (combined with 56,000 ha of native reserves) have underpinned an internationally successful business which has created jobs, added to the local community's wealth, provided foreign exchange for the nation, developed new technologies for the forestry, pulp and paper industry (not only in Brazil, but worldwide), and invested in extensive social and environmental programmes.

From an environmental perspective, the company has invested more than US$250 million on:

- Cleaner production technologies for its pulp mill;

- International award-winning research and development on fast growing and high-yielding hybrids, with seeds now being exported around the world;

- Establishment of a comprehensive environmental policy and management programme;

- Production of almost all the mill's energy needs through using biomass waste such as wood bark and black liquor;

- A conservation programme for the remaining 27% of the region still covered in original forest, which involves the planting of over 1.5 million native trees per year and which is providing a favourable ecosystem for some 150 bird, 36 mammal and 3,000 insect species;

- A community agro-forestry initiative, with Aracruz distributing seeds, advice and credit to local farmers, plus contracts to buy back the wood, to encourage the planting of trees on degraded land and discourage the felling of native species to sell for fuel;

- Numerous national and international initiatives to promote the concept of sustainable development and especially the need to link environmental conservation to socio-economic progress. One of these international initiatives was the launch, with the WBSCD and other industry peers, of a major research project to look at the entire life-cycle of the forestry, pulp and paper industry from the planting and cropping of trees, to the production of pulp and paper, to issues such as recycling. The International Institute for Environment and Development has recently published a report on the findings of this project.

The company's investment in social infrastructure around its mill – homes, hospitals, roads and schools – amounts to more than US$125 million. It has established a private pension fund and healthcare scheme for its employees, and invests money, material and managerial resources in efforts to improve the quality of local schools.

Aracruz was also one of the founding members of Ação Comunitária do Brasil (ACB) and recently co-founded ACB's affiliate in Espirito Santo. It offers both organisations financial support and management advice. Like many of its international peers, the company is currently reviewing its community activities and is recognising the need for a more strategic approach; one which focuses on fewer but longer-term partnerships, rather than responding piece-meal to endless and often ad hoc demands from government and local NGOs. The company is also considering the establishment of an Institute which will offer technical training and general management skills to people living in the area surrounding the mill.

The Mumias Sugar Company in Kenya

In a sector where the impacts of large-scale agribusiness and monoculture are often strongly criticised, the Mumias Sugar Company illustrates that it is possible to forge mutually beneficial linkages between large and small-scale enterprises, between the public and private sector, and between foreign and local entities.

Situated in a rural part of Kenya, the Mumias Sugar Project was established in 1971 with the express goals of: achieving production efficiency, in order to increase Kenya's self-sufficiency in sugar production; and meeting broader socio-economic criteria, such as providing rural-based employment and income opportunities through the process of rural industrialisation. The project consists of:

* A sugar processing factory;

* A commercially-run nucleus sugar estate;

* An outgrowers scheme, based on contractual relationships between the company which owns the factory and nucleus estate, and some 40,000 independent small-scale farmers, plus their representative body, the Mumias Outgrowers Company (MOCO).

The Mumias Sugar Company (MSC) has the following ownership structure: 71% Kenyan government; 17% Commonwealth Development Corporation (the private sector arm of the British ODA); 4.4% Booker Tate (a British-based multinational); and 7.6 % Kenyan financial institutions. Although not without its problems, this diversified ownership structure has enabled different partners to bring a wide range of resources and skills to the project. The government and the company have both made substantial investments in infrastructure development, such as roads, electricity, schools and hospitals; the government, company and financial institutions have determined the project's funding structure; and Booker Tate is contracted by the other partners to provide the management, technical expertise and training for the project.

As part of its management role MSC carries out various support activities for the small-scale farmers, ranging from the provision of agricultural extension services, credit, seed cane and fertiliser at lower prices than the farmers would pay if they were entering the market themselves; to technical support for major operations such as land clearing and harvesting. The farmers, who mostly have title to their own land, are responsible for planting and crop management, and their contract stipulates how they are paid for their cane. MOCO, an independent company in which MSC has no direct stake, plays a vital intermediary role, representing the farmers' interests in negotiations, disseminating credit, building local institutional capacity and gradually taking on responsibility for extension services.

The following statistics illustrate the project's impacts:

* Since its establishment in 1971 the company has increased direct employment to some 5,000 people, and the number of expatriates holding permanent senior management positions has decreased from 38 in 1971 to two today;

* The number of small-scale farmers with contracts has increased from 3,000 in 1971 to some 40,000 today, they have gone from producing 50% of the factory's needs to over 90% and most have seen substantial increases in their income;

* External and internal evaluations have estimated that the project has also provided economic and social benefits for a further 250,000 people in the Mumias district, through the provision of education, health, housing and social facilities, and the creation of farming and small-scale enterprise opportunities;

* It is now the largest producer of sugar in East Africa, the only sugar producer to consistently make a profit, the second largest source of tax to the Kenyan government and the basis of millions of dollars of savings in foreign exchange through reduced sugar imports;

* Environmentally the project has helped the small-scale farmers to improve their land management practices through its comprehensive extension services. The factory uses biomass for its energy, and new technology is being introduced to enhance recovery of sugar.

The key factors underpinning the success of this partnership have been: clear understanding of roles and responsibilities between the project partners, normally backed by contractual agreements; the establishment of two-way trust between the company and the outgrowers, facilitated by the intermediary role of MOCO and by the work of the company's extension officers; and the genuine commitment on the part of the company to continuously improve its social and environmental impacts. For example it undertakes efforts to: ensure that the farmers still grow food crops by restricting the amount of sugar cane they can grow to 50% of their plots and providing extension services for inter-cropping and various food hybrids; on-going capacity-building efforts with women's groups to increase their participation in decision-making, which is an area that still requires a lot of development; and efforts to involve the company's employees and the outgrowers in share ownership schemes, as part of the company's privatisation programme which is currently being structured.

Bamburi Portland Cement in Kenya

The Bamburi Portland Cement Company (BPCC) was established in 1954 to quarry limestone and produce cement on the Kenyan coast near Mombassa. Over the years it has played a key role in Kenya's economic development, producing cement for construction and industrialisation, and earning foreign exchange. In 1992 it became one of the first companies in the world to be awarded a UNEP Global 500 Award for Sustainable Development. Apart from being a corporate leader in energy management within Kenya, BPCC has also received international acclaim for its innovative quarry rehabilitation programme. This is an integrated rural development initiative which has turned the company's exhausted quarries into a profit-generating, employment-creating, forestry, aquaculture, agriculture and tourist business.

Bamburi's limestone quarries, like any others, have the appearance of a barren moonscape. In 1971, the company invited Rene Haller, (a Swiss agronomist with extensive experience in Africa), to try and turn its exhausted quarries to productive, profitable and aesthetically pleasing use. Twenty years later, with the full backing of the cement company and a team of well-trained and motivated local staff, Rene Haller has produced a project that is not only economically viable, but also ecologically sustainable and innovative. The initiative is now run as a separate subsidiary of BPCC, called Baobab Farm. It is designed to be a self-sustaining and fully integrated ecosystem, without the use of chemicals and artificial fertilisers and with all the activities structured to receive inputs from each other's waste products.

The core elements of the project are:
• **reafforestation**
• **an integrated aquaculture system**
• **other agricultural activities**
• **tourism**
• **education, research and consulting.**

Reafforestation
The first objective of the rehabilitation plan was to revegetate the quarries. Today there are over 200 hectares of forest with one million trees and 250,000 seedlings growing in Bamburi's exhausted quarries. Management of the trees is kept to a minimum – they are planted directly into the coralline stone, with a mixture of chopped up Casuarina root nodules and top soil, taken from established Casuarina trees. These carry various micro-organisms which help to establish the seedlings. Thereafter the trees grow fast and are well suited to natural pest protection and arid climatic conditions. Harvesting of the trees normally begins within two years when material for housebuilding and/or for animal fodder is cut out and either used on the farm or sold. Several years later trees can be cut for firewood, charcoal and

building timber, leaving behind nutrition-rich soils for reafforestation. Baobab Farm has established a woodfuel business with local communities, providing distribution and retail opportunities for local entrepreneurs, and serving to generate income and employment, as well as helping to alleviate the fuelwood crisis. All seedlings are grown on the farm and there is on-going experimentation with new varieties and methods.

The integrated aquaculture system
Over the last 16 years Baobab Farm has also developed an intensive Tilapia fish farming enterprise, which is today internationally recognised. It is estimated that by the year 2010 the predicted 70 million people in Kenya will require 245,000 tons per annum of fish, to sustain even current levels of protein consumption. Development of an intensive aquaculture industry, in Kenya and elsewhere in Africa, is one of the key solutions to this need.

The system combines fish farming, with rice and algae production, crocodile rearing, game farming, the production and use of biogas and biofiltration methods, horticulture and tourism. Its overriding objective is to make optimum use of available resources and to ensure both environmental sustainability and economic efficiency. Income is generated from the sale of fish, prawns, rice, vegetables and fruits to local tourist hotels and communities, and the use of crocodiles and wildlife as a tourist attraction.

Other agricultural activities
Baobab Farm also runs sheep, goats, cattle and broiler chickens. All are farmed on a small-scale basis, making maximum use of local, appropriate technologies. The project is used as a model farm to transfer skills, expertise and self-reliance to surrounding communities.

Tourism
The company has established The Bamburi Nature Trail around the aquaculture project. The nature trail now receives some 100,000 paying visitors a year, both locals and tourists. Apart from being a source of revenue generation, this also raises public environmental awareness.

Education, research and consulting
The lessons of Bamburi's rehabilitation project and its integrated aquaculture system are spread through an increasing number of education programmes, both for schoolchildren, local farmers and the general public. The company welcomes scientific researchers and a number of PhD. and MSc. theses have been completed on its various activities.

Hindustan Lever in India

DEVELOPING YOUNG MANAGERS AND COMMUNITIES

Vikram Grover is a young "high-flier" in the sales and marketing division of Unilever subsidiary Brooke Bond Lipton. Based in Bangalore, the "silicon valley" of India, Vikram has a Masters degree in Engineering from one of India's most prestigious universities and has spent his first 10 months as a graduate trainee moving around the company's core divisions: finance, production and marketing. He is now one of 50 young managers from the Unilever Group in India spending six weeks living and working with a family in a remote village in the Etah District of Uttar Pradesh, as part of Hindustan Lever's Integrated Rural Development Programme (IRDP). The experience is challenging his comfortable assumptions and opening his eyes to the harsh realities of life for many of his fellow Indians. It is also developing his leadership skills, his ability to work in a team, to improvise, innovate and negotiate. And the experience is increasing his understanding of the opportunities and constraints of rural markets, which are important areas of potential growth for his company. Hopefully the projects that he and his colleagues are working on with their local hosts will also leave behind tangible and sustainable benefits, ranging from new skills, to physical improvements, enhanced institutional capacities and improved health care. One young manager, for example, is working with a local NGO to organise a camp for 100 physically handicapped children living in the area; another is helping villagers to install a series of handpumps; a third is working with villagers to finish and equip a half-built school. After an initial briefing each of these young managers is required to consult with the people in their host village, identify an area of need and develop an action plan in consultation with the villagers for meeting this need. Their period of secondment is an integral element of the company's Integrated Rural Development Programme and of their own management development process.

The Integrated Rural Development Programme (IRDP) was established by Hindustan Lever (HL) in 1976 as a last effort to improve milk yields from its dairy factory. The company had purchased the factory in 1963, in response to the Indian government's call for rural industrialisation. Milk was supplied by local villagers, but after ten years of operation, despite efforts to introduce better cattle and livestock management practices, the milk supply was so poor and erratic that the plan°t was operating at 50% capacity and incurring substantial losses. HL realised that the problem could only be overcome by taking a more integrated approach and tackling not only livestock management, but the underlying poverty in the area. The IRDP was therefore launched to address the following activities:

- improved dairy production through better animal husbandry and milk collection practices;

- diversification to pigs, poultry, complimentary crops and dual use crops;

- development of other income generation projects;

- improved health care, especially immunisation for mothers and children;

- infrastructure development, especially the provision of basic services;

- literacy and training, especially improving access for women and girls; and

- establishment of village development committees.

Since 1976 milk collection has increased from 15,000 to 86,000 tonnes per annum and the dairy at Etah is now one of HL's most profitable business units. Over 10% of the dairy's pre-tax profit is currently invested in the IRDP which has also attracted increased government funding. It employs over 60 staff – mostly field officers who work with the village committees and the young managers during their six week secondments. From an initial six villages the programme now covers over 400, and plans to reach 700 by 1998. Not only has milk and factory production increased dramatically, but a 1991 evaluation also found improvements in other sources of village income, increased employment, literacy, health and leisure time. The company recognises that there is still room for improvement. PLAN International recently assessed the project against the following criteria – empowerment, gender equality, sustainability, quality and learning – and found a number of shortfalls, especially in the first two criteria. The company's willingness to participate in such an evaluation indicates its commitment to continuous improvement, and increased attention is now being focused on these areas.

There can be little doubt, however, that the villagers are enjoying a better quality of life now than they were in 1976. The on-going investment of Hindustan Lever, in terms of money, management secondments, technical expertise, budgetary discipline, senior management support and influence with local government departments, has played a critical role. The fact that the company is also benefiting from the programme, both directly through increased milk yields to its factory, and indirectly through the development of its young managers, is more likely to ensure long-term continuity and sustainability of the initiative, than if it was driven purely by corporate philanthropy.

Rio Tinto in Zimbabwe

Rio Tinto has had a long history in Zimbabwe, mining gold and emeralds, refining nickel and producing industrial goods. It has contributed not only to the country's industrialisation and economic growth, but also to social investment through the Rio Tinto Foundation. RTZ-CRA, the international natural resources group, owns 56.1% of the company's shares, with most of the remaining 43.9% held by Zimbabwean companies and individuals. The organisation therefore represents a long-standing and successful partnership between a foreign multinational and the private sector in Zimbabwe.

Given the nature of its activities Rio Tinto's social and economic impact has mainly been in rural areas and it has played a key role in promoting rural development and industrialisation in several areas of the country. It is bound by RTZ's international Environment, Health and Safety Policy and by adopting these international practices and standards, the company has taken a leadership role in building local capacity and promoting corporate responsibility in the area of environmental management. It was one of the first companies in Zimbabwe, for example, to undertake a comprehensive environmental impact assessment (EIA) in the early 1990s. A key aspect of this EIA was the involvement and training of local environmental experts, thereby building Zimbabwean capcity in this field.

The Tugwane Dam and Rupike Irrigation Scheme

Through its mining operations at Renco, in the arid lands of Zimbabwe's southern lowvelt, Rio Tinto came to know at first hand the effects of successive droughts on their neighbours the Nyajena. In the absence of stable water supplies these rural communities had little chance of growing self-sustaining food crops.

To address this problem Rio Tinto decided to fund and technically support the construction of a dam and irrigation scheme through its corporate foundation. Today the Tugwane Dam and Rupike Irrigation Scheme is occupied by some 200 farming families each on half-hectare irrigated plots, and is the springboard for local development, employment and small-scale business opportunities.

The scheme was funded primarily through the Rio Tinto Foundation. Established in 1974, by the donation of a block of one million shares in Rio Tinto Zimbabwe Ltd. by the parent company RTZ, the foundation

provides an interesting model of how a company has formalised its commitment to good corporate citizenship. A further one million shares was donated by RTZ in 1977 and the foundation's annual income is derived from dividends on the shareholding and interest on investments funded by these dividends. Its focus is on supporting rural development projects, which involve small-scale farming and other income generating opportunities, with a focus on those adjacent to Rio Tinto Group operations.

In consultation with the local people and working with government, Rio Tinto started to construct the 3.8 million cubic metres Tugwane Dam in 1987. By early 1988 it was 80% full, and the irrigation works and over-head spray system installed a year later. At each stage, Rio Tinto provided finance, technical and overall project management. Even in the drought of 1992 the Rupike farmers were able to sustain their crops. Literally, the desert has bloomed.

The first crops were traditional food staples – maize, sugar-beans and groundnuts. Soon the farmers were branching out and producing a range of vegetables with a surplus for the local market. Now the Nyajena have readily accessible water for their cattle, and the dam is stocked with fish, – additional free protein. Livestock, fish farming, orchards, woodlots and rabbit and chicken breeding are possible further developments. The powerline serving the project also supplies electricity to the Rupike township, where schools, housing, a clinic, the business centre and Rural Council facilities have been developed. Three grinding mills are in operation, and potable water for the township is now on tap. A number of small businesses providing services to the scheme have been set up by local entrepreneurs. Training the Rupike farmers has been given the same level of personal attention and expertise by Rio Tinto that went into the scheme itself. Training includes money management and the production, marketing, packaging and transport of crops.

In keeping with the Rio Tinto Foundation's policy to present completed projects to the appropriate authority, the $6 million Tugwane/Rupike scheme was handed over to the Ministry of Lands, Agriculture and Water Development on 30 June 1994, as a gift to the nation and local community.

Being a good citizen involves some demonstration beyond just behaving within the laws of the country. Rio Tinto Annual Report

Golden Hope Plantations in Malaysia

Golden Hope Plantations is a leading Malaysian corporation with diversified interests in plantations, resource-based manufacturing and property. Over the past 100 years, it has played an important role in developing the Malaysian plantations sector and contributing to the country's growing economic success. Equally important, it has gained an international reputation in the field of sustainable development and is one of the few companies to have been awarded a UNEP Global 500 Award. It is also one of the few large companies in the world that makes an explicit mention of its commitment to all stakeholders in its corporate vision statement.

Golden Hope currently owns and manages more than 172,000 hectares of oil palm, rubber, cocoa, coconut and fruit plantations. In recent years the group has diversified into value-added manufacturing of these resources, producing products such as refined edible oils, tropical fruit juices, oleochemicals, rubber footwear, fibreboard and furniture components. Although the bulk of its commercial activities take place in Malaysia, in recent years the company has made investments to establish a plantation in Indonesia, build and operate edible oils and fats refineries in Vietnam, China, Bangladesh and Tanzania, and pack and distribute the group's products in Europe and the USA.

Golden Hope has played a leading role in implementing practices such as total quality environmental management, zero burning and integrated pest management into its plantation operations and investing in zero discharge technologies in its manufacturing activities. It has also invested heavily in the training of it employees and in social services around the environs of its plantations. Some of the activities that the company has undertaken to implement its programme are as follows:

- **Total Quality Environmental Management (TQEM)** – on the first page of Golden Hope's 1996 Annual Report, the company states its commitment to TQEM for managing quality, health, safety and the environment in all its operations. It has incorporated TQEM into the Group's logo to signify adoption of TQEM principles as primary considerations in all aspects of the business. This statement is backed by plans to provide TQEM planning to all levels of estate employees, not only the managers, and by the fact that the Director of Quality and Environment has a seat on the Group's eight person Management Committee.

- **Zero burning** – the company was a leader in starting this practice in 1989. It is a replanting technique which deals with plantation crops that have reached the end of their economic life, such as old oil palms. They are felled, shredded and left to decompose in situ and unlike the conventional systems of clearing and burning, no burning is carried out This process not only helps to eliminate atmospheric pollution, but also replenishes soil organic matter, improves its physical properties and enhances it fertility, thereby reducing the need for chemical fertilizers;

- **Integrated pest management** – Routine monitoring for pest levels and the use of biological predators for pest control plays a central role in the company's plant protection practices and research and development is on-going to maximise the use of this approach over the use of chemical pesticides;

- **Zero discharge effluent systems** – since 1976, the company has invested in research and development efforts to monitor and treat effluent at its mills and factories. Today all its mills have effluent treatment plants to handle wastes and samples are analysed on a regular basis to monitor progress. In 1994, it collaborated with an Italian manufacturer to develop a new oil palm milling process that provides more efficient product recovery and reduces effluent output. The new technique has reduced biological oxygen demand loading (BOD) by 800%. In 1993 the company also developed a system to treat effluent from its latex concentrate production and the manufacture of its fibreboard products, which has also led to measurable environmental and efficiency improvements;

- **Use of wastes and by-products** – empty fruit branches and treated oil palm effluent which are rich in plant nutrients are recycled as organic fertilizers instead of being incinerated. Other by-products, such as kernel shell and palm fibre are used for power generation in the mills.

- **Human resource development** – the company pursues programmes for its employees well beyond the provisions of statutory requirements. It invests extensively in education and training (both for its employees and local communities), housing, child care centres, water and electricity supplies, health services, recreational and other community services. In recent years growing emphasis has been placed on the development of employee quality and decision-making teams, ensuring that the company's employees have a greater say in the company's workplace and community practices.

Golden Hope offers a good example of the growing leadership role in corporate citizenship which is being undertaken by local companies in some of the world's emerging markets. It also illustrates the growing importance of south-south investments and technology cooperation.

Our ultimate aim is to achieve zero waste generation and zero emission via an integrated two pronged approach. Firstly, we seek to continue improving the efficiency of our plantations and manufacturing operations to optimise inputs and reduce waste, and secondly, our focus is on increasing the value and extent of utilising the biomass and by-products from our activities. The education and training of our employee, suppliers, contractors and customers is an important part of this vision.   Teoh Cheng Hai, Director, Quality and Environment

B&Q IN PAPUA NEW GUINEA

Companies do not have to be located in rural areas themselves to make a contribution to sustainable rural development. Those that source raw materials, such as forestry products and foodstuffs, from developing countries also have a responsibility to ensure that these natural resources are being produced in an environmentally sustainable manner and in a way that benefits rather than exploits local rural communities. British-based B&Q offers a good example of a company that has invested in this approach.

B&Q is one of Britain's largest home-improvement retailers, with a nationwide network of some 280 stores, 500 suppliers of timber and other products, and millions of customers. Since 1990 the company has engaged in a detailed and costly programme to understand and act on the environmental and social issues related to its sourcing of products such as timber, and to educate its customers about these issues. During this process it has set up comprehensive supplier auditing procedures and worked closely with international environmental NGOs such as the Worldwide Fund for Nature (WWF) and the Forest Stewardship Council which are profiled on page 216.

It has also developed direct supplier relationships with community-based forestry projects in developing countries. One of these is the Bainings community in Papua New Guinea, with which B&Q established a relationship through the Ecological Trading Company. At the outset of the relationship, B&Q donated money to support the development of the Bainings project in a number of ways. This included an initial feasibility study prepared by the International Institute for Environment and Development on the potential for sustainable, community-based forestry in the area, followed-up by financial, technical and managerial support in helping the community to develop a forestry management plan, and purchase portable sawmills. In early 1994, B&Q also paid for an independent certification of the project, in line with the FSC's Forest Stewardship Principles, and is now stocking Bainings-sourced timbers in its stores in the UK. According to Max Henderson, a naturalised PNG citizen and liaison officer for the Bainings community, the initiative has resulted in: increased cash flow into the villages concerned; improved rural employment opportunities; reinforcement of the value of the forests to local communities; an increase in self-esteem among villagers; and a supply of sawn timber for improved housing in the villages.

The Odebrecht Corporation in Peru

The Odebrecht Corporation is one of Brazil's largest privately-owned conglomerates and offers another good example of south-south technology cooperation and corporate citizenship. The company's major business areas are engineering and construction, chemicals and petrochemicals, and equity investments in a variety of infrastructure projects, ranging from energy to transportation. Odebrecht employs 32,000 people, of which about 9,000 are outside Brazil, and currently has more than 100 job sites in over 20 countries in Latin America, the USA, Asia, Africa and Europe. In many of its activities the company is operating in remote rural areas and has developed a strong corporate vision and management system to support integrated rural development activities in these areas.

Three of the management structures that the company has established to promote socially responsible behaviour in its own activities and those of its business partners, are an integrated community relations system; a Social Expression Award; and a foundation, the Emilio Odebrecht Foundation, which is profiled on page 69.

The Community Relations system has been developed on a group-wide basis and is adapted to the local realities of each project. It is based on the premise that all projects must be accompanied by a systematic and integrated programme for interaction and consultation with local communities. A series of in-house manuals and practical guidelines have been developed, and in implementing the system, the company's project management teams are required to consider the whole range of business activities under their responsibility. The process includes:

- Identifying possible adverse impacts of the project and the communities most effected;

- Identifying and implementing actions to minimise such impacts;

- Implementing ongoing communication and information systems directed at the community;

- Planning other activities aimed specifically at the community; and

- Committing to a hiring policy that favours workers from the local community.

Linked to this approach, the company has a commitment to developing small-scale agricultural activities and rural businesses linked to some of its projects. In Peru, for example, the company has worked with the Peruvian government on the development of the Chavimochic irrigation project. From the outset it has invested in an integrated rural development programme to ensure the self-sustainability and self-financing of the irrigation project. Since 1993 this has included helping with the organisation of associated efforts by small-scale farmers to produce a range of non-traditional agribusiness products for local and export markets, and the establishment of other rural industries. These activities are producing a steady stream of revenues which are helping to cover project financing costs and creating new rural employment opportunities. A similar approach is being taken with irrigation projects in Ecuador and Angola, and in 1994 the former initiative won Odebrecht's global Social Expression Award.

2.7 Emergency Relief and Preparedness

Almost every week news of another disaster, normally in a developing country, hits the television screens and pages of the world's newspapers. The Red Cross estimates that the average number of people affected by natural and man-made disasters is growing by roughly 10 million a year. Billions of dollars of overseas development assistance goes on emergencies and the figures are growing. In 1971, for example, OECD emergency aid was US$200 million; in 1994 US$1 billion went to Rwanda alone. The astronomical economic costs of emergencies are matched by the enormous human and environmental costs, as entire communities face dislocation, despair and death.

Financially and politically, the "disaster business" has become a critically important component of international aid and development and there is an urgent need to search for ways to:

- Improve the effectiveness, efficiency, co-ordination and accountability of the immediate responses to emergencies and disasters;

- Integrate such responses into longer-term initiatives for rehabilitation and sustainable development; and

- Develop programmes and policies which minimise the likelihood of disasters and ensure better preparedness when they do occur.

None of these objectives are achievable by governments or humanitarian agencies acting on their own. Increasingly, nor are they achievable without the active involvement of the private for-profit sector which is becoming a major player in emergency relief, rehabilitation and preparedness.

More and more of the world's humanitarian agencies are starting to form strategic alliances with business, not only in fundraising and social marketing, but also in service and product delivery. One example is the partnership between CARE UK and the telecommunications giant Cable & Wireless to produce emergency communications kits, which is profiled on page 220. Humanitarian agencies and governments are also realising that private enterprises can often provide logistical serves on-site – such as transportation, managing feeding-centres, supplying water, medicine, temporary shelter, blankets and clothing   more cost-effectively and efficiently than either government or the voluntary sector. Equally important is the managerial, financial and logistical support role that business can play in emergency preparedness programmes – both in terms of industrial accidents, which are clearly the responsibility of business to avoid and manage, and natural and other man-made disasters.

This growing role of the private sector is leading to a fundamental change in the way the industry is managed and perceived, one reason why this year's first-ever World Aid expo and conference on emergency relief in Geneva has attracted hundreds of companies and aid agencies to debate the future of disasters.

RELIEF INC.

In flowing robes and suits they came from every part of the world to discuss the future of their business, a multinational with 128 million workers and a fast-growing annual turnover of around US$19 billion in 163 countries from America to Zimbabwe. But the hundreds of managers gathering in Geneva had no profit forecasts to read. Instead, at the quadrennial conference of the International Red Cross and Red Crescent Movement, the packed agenda covered war and hunger, refugees and disease and how to help the 250 million people affected every year by conflict, famine and flood. The movement is the world's most experienced, extensive humanitarian network. Its unique role is recognised by governments. Yet alongside fundamental principles of humanity and neutrality, it is increasingly run like a major global enterprise with professional marketers, accountants and managers, taskforces and strategic plans.

While the new professionalism is to be applauded, however, it is part of the struggle now raging for the soul of the aid industry. For although the relief agencies have much to learn from business, their work involves ethical decisions which need values and principles to back them up. In many cases the market model is irrelevant since "consumers" are the poor and powerless and decisions are made by the people giving the money, not taking it. As charities seeking efficiency become like companies, and companies seeking the "halo effect" offer aid, both must be keenly honest about where their respective strengths lie and must find new ways of working together if we are to get aid which is both low-cost and purposeful.

Take the intricacy of a Washington-funded deployment of an operation involving the US Army and a commercial Californian contractor, Portable Water Supply Systems (PWSS), to provide clean water in Zaire at the height of the 1994 cholera emergency. The contractor worked closely with the UN and non-governmental organisations (NGOs) and was vigorous in delivering water and promoting its success. The water company said it had halted a cholera epidemic and saved 140,000 lives at a cost of seven cents per life saved, claims which probably irritated relief agencies present in the camps at Goma.

From RELIEF INC, by Nick Cater, published in the Jan/Feb 1996 issue of World Link, magazine of the World Economic Forum. International consultant Cater – e-mail: cater@ifrc.org – is also external editor of the annual World Disasters Report from the International Federation of Red Cross and Red Crescent Societies, published by OUP.

While there is obvious uneasiness in some quarters about the "privatisation of disaster management" and much that needs to be tackled in terms of developing Codes of Conduct and improving understanding about the roles and responsibilities of different sectors, there can be no doubt that change is irreversible. A recent article captured some of the complexities and opportunities of this new paradigm, an excerpt of which is opposite.

A useful example of the changing nature of corporate involvement in disaster relief is offered by the Corporate Network for Disaster Response (CNDR) in the Philippines.

The CNDR is a network of private corporations, business associations and corporate foundations operating in the Philippines, which engages in disaster prevention, mitigation and preparedness programmes, and mobilises timely and appropriate relief response to disaster. Their goal is to collaborate with, rather than replace the efforts of government, international agencies and NGOs. CNDR was created as a result of the June 1990 earthquake in Luzon, which resulted in the death of thousands of people and billions of pesos of damage to properties and crops, and which demonstrated not only the critical role that corporations can play during disasters and other crises, but also displayed the problems associated with a lack of organised and co-ordinated effort in response to such situations.

At the time of the Luzon earthquake, Filipino companies and corporate foundations raised more than 1 million pesos in cash and in-kind to complement government relief efforts, and helped to raise an additional 53 million pesos from donor agencies and corporations for the massive rehabilitation programme. They established a task force to undertake this, which was later formalised into CNDR in October 1990. Over time this group has shifted its focus from a relief-oriented programme to a programme of preparedness/mitigation and prevention.

Its activities range from;

- training programmes covering corporate responses to crisis; drought planning and management; and earthquake preparedness, to

- relief operations in specific disasters, and

- network-building – for example the formation of regional corporate networks to facilitate disaster response in vulnerable areas.

The network has a core group of organising members which are the Philippine Business for Social progress, ABS-CBN Foundation, Andres Soriano Foundation, SGV and Company, United Planters Bank Foundation, Andres Soriano Corporation, PHINMA, DELBROS, Mabuhay Vinyl Corporation, San Miguel Corporation and the Makati Business Club.

All over the world from Japan to Zimbabwe, there are other examples of individual companies and groups of companies, sharing financial, technical and managerial resources to help deal with emergencies and disasters. One international initiative worthy of note is UNEP's APELL programme (Awareness and Preparedness for Emergencies at the Local Level) which is profiled on page 238.

III Multi-stakeholder Partnerships

The creation of new types of partnership between business, government and non-governmental organisations lies at the heart of economic progress, human development, social cohesion and environmental sustainability. The following section looks at 26 examples of partnerships between international NGOs and business, international agencies and business, and between groups of companies themselves, all aimed at achieving one or more of the above objectives.

The Partnership Multiplier of NGOs

International NGOs can play a vital intermediary role by: linking companies, governments and civil society organisations, at both a global and local level: mobilising financial, technical and managerial resources, and potentially reaching dozens of countries, hundreds of communities and thousands of people.

The following diagrams illustrate the multiplier impact of just three of the NGOs profiled in the following sector.

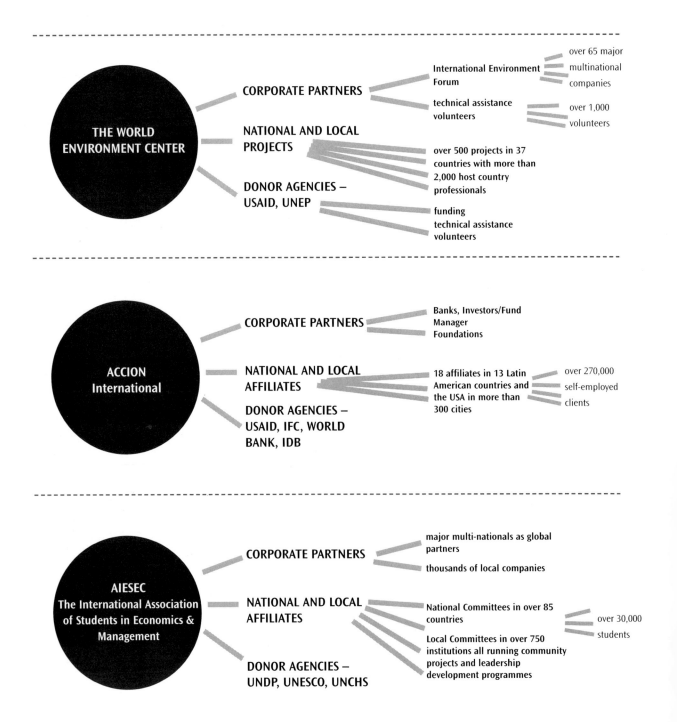

1 Partnerships between international NGOs and business

Many international NGOs, especially in the United States, have a long tradition of funding from corporate foundations and the philanthropic budgets of companies. Whilst these funding sources remain of great importance, both NGOs and the companies are recognising the need to move beyond the hands-off "cheque-book" approach of the past, to a more strategic and interactive relationship; one which matches the needs of the NGO and the beneficiaries it is serving, with the business strategy and resources of the company. The resources being provided are increasingly human, physical and technical, as well as financial.

The factors underlying these trends in corporate-NGO relationships have been discussed in earlier sections. The purpose of the following examples is to illustrate some of the ways in which international NGOs operating in developing and transition economies, are forging more complex and creative partnerships with multinational companies operating in the same economies. Such partnerships are certainly not without their problems, especially when they involve NGOs which have both a campaigning and a project management structure, and a need to keep the former independent from certain business interests, even if they are getting corporate support to run specific projects. However as both the NGO and business sectors become more important players in the development process there will be a growing need to find ways to move from confrontation towards consultation between the two, without totally losing the freedom to be confrontational when necessary.

Selected to represent a variety of objectives and activities, the NGOs include:

- three environmental organisations – the World Environment Center, WWF and Conservation International;

- two development and relief agencies – CARE International and ACTIONAID;

- ACCION International, a US-based organisation supporting small and micro-scale enterprises throughout Latin America and more recently in the USA – illustrating the growing commonality in social challenges and solutions between North and South America;

- Project HOPE, an international non-profit organisation dedicated to medical training and health-care education; and

- two youth organisations – one, the International Youth Foundation, targeted at helping marginalised youth around the world, the other, AIESEC, at mobilising the skills of university students to engage in community work and to promote sustainable development and corporate responsibility.

These cases are a small sample of the many non-governmental organisations which are developing closer links with both business and international agencies to implement projects in developing countries. Many national level NGOs in these countries, and increasingly even community-based organisations, are also starting to work more closely with business – both domestic companies and the local offices of multi-nationals. Relationships may include: strategic philanthropy (where a company matches its giving to strategic business interests); social marketing and licensing agreements; fee-based relationships where the NGO provides a service or product to the company; in-kind support from the company in the form of volunteers, managerial advice, technology or premises; and collaborative projects or formalised joint ventures. The potential is great and is only recently being explored.

1.1 The World Environment Center

The World Environment Center has played a valuable role in encouraging the responsible use of world resources. Its efforts to unite corporate and government leaders in developing solutions to environmental problems serve as a fine example of the benefits that can result when the public and private sectors work together.

President Bill Clinton

Developing comprehensive environment, health and safety programmes is a challenge for managers in any company. It is especially challenging for managers operating in the world's developing and transition economies, where access to information and capital is often limited, and where the pressures of rapid economic change and increased competitiveness, combined with weak regulatory systems, often push environment, health and safety issues off the core business agenda. Over the past 20 years the World Environment Center (WEC) has played a vital role in helping over 2,000 of these managers to make responsible decisions with favourable impacts on both the environmental and economic performance of their companies and surrounding communities.

From petroleum facilities in Pakistan, to pharmaceutical plants in Poland and pulp and paper factories in Turkey, WEC has now completed over 500 projects ranging from waste minimisation initiatives to local accident mitigation and prevention programmes. Every year the organisation mobilises over a hundred volunteers – environment, health and safety (EH&S) experts from leading multinational companies, government agencies, academic institutions and NGOs – to work with their counterparts in developing and transition economies and to find practical and locally relevant management solutions to common global problems. WEC and its network of programmes offers an excellent model of the leverage impact and added value of cross-sector and cross-cultural partnerships.

Established in 1974 with seed funding from UNEP, the World Environment Center is an independent, not-for-profit, non-advocacy organisation which contributes to sustainable development worldwide by strengthening industrial and urban environment, health and safety policies and practices. Over three decades it has quietly evolved into an effective, proactive and hands-on organisation by linking the "four Es" – environment, energy, education and economics. Today, with headquarters in New York, and offices in Bangkok, Jakarta, Mexico City, Prague, Geneva and Washington DC, it serves as a bridge for the exchange of information and expertise among industry, government, non-governmental organisations and the community on both a national and international basis.

WEC runs three complementary programmes:

- **The International Environment and Development Service** (IEDS) was established in 1982 to demonstrate to companies and government agencies that economic benefits can be derived from environmentally sound management. Initially a partnership between USAID and WEC, with 14 US corporations contributing human and material resources, the IEDS programme now receives funding and in-kind support from a wide range of sources including industry, the World Bank and private citizens. Since 1982 over 1,000 volunteer experts have helped IEDS to

INDUSTRIAL WASTE MINIMISATION IN CENTRAL AND EASTERN EUROPE
The International Environment and Development Service in Action

One of the largest and most comprehensive IEDS activities is the Industrial Waste Minimisation Programme, which is currently being implemented in twelve countries in Central and Eastern Europe. With financial support from USAID and in-kind expertise provided by some of the multinational companies which are members of its International Environment Forum, WEC has been demonstrating to companies and government officials in these countries the economic benefits of low-cost waste minimisation and cleaner production measures.

The programme consists of three stages, starting with waste minimisation demonstration projects in individual companies, where the WEC team works with a team established by the company to change management processes and implement specific projects; then moving on to train the trainer activities and local capacity-building work to decrease reliance on outside expertise, and culminating in the establishment of pollution prevention centres, established in collaboration with a local trade association or university and staffed by local environmental experts. The key characteristics of the WEC approach are:

- flexibility to meet rapidly changing circumstances and different levels of need and capacity in each country;
- working with the most appropriate partners in a particular country or region;
- finding solutions that are economically viable in local circumstances;
- focusing on changing management approaches and cultures vs. simply counting the number of workshops run and projects implemented; and
- building technical and managerial capacity in the local companies and government departments. The WEC staff act as facilitators rather than external experts with all the answers, and aim to build local confidence and expertise.

A recent evaluation of the Waste Minimisation Programme in Poland illustrates the potential of this approach. Since 1992 WEC has implemented 52 waste minimisation projects at 18 Polish companies representing the chemical, pharmaceutical, non-ferrous metals, meat processing and dairy industrial sectors. The results of this programme include:

- Economic benefits – the 18 participating companies saved about US$8 million a year. Since savings of a similar magnitude will continue in future years, the economic benefits gained by the companies are more appropriately expressed in terms of Net Present Value. The NPV of the economic benefits of the 52 projects has been calculated at US$24 million;
- EH&S benefits – by decreasing the use of resources such as energy, water and raw materials, and by reducing the generation of waste materials the companies were able to demonstrate improvements in their productivity, in their emissions to air, water and land, and in their health and safety records;
- Local management commitment and investment – in response to these initial benefits many of the participating companies have committed to make their own investments over and above the financial support initially provided by WEC, demonstrating a strong and hopefully permanent acceptance of the cleaner production philosophy and methodology.

> Our strategy is to go into a company and use a technical project as a vehicle to change the management culture and attitude. We usually start with a company saying it cannot afford all that 'environmental stuff'.
> When we finish a year later, they say they cannot afford not to deal with it.
>
> Antony Marcil,
> Chief Executive Officer,
> WEC

provide pro bono services in 37 countries and complete over 500 projects involving more than 2,000 host country professionals. Activities have included: industrial environmental reviews at national, sectoral and individual plants; waste minimisation demonstration programmes, in-country Pollution Prevention Centers; drafting environmental laws and regulations; workshops and training programmes; study tours and on-the-job internships for industry and government officials; and community-based Local Accident Mitigation Prevention Programmes.

- **The International Environment Forum** (IEF) – is a forum where senior policy makers and industry executives from around the world can meet for off-the-record discussions on environmental and resource management issues. Over 65 major multinational companies, representing ten industrial sectors and based in nine countries participate in the IEF, which holds regular meetings on leading-edge issues and publishes a series of Country Profiles covering a range of EH&S issues which are of interest to participating companies.

- **The WEC Gold Medal** for international corporate environmental achievement – plays an important role in building bridges, recognising excellence and raising awareness. The annual award has become a respected measure of multinational companies which have: established exemplary, inclusive, publicly-announced corporate environmental policies with a strong commitment to stakeholder consultation; clearly demonstrated a globally uniform and innovative implementation of this policy; and played an international environmental leadership role by extending beyond traditional corporate boundaries to larger societal issues, such as national development and environment goals.

1.2 WWF and the Forest and Marine Stewardship Councils

In a period of less than five years, the ambitious, and some said impossible, idea of developing an internationally agreed set of Principles and Criteria for the management of forests worldwide – coupled with a product labelling scheme to identify timber certified as originating from such well managed forests – has finally become a reality.

Dr Timothy Synott,
FSC Director

In the early 1990s, as consumers became more demanding about the environmental and social impacts of the products they were buying, a plethora of 'green' claims started to appear on everything from furniture to disposable nappies. In 1990 and 1991 WWF in the United Kingdom commissioned research into the claims of 'sustainability' being applied to wood and wood products. 626 companies were studied. Of those supplying tropical wood products 50% provided 'reassurance' as to the environmental acceptability of their materials, but of the 80 selected for further investigation only three were prepared to make a serious attempt to justify their claims. None were able to answer fully questions about their sources.

For the more progressive of these companies such as B&Q, a major DIY chain, and some of the country's other leading retailers, this set in process a wide range of individual corporate efforts to start auditing and working more proactively with their hundreds of suppliers around the world – many of them in developing countries. It also resulted in the launch of WWF-UK's 1995 Plus Group, which commits its member companies to work with WWF to phase out the sale and use of all unsustainable wood and wood products. Most importantly of all, the research emphasised the critical need for an international, independent, credible and verifiable labelling system.

Other organisations in other countries identified a similar need and in 1990 WWF-UK was part of a group of timber users, traders and representatives of environmental and human-rights organisations which met in California to discuss ways in which they could improve forest conservation and reduce deforestation. The group agreed to work together on creating an independent, internationally credible body which would set and maintain standards to which forests and forest products could be certified as environmentally and socially acceptable. The founding assembly of the Forest Stewardship Council (FSC) was held in September 1993 with a draft set of Principles and Criteria of Forest Management, which had been put together by WWF and other organisations, with financial and technical support from public and private sources, including B&Q. Today, after five years of consultations in some 25 countries, these guidelines have been put into operation as part of a systematic process of product certification and monitoring. The FSC now evaluates, accredits and monitors independent certification organisations, who in turn are responsible for inspecting particular forests and woodlands around the world, and certifying them if they are well-managed according to the ten FSC Principles of Forest Management. Retailers stocking these products can then sell them under the FSC Trademark.

The FSC Principles of Forest Management form the cornerstone of the certification process. They cover the following ten points:

1. Compliance with laws and FSC principles

2. Tenure and use rights and responsibilities

3. Indigenous peoples' rights

4. Community relations and workers' rights

5. Benefits from the forest

6. Environmental impact

7. Management plan

8. Monitoring and assessment

9. Maintenance of natural forests

10. Plantations

A detailed text can be obtained on the Internet at http: /antequera.antequera.com/FSC/

With funding from the governments of Austria and Mexico, WWF-Netherlands and the Ford Foundation, the FSC was able to become operational with headquarters in Mexico and a network of National Working Groups and members from different sectors. Today it is funded by foundations, government donors, membership subscriptions and accreditation fees. In order to maintain its independence it does not accept funding from industry, but the timber industry still plays a critical role in the success of the initiative by both applying for FSC certification on the production-side and agreeing to only stock FSC certified products on the retail-end of the supply chain.

In the UK, for example, the FSC initiative has received the endorsement and active commitment of over 50 leading companies, including major retailers such as B&Q, J Sainsbury, Tesco, W H Smith, and Boots the Chemist – who between them serve some 20,000,000 million customers a week – as well as smaller companies set up on sustainability principles, such as the Ecological Trading Company. The initiative is also supported by a broad coalition of NGOs including WWF, Greenpeace and Friends of the Earth, coupled with the support of government and the European Union.

In June 1996 the FSC held its first General Assembly in Mexico, attended by 132 delegates from 35 countries. Forests, covering over 2 million hectares have now been certified by FSC-accredited bodies in a number of countries, including Bolivia, Brazil, Costa Rica, Honduras, Mexico, Papua New Guinea, Poland, the United Kingdom, USA, and Zimbabwe. The initiative has not been without problems – some of them the inevitable result of partnership between a broad coalition of interests, others a result of the practical challenges of dealing with a complex supply chain. However as the process of certification and monitoring continues to be refined, and as more producers and consumers agree to participate, the FSC will provide a real opportunity to protect and sustain the world's forests and the lives that they support.

THE MARINE STEWARDSHIP COUNCIL

"The Marine Stewardship Council has the potential to significantly alter worldwide fishing practices in favour of more sustainable, less destructive fisheries. When Unilever and other major seafood companies make commitments to buy their fish products only from well-managed and MSC-certified fisheries, the fishing industry will be compelled to modify its current practices. Governments, laws, and treaties aside, the market itself will begin to determine the means of fish production."

Michael Sutton, WWF and Caroline Whitfield, Unilever

In February 1996 two global organisations formed a partnership in an innovative attempt to harness consumer power to tackle the global fisheries crisis. The two organisations have different motivations, but a shared objective: to ensure the long-term viability of global fish populations and the health of the marine ecosystems on which they depend.

• **The World Wide Fund for Nature** – the world's largest private, non-profit conservation organisation – runs an Endangered Seas Campaign and is committed to finding new approaches to ensure more sustainable management of marine fisheries.

• **The Anglo-Dutch company Unilever** – one of the 40 largest multinational companies in the world, a major buyer of frozen fish, and manufacturer of some of the world's best known frozen fish brands, is interested in long-term fish stock sustainability to ensure a future for its successful fish business.

Having signed a Statement of Intent the two organisations are committed to work together and with other organisations to establish a Marine Stewardship Council (MSC) by 1997. The MSC will be an independent, non-profit membership body, and will establish a broad set of principles for sustainable fishing and standards for individual fisheries. By 1998, products from fisheries certified to MSC standards will be marked with an MSC logo. An international, multi-disciplinary project team has been established to draft the principles, and will hold a series of national and regional consultations over the coming year with conservationists, representatives from the seafood industry, fishery managers and policy-makers, to refine these principles and develop a process for international implementation.

1.3 Conservation International

Conservation International believes that the earth's natural heritage must be maintained if future generations are to thrive spiritually, culturally and economically. With projects in more than 20 countries in Latin America, Africa and Asia, the organisation brings scientifically-based, economically sound and culturally sensitive conservation models to ecological hotspots – threatened rain forests and other ecosystems rich in biological diversity. Through model demonstration projects and technical support, it helps people to improve their standard of living while conserving their valuable natural resources.

> Just as business must be willing to take risks and innovate to stay at the leading edge, Conservation International has taken one bold step after another. For sheer scientific and technical innovation, CI is second to none.
>
> Gordon Moore,
> Chairman of Intel Corporation

Since economic problems are one of the greatest obstacles to sustainable development, CI has taken an entrepreneurial approach to demonstrate that business strategies – if creatively and responsibly applied – can be good for conservation in many of the world's most biologically important places. It works with several corporate partners to leverage their strengths – whether they are leaders in new technologies, consumer markets, or international finance – into innovative conservation solutions that improve the health of important ecosystems and the lives of people who live in them. The following examples illustrate this approach of working with business:

- In 1995 Conservation International joined forces with Intel, a corporate leader in computer technology, and the United Nations Scientific and Cultural Organisation (UNESCO) to equip 25 biosphere reserves around the world with sophisticated computer equipment and access to the Internet global information network. Under the agreement Intel provided about US$270,000 to pay for the costs of hardware and software, as well as technical support and training; Conservation International provided software for its Geographic Information System, the first multilingual geographic information software available which integrates geographical, biological and ecological data with social and economic factors; and CI and UNESCO together will provide training and support through a series of regional workshops.

> This project illustrates the power of partnerships. Intel provides the technology and financial support, Conservation International provides on-the-ground expertise, and UNESCO is the global umbrella for all the biosphere reserves. Together we're bringing the most sophisticated technology to bear on conservation and economic health.
>
> Peter Seligmann, Chairman and
> CEO of Conservation International

- Another example of CI's innovative approach to working with the corporate sector is its relationship with Japan's Keidanren – the Japanese Federation of Economic Organisations – which represents over 1,000 major corporations. As one of the world's major importers of natural resources from the tropics, CI felt that Japan was an important country to focus on, in terms of educating the Japanese public and corporate sector about the importance of biodiversity. It established a relationship with the Keidanren, which was the most effective and respected intermediary that it could work with to reach the corporate sector, and in 1992, when the Keidanren established its Nature Conservation Fund it agreed to make a grant of about US$400,000 to CI for two initiatives. The first was support for the Tagua Initiative (described opposite) in which the Keidanren offered not only financial assistance, but also assistance in identifying marketing opportunities and help with training workshop for Tagua nut carvers, drawing on Japan's expertise in this field with ivory. The second initiative was a series of workshops for Japanese

CONSERVATION ENTERPRISE DEPARTMENT
Linking economic viability and environmental sustainability

In 1990 CI established its Conservation Enterprise Department (CED) with the goal of helping local communities to establish enterprises based on the sustainable use of natural resources and to make the necessary linkages to bring these "biodiversity products" to market. These products range from tree oils and plant fibres, to nuts, timber, marine products and ecotourism. If managed and harvested well, they have the potential of creating jobs and other benefits for local communities on a more sustainable basis than other economic alternatives, thereby creating incentives for local people to conserve natural habitats. Staffed by a team of experienced business professionals, CED provides technical assistance to local enterprises in three key areas: management; market development; and finance.

Two of the projects currently underway are as follows:

1 The Croda–CI Partnership

Croda Inc., a worldwide leader in the development of raw materials for cosmetics, has joined forces with CI to refine and market rainforest ingredients which can be used in the manufacture of products such as shampoos, lotions, and other personal care items. Botanical products and oils are harvested by community enterprises in Peru, Guatemala and the Solomon Islands, purchased and processed by Croda and then marketed with CI's support and imprimatur.

2 The Tagua Initiative

The Tagua Initiative is the oldest of CED's initiatives, launched in 1990, and is now able to demonstrate encouraging results. Working in partnership with:

- CIDESA, a national community development organisation in Ecuador;
- residents of the Comuna Rio Santiaga Cayapas;
- Ecuadorian tagua processing factories;
- American, Ecuadorian, European and Japanese distributors, manufacturers and retailers of buttons, garments, carvings, and jewellery;
- the United States Agency for International Development (USAID)
- the Keidanren and JAIDO (Japan's International Development Organisation); and
- several academic and research institutes.

Conservation International has facilitated the sale of more than 2,000 tons of tagua nuts and 45 million finished buttons, creating over 1,800 jobs and developing a range of managerial and technical skills in the community. End-users of the buttons include leading garment companies such as: The Gap; Banana Republic; J Crew; Liz Claiborne; and Donna Karan New York. The initiative has also provided an economically viable example of alternative land use and thus played a role in persuading local people to reject a proposed 12,000 hectare banana plantation.

corporate executives, conducted in Tokyo by CI and the Washington-based Management Institute for Environment and Business, to demonstrate the vital linkages between biodiversity, local stakeholder partnerships and Japanese business. This relationship has played a valuable role in getting issues of global biodiversity onto Japan's corporate environmental agenda.

- In 1993 CI formed a partnership with McDonald's Corporation and Clemson University's Archbold Tropical Research Center, in the La Amistad Biosphere Reserve, a protected area covering 2.7 million acres in Costa Rica and Panama, to establish an integrated conservation programme aimed at testing the model of economically viable conservation. Called AMISCONDE (Amistad Conservation and Development Initiative) the programme combines business, education and scientific expertise with the community's desire to reverse soil damage, low crop yields and financial hardships. Within a year the programme's range had been extended to the Panamanian portion of La Amistad. After three years it has increased environmental awareness among local inhabitants, increased protection for the biosphere reserve and created new markets for conservation-based products from the region.

1.4 CARE International

CARE International is a confederation of 10 national members, working together to implement more than 350 development and emergency programmes in more than 65 countries. CARE reaches 30 million people in Africa, Asia, Latin America, the Middle East and Eastern Europe. With an annual project portfolio worth more than US$500 million, CARE International is one of the world's largest independent relief and development organisations. In the changing world of humanitarian aid, CARE International is striving to identify innovative and rewarding opportunities for its corporate partners.

Working relationships between CARE and the corporate sector go back a long time. In the aftermath of World War Two, corporations joined CARE in providing CARE packages containing desperately needed supplies to those left destitute in Europe and then Asia. Today, corporations continue to play a role by helping CARE to foster self-sufficiency within the developing world. CARE achieves this through mutually beneficial alliances which both respond to the commercial needs of its corporate partners and make a positive impact on the needs of the world's poor. These alliances take many forms and the following examples illustrate some of the ways in which CARE is moving from philanthropy to partnership with its corporate supporters.

Cable & Wireless lending commercial know-how to emergency relief

CARE's partnership with Cable & Wireless plc demonstrates how a global telecommunications group can lend its commercial know-how to improve the delivery of humanitarian aid. The company teamed up with CARE to develop specialist telecommunications kits for use in emergency situations.

The post-cold war era has seen a number of humanitarian emergencies such as Somalia and Rwanda. In each situation, CARE staff were on the ground saving lives amid chaos and large-scale suffering. Reliable communications were critical for both security and for the effective procurement of relief supplies.

The portable kits developed with Cable & Wireless contain radios, chargers and satellite telephones. This state-of-the-art equipment can be dispatched instantly to an emergency situation – anywhere in the world. The expertise of Cable & Wireless has improved CARE's emergency response capacity. "Good communications are at the heart of effective emergency management. Not only can we respond immediately but the quality of our response is greatly enhanced by keeping vital lines of communication open at all times", explains Will Day, Chief Executive of CARE International UK.

> Our partnership with CARE enables us to understand this specialist market and to improve the service we can offer to organisations like CARE on a global scale.
>
> Mary Godwin,
> Community Investment
> Manager, Cable and Wireless.

The scope of CARE programmes worldwide enable many corporations to enter truly global partnerships. On 2 May 1996, the first world-wide partnership between the global futures markets and CARE took place in 11 countries on five continents. More than 300 participants contributed an amount based on that day's trading volume or a fixed donation. At close of business, World Trading Day had generated over US$1 million.

World Trading Day saw participants from international futures exchanges, trading firms and other companies investing in the future of the world's poor. In the words of Anthony Belchambers, Executive Director of the Futures and Options Association: "We are delighted to have had the opportunity to promote this global initiative and to help raise awareness of this event among our members."

The benefits for Cable & Wireless are many. Through this innovative partnership, Cable & Wireless is developing its already large pool of expertise so that it can strengthen its position as *the* provider of emergency telecommunications for this specialist market. Through its field experience with CARE, the Cable & Wireless Emergency Response Unit is able to test and adapt its core products under demanding conditions. The corporate partnership also includes the invaluable secondment of Guy Lynch, one of Cable & Wireless's senior emergency response specialists, who has been working in CARE's own Emergency Response Unit designing the telecommunications kits as well as improving CARE's equipment infrastructure.

Starbucks Coffee Company working with coffee producers in developing countries

In the United States, Starbucks Coffee Company and CARE have worked together since 1991 to build more productive futures for people in coffee growing countries around the world. This unique partnership enables Starbucks to express its concern and commitment to the global community.

Through CARE, Starbucks is investing in projects that have a sustainable impact on the lives of people involved in coffee production. In the last five years, Starbucks has helped to raise almost US$1 million, touching the lives of more than two million people in Africa, Latin America and South East Asia.

This partnership was launched in September 1991 when Starbucks unveiled its CARE gift-pack: a selection of four coffees from Guatemala, Kenya, Ethiopia and Indonesia. The CARE gift-pack continues to represent a gift of universal goodwill. It is both a great introduction to four of Starbuck's favourite coffees and supports CARE's development programmes in these four countries by donating US$2 per sampler sold.

Starbuck's commitment to CARE extends to mobilising support to raise funds for CARE's work. In the summer of 1995, Starbucks sponsored Grammy award-winner Mary Chapin Carpenter's Stones in the Road concert tour. For the duration of the tour, coffee and merchandise sales helped to raise funds and awareness for CARE.

The Starbucks/CARE Partnership has led to increased awareness of CARE and heightened consumer loyalty for Starbucks. Most importantly, it has made a difference to the lives of people in the countries which supply Starbucks coffee.

The corporate benefits of partnership

A corporate partnership with an international organisation such as CARE provides many benefits. These include: high visibility among CARE partners including national governments, international donors such as the European Union, community leaders and beneficiaries; facilitating access to policy makers and opinion leaders; promotional and public relations opportunities to help boost product awareness and loyalty; staff participation; and a philanthropic association with one of the world s largest independent humanitarian organisations.

1.5 ACTIONAID

ACTIONAID is an international development agency focusing its work in twenty of the world's poorest countries in Africa, Asia and Latin America. Its mission is to tackle poverty by helping poor people gain more control and choice over the process of change which confronts them. It is headquartered in London and raises income of about UK£37 million from public and private sector sources, as well as from over 100,000 individuals. ACTIONAID has been one of the leaders in the NGO sector in actively seeking to forge practical partnerships with companies, as well as raising funds from them.

The agency recognises the immense impact which international business has on the world economy, not least in developing countries, but also recognises that this impact can in some circumstances be negative. Equally, it welcomes the vital role which economic growth has to play in providing resources for sustainable development, but recognises that such growth does not necessarily alleviate poverty, and can even exacerbate it. ActionAid's focus is therefore not on economic growth per se, but on human development – giving poor people and their children some control and choice over the process of change that affects them. The traditional view of charity towards developing countries tends to ignore the mutual self-help and initiative that actually characterises many poor communities and ActionAid's goal is therefore to be a catalyst for the realisation of this initiative.

The agency's ground-breaking work on adult literacy illustrates this approach to development. It also offers great potential for co-operation between the NGO, government and private sectors. The programme is called REFLECT – the F referring to the celebrated Brazilian educationalist Freire whose methods have been adapted for it.

REFLECT parts company with traditional adult literacy approaches by using participants' own knowledge and priorities instead of a conventional textbook. The process begins with finding out what issues matter to people, and what they would like to discuss. One common example would be their need to build up credit for small enterprises. Participants analyse a series of issues through the construction of graphics which are then used for reading, writing and numeracy work. This can provide an opportunity for literacy, improved business management and improved income-generating initiatives to go hand-in-hand.

Results of the trials in Bangladesh, Uganda and El Salvador have shown impressive success rates of 60-70% in literacy (compared to 25% in traditional approaches), and significant improvements in economic and social development in the community. The potential of the REFLECT approach has recently attracted funding from the British ODA, and US$500,000 from the Special Grants Programme of the World Bank.

ACTIONAID'S PARTNERS IN CHANGE programme in India

Established in 1993, this initiative is aimed at brokering practical partnerships between local not-for-profit organisations and companies operating in India. It focuses on raising awareness in the private sector about the potential for such partnerships and then putting them into practice.

As far as awareness-raising is concerned, ACTIONAID produces a quarterly publication aimed at the corporate sector called CHANGES, and also sits on a number of committees such as the Partnership Advisory Committee of the India Business and Community Partnership Initiative and the Health, Education and Rural Development Committee of the Confederation of Indian Industry.

In terms of practical brokerage, it now has some 20 companies – both foreign and Indian – actively working with local NGOs. For example:

- The British insurance firm Allied Dunbar seconds employees from the UK to work on capacity-building projects with NGOs in southern India, helping them to produce strategic plans and undertake organisational development;
- Titan Industries, part of the Tata group of companies, has a stated policy of working with the disabled and is working with a local NGO to establish a plant for making watchstraps which will employ disabled people. It also worked with an ACTIONAID partner on a drinking water project near its main factory, where the labour was provided by the community, technology and supervision by the NGO and the material supplied by the company;

- United Phosphorus Ltd., a leading agricultural inputs company, has appointed an ACTIONAID partner as its authorised distributor. It has also provided some equipment to the partner on a trial basis which it can subsequently acquire on easy terms; and is planning to undertake training and extension support to selected communities;
- Coats Viyella India Ltd. regularly donates used computer stationery to an ACTIONAID partner, the Spastics Society of India, and has helped another NGO purchase relatively expensive equipment, using its own purchasing channels and discounts;
- Brooke Bond Lipton India Ltd. now places orders with an ACTIONAID partner for cardboard cartons – a process which is based on commercial terms and therefore likely to be more sustainable;
- Goodricke India, a tea major, is supporting the publication and dissemination of ActionAid's disability newsletter;
- Kentucky Fried Chicken is working with ACTIONAID to assist the company in recruiting disabled people to work in its outlets, and is also looking for small-scale income generating projects which can supply packaging materials; and
- McKinsey & Co, the management consultants, have been working with several Delhi-based NGOs to help them address management issues such as systems and organisation structure.

ActionAid's corporate partnership team are in discussion with numerous other companies looking at ways to creatively match corporate resources – human as well as financial and physical – to community needs. Some of its staff have also visited Philippine Business for Social Progress to assess their model of corporate engagement, offering an example of the potential for sharing good practices between countries.

Why is effective literacy training of interest to companies? Evidence from around the world shows that literacy has a range of practical benefits. These include improved health through better take-up of services and safer health practices; increased productivity at an individual and corporate level; ability to use written information in the workplace, and perhaps most importantly the capacity to be trained in new job skills. In fact, it could be said that a non-literate workforce with non-literate families require special efforts from a company if an efficient working environment is to be created. ACTIONAID also sees that companies can make a social investment in the developing countries where they operate by supporting literacy programmes, and is reviewing this possibility with several companies.

ACTIONAID is also working with The Prince of Wales Business Leaders Forum and other partners in Pakistan, on a feasibility study for a business-supported partnership initiative there, and in Bangladesh it is reviewing its potential role in monitoring how local manufacturers are complying with their Western purchasers' codes of conduct on employment, child labour, education and health and safety. With its experience of child labour issues and its neutral reputation, the agency is well placed to: help multinational companies monitor their global sourcing codes; assist local companies in meeting these requirements and in improving their own management practices.

1.6 ACCION International

Victoria Tikona has sold vegetables in a busy street market in La Paz since she was orphaned at the age of five. For many years she had to buy produce on consignment, paying a 10% premium and having to accept a poor variety and quality because she lacked the cash to be a more demanding customer. In 1987 she joined three friends and together they applied for a "solidarity loan" from a private credit organisation called PRODEM. With her US$50 portion of the group's US$250 loan she was able to buy better produce at better prices and her income immediately increased by 30%. Today she has her own sales outlet and a much larger inventory. Her family's standard of living has improved and she says, "Now I have hope in the future."

Amid the poverty of Latin America's shanty towns there is a quiet revolution underway. It is resulting in increased production, sales, exports, incomes and employment. It is helping to improve standards of living, education levels, women's prospects and hopes for a better future. A better future not only for the individuals who are spearheading the revolution, but also for their communities and their countries. It is being fuelled by the entrepreneurial spirit and personal persistence of millions of people like Victoria. It is being supported by a dynamic partnership between these people and the local affiliates – such as PRODEM – of a US-based private not-for-profit organisation called ACCION International.

Founded in 1961 to fight hunger and unemployment by encouraging the economic self-reliance of impoverished women and men in the Americas, ACCION International currently operates through a network of 18 affiliated institutions in 13 Latin American countries and nearly 300 Latin American cities. A few years ago it transferred its methodology to the United States and now operates similar programmes in six communities in North America. In 1995, the ACCION network disbursed US$331 million in loans averaging US$591 each, to 277,000 self-employed clients. Its active loan portfolio of US$156 million at year-end 1995 is a result of 78% per annum growth since 1990, and it has maintained a long-standing loan repayment rate of 98%.

Although the core services of the ACCION Network are the provision of credit and basic business training to micro-entrepreneurs, it has had an impact far beyond this. For over 30 years it has acted as a strong advocate for the enormous potential of micro-enterprise and for the commercial viability of micro-finance intermediaries. It has worked with governments throughout Latin America and donor agencies such as the Inter-American Bank and USAID, to influence the policy agenda and to create a more enabling environment for micro-enterprise. Today it is an internationally recognised leader in the field of micro-enterprise development; a field which is itself finally becoming internationally recognised as being a critical component of sustainable development. As a member of the advisory council of CGAP, the World Bank's recently established micro-finance initiative, and an advisor to the forthcoming Micro-credit Summit in 1997, ACCION is in a good position to share its philosophy and methodology with other parts of the world.

A business-driven, entrepreneurial approach has been central to this philosophy and methodology. This is reflected not only in the way that

CREATING NEW MODELS OF FINANCIAL INTERMEDIATION

Many of ACCION's affiliates have outstripped traditional non-profit funding sources, as well as the capabilities of local banks to serve corporate customers like the ACCION affiliates which do not have significant tangible collateral. In response, ACCION is working to create new models of financial intermediation – fusing social mission with the capacity to access the vast resources of international financial markets. It is creating these models at both the local, "point-of-delivery" level and at the international "capital-mobilisation" level.

At the international level ACCION has developed a number of innovative mechanisms in partnership with other private sector and donor organisations, to mobilise funds from the USA and other capital markets to support lending programmes in Latin America:

• The recently launched **Pro-Fund** is an investment fund established by a partnership between ACCION, FUNDES (another privately-funded organisation headquartered in Switzerland with a strong market focus, support from a wide range of Swiss and Latin American companies, and a network of financial intermediaries in 10 Latin American countries), Calmeadow (a Canadian-based organisation with similar objectives and methodologies) and Societe d'Investissement et de Development International, a consortium of French NGOs investing in SMEs world-wide. Apart from these four non-profit sponsors, each of which is supported by a variety of corporations and international organisations, other members of the investor group include the IFC, the Multilateral Investment Fund of the InterAmerican Development Bank, Corporacion Andina de Fomento, Calvert Social Investment Fund, Rockerfeller Foundation and the Swiss Government. Operating out of Costa Rica with an initial capitalisation of US$17 million, Pro-Fund operates on a for-profit basis and makes equity and quasi-equity investments in: established NGOs servicing the SME market and seeking to become formal financial institutions; new financial institutions dedicated to SME finance such as BancoSol; and established financial institutions seeking to enter the SME market.

• For over a decade ACCION has operated a **Latin American Bridge Fund**, which is capitalised with loans and donations from individuals, foundations and ethical investment institutions. These funds are deposited in a trust account at Citibank and invested in bonds rated A- or better, based on social investment screens as advised by Kinder, Lydenberg, Domini & Co. The income from these investments help to cover the interest payments due from the Bridge Fund to its lenders.

At the same time, these assets are used as collateral to back guarantees in the form of standby letters of credit issued by Citibank, in favour of local banks in Latin America. Anchored by the L/C, these local banks then make lines of credit available to ACCION's affiliates, who can then on-lend the monies to their micro-entrepreneur clients. One of the most exciting aspects of the Bridge Fund is its leverage impact. Citibank has agreed to issue L/Cs of US$1.30 for every US$1.00 invested. As a result, a US$10,000 loan to the Bridge Fund enables ACCION to issue US$13,000 in L/C guarantees, and given that local banks will provide credit facilities averaging 2.5 times the amount of a guarantee, US$10,000 supports US$29,250 in local bank loans to ACCION affiliates. And since most of their loans to micro-entrepreneurs are for four month maturities, this loan gets lent out three times during the year. In short US$10,000 invested in the USA provides US$87,750 in micro-loans annually in Latin America – an incredible leverage of 8.8 to 1 on the initial loan.

ACCION is taking a similar innovative approach to financial intermediation at the local level:

• In Bolivia ACCION worked with a major local bank, the IFC, USAID, IDB, and FUNDES to create one of the world's first private commercial banks, BancoSol, dedicated exclusively to serving micro-entrepreneurs. Established in 1992, BancoSol already reaches more clients than any other bank in Bolivia with a high return on assets and a loan repayment of nearly 100%. BancoSol projects that it will provide credit to 38,000 new micro-entrepreneurs by the end of 1998, representing a 48% rate of growth. ACCION also manages a Time Deposit Programme for BancoSol, helping to place US$ denominated Bancosol Certificates of Deposit (CDs) with individual and institutional investors in the USA. The CD proceeds are used by Bancosol to fund short-term US$ denominated micro-loans in Bolivia.

• In Peru, ACCION's affiliate (ACP) is in the process of creating a finance company which will be a regulated financial institution capitalised with a relatively small initial equity base of US$256,000. Once established, ACP projects it will reach 28,000 new clients by 1999.

• ACCION's Ecuadorian affiliate (FED) is working to create a "Special Purpose Corporation" which will purchase FED's loan portfolio and that of other micro-lending organisations, and issue debt backed by the micro-loan portfolios. Such securitisation measures will allow this affiliate to increase the amount of credit it can extend by 193% by 1998, reaching some 21,000 new clients.

ACCION and its affiliates have structured their lending programmes and organisational development, but also in the working relationships which they have developed with the formal business sector, especially the financial sector, both in the USA and Latin America. Business leaders throughout the region offer their time and advisory support to ACCION and its affiliates; companies are engaged with different affiliates in activities to promote franchising, subcontracting, purchasing and distributor agreements with ACCION's micro-entrepreneur clients; US-based investors, foundations and charities are investing in, or donating money to, ACCION's various funding initiatives; and banks throughout the region are working with ACCION to increase the leverage of its loan portfolio and to develop innovative financing mechanisms, such as those described above.

1.7 Project HOPE

Project HOPE's simple philosophy – "Go only where invited, and help people help themselves" – underpins every health education programme undertaken by the international non-profit organisation. Created in 1958 by William B Walsh MD as Health Opportunities for People Everywhere, Project HOPE now conducts medical training and health education programmes in North and South America, Central and Eastern Europe, the former Soviet Union, China, the Middle East and southern Africa. HOPE has now worked with more than 5,000 health-care professionals and volunteer educators in more than 70 countries around the world, and currently provides approximately US$100 million worth of resources to 20-30 countries per year.

> The HOPE/Chevron alliance is a very powerful example of how philanthropic efforts and successful business strategies can work together to solve critical needs in a community.
>
> Ken Derr,
> CEO, Chevron

In addition to health education, Project HOPE provides health policy research and emergency medical assistance. To support programmes and to help insure their long-term sustainability, HOPE actively facilitates partnerships between a number of organisations and individuals who combine skills and resources both internal and external to the host country.

Long-term solutions to health problems

Although immediate humanitarian assistance is often an element of its activities, Project HOPE aims to support long-term systemic solutions to health-care problems. As a result, all programmes are aimed at educating health professionals about successful processes and procedures. Programmes cover the development of health-care facilities as well as the newest medical techniques for doctors, nurses, engineers and managers. Education initiatives include: health promotion; disease prevention; community health; specialist hospital services; biomedical engineering; and health care management.

Health policy research

While developing practical solutions on the ground, Project HOPE also allocates resources to researching, understanding and disseminating information about health policy. The health economists at Project HOPE's Center for Health Affairs (CHA) analyse the political, economic and social factors, and technological trends which determine the cost and quality of health care. Project HOPE's health policy journal, Health Affairs, was founded in 1983 and has developed a world-wide reputation for dissemination and discussion of policy and management issues.

The facilitation of partnerships

The basis of all HOPE's programmes is partnership. Partners may include government departments, health-care institutions, health-care professionals, funding organisations and private companies. Each programme partner agrees to contribute a range of resources and expertise to meet the designated project plan, which is designed, agreed upon, and implemented by HOPE health care educators working with their host counterparts.

The business sector has been a long time supporter of Project HOPE's work around the world. In recent years, there has been a growing emphasis on working with companies in a more creative manner which draws on their management skills and seeks to help them meet their corporate responsibility objectives in countries where they do business. The brief profiles below give an indication of how some of these partnerships between Project HOPE and major companies are evolving.

Project HOPE and SmithKline Beecham in Hungary

In Budapest HOPE, along with local medical universities and SmithKline Beecham is sponsoring the Family Medicine Model Community Practice, designed to greatly improve the quality and efficiency of health-care for Hungarian families. By promoting healthy lifestyles in a more family centred atmosphere, the Practice supports recent government health care reforms which promote a shift away from hospitals to more easily accessible and less costly health-care in the community. Project HOPE is providing training for the general practitioners and family medicine residents working in the practice.

Project HOPE and Chevron in Kazakhstan

In a broad initiative funded by Tengizchevroil (a joint venture between Chevron and the Kazakh government) HOPE has been working to improve health care for the 450,000 residents of the Atyrau region of Kazakhstan. Most recently, HOPE worked with the Kazakhs and Tengizchevroil to develop a new ambulatory care clinic in Kulsary. After conducting the needs assessment and determining priorities, HOPE staff and volunteers designed the facility, and specified and co-ordinated the purchase of the medical equipment for its emergency care unit, surgical and ICU facilities, pharmacy, blood bank, labour and delivery unit, and X-ray facilities. The clinic is serving the local Kazakh population, as well as expatriate Chevron employees.

In addition, HOPE has worked with local medical professionals to upgrade infant and maternal health, cardio-vascular and emergency care, pediatric intensive care, and tuberculosis diagnosis and treatment. Citing HOPE's TB programme, the first in the former Soviet Union, Chevron's CEO Ken Derr maintains that HOPE has added real value to Chevron's corporate initiative in Kazakhstan. "In less than three years, we are seeing real improvement in the health of the local people."

HOPE in China

Project HOPE's largest single project is the development of a national children's hospital in China. Funded in large part by the Chinese government, the Shanghai Children's Medical Center will serve as a national training and referral centre and will impact pediatric practice throughout the country. Scheduled to open in 1997, the hospital will care for more than 250,000 acutely ill children per year and will enable the Chinese to utilise advanced technologies which are saving children's lives elsewhere in the world. Multinational companies with business interests in China are making it possible for HOPE staff and volunteers – health-care professionals from leading universities and medical centres – to train the future Shanghai Children's Medical Center staff in the newest technologies in pediatric care and hospital management. In addition, the support of the medical equipment industry is enabling Project HOPE to ensure that key areas of the Center have the most up-to-date diagnostic and treatment equipment, as well as the training needed to maintain and service it.

HOPE in Malawi

HOPE health education programmes in Malawi have been so successful that they have been expanded from one programme in one district in 1989 to four programmes in eight districts in 1995. In partnership with the management of private tea estates in Malawi, Project HOPE trains health workers who provide on-going support and education to the agricultural workers and their families who live and work on the estates. They teach families how to prevent potentially fatal diseases such as pneumonia, AIDs, and malaria, and provide guidance on healthy nutrition and personal and community hygiene. In a recent evaluation, tea estate managers pointed to improvements in the general health of the workers and their families, and indicated that the changes are being sustained over time. According to Hugh Miller, Manager of Gotha Tea Estates Ltd., in Thyolo, "Since Project HOPE became involved with this estate, there has been a noticeable improvement in basic health-care."

1.8 The International Youth Foundation

This is the most critical time in the history of the planet, because never before have so many people, such a high proportion of the world, been under the age of 20. I think there is no more fundamental issue for the future than how we engage that group of people.

David Bell,

Chief Executive,

The Financial Times

Established in 1990 with start-up funding from the Kellogg Foundation, The International Youth Foundation (IYF) works with local partner organisations and companies in nine countries with developments underway in 10 others. IYF helps improve the lives and opportunities of children from the age of five to 20 so they may have healthy and productive futures. The organisation is built on a simple premise. As its founder President and CEO, Rick Little explains, "Although the problems of young people are mounting in many cultures around the world, there are programmes and activities that exist to solve these problems. We don't reinvent the wheel. Instead we find what works and expand its effectiveness."

The organisation employs four basic strategies to bring effective programmes to more children in need:

1 It has created an interconnected global network of national grant-making foundations focused on supporting local children and youth development projects in their native countries. These national foundations share ideas and information about "programmes that work" on an international basis, but set their own priorities, funding and operational strategies which meet their local needs, with financial and technical assistance from IYF. They act as valuable intermediaries between the global leverage and presence of IYF and the local needs and specific characteristics of small, grassroots projects in their own countries.

2 It improves the quality of youth programmes through research and communication about what works and by promoting rigorous evaluations of programme efficiency and effectiveness. A key aspect of this strategy has been the establishment of YouthNet International, a global exchange of effective programmes (currently numbering some 135 in 30 countries) all of which have been evaluated according to a clearly defined set of 17 criteria.

3 It raises the issue of children and youth to higher prominence through a diverse and committed network of influential people, businesses and institutions.

4 It mobilises more resources – through an inter-connected global network of national grant-making foundations.

The concept of leverage plays a central role in the IYF philosophy and strategy. Funds raised at the international level, for example, are leveraged through matched funding and innovative mechanisms such as debt swaps, to achieve a positive multiplier effect by the time they reach local projects. Ideas and innovations are also "leveraged" through the YouthNet International system, which provides a wide, efficient and flexible communication mechanism which can be accessed by donors, companies, youth programmes and other non-governmental organisations from a wide variety of countries.

IYF WORKING WITH COMPANIES IN SOUTH AFRICA and THE PHILIPPINES

The following examples illustrate how IYF is working with two companies on local projects.

- **In South Africa**, IYF is working with the **Kellogg Company** to strengthen the management and increase the outreach of a South African managed foundation called the Human Resources Trust (HRT). The Kellogg Company is working with HRT to run leadership training programmes for youth administrators, support programmes for AIDS prevention and promote youth development through advocacy. Kelloggs also helped to launch this partnership with core support for administrative costs. IYF is also working with Kellogg South Africa on developing a children's nutrition campaign. Kellogg production plants in South Africa will overproduce capacity and donate free breakfast cereals to the townships, thereby helping young children enjoy a nutritional start to the day and promote their learning capacity in school. The company is engaging other corporate interests in South Africa through IYF in a collaborative effort to procure milk and juice to provide 20,000 meals/day for the next five years. After the programme is established and evaluated in South Africa, the Kellogg company and IYF hope to implement similar initiatives on a partnership basis in both China and India.

- **In the Philippines** IYF's local partner organisation is **The Children and Youth Foundation of the Philippines** (CYFP) which has developed a multi-level partnership with the Ayala Corporation, the country's largest and one of its most successful holding companies. Jaime Augusto Zobel de Ayala sits on the Board of IYF's Directors and acts as Chairman of CYFP. Through its Chairman the Ayala Corporation has initiated multi-lateral talks with the Philippine government and the Asian Development Bank, as well as supporting efforts to build a consortium of private multinational corporations to focus on the issue of children and youth and how they can be engaged collaboratively to invest in youth enterprise initiatives. CYFP's public-private supported Don Bosco training centres are expanding in number and provide much needed skills training for the Philippine economy.

From the outset, working directly with the private sector and adopting a business-like approach to efficiency, evaluation and effectiveness have been key elements of the IYF approach and its success both at the international and national level. In particular, IYF works with companies to:

- utilise the expertise and influence of business leaders as policy advisers and as champions for the cause of children and youth;

- develop joint international programmes and local projects; and

- source funding and other types of support from the private sector, which currently accounts for 74% of IYF's financial support.

Two examples of this business-led approach at the international level are IYF's Ecuadorian debt conversion and its **Companies Caring for Children** programme:

- In 1992 IYF worked with JP Morgan to establish one of the first debt conversions for youth between the USA and Ecuador. Working with JP Morgan and other creditors, the banks were able to reduce their exposure by writing down foreign debt bonds with a face value of US$5 million. IYF bought these for US$1.04 million and converted them to the Ecuadorian government for US$2,271,501 for projects specifically aimed at social development and children and youth issues. Thirty two projects were approved as a result of this capital being created and it was a classic win-win for all concerned.

- The organisation is currently working with a small group of outstanding multinational companies to launch an international programme called **Companies Caring for Children** which will encompass not only financial support, but also more integrated and tailored initiatives for each company, aimed at matching specific youth issues and initiatives to the company's strategic business interests, and ensuring that both the company and the IYF network produce the greatest, most efficient and effective return possible on their joint investment in youth.

The programme will have four main goals, which companies will be asked to support in a variety of ways as deemed appropriate to the interests and resources of each company:

1 Mobilising more funds and using them more effectively

2 Increasing the involvement of employees and their families in youth action either through volunteering, or matched funding schemes

3 Going beyond cause-related marketing to the use of solution-related marketing aimed at promoting youth programmes and replicating them in other countries

4 Establishing and spreading standards for responsible business policies and practices, to ensure that companies produce and market their products and services in a way that does not harm children or their prospects.

This proposed programme offers a good example of how an international non-profit organisation such as IYF can engage with a multinational company: through a wide range of its core business activities (not just its philanthropy function); in a wide range of countries; and in a way that has direct benefits for both organisations, while at the same time increasing the potential leverage and efficiency of resources going to ultimate beneficiaries.

1.9 AIESEC

The international Association of Students in Economics and Management (AIESEC) is the world's largest student-managed education association. It operates in more than 750 academic institutions in over 85 countries – including many of the world's developing and transition economies – and aims to educate students to be globally-minded and responsible members of society. It meets its objectives through a wide range of multi-cultural meetings, leadership workshops, exchange programmes and a Global Theme Programme, all of which encourage students to think about, and most importantly act on, issues in society.

The Global Theme Programme in particular encourages students to identify local development needs in their own communities – ranging from small and micro-enterprise development, to literacy training and environmental education – and to design, implement and manage projects to meet these needs, often in partnership with other NGOs or companies. At the same time the programme has a critical international dimension through which AIESEC's international team liaise closely with agencies such as UNDP, UNESCO and UNCHS, as well as multinational companies, to provide a youth input to UN conferences and other policy dialogues, and to hold a major Global Theme Conference for about 600 students and global leaders every three years.

Since the launch of its Global Theme Programme (GTP) in 1989, AIESEC has addressed issues such as sustainable development, corporate responsibility and entrepreneurship, and education for international and multi-cultural understanding. Its national and local committees around the world have run hundreds of education and awareness-raising programmes in their universities, schools, and local communities, and many local committees in developing countries – such as Colombia, Brazil, Botswana, India, Kenya, South Africa and the Philippines, have also implemented income generating and poverty alleviation projects in marginalised communities. At the international level AIESEC has produced student action guides on each of the above subjects, which have been disseminated around the world, and it sent large youth delegations to the Rio Earth Summit, the Copenhagen Social Summit and the Istanbul Cities Summit. It also operates a Youth Emissaries Programme with UNDP which enables university students to work on development projects.

AIESEC's international partners represent companies and institutions which are international leaders in their respective fields. They recognise and support the need to develop a core of global citizens who:

- are able to work effectively in different nations and cultures

- understand the ethical, social and environmental responsibilities of the private sector

- have a strong sense of voluntarism and commitment to the development of their communities.

At the same time, many of them are in a position to work with AIESEC at a national, and even local level, in countries around the world. The profile on the left gives an idea of the way just one these partnerships works in action.

THE PRICE WATERHOUSE RELATIONSHIP with AIESEC ranges from its role as AIESEC's International Financial Systems Partner, to links with AIESEC committees in nearly 40 countries. As AIESEC's financial systems partner the company gives the organisation advice on its financial management procedures and systems – which is critically important, bearing in the mind that AIESEC is run totally by recently-graduated students who undertake enormous complexity and responsibility in running a large budget with a network of affiliates in over 85 countries. Apart from this financial advice, Price Waterhouse also offers the organisation legal advice, audit services, traineeships for its International Exchange Programme, training in management and leadership skills, support on Boards of Advisors at both the international and national levels, and sponsorships of international and regional conferences and award programmes. In return Price Waterhouse gets access to a large group of well-qualified students from around the world, many of whom have developed valuable leadership skills and a strong sense of social responsibility through their work with AIESEC.

2 Partnerships between international agencies and business

Recent years have witnessed growing levels of dialogue and practical co-operation between the international business community and the world's bilateral and multilateral development agencies. Co-operation between these two groups can occur at a number of levels:

1   Working together to give advice and technical support to national governments on improving the enabling environment for private sector development e.g. regulatory and legal systems, privatisation programmes, establishing stock exchanges and banking systems etc.

2   Co-financing commercial projects such as infrastructure development.

3   Commercial procurement and contract relationships between bilateral and multilateral agencies and companies.

4   Co-resourcing social and community projects, with funding and other types of resources.

Co-operation between publicly accountable institutions and privately-driven businesses can raise various political, procedural and practical challenges, ranging from issues of sovereignty and accountability, to legal and mechanistic questions of how to channel funds from one entity to the other, to basic practical differences in culture and management. The private sector funding arms of various development institutions, such as the IFC and Commonwealth Development Corporation, obviously have a long tradition of structuring commercial partnerships with the private sector and many private sector entities tender for consultancy contracts with the World Bank and other international agencies. However when it comes to the public and private sector working together on social and human development projects the situation tends to become more complex and politically sensitive. This is especially so for the multilateral agencies which are accountable to more than one government, and also tends to be more difficult when an individual company and corporate "brand name" is involved rather than a consortium of companies. However the need for public and private entities to work together on solving societal problems is simply too great not to search for ways around the obstacles.

One mechanism which appears to be working well is co-operation between a multilateral or bilateral agency and a group of companies. This group can be representative bodies i.e. the International Chamber of Commerce, national and local chambers of commerce or trade associations or business-led networks with a clear societal and/or sustainable development mandate i.e. the PWBLF, WBCSD, Rotary and their national equivalents.

The following profiles offer a small sample of these different approaches, drawing on examples from several multilateral and bilateral agencies and a range of business associations and companies. Although not profiled here, UNIDO also works closely with the private sector and is forging new types of advisory and project partnerships with multinational companies.

2.1 The World Bank's CGAP Programme

In developing countries throughout the world there are at least 500 million low-income people active in micro-business of one kind or another. They and their businesses represent one of the greatest hopes for achieving sustainable development – and one of the greatest challenges. Giving these people access to credit is one of the surest paths to poverty alleviation. They do not need subsidised loans and they certainly do not need charity. They are business people, many of them entrepreneurs, capable of demonstrating enormous productivity gains and return on investment for every dollar loaned to them. When they are lent money, at rates which reflect the full costs of lending to this sector, they have demonstrated in countries as different as Bangladesh, Indonesia and Colombia, that they are capable of maintaining repayment rates in the 90 percent range. Despite this, there are very few commercial banks in the world either organisationally equipped or strategically interested in lending to them.

There are however a number of specialist micro-finance intermediaries (MFIs), such as Women's World Banking, members of the ACCION Network, the Grameen Bank in Bangladesh, Bank Raykat in Indonesia and KREP in Kenya, which are successfully reaching millions of these borrowers and demonstrating commercial viability in the process. The problem is that they are only reaching the tip of the iceberg, and the development challenge is to replicate and scale-up these models to greatly increase their outreach and their impact.

In June 1995, a group of bilateral and multilateral donors, spearheaded by the World Bank, formed the Consultative Group to Assist the Poorest (CGAP), with the goal of tackling this challenge. The main objectives of the CGAP programme are to:

- support micro-finance intermediary institutions that deliver credit and/or savings services to the very poor on a financially sustainable basis or that are capable of becoming financially sustainable;

- increase learning and dissemination of best practice for delivering financial services to the poor;

- strengthen donor co-ordination for systematic financing of such programmes;

- help to create a positive policy environment for micro-lending institutions. The performance of many MFIs is adversely affected by regulations, such as interest rate caps or an inability to mobilise savings amongst the poor without being a full-scale commercial bank and meeting the necessary capital adequacy ratios to be so;

- support innovative or experimental practices in the micro-finance field, or entry into new markets;

MOBILISING THE CITY OF LONDON

The City of London is one of the world's major financial centres – renowned worldwide for its ability to mobilise funds and create innovative financing mechanisms. Despite this fact, and despite the long-standing relationship between the United Kingdom and many developing countries, the UK lags behind the USA in terms of having organisations such as ACCION International capable of tapping the capital markets to support micro-finance initiatives. In June 1996 the British ODA, in partnership with the Centre for the Study of Financial Innovations (CSFI), The Prince of Wales Business Leaders Forum (PWBLF) and CGAP started a process of consultation with city institutions from the banking and fund management sector, to assess the potential of increasing support for micro-finance initiatives in developing countries. Leading micro-finance practitioners and supporters from around the world, ranging from ACCION, to Triodos Bank and the Citicorp Foundation, shared their perspectives on the commercial viability and potential for micro-finance lending. As a result of the meeting, a task force is being established which will meet on a regular basis to look at key issues associated with commercialising micro-finance and accessing the City of London's capital markets.

Harnessing the spirit of enterprise

It's 6.30 am. on a cold and windy morning in La Paz. In the city centre the main street is almost deserted. The banks and modern office buildings stand silent and empty. The world is just waking up. Or so it seems. Less than five minutes away several thousand business people have already been at work for almost an hour. Many of them have been awake since 4.00 am. By the time the city's bankers and captains of industry have arrived at their comfortable offices these thousands of people will have exchanged thousands of products, worth thousands of dollars, providing livelihoods for thousands of people. By 9.00 am. many of them will have finished selling for the day and will be returning to their workshops and tiny factories to produce merchandise for tomorrow's market. Their places will be taken by another group of sellers, mostly traders rather than producers, who will keep the winding side-streets filled with colour, noise and enterprise for several more hours.

Traditional herbs and medicinal plants are sold alongside brightly coloured plastic buckets, hand-made broomsticks, imitation designer jeans and richly textured ponchos. Fruit, vegetables, dry goods, batteries, cloth, meat, hot meals, ceramics, shoes, electronics, tobacco, cosmetics...the list is endless. If there are customers who will buy the goods, there are entrepreneurs who will find and sell them. What is more they will sell them in the exact amounts that their customers need and can afford. Flexibility and customer service is the name of the game. It is the only way to survive when there are a dozen competitors, all operating within a few feet of each other. The competition is fierce and unrelenting. Demanding buyers and aggressive sellers haggle over prices and a few traders use megaphones to get their message across. It is difficult to imagine a scene more competitive, more enterprising, or indeed more hopeful, than this Bolivian street market and others like it.

Almost all of these businesses are unregistered and are variously described as being part of the informal or invisible sector. However there is nothing invisible about the economic and social contribution that they make, both locally and nationally. This contribution may not show up on the government's official economic statistics, but it is real and absolutely vital to the economic growth, social equity and political stability of the country, and many other countries like it.

- increase micro-finance activity within institutions such as the World Bank itself; and

- attract private-sector support from the formal banking system.

It is not the goal of CGAP to deliver services directly to ultimate beneficiaries, but to strengthen the capacities of those institutions that have, among other things, proven track records of reaching large numbers of the poor, sound financial policies, high cost-recovery and loan-repayment rates, and a demonstrated ability to mobilise matching funds, preferably from private sector, or non-traditional donor sources. The ultimate goal is to enable these institutions, and others with potential but which are still at an earlier stage in their development, to get to the point where they can access the capital markets directly.

CGAP is governed by a donor committee of bilateral and multilateral donors, which currently include: Canada, France, the Netherlands, the United Kingdom, the USA, Switzerland, Sweden, Norway, Luxembourg, Germany, Finland, Denmark, Belgium, Australia, the International Fund for Agricultural Development, the Asian Development Bank, the African Development Bank, the European Commission, the International Labor Office, the Inter-American Development Bank, the United Nations Development Programme, and the United Nations Capital Development Fund. It is supported by a Policy Advisory Group, chaired by Dr Muhammad Yunus, founder of the Grameen Bank, and a group of 10 other leading practitioners in the field of micro-finance. It is administered by a small secretariat in the World Bank's Private Sector Development Department. To-date, the projects being supported by CGAP range from an MFI in Mexico, to a network programme in Vietnam and a policy forum in Mali for 16 West African countries.

One of the key objectives of the CGAP initiative is to encourage greater private sector support for assisting micro-finance programmes. There are a number of ways that the private sector can play a more active role in this field. These include the following:

- Contributing capital and financial services to MFIs, either on a commercial basis by: extending loans and lines of credit, as a number of Latin American banks are doing with the ACCION Network, profiled on page 224, investing equity as a number of private sector companies have done with BancoSol in Bolivia, or underwriting financial instruments, as CitiTrust is doing for RepFin SA in Colombia; or on a social investment basis by making grants through corporate foundations or community investment arms, as the Citicorp Foundation is doing with its Banking on Enterprise initiative, profiled on page 119;

- Providing technical assistance and business skills training;

- Developing increased business linkages with micro-enterprises through outsourcing and subcontracting of non-core services, as has been done by the companies profiled on pages 114 to 121;

- Advocating for policy reform to create a more enabling environment for small and micro-enterprise development;

- Supporting research projects and case studies on "good practice" in the private sector

- Creating award programmes and encouraging media coverage for outstanding MFIs, or individual practitioners and entrepreneurs working in the field of micro-enterprise.

2.2 The World Bank's *info*Dev Programme

For developing countries, the revolution in communications and information technologies, and the new world economy that it has helped unleash, is a double-edged sword. On the one hand, all countries, even the poorest among them, now face a rising competitiveness threshold. On the other hand, these new and increasingly low-cost technologies offer extraordinary opportunities for developing countries – opportunities that are unprecedented, and that have a lot of "development leverage"...we would like to see how we can forge a partnership with the private sector to help bring the developing countries, and particularly the poorest and most vulnerable groups within those countries, into the information age.

Jean-François Rischard,
Vice President Finance and Private
Development, The World Bank

In September 1995 the World Bank launched an innovative public-private sector initiative called the Information for Development Programme (*info*Dev) aimed at helping developing economies to fully benefit from modern information systems.

Managed by the Bank's Industry and Energy Department, *info*Dev is governed by a Donors' Committee consisting of bilateral and multilateral donors and private companies, and is advised by a Technical Advisory Panel of six prominent experts from Egypt, France, Japan, South Africa, Tunisia and the USA, with backgrounds in information technology, telecoms, internet, regulation, broadcasting and education. *info*Dev brings together the financing and expertise of private organisations, governments and multilateral donors – linking the market-opening interests of eventual investors to the objectivity and long-term development goals of public donors. *info*Dev finances projects with the following objectives:

- create a market-friendly environment to accelerate access to information technologies;
- reduce poverty and economic exclusion;
- promote education, health and the environment;
- improve the efficiency and transparency of governments.

Since its launch in 1995 *info*Dev has mobilised funding from Belgium, Denmark, Finland, France, Luxembourg, Netherlands, Sweden, Switzerland, the UK, the European Union, the World Bank and on the private sector side from IBM. *info*Dev has approached the private sector not only to improve its financial base, but to benefit from private corporations' familiarity with the market and with rapidly evolving technologies. *info*Dev projects hold great potential for the private sector, emphasising as they do market liberalisation and market development. The future markets for investment in this field are mostly in Asia, South America, Africa and Eastern Europe. However, before successful investment can be made these markets have to be developed. *info*Dev is helping governments to address strategic issues such as regulatory reform and tariff restructuring, and channelling policy and technical advice to governments, as well as supporting specific information technology projects.

Supporting public-private partnership projects

Within *info*Dev's first year of operation over 140 proposals were received for funding, covering an enormous diversity of objectives, geographies and sectors. To-date *info*Dev has approved funding for four initiatives: the African Virtual University; the Sixth International Telecommunications Union Regulatory Colloquium and the following two public-private partnership projects:

- The South African-based Telematics for African Development Consortium is focused on utilising information and telecommunications for community development and education. Its immediate focus is developing distance education at secondary and tertiary levels. Six pilot projects are under way focusing on curriculum development and management, and the provision of information services to marginalised communities. The membership of the consortium is wide-ranging and includes: CSIR – a leading South African government research institute; multinational and South African companies – IBM, Hewlett Packard and Telkom (SA); the Ford Foundation; the Universities of Pretoria and South Africa (already a leader in distance learning); the South African Broadcasting Corporation; and St Albans, a leading private school which has been a pioneer in using technology for education and community outreach.

- The Jamaican-based **Partnership for Technology in Basic Education** shares the same cross-sector approach. Its key partners include: Jamaica's Business Partners for Education (a group of private sector companies and individuals providing funding and advocacy for educational improvement); the Jamaica Computer Society Education Foundation; the University of the West Indies; the Ministry of Education and primary and secondary schools. Business Partners for Education have played a key role in providing computer equipment and software, training teachers, conducting workshops and promoting the use of technology in education through public information campaigns. The programme, supported by the World Bank, with support also from the Inter-American Development Bank, will pilot and evaluate alternative approaches to the use of computers in education.

2.3 UNDP's "Money Matters" Initiative

The basic issue is whether global pension funds, totalling US $7 trillion and global mutual fund assets of US $ 4.3 trillion, can assist in growing developing economies through financially sound investments. What has to be done within the developing economies to attract these investments, and what are the expectations vis-à-vis return, stability, securities structures, social and economic development of the 'pooled asset' and investment management industry? These are the key questions we are addressing – I think we can find answers.

Marshall Carter,
Chairman of State Street Bank and
Trust Company

How to draw the rest of the developing countries into the arena where bulls and bears operate? Is this the responsibility solely of the developing countries to dress themselves up for foreign capital in the hope that they don't get raped? If it is, is it possible that the money managers can help through dialogues like this? Generally, foreign capital is attracted to already successful countries. The historical experience is against the kind of partnership that we are talking about. The real challenge is how to foster sustainable development. Sustainable development in the developing countries is defined very clearly as 'growth plus'. Growth plus equity, growth plus environmental concern, growth that is pro-poor, pro-jobs, pro-nature, and pro-women.

Solita Monsod, former
Cabinet Minister of Economic Planning,
the Philippines

Public sector finance is under pressure all over the world. Long-running budget deficits, rising public debt and a declining public sector asset base have put growing pressures on scarce public resources, leading to a fiscal crisis of the state.

Many public policy initiatives have been postponed or curtailed, putting at risk future economic growth, social progress and environmental sustainability. It is not surprising that official development assistance (ODA) is also affected and stagnates around $60 billion a year, forcing development agencies to search for both a meaningful role to play in the process of globalisation and for new sources of funding. While the constraints on public resources are growing, global private finance is booming as a result of fundamental changes in financial markets and institutions, as well as accelerating deregulation. Private capital flows to developing countries are rising sharply: from 1990 to 1995, net private flows to developing countries almost quadrupled from $44 billion to $167 billion, accounting for over 70% of all flows to developing countries. In view of these new financial realities, ODA can no longer be the only source of finance to achieve sustainable human development: a much more intense public-private partnership for development funding is urgently needed. This need has led to the creation of the *Money Matters Initiative*.

At the World Summit for Social Development in Copenhagen, March 1995, a first meeting called "Money Matters: Financing Social Development in the 21st Century" was launched. The driving force behind the initiative were leading private investors, such as State Street Bank and Trust Company, Fidelity Investments, and Arthur Andersen, in close cooperation with UNDP, and facilitated by a 'neutral matchmaker', The World Times Inc. of Boston. The meeting brought together 75 leaders from both the private financial sector and the public sector to mobilise financial and political support for constructive reform of monetary, financial and development institutions.

The follow-up action has been encouraging:

- A second annual global meeting took place in Boston, March 1996, entitled "Money Matters II: The Role of Private Finance in Fostering Sustainable Development", attended by a group of 90 bankers, business people, government officials, members of UNDP and the World Bank, as well as academics and journalists. Since March 1995, regional *Money Matters* meetings have also been held in Malaysia, Tunisia, Chile and Zimbabwe.

- A working committee consisting of twelve senior executives from private financial firms and public officials from the UN system and developing countries has established the *Money Matters Institute*, administered by the World Times Inc. So far, Banque Nationale de Paris, State Street Bank and Trust Company, Lamalie Amrop International, UNDP and The World Bank Group have joined the institute. The *Money Matters Institute* focuses on best practices in two research areas: how can private capital be used for sustainable human development; and what is needed in developing countries to attract and retain such private capital, and to transform it into development?

2.4 The UN's EMPRETEC Programme

EMPRETEC promotes entrepreneurship and provides assistance in the establishment and expansion of small and medium-sized enterprises (SMEs) in developing countries and those with economies in transition. The programme is designed to meet the diverse and changing needs of entrepreneurs and make available to them the training, technical assistance, financial advice and business opportunities required to start and operate successful and innovative businesses.

> **EMPRETEC has helped my company to diversify the product line and establish trade arrangements with other EMPRETEC companies in Latin America.**
>
> **Ms Ruth Pasipanodya,**
> **President, Escapades** *(ladies and*
> *children's garments)*, **Zimbabwe**

The fundamental goal of the programme is to establish in each country an institutional base of public–private sector partnerships which will support the creation, development and expansion of SMEs. Empretec is a technical co-operation programme of the United Nations Department for Development Support and Management Services (DDSMS), and UNCTAD. In Africa, it has been launched with funds from UNDP, while working from a broader base of donors in Latin America.

Serving Latin America and Africa

The first national programme was established in Argentina in 1988. Currently, the programme operates in ten countries in Latin America and Africa, namely: Argentina; Brazil; Chile; Colombia; Ethiopia; Ghana; Nigeria; Uruguay; Venezuela; and Zimbabwe. Programmes are set up through a partnership among the UN partners and national public and private sector institutions. The programme requires the formation of an active coalition between the public and private sector which materialises in the national executive committees, many of which include prominent business leaders from local and multinational companies operating in the country. These have proven invaluable in setting the institutional base of the programme and in securing its capacity for self-financing after initial donor funding has launched them.

> **EMPRETEC was instrumental in helping Micap negotiate with potential joint-venture partners.**
>
> **Mr Michael Appiah,**
> **President, Micap Computer**
> **Services, Ghana**

Building capacity and an enabling environment for entrepreneurship

To meet the changing needs of SMEs, EMPRETEC fosters an enabling environment at two levels: influencing national policies; and capacity-building of both national institutions and individual entrepreneurs.

- EMPRETEC's involvement on national policy issues centres on the creation of an appropriate legal framework. By working closely with host governments, business organisations, and the SMEs themselves, EMPRETEC provides guidance in the areas of taxation, insurance and labour law, and helps to create business support centres, entrepreneurs' associations, co-operatives and international networks. Training of public and private sector officials is another key aspect of capacity-building of national institutions.

- Capacity-building of individual entrepreneurs is the final component of the EMPRETEC approach. This active coalition between public and private sectors succeeds in providing a sturdy foundation for achieving the shared goal of SME establishment and growth.

EMPRETEC GHANA

By the end of the eighties, when the Government of Ghana had just started with its structural adjustment programme, the Government identified the need for strengthening the available entrepreneurial talents in Ghana. The goal of the EMPRETEC programme was, and continues to be, "to act as a catalyst for, and accelerate the content of, private sector participation in national economic development."

Established in October 1990, EMPRETEC Ghana began as a technical co-operation program of the United Nations Centre on Trans-National Corporations (UNCTC) and the United Nations Development Programme (UNDP) at the request of Government of Ghana (GOG). After a successful start, EMPRETEC Ghana became a fully fledged private non-profit organisation. Since its inception, EMPRETEC has not only grown in influence but has assumed the pivotal role as a business development organisation in the promotion of the private sector, focused in particular on the development of small and medium-scale industries.

EMPRETEC Ghana has developed a core competence in "Entrepreneurship Development Training (EDT)" and offers a variety of services including: training; business consultancy and extension services; credit sourcing, facilitation and syndication of financing for SMEs; networking and linkage development; and business communication services.

Over the last 5 years, its achievements include:
- 2000 entrepreneurs, 30% of whom are women, benefited from EMPRETEC workshops;
- Over 35 business linkages have been initiated and established between individual EMPRETECOS and multi-nationals, both local and foreign. Informational seminars such as *How to do business with foreign companies*, *Developing subcontract relations with large companies* and *Marketing Ghanaian products in the USA* have attracted the active participation of 354 companies.
- EMPRETEC assisted businesses in their efforts to enhance their operational capacity and efficiency, particularly in the fields of financial management, marketing management, and production management, by organising needs-based training programmes.
- More than 40 businesses have been assisted in preparing business plans and EMPRETEC assisted 39 of these companies to raise capital or obtain finance from local financial institutions.

In order to sustain and nurture the momentum among the trainers and graduates of the "Entrepreneurship Training Programmes" generated by the EMPRETEC training, an autonomous association, EMPRETEC BUSINESS FORUM was formed in February, 1991. The purpose of this Forum is to provide a platform for its members to interact and exchange business information, find solutions to problems common to their individual businesses and to relay information relevant to the sustainability of the EMPRETEC program. The membership currently stands at 400.

From October 1990 to August 1994, EMPRETEC Ghana was largely funded by the UNDP. In its current form, the EMPRETEC Ghana Foundation is supported by a consortium of donors including UNDP, the British Overseas Development Administration (ODA), the World Bank Group, European Union (EU),the Ghanaian government through the National Board for Small Scale Industries (NBSSI), and Barclays Bank of Ghana.

Transnational companies supporting EMPRETEC in Latin America and Africa

Abbot Lab • Agfa Gevaert/Bayer • Agip Nigeria • Amco Informatic • Anglo-American • Augusta (EFIM) • Ashanti-Goldfield • Banca Nazionale del Lavoro • Bank of Boston • Barclays Bank • Coca-Cola Company • Coopers & Lybrand • DuPont • Enichem/ENI • Hoescht Ltd • IBM • ITT • Leyland • Lonrho • Marks & Spencer • Merrill Lynch • Mobil Oil Nigeria • Ogilvy & Mather • Olivetti • Price Waterhouse • Sevel/Fiat • Shell • Siemens • Sudamtex • Techint • Total • Volkswagen

Evaluating the impact

The programme has demonstrated success in identifying, selecting and motivating entrepreneurs, and providing them with training, advice and assistance to enable them to develop their projects and turn them into profit-making enterprises. More specifically:

- EMPRETEC has provided training and technical assistance to over 5,000 entrepreneurs, who were identified through a rigorous selection process;

- Some 25% of the participants are women;

- EMPRETEC has generated over 150 entrepreneurship and management training workshops in ten countries in Africa and Latin America;

- It has trained and certified over 50 local instructors in three languages as EMPRETEC workshop trainers;

- 22 EMPRETEC support centres have been established in ten countries, 14 of which are currently self-financing with support from international donors, host governments and private sector companies;

- 23 active entrepreneurship associations have been established in ten countries;

- 4 global and regional fairs have been held, which resulted in the establishment of business linkages and the exchange of business information between entrepreneurs both regionally and internationally; and

- EMPRETEC programme country directors have tailored their services to the needs of the local entrepreneurs, offering specialised services on topics such as marketing, total quality management, finance, negotiations, and technology transfer.

An indicator of success is that two thirds of these centres are self-financing. Specific economic results of EMPRETEC programmes include increased employment, increased sales volume, increased assets and exports, increased attention of multilateral organisations and donor countries, expansion of business associations, and involvement of the corporate private sector. More than 30 major multinational and regional companies are supporting the programmes in Latin America and Africa.

2.5 UNEP's Cleaner Production Programme

APELL
Preventing Industrial Accidents and their Impacts

APELL
Preventing Industrial Accidents and their Impacts

The APELL programme was launched by UNEP in 1988 in co-operation with the chemical industry, represented by several national organisations and the International Council of Chemical Associations, following various accidents in both industrialised and industrialising countries. It is a joint initiative between international organisations, national and local governments, industry associations and companies, non-governmental organisations (NGOs) and local community groups. The goal of the initiative is to prevent technological accidents and their impacts by assisting decision-makers and technical personnel to increase community awareness of hazardous installations and to prepare response plans in case unexpected events at these installations should endanger life, property or the environment.

APELL has been designed to be an on-going, flexible process – adaptable to a variety of potential risks posed by different cultures, value systems, industries, community resources, response capabilities, legal systems and regulatory requirements. Locally-established co-ordinating groups are created to consult with a wide range of organisations in the community to gather facts and opinions, assess risks, evaluate approaches and organise available personnel and resources to produce an emergency response plan. UNEP-IE, with the support of its network of international experts from industry and elsewhere, provides technical expertise at the request of national governments to help launch local APELL activities. This assistance takes the form of seminars, workshops, evaluations, advice, and a range of publications including a regular newsletter, case studies and a handbook outlining the ten-step guide to the APELL process which has now been translated into 20 languages. The APELL process has now been implemented in over 30 countries in Asia, Latin America, Africa and central and eastern Europe.

UNEP'S Industry and Environment Office (UNEP-IE) was established in Paris in 1975 with the aim of bringing together industry, government, and non-governmental organisations to work towards environmentally sound forms of industrial development.

It goals are to:

- define and encourage the incorporation of environmental criteria into industrial development;

- help formulate policies, strategies and management tools for sustainable industrial development and build the capacity for their implementation;

- promote preventative environmental protection through cleaner, safer production as well as other pro-active approaches; and

- stimulate the exchange of information on environmentally sound technologies and forms of industrial development.

UNEP-IE also carries out the clearing-house function for the implementation of the Montreal Protocol on Substances that Deplete the Ozone Layer.

Its activities include: regular dialogue and meetings with industry associations in a number of different sectors; a tourism programme looking at environmental management issues in what has become the world's largest industry; the production of training manuals and workshops (such as a recent initiative with the International Chamber of Commerce and the International Federation of Consulting Engineers to help companies implement the ICC's Charter for Sustainable Development); the publication of a variety of newsletters, management guidelines and technical papers; research on key environmental management issues, such as the project Engaging Stakeholders described on page 85; environmental technology assessment; work on energy and transportation and major world-wide programmes such as The Cleaner Production Programme and APELL (Awareness and Preparedness for Emergencies at the Local Level).

UNEP IE works with industry associations and individual companies in all of its activities. It offers a good example of the potential leverage and outreach effect which a public entity can have by working in partnership with the private sector and with other public sector organisations. UNEP-IE's success in covering a wide range and depth of issues and reaching a large number of countries, companies and industry associations is especially notable given that its permanent professional staff is only in the region of eight people, although it is also supported by government and industry secondees and in-house consultants.

The APELL and Cleaner Production programmes offer good examples of how UNEP-IE leverages its multi-stakeholder partnerships to increase both the reach and impact of its activities.

THE CLEANER PRODUCTION PROGRAMME

Current trends in population, industrialisation and consumption continue to release wastes and pollutants faster than the earth can absorb them. Natural resources are consumed faster than they can be restored. The need to reorient production processes, products and services, as well as consumer demands is a key issue on the sustainable development agenda. Launched in 1989, UNEP's Cleaner Production Programme is one of the international initiatives aimed at tackling these challenges.

Cleaner Production is the continuous application of an integrated preventative environmental strategy applied to processes, products and services to increase eco-efficiency and reduce risk to humans and the environment.

The programme's objectives are to:

- Increase world-wide consensus on a "cleaner production" vision;

- Catalyse the implementation of policies, strategies, environmental management systems, and environmentally sound technologies;

- Promote the establishment of National Cleaner Production Centres;

- Support the growing network of organisations dedicated to promoting cleaner production and eco-efficiency activities;

- Help enhance capabilities through training and education;

- Support demonstration projects and provide technical assistance.

The Cleaner Production programme is structured as an international network of partner organisations consisting of more than 100 organisations in over 60 countries. Financial and/or in-kind support has come from a combination of some 14 governments, multilateral agencies and industry associations, operating at both national and international levels. Some of the key partner organisations have included the European Union, UNIDO, UNCSD, The International Maritime Organisation (IMO), the International Labour Office (ILO), OECD, The International Chamber of Commerce (ICC), the World Business Council for Sustainable Development (WBCSD), the World Bank and the World Environment Center (WEC).

This network of partners, together with individual companies and industry experts work together in a variety of ways ranging from: capacity-building activities such as training workshops and demonstration projects; the production of newsletters, training manuals and case studies; regular up-dating of The International Cleaner Production Information Clearing House (ICPIC) which is available on-line via the Internet; and the establishment of working groups covering key sectors and issues.

An important initiative has been a joint venture between UNIDO and UNEP to establish National Cleaner Production Centres in eight countries: Brazil; China; the Czech Republic; India; Mexico; the Slovak Republic; Tanzania; and Zimbabwe. The purpose of these centres is to build local capacity to introduce, implement and develop cleaner production initiatives which are adapted to local conditions rather than imposed from outside. Working in partnership with host organisations, such as the business-led Environmental Forum of Zimbabwe and the Czech Environment Management Centre, UNEP and UNIDO are supporting policy analysis, training activities, in-plant demonstrations and information networking in these rapidly industrialising economies.

> Much of the current thinking on environmental protection focuses on what to do with wastes and emissions after they have been created. The goal of cleaner production is to avoid generating pollution in the first place – which frequently cuts costs, reduces risks and identifies new opportunities.
>
> Jacqueline Aloisi de Larderel,
> Director,
> UNEP IE

2.6 The ILO, IILS and World Business Academy STEP Programme

The World Business Academy recognises that business executives need more than vague, abstract notions about how they can combine profitability with social responsibility. They need practical tools and education in business renewal methods and technologies, and they need this not only in OECD economies but everywhere in the world. In order to help companies to develop these tools, WBA has joined forces with the International Labour Office (ILO) and the International Institute of Labour Studies (IILS) to undertake a major research, resource development and relationship-building initiative. This will be aimed at empowering enterprises to manage rapid change and organisational transformation, in a socially responsible manner.

The initiative is called The Social Transformation and Enterprise Performance (STEP) in a Global Economy project. It will provide practicing managers with down-to-earth knowledge and practical tools for improving the performance of their business in a socially responsible manner. It will draw on the global network of WBA's fellows and members, and on the extensive research and analytical skills of the IILS. It will also build on the ILO's ability to provide socially responsible business leaders with the opportunity to influence policy and legislation of governments in areas which directly affect their business and industry as well as the wider society. In this connection, ILO has developed an enterprise strategy to consolidate and leverage the activities of its own office with those of the private sector, in order to be a positive joint force for social change. One element of this strategy is to conduct regular enterprise forums, starting in November 1996, to maintain a dialogue with the private sector and other ILO partners.

The STEP project will begin with a comprehensive global research study into best practices which mutually support social responsibility, performance improvement and the development of human capital. Case studies will be developed looking at various areas of business renewal and performance improvement, commencing with examples of human-centred restructuring for competitiveness. The case studies will be assembled into a Global Resources Bank which will be accessible by Internet as well as other means.

Based on the best of these inputs, selected World Business Academy fellows and members, together with other leading edge scholars, will be invited to participate in the development of training programmes which will be offered to companies around the world to improve their capability in socially responsible business renewal. These training programmes will be initiated in a number of developing countries, such as India, Thailand, South Africa, Kenya, Brazil and Argentina, as well as the transition economies of central and eastern Europe.

STEP will also focus on the identification and promotion of opportunities for business enterprises to link with other social partners such as employer organisations, trade unions, NGOs, business schools, government institutions, and international agencies in strategic alliances which will facilitate improved business performance in ways which benefit the wider community.

STEP is a global research, resource development and network initiative, which will focus on best practice case studies, training programmes, regular enterprise forums and strategic alliances. It offers great potential for both dialogue and action.

THE WORLD BUSINESS ACADEMY

The World Business Academy is a global membership-based, non-profit organisation aimed at creating a better world through business. Its work is focused on three areas: new business paradigms; sustainable business strategies; and development of human potential. Operating through a membership network of visionary business leaders and academics and a select group of WBA fellows, the organisation develops educational and training materials, workshops and senior level consultations around these three core areas. Everything it does is based on the premise that recent profound world changes require business, now the most influential force in society, to accept greater responsibility in partnership with other social actors, and to accept, what WBA describes as the "double-bottom line – coupling profitability with social responsibility, and human development with business performance."

2.7 The IFC's Technical Assistance Programme

AMSCO was established in 1989 with the IFC, UNDP and the African Development Bank as the project sponsors to provide management training and support to African entrepreneurs. It also pioneered the approach of bringing in private sector partners through an Industry Council for Development Services and today has private shareholders, mostly large companies, from Belgium, Cameroon, Canada, Denmark, Finland, France, Hungary, India, the Netherlands, Pakistan, Portugal, Switzerland, the United Kingdom, and the USA. These companies include Nestle, Accor, Banque Nationale de Paris, Philips, Bata Ltd., British Petroleum, Booker Tate, Standard Chartered Bank, Barclays, IBM World Trade Corp., the Tata group and Nabisco. Since its inception, AMSCO working in partnership with a UNDP project called African Management Training Services, has provided management services to over 70 companies in some 17 countries throughout Africa. The average number of employees in these companies has been 100 and approximately 6,000 jobs have been created. Most of the support has been in the services and manufacturing sectors, although there have also been projects in food and beverages, tourism, agriculture and agro-industry. In mid-1995 AMSCO and the UNDP Private Sector Development Programme co-sponsored an in-depth study, conducted by an independent firm, to analyse the actual changes in the financial and productivity performance of eleven client enterprises during the period of AMSCO's involvement with them. The conclusions of the study were that during this period client companies saw: average annual turnover doubled; net annual losses of US$55,000 turn into net annual profit of US$400,000; labour and capital productivity increase on average by more than 100%, average export earnings more than double and import substitution increase in US dollars by almost 50%.

The International Finance Corporation, an arm of the World Bank group, is the largest source of direct project financing for private investment in developing and transition economies. Its primary goal is to stimulate efficient and environmentally sound private sector development in these emerging markets through providing investment, mobilising other public and private investors and helping to improve the policy and regulatory framework to encourage private domestic and foreign investment. In order for the IFC to achieve these objectives, potential projects need to be technically, financially and economically attractive, as well as environmentally sound. Thorough, detailed project preparation is therefore essential, as is a market-friendly and responsible approach to policy formulation and regulations. Many local policy makers, project sponsors and business people may not have access to the expertise required; however, such technical assistance falls outside the normal scope of the IFC's project appraisal work and profit-driven mode of operating. To overcome this, in the early-1980s the IFC established a comprehensive Technical Assistance programme.

The programme has developed into a wide range of initiatives including:

- **The Technical Assistance Trust Funds programme** – a group of over 20 trust funds established by contributions from bilateral and multilateral donors and managed by the IFC – which help to fund a range of activities such as sector studies; project feasibility assessments; project identification and linking of partners; pilot plants and operations; project rehabilitation and privatisation support. Current projects range from work in capital markets development to technical support for privately funded environmental and social projects. For example, the TATF programme is helping establish an Environmental Assistance Fund for SMEs in Africa; a best practices programme on private sector education in Pakistan; the design of a mutual funds system in Peru; a training programme on environmental risk management in Asia; and a global survey of investment opportunities in the hospital sector.

- **Project Development Facilities and Business Advisory Services** in a number of regions and countries, which include: the Africa Project Development Facility; the African Management Services Company (AMSCO); the Mekong Project Development Facility; Business Advisory Services for the Caribbean and Central America; the Polish Business Advisory Service; and the South Pacific Project Facility.

- **The Foreign Investment Advisory Service** which was created in 1985 to advise developing country governments (and now transition economy governments as well) on how to enhance their policies, programmes and institutions to attract more beneficial foreign direct investment.

Partnership is crucial to both the funding and implementation of these activities. The technical assistance programme is supported by about 30 bilateral and multilateral donors and by an Industry Council for Development Services (ICDS) which played an important role in the establishment of AMSCO. The donors and supporting companies not only provide financing, but also offer "in-kind" support through the identification of technical experts. The role of private sector companies in this process is one which has great scale-up potential in future years.

2.8 WHO, UNICEF and Rotary's Polio Immunisation Programme

ROTARY HAS MOBILISED PEOPLE AS WELL AS MONEY:

- In Bulgaria, Rotarians convinced the Gypsy community to participate in National Immunisation Days, despite traditional distrust of government programmes;
- Rotarians in Peru were often the only means of reaching children in areas of guerrilla conflict, taking vaccines to regions where government health workers could not travel;
- Thai Rotarians created posters for three national campaigns and provided funds to train Laotian health workers;
- Rotarians in Ecuador, with support from a local company, supplemented their government's surveillance system with a reward programme promoted by the national media;
- Rotarians chair many of the Inter-Agency Co-ordinating Committees which have been established in different regions of the world;
- Rotary worked with pharmaceutical manufacturers to increase donations of vaccine;
- In Nigeria, Rotarians formed a national umbrella organisation to co-ordinate all non-governmental support for health, including immunisation;
- Rotarians from the USA, Australia and New Zealand helped to equip laboratories in Ethiopia, Russia and India.

The other partner organisations have also played a critical role:
- WHO's Expanded Programme on Immunisation (EPI) is the primary global vehicle for immunising children against polio and other major vaccine-preventable diseases;
- UNICEF is the major provider of vaccines and immunisation equipment, as well as playing a key role in social mobilisation;
- Pan American Health Organisation – spearheads implementation of EPI in the Americas;
- The US Centers for Disease Control and Prevention (CDC) is a US government agency which provides technical, laboratory and programmatic assistance to polio eradication;
- Task Force for Child Survival and Development – sponsored by WHO, UNICEF, the World Bank, UNDP and the Rockerfeller Foundation, assists through research, surveillance and the exchange of information.

In 1985 polio claimed the lives of some 600,000 people around the world. Only 74 countries reported no cases of the disease. By 1993 there were only 120,000 victims and 144 countries reported no cases. Over that period of time, an international partnership of leading global health agencies, non-governmental organisations and companies, worked together to immunise more than 80% of the world's children against polio and other diseases. The project has been hailed as one of the "greatest public health success stories of the past decade." Central to the success of the initiative was the role played by Rotary International through its PolioPlus programme. It offers a fine example of the power of the private sector to achieve social goals if it can be mobilised on a global scale.

Rotary International is the association of the world's 27,000 Rotary Clubs, an organisation of some 1.2 million business and professional men and women from around the world. Founded in Chicago in 1905, Rotary provides humanitarian service, encourages ethical standards in business and other professions, and helps to build goodwill in the world. Each club serves first and foremost its own community, but they are all connected through an international network and the work of the Rotary Foundation.

In 1985 Rotary launched PolioPlus as a world-wide programme to raise funds to immunise some 100 million children a year for five years. Drawing on the strength of Rotary's international network, the organisation raised more than US$246 million, of which more than US$200 million was distributed by the Rotary Foundation to immunisation and eradication efforts in 103 nations.

The initiative went much further than fundraising. In project countries Rotarians have mobilised tens of thousands of volunteers, and provided community-based leadership and resources for social mobilisation efforts such as transportation, logistical support and communications. Rotary Clubs also sponsor and equip laboratories and provide disease surveillance.

The six partners have now formed the Polio Eradication Network to meet the target of eradication by the year 2000, the goal set in 1988 by the member countries of the World Health Assembly.

2.9 UNICEF's Social Marketing Campaigns

The United Nations Children's Fund, the only UN organisation dedicated exclusively to children, works with other UN agencies, governments, non-governmental organisations and the private sector, to provide community-based services in primary health-care, nutrition, basic education and safe water and sanitation in over 140 developing countries. It aims to reduce the terrible toll the lack of such services takes on the world's youngest citizens.

UNICEF was created in 1946 to meet the emergency needs of children in the aftermath of World War II in Europe. As the organisation celebrates its 50th anniversary it can also celebrate the fact that the past 50 years have witnessed great progress for the world's children than the previous 2000 years of human history, however much remains to be done. UNICEF is working closely with the business community and encouraging companies to support its efforts in a variety of ways, including the following examples of social or cause-related marketing.

THE POWER OF SOCIAL MARKETING

British Airways launched its "Change for Good" campaign in April 1994. The concept is a simple one. During their flights passengers are encouraged to gather the remains of their foreign currency and donate it to the "Change for Good" fund rather than taking it home to end up cluttering wallets and drawers. The spare change is collected by the British Airways crews and the airline then passes it over to UNICEF. Although the donations may represent spare, unwanted change to the passengers, when it is pooled together it can generate substantial income to help the world's children. By the end of 1995 the British Airways "Change for Good" programme had raised over US$3.8 million. This money has helped to support specific projects such as:

• HIV/AIDs education in Zimbabwean schools;
• mother and child health programmes to tackle diarrhoea in Mexico;
• relief programmes in India;
• training of village health workers in Tanzania; and
• a special appeal on the airline which raised support for the massive relief effort in Rwanda in 1995.

UNICEF is now running this scheme with 12 other airlines and as at April 1996 the airlines' passengers had raised over US$8 million.

The benefits are not only financial. In addition to the monies raised, over 84 million people a year have been exposed to the initiative and to the work of UNICEF and the help it provides to improve the lives of millions of children.

ITT Sheraton has introduced a simple but highly effective "Check Out for Children" initiative in 70 of its European hotels. On arrival at the hotel, guests are advised that on check-out they will be invited to add one dollar (or local currency equivalent) onto their bill, which will be donated to UNICEF. The European hotels aim to raise US$750,000 by the end of the financial year. The programme has already raised more than half this amount in its first six months of operation. ITT Sheraton are now discussing ways in which to introduce the scheme to all 420 of their properties around the world.

Inter-Continental Hotels and Resorts launched a "Round Up for Children" campaign in all of its 170 hotels worldwide in January 1996 whereby guests are invited to "round up" their hotel bill with the additional amount going to UNICEF. In its first six months of operation the scheme has raised over US$300,000.

Sumitomo Bank in Tokyo also runs several programmes encouraging its employees and customers to support fundraising efforts for UNICEF. It offers clients Charity Accounts, for which all after-tax interest is automatically paid to UNICEF, with the bank providing a matching donation. It also operates a foreign coin collection programme which has raised more than £100 million for UNICEF

In each of these examples all the participants have gained. UNICEF has received additional funding and has raised its own profile. The individual organisations have benefited through demonstrating a commitment to be caring companies, through local publicity and by encouraging staff support and participation. Most importantly of all, the welfare of the young people of the world who are being helped by UNICEF has been improved, to the benefit of all.

2.10 Partnerships between business and the bilateral development agencies

NORDIC RUSSIAN LEADERSHIP EXECUTIVE TRAINING (NORLET)

The objective of this project is to accelerate the development of managerial skills needed to support and speed up the necessary restructuring of the Russian economy and industry. The project is the practical follow-up to research carried out by the World Business Council for Sustainable Development on investment barriers in central and eastern Europe, and a joint study on management training needs in the region by the WBCSD and The Prince of Wales Business Leaders Forum in 1994.

The project is financed by a grant from the four Nordic governments of Norway, Finland, Denmark and Sweden. This grant is matched by in-kind contributions to an equivalent value from a consortium of participating Scandinavian companies: ABB, Norsk Hydro, Tetra Laval, Statoil, Neste, Danfoss and Finnish Tele.

During the first three years of the programme 600 managers with high leadership potential will participate from Russia and to some extent from surrounding states in the former Soviet Union. These participants are selected from the Russian joint venture companies of the consortium members, as well as from Russian customers and suppliers of these JV companies and other companies of key importance to the economy. The programme for each participant lasts one year during which there is three weeks of classroom based training in St Petersburg, the creation of a mentor relationship with an experienced manager, and the organisation of an internship with a western host company. During the year the participant also carries out a development project in his/her company.

An important "train-the-trainers" programme is also included in NORLET. Local trainers will gradually take over responsibility for the programme in order to run the initiative as a commercial entity after the three-year project is completed.

NORLET is a capacity-building project, business-driven but with management development benefits that reach far wider than the immediate companies involved. It has a genuine win-win profile and is therefore more likely to be sustainable in the long run.

Non-commercial linkages are beginning to be developed between business and bilateral development agencies (BDAs) in a number of ways:

- **Indirectly through NGOs** – in recent years the BDAs have made great strides in working more closely with non-governmental organisations. In some cases they have established major programmes to achieve this, such as the New Partnerships Initiative of USAID and the Joint Funding Scheme of the British ODA, which is currently supporting over 100 NGOs and providing half the costs for 1,800 projects – most of which involve British NGOs working with their local counterparts in developing and transition economies. In a growing number of cases these NGOs are also getting support from the corporate sector, with the result that individual companies or groups of companies may be supporting the same NGOs or the same projects as bilateral agencies, without there being a direct link between the companies and the BDA. For example, WEC receives support from both USAID and a number of leading American and non-American companies, and in India the British-based NGO ActionAid has been supported by ODA and by British companies in its activities.

- **Through support for business-led development organisations** – such as those described in the following section. Organisations such as Philippine Business for Social Progress, the National Business Initiative in South Africa and the Thai Business Initiative for Rural Development, for example, are all receiving support from different BDAs ranging from USAID to AUSAID and NORAD. These are clearly business-led initiatives, but they are also not-for-profit, and are legally constituted as such.

- **Directly through joint public-private projects** – in a small, but increasing number of cases – bilateral agencies are entering into joint initiatives directly with individual companies or groups of companies headquartered in their home country, to undertake environmental, human and social development projects in developing and transition economies of mutual interest to both the agency and the companies concerned. These are not projects where companies are commercially contracted by a bilateral agency to fulfil a particular job, which is a long-standing practice, but joint resourcing programmes where both the companies and the agency jointly provide funding and/or in-kind support to a development project. The NORLET programme described on the left is an example.

- **Strategic level dialogue** – in some donor countries efforts are underway to establish a more co-ordinated and strategic dialogue between locally headquartered multi-nationals and the country's BDA to assess the potential for greater public-private collaboration towards sustainable development in developing countries. In the United Kingdom, for example, the ODA in June 1996 hosted a consultation with a group of British companies all of which have interests in emerging economies, brought together by The Prince of Wales Business Leaders Forum and WorldAware. The purpose of this consultation was to review the potential for greater public-private collaboration in development.

3

National business partnerships for development

The following section looks at seven examples of partnerships which are:

a) national in scope

b) business-led, and

c) focused on applying the resources of the business sector (not only financial, but also managerial and technical, as well as the infrastructure, connections, influence and culture of the business community) to the service of national development.

These partnerships are not mandated representatives of organised business, such as Chambers of Commerce, Confederations of Industry, Institutes of Directors or sector-specific trade associations, the role of which has already been covered in a previous section. These are examples of partnerships which have been established by groups of companies with the specific purpose of:

a) tackling a range of broader societal and developmental challenges, and

b) promoting and demonstrating through action, the broader role of business in society as a good corporate citizen.

In each of the examples the partner companies are drawn from a wide range of different sectors and are a mixture of both local and multinational companies. All of the partnerships are addressing a number of different development issues, rather than being single-issue focused – although there are countless examples of single-issue partnerships in areas such as business and education, and business and the environment, some of which have been described in previous sections.

Five of the examples are drawn from developing and transition economies and two from OECD economies. All are slightly different in the strategy they employ, although they each have elements of: managing or helping companies to manage community projects; running awareness-raising campaigns about the business and societal value of corporate responsibility; and influencing the policy dialogue. The main characteristic they share in common, other than their business leadership, is their role as catalytic intermediary bodies acting as a vital link between the business sector on the one hand, and government and community-level organisations on the other. Each case study is also an interesting model of how groups of companies – often competitors – are working together with each other and with other sectors, and each of them has the potential for replication or adaptation elsewhere.

3.1 The National Business Initiative
for growth, development and democracy in South Africa

There are many ways in which the special skills and know-how of the business community can help the Government of National Unity to achieve its development objectives. The original thinking which has gone into the launch of the National Business Initiative is very much appreciated and I give it my unqualified support.

President Nelson Mandela

Two years after South Africa's first democratic elections the sense of miraculous transformation is increasingly tempered by the need to make visible and substantial progress in tackling the country's enormous socio-economic challenges. In particular there is the need to grow the economy, consolidate and strengthen democratic institutions, and develop policies and programmes for improving the lives of the majority of people. The South African business community and international investors have a pivotal role to play in this process and in March 1995 The National Business Initiative (NBI) was established to promote and facilitate this role. Within its first year of existence, the NBI has already mobilised support from 132 major companies and is working in partnership with government and other interests to establish programmes in areas of strategic national importance. These programmes are aimed at: building effective governance; developing income generating strategies for the country's high levels of unemployed people; and tackling critical issues associated with education, training, and urban development.

BACKGROUND

The NBI was established by the merger of two existing business-led organisations, and therefore started with the advantage of their combined skills, resources and reputations. These two organisations were The Urban Foundation and The Consultative Business Movement.

The Urban Foundation was created in 1977 by a group of business leaders including Sir Harry Oppenheimer, chairman of the Anglo American Corporation, with support from black community leaders in response to the Soweto riots of 1976. The initiative was aimed at developing private sector-community driven solutions to improve the socio-economic and political conditions of the disadvantaged and the poor, especially in urban areas. It carried out its task by:
• researching and influencing government policy;
• developing appropriate institutions and systems; and
• managing and supporting community development projects.

During its 18 years of existence the Urban Foundation developed a reputation for both its research and policy formulation capabilities, as well as some of its innovative, market-driven solutions to problem areas such as education, housing and community-based facilities. Among other things it

The NBI's mission is to enhance business's collective contribution to make our country and society work for all by:

- **Promoting increased economic growth**
- **Reducing poverty and socio-economic inequality**
- **Supporting effective and efficient governance**

helped to establish: the Joint Education Trust, a multi-million rand initiative funded by business, which still supports leading edge education projects today; a Home Loan Guarantee Company and Group Credit Company; a number of informal settlement upgrading projects; and several community centres. It also spearheaded business initiatives to abolish influx control and establish property rights for black South Africans.

The Consultative Business Movement was established by a group of business leaders in 1988 after intensive consultation with community and political representatives. It was focused on building better understanding between business and the different political and economic actors in South Africa. Its first phase of activities focused on structured contact between business and political groups across the political spectrum. This was followed by workshops aimed at facilitating a more mature debate and co-ordinated approach to the way companies were preparing for their role in the rapidly changing South Africa, resulting in several books on the role of business in transition. As its reputation as a catalyst and facilitator grew, the CBM was called on: to help with the process which led to the country's National Peace Accord; to serve as a secretariat for various Regional Dispute Resolution Committees; to provide secretariat support for the National Economic Forum and dialogue between business and organised labour; and finally, to render process and secretariat services to the Convention for a Democratic South Africa (Codesa) which led to the 1994 election. In the lead-up to the election CBM was also active in mobilising business participation in a massive voter education programme for the millions of South Africans who had never voted before.

This brief description of the two business-led organisations that underpin the NBI gives some indication not only of the base on which the NBI has been built, but also of the leadership role that the South African business sector played in supporting disadvantaged communities and promoting and facilitating political change during the uncertain period from 1976 until the 1994 election. In doing so it also had an interest in protecting its long-term strategic interests and ensuring the survival of a market economy (which was by no means a certain outcome in the 1980s). This added to the benefits that business involvement brought to the process of political transition, and is an example of how business can support societal change in a win-win manner.

THE NBI'S STRUCTURE AND STRATEGY

Each NBI member company is represented on its Board of Governors which represents both its business members and community leadership. They in turn appoint a national Board of Directors, consisting of a mixture of business and community leaders. There are also provincial boards and over 250 business leaders get actively involved in activities at this level. The membership fees of participating companies cover the NBI's core costs and some of its initiatives, but it also obtains targeted business funding, as well as government and international donor support for specific initiatives.

The NBI has structured itself to be:

- **A problem solver** – bringing business skills and resources to focus on those issues, which if resolved could produce a valuable multiplier effect of positive results for the nation. In doing so this enables business to act collectively and enhance its influence, build positive relationships with government, labour and community interests, and support the process of reconstruction and development.

- **A think tank** – with the intellectual and research capacity to identify, consider and research important issues. From this process the NBI supports the process of policy change and produces regular newsletters, briefs and meetings to provide information on critical development issues, policy proposals, strategies for addressing national problems and probably most important of all, concrete plans for delivery mechanisms.

- **A facilitator** – which through its independence, legitimacy and mobility, can help different actors to achieve consensus and move towards common goals.

The NBI's current programme focuses on the following areas:

The NBI's Strategic Programme for 1996/97

OPERATING AREA	FOCUS	BROAD INITIATIVE
Effective Governance	**Public Sector Support**	Public Sector Transformation Management Development Local Government Training
	Consolidating Democracy	Business Against Crime KwaZulu-Natal Political Process
Economics	**Income Generating Strategies**	Public Works Programme Local Economic Development and Local Business Service Centres SMME - Facilitating capital flow Infrastructure Investment Task Team
Development	**Education & Training**	Education Quality Support Teacher Development Further Education and Training Financing Crisis in Education
	Development Facilitation	Housing Delivery Task Team Urban Development Partnerships

---

It tackles each of this issues in partnership with other sectors, as illustrated in the following diagram:

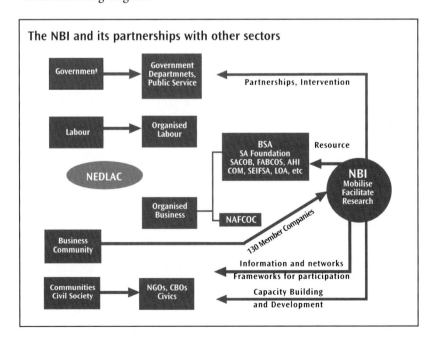

The NBI and its partnerships with other sectors

1) The Economics Programme

With unemployment in South Africa already at unacceptably high levels, the prospect of jobless growth poses a serious threat to work place stability, and hence the sustainability of the country's current growth trend. The NBI and its members recognise that both the private and public sectors must offer concrete programmes for income generation, albeit short term, to the unemployed and those segments of the community that will be adversely affected by job losses, in order to bridge the gap between social imperative and economic sustainability.

To this end it is:

- working with government departments on the development of subsidy and incentive schemes aimed at enhancing private sector involvement in public works programmes;

- mobilising its member companies to assist in the establishment of local economic development initiatives using a resource kit developed in partnership with government; and

- facilitating a cross-sector Infrastructure Investment Task Team to help implement a market-friendly framework to encourage private sector participation in the financing and delivery of infrastructure projects.

2) The Effective Governance programme

The rapid political transformation in South Africa has created new hope and opportunities for the structure of governance at national, provincial and local levels. However from a practical perspective, the election of hundreds of new political leaders and the integration of thousands of new, mostly untrained public servants into the country's fragmented and cumbersome government structure has placed enormous pressure on the process of governance. There is an urgent need to increase the level of training and mutual understanding between government and other sectors.

Under the auspices of its effective governance programme the NBI has undertaken a number of initiatives such as:

- co-hosting a workshop with UNDP on local government training;

- producing a booklet of policy recommendations on local government training;

- using business resources to assist the South African Parliament to restructure its administration;

- reviewing international best practice in Industry and Parliament dialogue mechanisms with the aim of establishing a structure in South Africa to facilitate a non-partisan, honest sharing of information between industry and members of parliament;

- assisting in the secretariat for the Presidential Review Commission on the transformation of the public service;

- working with various universities and the South African Management and Development Institute to increase private sector contribution to the management training of public servants; and

- arranging visits from international experts on topics such as reinventing government, backed by newsletters on international best practice in this area.

One of the NBI's major activities in its Effective Governance programme is the Business Against Crime Initiative, which was profiled on page 173.

THE LOCAL ECONOMIC DEVELOPMENT RESOURCE KIT

The NBI has recognised that Local Economic Development (LED) is critical to increasing employment and has launched a programme to mobilise local capacity and resources at the community level. It has developed an LED Resource Kit – which it plans to distribute throughout the country, backed up by the training of facilitators, the dissemination of international and South African best practice in local economic development, and the identification of pilot projects which will involve member companies. LED Resource Kits have been distributed to member companies, local and provincial government and community-based organisations in the Gauteng region.

3) The NBI Social Development Programme

The worst scars of apartheid mark the low level of development of South Africa's human resources. This is evidenced in the poor quality of education, low level of skills and inadequate access to housing, transport, health and social services. These problems are exacerbated by inefficient patterns of urban development of the apartheid city. The NBI's Social Development Programme focuses on improving the quality of education and training and developing innovative responses to housing and urban development challenges.

The NBI's Education Policy and System Change Unit (Edupol) is the leading initiative devoted to bringing the resources and logic of business to the process of education change. It has:

- Encouraged the government to adopt an Education Quality Improvement Programme (EQUIP) and developed a business support project to support that initiative (as described on page 130);

- Undertaken an audit of national teacher education (which surveyed nearly 300 training institutions and 490,000 teacher training students) and made recommendations on how to improve efficiency and quality of teacher training;

- Managed a commission by the Danish aid agency, DANIDA, to support the development of teacher policy at both provincial and national levels;

- Undertaken several major studies on the financing and governance of further education and training – looking at both the South African system and international practice in some of the country's key competitive nations; and

- Participated in numerous government commissions, for example, on the development of a new schools bill and the improvement of education management development.

In the area of housing and urban development, the NBI has:

- Undertaken extensive research into the process of informal settlement upgrading (this focused on eight settlements around the country and included interviews with over 1,500 informal settlers). It produced evidence of the viability of incremental informal settlement upgrading and was used to support the implementation of a capital subsidy scheme for low income households;

- Interacted with government on key policy initiatives, such as the New Urban Development Strategy, the government's White Paper on A New Policy and Strategy for Housing, and the Housing Bill 1996;

- Established a Housing Delivery Support Team to mobilise a collective business contribution to accelerating housing delivery. South Africa's housing crisis is one of the major political challenges facing the country. The NBI's Housing Delivery Support Team was established after consultation with the Department of Housing and set up outside the formally mandated and representative business structures – with an eye on national rather than sectoral interest and the flexibility to respond to rapidly changing issues. The Task Team involves senior individuals from major business bodies under the chairmanship of the NBI's Development Board chairman. The Ministry of Housing has appointed the NBI as the implementing agency to establish provincial expediting teams to expedite housing projects for over 250,000 families. This partnership to expedite housing will be funded by the government,

> Private companies need three thing to succeed: the capacity to produce goods and services profitably; a policy and regulatory environment that makes that possible (i.e. trade legislation, competition policy, labour law and the like); and social institutions that work (where the interaction of private firms with one another, customers and others, is regulated by the rule of law, and also through whih basic social needs of the majority of citizens for houssing, health ad education can be met).
>
> Brian Whittaker
> Executive Director, NBI

A sample of member companies:
ABSA • AECI • Afrox • American Airlines • Andersen Consulting • Anglo American Corporation • Anglovaal Group • Arthur Andersen • Barlow Ltd • BMW SA • BP SA • Caltex • Coca-Cola• Commercial Union • Coopers & Lybrand • CSIR Deloitte & Touche • Edgars • Engen • Ernst & Young • Eskom • First National Bank • Gemini Consulting • Gencor • Gilbeys • Gillette SA • IBM • Johnson & Johnson • Kellogg Co • Liberty Life • Lonrho • Mercedes Benz • Munich Re • Murray & Roberts • Nampak • Nedcor • Nestle SA • New Age Beverages • Norwich Life • Ogilvy & Mather • Old Mutual • PG Bison • Premier Group • Price Waterhouse • Rio Tinto SA• SA Breweries • SA Philips • SA Sugar Association • SBC Warburg • SC Johnson Wax • Shell • Sentrachem • Siemens• Smith & Nephew • SmithKline Beecham • Standard Bank• Swiss Re • 3M• Tioxide SA • Tongaat-Hulett • Toyota SA • Unilever

managed by the NBI and supported by business leaders and NBI member companies;

- Developed a framework that describes public and private roles in the housing process in order to try to encourage greater involvement of private funders, developers and builders on which effective delivery relies. This is in response to the Department of Housing's considerable effort in creating institutions to support private delivery such as the Mortgage Indemnity Fund, the National Housing Finance Corporation and the Home Owners Defect Warranty Scheme;

- A programme to encourage greater employer involvement in the provision of housing for employees, is currently under investigation.

KEY SUCCESS FACTORS AND LESSONS

It is still too early to undertake a structured evaluation of the NBI's success and impact, however there are already clear indications of the value-added that a business-led partnership of this type can offer to both the private sector and the nation.

- To date NBI has made a point of focusing on the core competencies that business can bring to a particular problem (such as management expertise, capacity to take risk, ability to manage resources efficiently, innovation etc.) and then working in partnership with other sectors to mobilise their core competencies, rather than trying to do everything itself.

- It has developed a solid research and policy base, which underpins all its work.

- It has a clear strategy of piloting and evaluating initiatives first before undertaking public relations efforts and potentially raising unrealistic expectations of what business is capable of doing.

- Its focus is to build credibility and trust – not only as an effective and honest facilitator, but also as a deliverer of achievable solutions rather than unrealistic promises and demands.

- It has also emphasised the value of learning from best practice – both within South Africa and internationally – thereby minimising the chance that scarce resources and time will be wasted in "reinventing the wheel".

Although it is still early days for the NBI, it is fair to say that there are few, if any, other models in the world where a single business-led partnership is taking such a proactive, strategic and consultative approach with government and other key stakeholder groups, to help shape policies and programmes in such a wide range of crucial national issues.

3.2 Philippine Business for Social Progress

PBSP'S MISSION

To make a significant contribution to the development and delivery of solutions to poverty by promoting business sector commitment to social development, harnessing resources for programmes that promote self-reliance, and advocating sustainable development as fundamental to overall growth.

Philippine Business for Social Progress (PBSP) was founded by a group of 50 companies in 1970 in response to a period of economic decline, runaway inflation, growing poverty, social unrest and political insurgency. Today it has over 180 member companies, relationships with major international donors, regular policy dialogue with government and a proud history of organisational and programme management, having worked with some 1,000 partner organisations, and supported over 3,000 projects with funding in the region of US$50 million, which have benefited around 1.6 million Filipinos throughout the country. PBSP offers one of the best examples in the world of a business-led partnership that is tackling the problems of poverty and social unrest at both the grassroots level (by funding, capacity-building and sometimes directly running community projects) and at the strategic policy level (by influencing both corporate strategy and government strategy).

BACKGROUND

In the Philippines of the 1960s and early 1970s the business community was viewed by most of the population with enormous distrust and resentment and seen as a driving force behind the imperialism, feudalism, and political corruption and patronage which was crippling the livelihood opportunities of the poor and ripping apart the country's social fabric. A small group of visionary business leaders and their organisations joined forces to review and improve the contribution of business to society. Led by the Economic Development Foundation of banker Sixto Roxas, the Association for Social Action headed by Howard Dee of United Laboratories, the Council for Economic Development, and the industrialists Jose and Andres Soriano of the San Miguel corporation – the small group convinced 50 other business leaders to join them.

At the time Lucio Mazzei, a Venezuelan, was head of Shell Philippines. Aware of a similar business-led organisation in his home country called Dividendo Voluntario para la Communidad. He provided a grant from Shell for these business leaders to visit this initiative in Caracas. PBSP was initially modelled on this Latin American organisation and is thus an early example of the role that a multinational company played in helping to transfer socially innovative ideas from one country to another – both in terms of knowing about the ideas in the first place as a result of its global network, and in terms of providing the funding and other resources to encourage the transfer to take place.

STRUCTURE AND STRATEGY

From the outset PBSP was founded on two basic premises:

- The melding of strong business discipline with equally strong social development expertise.

- The active involvement of business supporters beyond the writing of cheques (as important as these were and to a lesser extent still are to the organisation's survival).

Over the past 25 years the organisation has fundamentally restructured both its funding and operational strategies in response to changing conditions and experience, but these two principles have remained paramount and are key to the organisation's success and sustainability.

FUNDING

Each member company signs a statement of commitment when it joins PBSP, in which it agrees to follow several principles of corporate responsibility and more specifically to set aside 1% of net income before taxes. Of this, 60% was originally channelled through PBSP and 40% retained by the company for its own community investment activities. In 1989 this balance was amended to reflect the increasingly proactive stance of many companies in managing their own community investment activities, with the result that today 20% is channelled through PBSP and 80% is retained by each member company (although in a number of cases the companies then contract PBSP to run specific programmes on their behalf). This funding structure allows for a clear delineation between funding operating costs and programme costs, and also allows for flexibility on the part of member companies in terms of how they balance their community spending between their own corporate-managed projects and using PBSP as an intermediary organisation.

However during the oil crisis and economic recession of the late 1970s, and in the face of declining membership, PBSP realised that it needed to broaden and diversify its funding strategy. It has done so in a number of ways:

- establishing and professionally managing a capital fund;

- starting to co-finance programmes with donor agencies;

- placing more emphasis on loans instead of grant assistance in project financing;

- generating income from services such as running training courses and consultancy; and

- reducing operating costs.

All are management approaches which would be familiar to any well run business, but in the case of PBSP they are taken to maximise the leverage and efficiency of funding in order to ensure that more resources directly reach the poor. Today more and more international donors, as well as the Philippine government and business community, view PBSP as a highly credible and effective conduit for channelling both public and private funds to local community projects.

OPERATIONS

Over the past 25 years PBSP has also undertaken several strategic changes in its operations focus, based on its growing experience and knowledge base of what works and what doesn't, as well as its readiness and ability to respond to changing conditions in both the needs of its business supporters and society at large. Over the years it has: supported projects in selected communities; run programmes to build the capacity of its grantee and partner organisations; managed projects around key themes, such as community organising, livelihood and social credit, basic services and appropriate technology; helped to establish "PBSP-clone" organisations at local and provincial levels; and established its own provincial network of offices to ensure that its service delivery is as localised and as appropriate as possible.

The organisation's current operations strategy reflects its recognition of two key factors:

1) The need for a more integrated, multi-disciplinary and resource-based approach to the challenge of poverty alleviation; and

2) The need to get more involved in the policy debate and to take a more strategic view and action on the role of business in society, beyond philanthropy and community investment activities.

In response to the first factor PBSP is now running all its programmes under an Area Resource Management (ARM) framework, which works through multi-sector partnerships between private entities (both business and NGOs) and local government to achieve the most efficient and equitable use of resources in a specific area, taking into consideration the socio-economic, ecological and organisational systems.

As far as the second factor is concerned, in 1992 PBSP established a Center for Corporate Citizenship, dedicated to promote the practice and critical review of corporate citizenship among chief executive officers and other senior level managers and decision-makers in the country. This centre is increasingly being encouraged to take a view of corporate citizenship that moves beyond the philanthropy and community relations activities of companies, to look at core business policies and practices and their impacts on society, on the environment and on development in general. The centre supports research and holds an annual conference attended by the President of the Philippines and/or cabinet ministers and prominent leaders from the private sector. It also works with a number of Chief Executives through a series of Consensus Groups, looking at specific societal issues to which business can offer solutions in partnership with the public sector. To date the issues covered have been:

- **Business and Education**

- **Business and the Environment** – in co-operation with the active and highly respected organisation Philippine Business for the Environment

- **Business and Countryside** (rural) **development**

- **Business and Local Government**

The formation, the management and the findings of these consensus groups have applicability in countries all over the world.

PBSP's Area Resource Management Strategy

●●

Since 1991 the three-pronged ARM approach has focused on the following interdependent systems:

• Within the socio-economic system it aims to help poverty groups gain control over resources and eventually be owners of anchor enterprises. Its efforts are focused on the development and optimum use of coastal, lowland and upland resources.

• Within the ecological system its goal is the balanced use of conservation, preservation and regeneration (as needed) of natural resources. This is aimed at ensuring that land and marine resources are preserved, while they are being harnessed for optimum production.

• Within the organisational system, the ARM's goals are to: develop public-private partnerships to facilitate development work; strengthen and consult NGOs and people's organisations; encourage the corporate sector, international and local donors to invest their resources; and encourage active government participation in poverty alleviation through appropriate legislation, policies and delivery of basic services.

This strategy is implemented in selected geographic areas, with the key beneficiaries usually being small-scale farmers, fishermen and local communities. An example of the ARM approach in action is the role that has been played by PBSP over the past five years in helping the Cebu City government establish an integrated rural development programme to restore the productive capacity and environmental quality of the region's badly eroded and deforested hilly land.

The initial partners in the programme were: the Cebu City government; PBSP's regional office which acted as programme manager and catalyst; over 60 private companies which provided various financial, technical, managerial and material inputs, including equipment and training; and some 330 upland farmers. As the programme has evolved other partners have joined such as international NGOs, including the New York-based Trickle-Up programme and the Tokyo-based Asian Community Trust; Cebu Hospital which now runs regular medical missions to the area; city hotels which are offering a market for the farmers' produce and various specialist government offices and academic organisations.

At the outset of the programme the PBSP project managers undertook consultations with the farmers and local communities to agree on targets for poverty reduction, reforestation, land reform and access to basic services. These have formed a key element of regular consultations and feed-back sessions with the programme partners, and have been a useful guide for evaluating project progress within the

organisational, ecological, and socio-economic framework of the ARM approach. Several community groups have been established and have undergone training and capacity-building in technical and leadership skills. A youth project has also been established to develop tomorrow's community leaders. Several demonstration farms have been set up and over 400 farmers have had access to financial and technical assistance. Some have introduced high-value crops and poultry and increased incomes by 200% as a result. Attention has been paid to the environmental impacts of farming methods and several hundred hectares of land have been reforested. Basic services such as potable water and health consultations are being provided by different programme partners and capital build-up schemes are being implemented to ensure better financial sustainability.

Many of the upland farmers entered the project reluctantly and with great scepticism, having seen many cycles of unsuccessful "projects imposed from the outside". While progress of the ARM approach has not been without its problems, there is a much greater sense of optimism and self-help five years later and a more sustainable base on which to continue building in terms of the access to new skills, technologies, funding sources and markets which the project has facilitated. PBSP and its supporting companies played a critical role in facilitating this change in local circumstances and local attitudes.

KEY LESSONS AND SUCCESS FACTORS

In recent years PBSP has undergone a number of external assessments and evaluations by donor agencies and recently as part of an international study on foundations in developing countries, commissioned by the New York based Synergos Institute. In every case the assessment has been generally positive, suggesting that PBSP is a model worth serious consideration in other countries. A few key success factors are regularly cited by external observers, PBSP staff and business supporters alike. They are as follows:

1) Commitment and level of active involvement of business leaders

A core group of prominent business leaders have a highly active and hands-on involvement with PBSP. They are part of a working board not only in terms of managing the foundation, but also in terms of having regular field exposure to projects and problems at the grassroots level. Equally they are active in the PBSP's increasingly strategic approach to key policy issues and have the necessary access to government ministers to bring these issues to the table. Over half of PBSP's founding member companies have remained as members and in most cases their Executive Officers have played a continuous and active voluntary role.

2) Melding of sound business principles and social development expertise

Described by one of PBSP's founders as "A heart with a mind and a mind with a heart", this approach has been central to the organisation's success. Its rigorous approach to consultation, organisational and programme planning, monitoring, evaluation and resultant learning and adaptation brings together the best of business and social development disciplines, and demonstrates that the two approaches can work well together and learn from each other.

3) The continuity of management, expertise, professionalism and commitment of staff

Many of the PBSP's senior management team have been with the organisation for over 10 years and have undergone extensive training and exposure to different elements of the organisation and the societal issues it is trying to address. All staff are selected on two key criteria: experience and commitment to social development work. They undergo regular training (sometimes supported by member companies) on both the technical and vocational aspects of PBSP's work and to build skills in teamwork, leadership, communications, stakeholder consultation and problem solving. They are also supported to take sabbaticals and external training and education courses in their field.

4) A learning organisation

Any assessment of PBSP cannot fail to note the organisation's "learning culture" defined by both its willingness and its ability to constantly review and renew itself, based on experiences of the past and predictions of the future.

5) An intermediary organisation in touch with policy-makers and the grassroots

Probably one of PBSP's greatest success factors stems from the fact that its managers have access to, and dialogue with, an extremely wide range of stakeholders – from the poorest of the poor to the most prominent politicians and business leaders in the country. This access is facilitated not only by the organisation's mission and its structure, but also by the training

A sample of member
companies:

Aboitiz Corp. • American Wire &
Cable Co. • Andres Soriano Corp.
• Asia Industries • Atlas Co. •
Bayer • Citibank • Davao Co. •
Del Monte • Dow Chemical •
Far East Bank and Trust Co. •
First Philippine Holdings • IBM •
Iligan Co. • Jardine Davies •
Magellan Capital Holdings •
Makati Stock Exchange • Manila
Stock Exchange • MCCI Co. •
Morgan Guaranty Trust • Nestlé
• Phelps Dodge • Philippine
Airlines • Philips • Phinma •
Pilipina Kao • Pilipinas Shell •
Pioneer Co. • Philtread •
Planters Development Bank •
Prudential • Roxas and Co. •
RGV Real Estate • San Miguel
Corporation • Sycip, Gorres,
Velayo and Co. • Unisys •
United Laboratories

and managerial skills that its staff have, which enables many of them to cross what would normally be an enormous divide. They are therefore ideally placed to make a difference in society.

6) Commitment to "division of labour" and "purposeful partnership"

At the outset, PBSP focused on being a grant-making foundation channelling corporate philanthropy money to local non-governmental organisations to run specific projects in specific communities. It still undertakes this function today, but in the past 25 years it has not only expanded the range of its own functions and activities, but also formed a multitude of other partnerships to fulfil its mission. It is increasingly focusing its attention on assessing which partner can most effectively and efficiently deliver which products and services in any particular programme, and then structuring these programmes accordingly.

7) Leveraging resources

Linked to the above PBSP has been able to attract and leverage funding and other resources, such as management advice and expertise, from a wide variety of sources in the business, government and international donor community. Again it can use its high-profile and well-respected position as a national organisation to access these resources and then its extensive network of partner organisations to add further value to these resources and deliver them in a way which meets local needs.

In summary, after 25 years of existence and with managerial experience of over 3,000 projects targeted at alleviating poverty, PBSP can comfortably claim to be one of the most sustainable and successful national non-governmental organisations in the world. The leadership role played by individual business people and their companies has been a critical factor in this achievement and will continue to be so in future, as PBSP expands its role from project management to policy dialogue and to influencing the strategic business agenda of companies in the Philippines.

3.3 The Thai Business Initiative in Rural Development (TBIRD)

TBIRD'S MISSION

The Thai Business Initiative in Rural Development aims to mobilise the corporate sector to bring its business expertise to poor villages in Thailand. By sharing valuable resources, skills and knowledge, businesses can make a vital contribution to rural development, offering villagers access to information and opportunities that would not otherwise be available.

Despite Thailand's impressive rate of economic growth in recent years, wide income disparities remain between the urban rich and the rural poor. In the north-eastern part of the country especially, high levels of poverty, inadequate opportunities for local employment, declining agricultural productivity, lack of water and deteriorating environmental conditions, are resulting in continued migration to the cities – especially by the most entrepreneurial rural villagers – further undermining rural prospects and straining already overburdened urban infrastructure. In order to address this situation rural villagers need access to education and training, income-generating opportunities, credit, markets, basic services and support in institution-building and organisational skills. The Thai Business Initiative in Rural Development (TBIRD) was launched in 1988 to share the financial, technical and managerial resources of the private sector with government and community initiatives, in order to tackle this challenge. Today nearly 100 companies – ranging from medium-sized Thai businesses to major multi-nationals with investments in Thailand – are actively involved in TBIRD, which is run by the Population and Community Development Association (PDA). The programme is reaching villages throughout the country, improving the livelihoods and quality of life of thousands of rural inhabitants, and increasingly serving as a model for other countries in the region.

BACKGROUND

TBIRD was the brainchild of Mr Mechai Viravaidya, Chairman of Thailand's Population and Community Development Association (PDA), and well known throughout the country as "Mr Condom" for his leadership role in the country's highly successful birth control programme. At the time of TBIRD's inception in the late-1980s Mr Viravaidya was Deputy Minister of Industry and was very aware of the growing importance of foreign investors in Thailand's economy. Whilst the growth in the country's industrial workforce and output was concentrated in the cities, he believed that the foreign and Thai companies driving this growth had both the resources and the responsibility to participate in rural development. He convinced the government's National Rural Development Committee to review the role that business could play in this process. Swedish Motors Co. were the first company to get involved with the project and in 1989, with government support, the PDA and the Thai Chamber of Commerce jointly launched TBIRD.

> We didn't want to just give money to the villagers. The important thing was to spend time to teach them how to use it properly.
>
> Thamnu Wanglee,
> President,
> Nakornthorn Bank

TBIRD is essentially a network of partnerships between individual companies and individual villages, which is catalysed, facilitated, supported, monitored and evaluated by PDA. With over 20 years of experience in rural grassroots development, PDA has pioneered some of the most effective integrated community-based development projects in Thailand, based on the principle that local participation and initiative are essential for self-reliant growth. Today it operates a range of programmes in water resource development, vocational training, HIV/AIDS prevention, education, income-generation, environmental conservation, population and primary health-care from its head office in Bangkok and its 12 rural development centres in north-east and northern Thailand. It is therefore an ideal intermediary organisation to:

- promote the concept of corporate-community partnerships to companies, and

- help the companies and communities make these partnerships work in practice through helping to bring together appropriate partners, facilitating corporate-community consultation and project planning, providing technical assistance and co-ordinating with local government agencies and other NGO partners.

TBIRD PROJECTS

The activities carried out in different projects vary depending on the differing needs, wishes, skills and conditions of individual villages and companies. However most of them encompass the learning and dissemination of skills in four essential areas: organisational; financial management; production and marketing.

Most projects include income-generating activities – usually agricultural, cottage industries or small-scale enterprises which in some cases act as suppliers for the supporting company. Many of the projects also have a community development dimension, which can range from the establishment of small loan funds, to education support, vocational and computer training, environmental projects and local infrastructure development. The following three examples illustrate the variety:

- One of the largest contributors to TBIRD has been **PTT Exploration and Production** – a division of Thailand's petroleum authority. In 1995 it gave US$1 million to set up an endowment capital fund for TBIRD. It has also launched a landmark programme to implement TBIRD projects in 36 villages. These projects will include components such as: a scholarship endowment to enable rural students to gain access to tertiary education, based on the condition that they return to work for the villages when they have finished their studies; construction of community development centres; a school lunch programme where food is grown by teachers, students and parents; work to improve rice yields and production methods, in co-ordination with the International Rice Research Institute; an irrigation programme in several villages; and a loan fund for housewives to help finance their local silk production activities.

- **The Bata Shoe Company** joined TBIRD in 1990 and its approach was to build a shoe factory in Buri Ram province. From small beginnings with a nucleus of five women, who Bata trained intensively in Bangkok not only to produce shoes, but also to manage the production process and to train and supervise others, Bata has subsequently set up co-operatively owned factories in three other villages. It owns and runs a training factory in the area, but the co-operatives are owned and

TBIRD's Five Steps to Corporate-Community Partnership

At the outset of TBIRD in 1989 a group of PDA staff and Harvard Business School graduates worked together to produce a 10-step plan for company-village partnership. Today this has been refined to the following five-step approach:

1 TBIRD Presentation

PDA and TBIRD staff present the TBIRD concept to potential corporate partners, complemented by slides, examples of on-going projects and project documentation.

2 Task Force Formation

After agreeing in principle to join TBIRD, the company forms a small staff team to plan and manage its project and to co-ordinate with PDA. This task force normally draws together middle-management and professional employees from different departments with a variety of business experiences, talents, and skills. PDA assist the task force in identifying potential project villages. These may be villages where company employees have connections, where the company has long-term market potential, or where the company has no immediate business interest at all.

3 Village Visit

The task force visits potential project villages to meet community leaders and villagers. Discussions, facilitated by the community development experts from PDA, allow villagers and the company task force members to assess village needs and potential and to discuss possible income generation and community improvement activities.

4 Project Planning

After agreeing on a partner target village, the task force and villagers develop a simple work plan detailing project goals, activities, responsibilities, timeline and budget. This must be mutually agreed by both the villagers and the task force before the project proceeds and is therefore regarded as an informal contract of co-operation.

5 Corporate Approval

The work plan and corresponding resource commitments – which may be financial, managerial, technical, in-kind, or a combination of all – are approved by senior management or the board of the company, before the project is finally launched. Funds spent by the company are tax deductible through PDA.

---

operated by the villagers themselves. Bata provides the raw materials and covers the transportation costs, which the company says are offset by the high quality of workmanship in the TBIRD/Bata factories compared to most Bangkok-based shoe factories. The village co-operatives manage all aspects of the production and pay all the other overhead costs. They are paid a market-price by Bata for the shoes they produce, so Bata is not subsidising the transaction which ensures a more sustainable commercial relationship in the long-term. The co-operatives now employ several hundred villagers, each making between 100-120 baht a day – three times the average wage in the north-east and equivalent to wages in Bangkok. An evaluation of the project has also shown that two-thirds of the women employed in the co-operative factories are former migrants who have returned from Bangkok once viable and healthy employment was available in their home villages.

- **Nakornthon Bank**, one of the smallest commercial banks in Thailand, joined TBIRD in 1991. After consultations with the villagers of Ban Hua Krok, the Nakornthon task team have helped to support training and study tours to other villages and agricultural institutes; made sure that specialists from government research centres make follow-up visits; funded extra training where needed; helped to set up a revolving loan fund for the villagers; and made regular visits to the village to explain basic concepts of money management, marketing, bookkeeping and other business skills.

- In 1995 the **Australian Agency for International Development** (AusAID) agreed to fund a one year Australian-Thai Business Initiative in Rural Development (RooBIRD) aimed at getting the many Australian companies with investments in Thailand mobilised to support the programme. This approach has interesting implications for the other bilateral donor agencies operating in the country, where their national companies have a presence.

A sample of member companies:
3M • American Express •
American International
Assurance Co • Australian Stock
Exchange • Bangkok Glass
Industry Co. • Bank of Asia •
Bata Shoe Co • Berli Jucker •
Body Shop • Bristol Myers-
Squibb • Capital Nomura
Securities • Carnaud Metalbox •
Castrol • Design 103 • Diethelm
& Co • Dusit Thani Hotels •
Embassy of Australia • Embassy
of Japan • Ericsson • Gemcrafts
• IBM • Industrial Finance Corp
of Thailand • International
Herald Tribune • Lever Brothers
• Mobil Oil • Nakorhthon Bank
• National Australia Bank •
Nestlé • Oriental Hotel • Pacific
Islands Club • Pan Asia
Footwear • PTT • Rotary •
SC Johnson & Son •
Scandinavian Airline (SAS) •
Schering • Shangri La Hotel •
Siam Agroforestry • Siam
Occidental • Siam Unisys •
Singer • Swedish Motor Co. •
Thai Bridgestone • Thai Farmers
Bank • Thai Fuji Xerox • Thai
Invest & Securities • Thai Oil •
Unocal • Upjohn

- Many other inspiring examples exist: **3M** in Thailand has established a company task force which is working with a group of villagers in the Buri Ram province to improve the production of silk – using the skills of an agricultural consultant – and the marketing of the silk products – using the expertise of 3M staff; **Bristol-Myers Squibb** have helped villagers to access the skills and resources they needed to improve agricultural techniques and to set up a "vegetable bank" – a model which has now been replicated in over 40 other villages; and the **Singer** company in Thailand, well-known for its production of sewing machines, has established two centres in Khon Kaen province to provide training in commercial sewing skills. The centres are not only being used by local villagers, but also by others involved in TBIRD projects.

CONCLUSIONS AND SUCCESS FACTORS

In 1993 The United Nations Economic and Social Commission for Asia and the Pacific (ESCAP) awarded a Certificate of Merit to TBIRD for its success in alleviating rural poverty. It also co-funds an international training course on the TBIRD approach which it has nominated as a key strategy for improving human resources in Asia. Harvard Business School have also written a case study on the TBIRD approach as an example for their courses on corporate social responsibility and private investment in developing countries.

Some of the key factors underpinning TBIRD's success have been:

- the individual vision and leadership of the project's founder Mr Mechai Viravaidya;

- the vital intermediary role played by the PDA as a link between the companies and the villages;

- the emphasis placed on companies not just giving money, but also encouraging their employees to get involved. Many of the participating companies believe that this has given their mostly urban employees valuable first-hand experience of the rural realities in their country, increased morale and been beneficial to the company's reputation;

- government endorsement and support for the programme, emphasised by the fact that all project expenses to TBIRD are tax-deductible; and

- a high-profile campaigning element – supported both by donor funds and the role played by individual corporate "champions" who are often prominent business leaders.

In the last couple of years PDA's international training unit – The Asian Centre for Population and Community Development – has organised study tours and training courses on the TBIRD concept for participants from a number of other countries around the region, including Cambodia, Laos, Vietnam, Nepal, Sri Lanka and China's Yunnan province.

3.4 The Business Leaders Forum in Poland

Multi-nationals doing business in Poland have an obligation to do more than just enrich their share-holders. They must also set a good ethical example, aid in promoting the overall health of the business environment and help the less fortunate to help themselves.

Janusz Golebiowski
BOC Gazy and
President of the BLFP

Poland has made good progress in the transition to a market economy and remains an attractive destination for foreign investors. However economic growth, competitiveness and social stability will not be sustained in the medium to long-term without the public and private sector working together to address the high social costs which have accompanied rapid transition and restructuring, and some of the other obstacles to progress such as: shortages in managerial and certain technical skills; institutional inadequacies in the legal, financial and regulatory systems; environmental problems; and the need for continued public sector reform and the strengthening of civil society. In 1993 the Business Leaders Forum in Poland (BLFP) was established, with support from The Prince of Wales Business Leaders Forum, to mobilise the support and resources of foreign and Polish companies in addressing some of these issues. Working with member companies and partner organisations, the BLFP is focusing on a range of initiatives in the education and training field, public safety and public-private sector dialogue.

STRUCTURE AND STRATEGY

The BLFP works with its member companies and other partner organisations to:

- demonstrate that environmental and social responsibility are, and should be integral to core business activity;

- help publicise the wider social benefits of business and spread corporate good practice;

- help build and publicise successful partnerships between the private sector and other groups in society.

It meets these objectives through: designing and managing programmes that companies can support both financially and in-kind; profiling and publicising corporate good practice; and running regular meetings and consultations between companies, public officials, international visitors and civil society organisations to discuss specific policy issues or project ideas.

ACTIVITIES

Apart from a recently launched initiative on public safety in Warsaw, the BLFP has concentrated its programmes on education, training and youth initiatives, often working in partnership with other organisations. For example it has been involved in: a career advisory service run by the Progress and Business Foundation in Krakow; an executive receptionist training and work placement programme for the physically handicapped in collaboration with the Stefan Batory Foundation; a Women as Entrepreneurs initiative in

Sample of member companies:
ABB • American Express •
Amoco • WS Atkins • BDK • BOC
Gazy • British Gas • British
Petroleum • Coca-Cola •
Commercial Union • Coopers &
Lybrand • DHL • Enpol • ERM •
Gaspol • Huta Sendzimira • ING
Barings Bank • Monolit-Montex
• Mostostal • Nabarro
Nathanson • Price Waterhouse •
Proctor & Gamble • Protektor •
Ryder Polska • SmithKline
Beecham • Smirnoff •
SugarPol • Wega

THE MASTER CLASS ADVICE SCHEME FOR SMALL BUSINESS OWNERS

The Master Class programme is designed to give small business owners an opportunity to discuss some of the practical problems they face with selected executives from major companies during informal small-group discussions. This low-cost programme is intended to complement more formal business advice services across Poland.

The Business Leaders Forum in Poland runs the programme in partnership with:

• FISE (Fundacja Inicjatyw Spoleczno-Ekonomicznych) which has 13 Agencies for Local Initiative around the country and
• Polish-American Enterprise Clubs.

The two partner organisations are responsible for identifying the small business owners (who are normally experienced entrepreneurs who would benefit from sophisticated advice and problem-solving support, but cannot afford to pay consultants to give it to them), while the BLFP arranges for suitable corporate executives to run and participate in the meetings, based on the information they are given by these entrepreneurs and the two partner organisations.

To date Master Classes have been held in Warsaw, Lublin, Kielce, Piaseczno, Gorlice and Pulawy, on the basis of about one a month. Companies such as Commercial Union, British Gas, ABB, Amoco, Coopers & Lybrand, BOC Gazy, DHL, Proctor and Gamble and BDK have met with over 50 small business owners and the co-ordinators of Polish-American enterprise clubs.

FISE and BLFP have established a system for tracking the feedback and progress of selected participants in the programme. Feedback to date indicates that the programme is beneficial to both the small business owners – who gain unparalleled access to senior executives and experts from some of the most successful companies in the world, and to the executives who meet entrepreneurs at the grassroots level of business development in Poland.

AUTOKREACJA

"AUTOKREACJA" is a youth leadership and development course which is based on a similar programme run by The Prince's Trust in the United Kingdom. It was piloted in Poland in 1995 with major support from Levi Strauss, and input from DHL, BOC, Xerox, ICL, Smirnoff and other companies in the south-east region of Poland. The companies not only provided financial and in-kind sponsorship, but also employee participation in selected workshops during the course.

50 long-term unemployed Poles between the ages of 18-25 participated in the pilot programme, which focused on enhancing their skills in job-finding and constructive social activity. The goal of the programme is to help participants increase their self-esteem, increase their chances of finding work or further training, and, if they stay unemployed, to find constructive and socially responsible ways to spend their time – for example in volunteer work.

Within two months 60% of the young people on the pilot course had either found work or gone into training. This success has attracted the interest of the National Labour Office in Poland and the media, and The Business Leaders Forum in Poland will be co-ordinating a second course in 1996.

Lodz with the Edinburgh Chamber of Commerce; and a leadership enhancement programme run by the Polish Children and Youth Foundation. Two of its major programmes are described in the box above.

The BLFP has also collected a wide range of case studies on corporate responsibility in Poland, ranging from Coca-Cola's professional training support for the retail sector and its "whole village" recycling scheme, to projects such as: American Express's customer service workshops and training programme; ABB's state-of-the-art training centre and its small-scale business development initiatives in which it has helped over 120 employees establish some 15 new businesses as part of its restructuring programme; Huta Sendzimira's work in restructuring and managing change; BOC's welding school; Commercial Union's banking and insurance training.

3.5 The India Business and Community Partnership

India is a country with immense opportunities and equally large social problems. Its business community has a long-standing tradition of philanthropy – supporting projects and organisations of benefit to the community, such as schools, hospitals and charitable trusts, through cash donations and in-kind support. The need for such support has not disappeared, but there is growing pressure on companies – both Indian and foreign – to move beyond the traditional approach of philanthropy and paternalism, to a more strategic approach which makes greater use of the full range of business skills and resources in tackling the country's social challenges. This pressure is especially strong on international investors which are becoming significant partners in India's economic development as a result of trade liberalisation, and many of which are facing tough challenges in establishing their Indian operations and reputations. In 1995 the India Business and Community Partnership (IBCP) was established by The Prince of Wales Business Leaders Forum, with support from the Confederation of Indian Industry, to work with international companies and their business and community partners in India.

STRUCTURE AND STRATEGY

IBCP has a two-pronged structure for meeting its objectives. It works closely with its member companies to fulfil its objectives, but has also established a Partnership Advisory Group consisting of representatives from non-governmental organisations, government bodies and international donor agencies, including: USAID; ActionAid; Athreya Management Systems; Bombay First; Oxfam India; the National Foundation for India; British ODA; and Save the Children Fund. The role of the PAG is to maximise IBCPT's effectiveness by providing expert advice, briefing and initiatives to the member companies. In particular the aim of the newly established group will be to:

- provide advice on India's development needs and on how companies can best meet them;

- identify suitable partners for member company initiatives;

- promote the benefits of good corporate citizenship activities to business, government and NGOs;

- participate in the PWBLF's International Partnership Network, which is a network of over 500 "partnership practitioners" – people from business, NGOs, government and international agencies, developing partnership projects around the world.

IBCP's MISSION

To demonstrate the character and importance of good corporate citizenship in the context of India to companies, government and public authorities, non-governmental organisations, opinion formers and the media by:

- providing opportunities for new entrants to the market to establish their own community programmes in a cost-effective way;

- working with NGOs to build their capacity;

- publicising Indian good practice internationally and disseminating information about international good practice in India.

This strong link between a business-driven initiative supported by companies which are focused on their commercial interests, but wanting to optimise their "spin-off" for meeting national development objectives, and an external advisory group of organisations whose purpose is to meet development needs, but who recognise the need to involve the private sector more actively, will offer an interesting model for evaluation once it has been in operation for a few years. The India Business and Community Partnership has a three-pronged strategy as follows:

Sample of member companies:
ABB Ltd • Bajaj Auto Ltd •
British Gas • Burson-Marsteller
Roger Pereira • Cadbury India
Ltd • Coca-Cola India • Eagle
Star • ICI India Ltd •
International Distillers •
National Power • Seagram •
SmithKline Beecham •
US WEST

• Brokering Partnerships between individual companies, NGOs and donors

India has a tremendous resource of community organisations working at the grassroots level on issues such as education, employment generation, health-care, literacy training, child welfare and integrated community development in both rural and urban areas. The IBCP works with companies to help them formulate their community investment strategies and then to source reliable partner organisations, implement community programmes, monitor progress and maximise the benefits to both the company and the community partners. As part of this process the IBCP will also be working with companies to run workshops for the NGOs on management skills such as marketing, budgeting, TQM and fundraising from business, and also some awareness-raising workshops for the companies on issues faced by the NGO community and development professionals.

Two of the examples of brokerage that the IBCP have been involved with are as follows: working with United Distillers, the Grand Metropolitan Foundation and the Bharatiya Yuva Shakti Trust (which is modelled on The Prince's Trust in the United Kingdom) to establish a youth enterprise programme in Pune; and working with Seagram to develop a community investment strategy which will encompass a wide-ranging support package for an urban development NGO operating in Delhi.

• Acting as a catalyst for joint projects

The IBCP is currently identifying areas where corporate interests coincide with the nation's major development priorities. The first of these areas is likely to be literacy and the organisation will be working with member companies, such as Cadbury India, which are already running literacy projects to spread their good practice more widely in the business community. It will also consult with NGO partners such as ActionAid which is developing a World Bank supported literacy programme called REFLECT, to encourage corporate involvement in this initiative.

Another programme of joint corporate activity that IBCP is developing is one on road safety. Working with a major insurance company, telecommunications company and paint manufacturer, with involvement from local hospitals and the municipal government, the programme will encompass a package of products and services, ranging from the supply of mobile phones to the ambulance service, to insurance funds and safety materials and bright paints for small road vehicles such as bicycles and motor bikes.

• Spreading the word

The IBCP organises national and international conferences, project visits and workshops to disseminate examples of best practice. In March 1996, for example, it co-hosted a major conference in Delhi on "Business as Partner in Social Development" which was attended by international and national NGOs, senior managers from about 25 companies and representatives from 10 of the major multilateral agencies and embassies. Drawing on a series of case studies which had been produced by the UK-based New Consumer organisation on ways that multinational companies are contributing to the goals of development, the conference provided one of the first platforms of its type for different sectors to review and discuss the developmental impact of the private sector.

3.6 Business for Social Responsibility in the USA

BSR's mission is to help member companies implement policies and practices which contribute to their long-term sustained and responsible success, fairly balancing the competing claims of key stakeholders – investors, employees, customers, business partners, communities and the environment.

It is increasingly clear that the next step in transforming American corporations is to transform the relationship between business and society

Rosabeth Moss Kanter
Harvard Business School

Even in the United States, which has a long history of corporate philanthropy and employee volunteering, the broader questions about the role of business in society, and its relationships with stakeholders other than shareholders, have only recently moved from being a community affairs or corporate foundation issue to a strategic management, boardroom level issue. Over the past five years in particular, numerous city-wide partnerships have been created between business and other sectors – several of which have been profiled in an earlier section – as have a number of issue-specific programmes aimed at developing better public-private partnerships to tackle education, crime prevention, community empowerment and environmental issues. On a broader level organisations such as the World Business Academy, the Social Venture Network and the Business Enterprise Trust, consisting of some of the country's most visionary and entrepreneurial business leaders, have played a pioneering role in resurrecting and reshaping the debate on business in society. In 1992 their vision helped to pave the way for the establishment of a national alliance of businesses called Business for Social Responsibility, which today has over 1,000 members – many of them medium and small-scale companies that are rarely represented on organisations of this type. The organisation runs programmes on a number of corporate social responsibility themes, including one which addresses the broad range of human rights issues which American companies face when they are sourcing and manufacturing in developing countries.

STRUCTURE AND STRATEGY

BSR operates as an alliance of companies, with a Board of Directors drawn from a combination of major companies and small-scale, entrepreneurial start-ups. It has offices in Washington DC, San Francisco, Boston and Denver and is funded by its membership fees and other voluntary contributions from corporations and corporate foundations. BSR also operates the Business for Social Responsibility Education Fund (BSREF) which is a non-profit research, education and advocacy organisation to promote more responsible practices in the broader business community, beyond BSR's immediate membership.

BSR'S BUSINESS AND HUMAN RIGHTS PROGRAMME

This programme helps companies address the broad range of human rights issues they face in sourcing and manufacturing in developing countries – e.g. worker health and safety, child labour, prison labour, wages and hours, working conditions and environmental standards.

The programme acts as a resource for companies by:

- Providing technical assistance and consulting to help companies develop and implement corporate human rights policies;
- Conducting educational workshops and training sessions;
- Facilitating a dialogue between the business community, human rights organisations, government officials and labour unions;
- Researching and publishing materials concerning global sourcing and human rights; and
- Creating a database of corporate "best practices" on these issues.

BSR has convened an apparel and retailing working group and an independent monitoring working group. The latter was convened at the request of The Gap company, the Interfaith Center on Corporate Responsibility (ICCR), and the National Labor Committee (NLC) to develop and help to implement independent monitoring at The Gap's manufacturing facilities in El Salvador. Several workshops have been run for large medium and small-scale companies and senior representatives from government and human rights organisations, to discuss companies' audit procedures, development of voluntary codes of conduct, and business and human rights in China.

Sample of internationally active member companies:

AT&T • The Body Shop USA • The Clorox Company • Coopers & Lybrand • Dreyfus Fund • Fannie Mae • Federal Express • The Gap • Home Depot • Honeywell • Levi Strauss and Co • Lotus Development Corporation • Marriott International • Patagonia • Polaroid Corporation • Reebok International • Revlon • Taco Bell • Time Warner Inc • Shorebank Corporation • Starbucks Coffee Company • Timberland Company

BSR works with its members in a variety of ways, as follows:

- **Research and publications** – including "best practice" research on a range of issues such as employee benefits and global codes of conduct, plus the publication of a regular newsletter, reports and a recent book entitled *Beyond the Bottom Line*;

- **Conferences, meetings and seminars** – including a national annual conference bringing together some 450-500 leaders from business, government and the independent sector to exchange views about current and emerging issues of great import (the 1995 conference focused on ethics, workplace policies and practices, community involvement, the environment, market-place issues and global sourcing and human rights;

- **Issues monitoring** – through monitoring the media, regular contact with public officials, advocacy groups, member companies etc.;

- **Technical assistance and advice** – including the sharing of tools and models for analysing and improving corporate policies and practices, such as company social responsibility self-assessments and comprehensive environmental audits;

- **Outreach and education** – with other business organisations, elected and appointed public officials, advocacy and public interest groups, scholars, community leaders and the media;

- **Public policy** – BSR informs members about a limited number of key national public policy issues and produces a quarterly report covering these, although BSR itself does not take positions on public policy issues;

- **Publicity for members' business product**s, services and "best practices";

- **Business-to-business exchange**; and

- **Establishment of regional networks.**

PROJECTS AND ACTIVITIES

Apart from its annual conference, regular newsletter, public policy reports and tailored member services, BSR operates specific programmes on:

Business and the Environment · Business and Human Rights in Developing Countries · Workplace Policies and Practices · Community Involvement · Affirmative Action

In May 1996, it also recently played a key role in helping to convene the White House Conference on Corporate Citizenship.

3.7 Business in the Community
in the United Kingdom

The inner-city riots that ripped through several of Britain's major cities in the early 1980s, causing severe injuries and millions of pounds worth of damage, sent a strong message to the country's business leaders: "wealthy high streets need healthy backstreets." It was clear that the British business sector would need to take a more proactive role in community activities in order to help tackle problems of rising unemployment, inequality, crime and inner-city violence. The result was the establishment of Business in the Community in 1982. Today the organisation works through 400 member companies, including the vast majority of Britain's major corporations, runs six national campaigns and operates through ten regional offices to: raise business awareness of community issues; promote business action; encourage partnerships between public, private and voluntary sectors; and match business resources to community need.

Businesses everywhere are finding themselves involved in a debate about their role in society. Customers, employees and local communities expect business to contribute to society, while more and more executives accept that their business success depends on the health of the community in which they operate.

**Lord Sheppard,
Chairman of Grand Metropolitan
and Business in the Community**

STRUCTURE AND STRATEGY

Business in the Community (BITC) is headed by its President, HRH The Prince of Wales, and governed by a board of 30 business, public and voluntary sector leaders, including heads of The Confederation of British Industry, the Trades Union Congress, the National Council for Voluntary Organisations and the Association of Metropolitan Authorities. It has about 200 staff based in London and in ten regional offices. For each of its major programme initiatives BITC establishes a Leadership Team, consisting of prominent business and community leaders, including civil servants from relevant government departments, who champion and help to direct the programme. This approach has been a critical factor in the success of the organisation and its campaigns.

The organisation currently has five key objectives, against which it monitors and measures its achievements. These are as follows:

1. To measurably raise the quality, impact and sustainability of business involvement in the community;

2. To increase the number of companies involved in their communities;

3. To act as an effective broker matching company resources (which BITC refers to as the 5Ps – profits, people, premises, products and power) to community needs;

4. To influence business attitudes and behaviour through campaigns; and

5. To serve as the leading authority in the United Kingdom on corporate community involvement.

BUSINESS IN THE
COMMUNITY'S MISSION
To support the United
Kingdom's economic and social
regeneration by raising the
quality and extent of business
involvement in the community
and making that involvement a
natural part of successful
business practice.

Its strategy for meeting these objectives is to work as: a campaigner creating awareness of community issues and gaining business commitment to practical action; a catalyst bringing partners together from the private, public and voluntary sectors; a broker matching resources to needs; an advisor offering expert guidance to companies and encouraging government to involve business more effectively in public policy; and an information source, sharing best practice and research.

PROGRAMMES AND ACTIVITIES
a) Campaigns
Business in the Community currently runs six nationwide campaigns:

Economic Development · Education · Environment · Employee Involvement · Opportunity 2000 aimed at increasing employment and status of women · Race for Opportunity aimed at boosting the economic activity of the UK's ethnic minority communities.

Each of these campaigns, and the specific projects which they support, have potential relevance and applicability in other countries not only in the OECD, but also in developing and transition economies. The following page summarises the activities of each campaign during 1995, and is a useful illustration of the enormous outreach and potential multiplier effect that initiatives of this type can offer. Many of the specific projects also demonstrate how Business in the Community has leveraged both private and public funding to meet broader societal objectives.

b) Programmes to engage companies and business leaders
BITC also runs a range of activities to engage business attention and support. These include:

- the **Professional Firms Group**, which brings together providers of professional services to discuss ways in which these services can be offered for maximum impact to meet local community needs;

- the **Per Cent Club** in which all the companies that join pledge to contribute 0.5 of UK pre-tax profits or dividends to community investment;

- several **Awards programmes** to raise the profile of outstanding companies and the projects which they are supporting;

- **advisory services** to help individual companies tackle specific issues or develop tailored programmes;

- **a business strategy group** which provides advice on public policy and tracks economic and social trends relevant to companies and their community involvement; and

- the **Seeing is Believing** programme which takes senior business executives on visits to corporate-community projects with the aim of motivating and mobilising them to take action. In 1995 over 500 top executives went on 50 visits to projects all over the country.

CAMPAIGNING and MOBILISING BUSINESS TO TAKE ACTION
a sample of one year's achievements in 1995.

● ●

The approach of working with a network of influential companies, government departments and voluntary organisations, all of which have a national and a local presence, enables Business in the Community to achieve an impressive leverage effect on the time and money it invests in its campaigns. In a one year period its message will reach hundreds of companies and thousands of stakeholders, many of which will get involved in some way – either changing attitudes or undertaking actions – which probably would not have happened otherwise.

EDUCATION: There is a compelling case for business to make a sustained investment in education to help build a globally competitive workforce and cohesive society. Aim High is BITC's campaign to encourage companies to work with schools and colleges to raise the quality of young people's aspirations and achievements. In 1995 the Aim High Campaign:

- Supported 150 companies in developing quality education programmes and monitoring their impact on student performance;

- Delivered major education projects including: Compact Plus jointly sponsored by Marks & Spencer and the Department of Education and Employment supporting 3,000 students in 150 schools; Toyota's Science and Technology Education Fund, distributing UK£600,000 to more than 600 schools; Royal Insurance Core Skills Portfolio being developed in 20 schools; and KPMG's mentoring programme for 20 headteachers;

- Established a steering group to look at social marketing programmes which combine business and community benefits;

- Continued to support hundreds of Education Business Partnerships and Compacts nationwide; and

- Attracted nearly 400 entries to the annual Aim High Awards to identify and celebrate outstanding business-education partnerships.

ECONOMIC DEVELOPMENT: This campaign harnesses the resources of major companies to support local partnerships working to create jobs and regenerate communities. In 1995 it:

- Delivered more than UK£1million worth of free professional advice through BITC's Professional Firms Group of lawyers, accountants and other service providers;

- Initiated the Business Bridge Project to stimulate the growth of small firms through large company advice and expertise, backed by Touche Ross and the Department of Trade & Industry;

- Launched the Partnership Exchange to increase the development and transfer of skills, expertise and support between public-private partnerships;

- Established a UK£3million Local Investment Fund as a new source of financing for community groups, with support from NatWest Bank, the Department of the Environment and 25 other companies;

- Supported the forum of 250 leading developers which promote the Urban Villages concept of mixed use, sustainable urban development and have published research to demonstrate the economic viability of the approach; and

- Managed a series of Award Programmes for Community Enterprise and Innovation.

ENVIRONMENT: For British companies environmental awareness has increasingly become a financial imperative and not just an ethical option, as evidence grows that good practice can generate economies. Business in the Environment campaigns for good environmental management by encouraging companies to work with their suppliers; raising awareness in the financial sector; and working through business support organisations and trade associations to reach smaller companies. In 1995 Business in the Environment:

- Helped numerous companies to integrate environmental considerations into their purchasing policies, through an initiative with British Telecom, the Department of the Environment and the Chartered Institute of Purchasing and Supply. It has produced a resource pack, Supply Chain – the Environmental Challenge; helped 30 major companies work with suppliers and supported seminars for individual companies such as Pilkingtons, Manweb, Thames Water and National Power involving more than 140 suppliers;

- Helped companies of all sizes audit their environmental performance and develop policies by producing a learning pack, Profit from Environmental Management, in partnership with the Open University;

- Launched a second edition of a self-assessment Environmental Review for Companies, with support from Coopers & Lybrand, the European Union and the Government's Environment Agency;

- Continued to develop relationships with the financial sector, building on a survey carried out with EXTEL on the attitudes of financial analysts to environmental issues, working with environmental risk agencies and developing an index against which to rate corporate performance; and

- Established networks in Wales and Northern Ireland to more efficiently and effectively co-ordinate different organisations promoting good environmental management and launched campaigns in several parts of the country.

EMPLOYEE INVOLVEMENT: is one of the fastest growing areas of corporate community involvement as companies recognise the benefits that employee volunteering can bring to the community, the company and the individuals themselves. BITC is the leading campaigner in the UK for this activity and the leading broker of community placements and secondments. In 1995 it:

- Provided advice and information to over 200 companies through a series of meetings and workshops supported by the Financial Times newspaper;

- Advised some of the country's major companies on more detailed strategies;

- Supported leading edge research on the business benefits of employee involvement;

- Attracted over 200 entries to the Employees in the Community awards; and

- Ran "good practice" workshops hosted for more than 50 other companies by eight of the country's leading businesses in this field.

OPPORTUNITY 2000: Launched in 1991 this campaign now has over 300 member organisations, who employ over 25% of the country's workforce, and who all commit to implement programmes of action to increase employment opportunities for women at all levels. In 1995 the campaign:

- Reviewed all its members and demonstrated that the number of women directors in these organisations had doubled from 8% in 1994 to 16% in 1995 (vs. the national figure of 3%);

- Implemented a high-profile award programme;

- Ran nine regional networks and a series of "good practice" visits and workshops to share ideas and examples with companies all over the country;

- Ran a Black Women's conference with support from the BBC;

- Published a booklet on "good practice" with case studies on the recruitment and retention of women in science, engineering and technology, in partnership with the government's office of Science & Technology;

- Organised a programme to help 120 employers and educationalists to encourage girls and young women to gain qualifications to equip them for careers in science, engineering and technology.

RACE FOR OPPORTUNITY: was launched by BITC in 1995 with the aim of boosting the economic activity of the UK's ethnic minority communities by harnessing their enormous business potential and entrepreneurship. In 1995 the programme:

- Consulted more than 500 public, private and voluntary organisations in 10 regions to set the priorities for the national campaign, prior to launching it at a conference for 400 delegates[o] and establishing pilot projects in five major cities;

- Gained the commitment of 18 of the UK's leading businesses to act as "champion" companies – British Airways, Barclays Bank, the BBC, Boots, GrandMet, Littlewoods, Lloyds Bank, McDonald's, Leo Burnett, Midland Bank, NatWest, Northern Foods, T&G, TSB Group, Voice Group, WH Smith; and

- Published, with Midland Bank, a new report on the economic and educational status of the UK's ethnic minority communities.

A sample of member companies
*(drawn from members of BITC's
Board and Campaign Leadership
Teams)*:
British Airways • Zeneca plc. •
AEA Technology • Prudential
Corp. • Wessex Water • United
Biscuits • IBM UK • WH Smith •
Olayan Europe • Welsh Water •
BOC • Coopers & Lybrand •
John Laing • Ford Motor
Company • Unipart • British
Gas • GE Power Systems • Marks
& Spencer • Video Arts •
National Westminster Bank •
British Telecom • Grand
Metropolitan • KPMG •
National Power • NYNEX Cables
• The Post Office • Royal
Insurance • Toyota • Whitbread
• Burson-Marsteller • McKinsey
& Co. • Nestlé Rowntree • News
International • WPP Group •
General Accident • 3i Group •
SC Johnson Ltd. • Norsk Hydro •
Powergen • Cadbury Schweppes
• Lever Brothers • Abbey
National • Avon Cosmetics •
Midland Bank • Rank Xerox •
Spencer Stuart Assoc • Barclays
Bank • Deloitte & Touche • BBC
Radio • Fishburn Hedges •
The Rover Group

KEY SUCCESS FACTORS

As it approaches its 15th Anniversary, Business in the Community is in a good position to assess what has worked and what has not, and to share these insights with companies and business partnerships in other countries. Most of the factors that it attributes to its success are not unique to the United Kingdom or to an OECD economy, suggesting that both its programmes and its strategy could be adapted in developing and transition economies:

- **Individual leadership** – The methodology of establishing leadership teams, each headed by a prominent and well-respected Chief Executive has paid enormous dividends – not only in terms of getting the individuals in question and their companies more proactively involved, but also in terms of influencing others to get engaged. In the case of BITC the leadership role played by HRH The Prince of Wales has also been key, and although not directly replicable in other countries, the idea of a nationally respected individual playing a "champion" role is one that can be replicated.

- **Government support** – BITC have made a consistent effort to get different government departments involved with their programmes – both as co-funders and useful supporters, advisers and influencers. At the same time they have consulted with opposition parties and aimed to get all-party support for their approach and activities. To-date the focus of their government relations has been on running practical campaigns and projects, rather than influencing public policy, although this is likely to change as the issues which BITC focuses on become increasingly strategic for both business and political leaders.

- **Adaptability** – The organisation has regularly revised its approach based on its experience of what works and on the changing demands of member companies. For example, they are currently increasing their focus on the development of more targeted products and expert advice through which to channel business resources more effectively into communities, while still remaining a campaigning organisation which offers a more general message for corporate involvement.

- **Building the "business case" for action** – From the outset BITC has emphasised the business benefits of community involvement and has made an effort to avoid being driven purely by the philanthropic considerations of business, totally separate from mainstream management. In recent years the organisation has become increasingly sophisticated in its approach to the business case, and is now utilising high quality research and rigorous analysis to quantify the business benefits of community engagement. The time has never been better to build a case for these issues to be seen as strategic business imperatives, rather than "nice-to-do" feel-good community projects.

4 Learning from "good practice"

The 26 partnerships profiled in this section and other examples throughout the publication, give some idea of the enormous richness and diversity of multi-stakeholder partnerships. They all reflect examples of voluntary and mutually beneficial collaboration between different organisations aimed at tackling the challenges of sustainable development. Beyond that however, it is almost impossible to develop a universal system of classification for different types of partnership. Such is the complexity of different players, issues and geographies, let alone motivations, structures and outcomes, that few partnerships are the same. Nor are they static. Despite this, useful comparisons can be made and much can be learnt from looking at different examples.

One thing is clear. Building multi-stakeholder partnerships is not easy. Such partnerships require a difficult balance of idealism and pragmatism. They require vision and a strong sense of mission, combined with practical and often frustrating hard work. They require demonstrable results if they are to survive, but at the same time persistence and patience when results are not forthcoming. Many are based on a strong commitment to principles, but must also reflect a willingness to accept, respect and respond to other perspectives and different ways of doing things. When partnerships are being built across borders and between different nationalities, which is increasingly the case in today's globally inter-dependent world, the complexity of working with the different cultures and approaches of the government, private and non-governmental sectors, is multiplied by different national cultures and approaches.

It is not surprising that many partnerships fail to live up to their expectations. Even partnerships that are heralded as "successes" are normally far from perfect when they are systematically evaluated. Despite all of this, even "imperfect" partnerships have an enormous amount to offer. It is fair to say, for example, that every single one of the 26 partnerships described in this section has resulted in some benefit, both for the partners involved and society at large. All of them could have done some things differently; all of them could probably be improved in some way. But they are all an improvement on not doing anything at all. These new types of multi-stakeholder partnership, and many others like them, undoubtedly offer one of our greatest hopes for a more sustainable future. It is therefore worth investing time and effort in studying them and trying to understand what works and what does not.

The concept of identifying, analysing and sharing "good practice" which has become such a valuable tool in the business sector, is one which has relevance here. Even if it is impossible to fit different types of stakeholder partnerships into neat categories, it is possible to develop a common language and to draw general lessons on what works and what doesn't. The following section offers a few of these lessons and observations of "good practice".

Three key groups of lessons or success factors are identified:

- Purpose
- Process
- Progress

THE USE OF BEST PRACTICE

There is a new and astonishing resource in the business world: the best practices database. Collecting descriptions of optimal business practices from around the world and recording these practices in a form that favours comparability, such a database makes it possible for companies within the same industry and in remote industries to "talk to each other" and learn from each other. Can a packaged-foods company learn anything really useful from an aerospace company? Yesterday's answer, sensibly enough, was "No, of course not." Today's answer is "Very probably – let's take a look." For profitable companies linked only by their pursuit of excellence, there must be a roundhouse: a point where all good things potentially connect.

A best practice is a deliberate pattern of business activity that accomplishes its objective with outstanding efficiency and effectiveness, and contributes to exceptional performance. It is often applicable across industry boundaries.

Paul O. Pederson
Price Waterhouse

Throughout the world, industry associations and individual companies are using "best practices" – examples or case studies drawn from their own industry sectors and others – to enhance the efficiency and effectiveness of their performance. The term is becoming so well-accepted in the business community that it is easy to forget that it is a relatively new approach to enhancing corporate performance; one driven by increasing competition and a growing need to understand *how* business is conducted.

Paul Pederson, who championed the development of Price Waterhouse's international best practices database called KnowledgeView℠ argues that the use of best practices offers companies an array of goals and advantages. These include:

Encourage transfer and acceptance of new ideas across industries

Support development of credible performance goals, measurements and results

Provide ability to learn from world-class leaders

Make employees surer and braver

BEST PRACTICE

Motivate continuous improvements

Stimulate greater openness among employees to change

Galvanise management action

Generate faster and more cost-effective attainment of performance improvements

Enhance key financial operational, and other business processes

This growing emphasis on understanding processes and how they effect outcomes, and the use of "best practice" case studies to do so, is not unique to the business world. Governments and non-governmental organisations are also starting to look at models around the world, both within their own sector and increasingly within the business sector, to review how they can manage limited resources and complex challenges in a more effective and efficient way.

There is enormous potential for using such an approach to understand and improve the impact of multi-stakeholder partnerships. In the case of such complex relationships between different sectors and organisations with a wide range of different characteristics, cultures and motivations, it is probably wiser to use the term "good practices" instead of "best practices" but the basic approach is the same. Namely: identifying and analysing partnerships that are working well; drawing out lessons; communicating these lessons in a common language; and putting them into practice in different situations.

Based on this approach, what are some of the key lessons, or good practices, that come out of:

- the preceding profiles of partnerships between business and other sectors; and

- other research on multi-stakeholder partnerships?

Three key themes appear again and again as the broad parameters that determine successful partnerships: Purpose, Process and Progress;

PURPOSE	• clear and common goals based on mutual benefit
PROCESS	• role of intermediary leadership • understanding and consulting stakeholders • clarity of roles and responsibilities • understanding resource needs and capacities • communication – regular, open, transparent, accountable structures for joint decision-making and conflict resolution
PROGRESS	• evaluating and celebrating success • continuous learning and adaptation

None of these are easy to achieve and some will be more important than others depending on the partners, their purpose and their circumstances. There is no blueprint. Almost all the partners profiled however, claim that one or more of these factors have been crucial in the success of their partnership.

(i) Clear and common goals based on mutual benefit

Partnership is not an end in itself, but a mechanism to achieve some greater goal that couldn't be achieved by the partners acting on their own. Partnership without purpose is doomed to failure. So is partnership where the purpose is not clearly defined and commonly "owned" by all the partners. They may have different motivations for wanting to achieve a certain goal – which is usually the case in multi-stakeholder partnerships – but they have to have agreement on the goal or purpose they want to achieve.

Equally important, there must be a sense of mutual benefit. As with motivations, the specific benefits may be different for each partner, but each has to feel that they are getting value from the time, cost and effort which inevitably goes into building cross-sector partnerships. The more these perceived benefits can be articulated and shared, the more likely it is that the partnership will be built on the mutual trust and understanding that is necessary for successful co-operation. The fact that many businesses are openly looking to link their social investment activities and their partnerships with NGOs, to strategic business interests is a clear example of this search for "benefit" or to use business terminology, "return on investment".

(ii) Role of intermediary leadership

One of the single most important factors in most successful partnerships is the role played by an individual or an organisation acting as the intermediary between different partners, and the mediator between different motivations, needs and resources. Most research on partnership emphasises the crucial role of leadership – often individual leadership. This is certainly important, but it is a special type of leadership that is called for – a

Most research emphasises the crucial role of leadership. This is certainly important, but it is a special type of leadership that is called for – a consultative or facilitative leadership.

consultative or facilitative leadership – capable not only of bringing together diverse interests, but also ensuring a sense of equity and "common ownership" when different partners have unequal amounts of power or resources, which is often the case when large companies are trying to reach out to community-based organisations.

This intermediary leadership function can be played by a person or organisation from any sector. In many of the cases in the preceding pages for example, it is played by the NGO being profiled in Section I or the business-led organisation in Section III, where these organisations are acting as intermediaries between individual companies, international donors and ultimate beneficiaries. There are countless examples, however, where a large multinational company has formed successful and mutually-beneficial partnerships directly with a community-based organisation or an environmental NGO without an intermediary organisation serving as an interlocutor. In almost all of these examples it is possible to find visionary individuals, in both the company and the community, who have formed the personal relationship necessary for "David to meet Goliath" on more equal, non-paternalistic terms.

(iii) Understanding and consulting beneficiaries and stakeholders

It is common to talk about partnerships between a company and an NGO, or between a group of companies, or between international donors and business, which are aimed at achieving some social objective, without referencing the ultimate beneficiaries or stakeholders of these partnerships. Organisations such as Tata Steel's Rural Development Society, PBSP and TBIRD are discovering, as are more and more companies, that no matter what partnerships are formed and with whom, they are unlikely to be successful unless there is some form of consultation with ultimate beneficiaries, or with stakeholders who may not be a formal part of the partnership but consider that they have a stake in its impact. Taking as inclusive an approach as possible, and developing mechanisms which enable stakeholders to participate and feel a sense of ownership in the outcomes of a partnership is absolutely crucial. It is what makes the difference between paternalistic philanthropy and genuine partnership.

(iv) Clarity of roles and responsibilities

This should go without saying and yet many partnerships fail because of unrealistic expectations about issues such as funding, timescales and division of labour. Establishing clear structures for operations, decision-making, conflict resolution and evaluation processes is critical. In some cases this is part of a formal signed agreement or statement of intent, in others it is based on mutual understanding, which is obviously easier if the partners already trust and respect each other.

(v) Understanding resource needs and capacities

Linked to the above, a common downfall in development projects is "throwing resources at a problem" which may be inappropriate, or too much for local capacities to absorb, or not the most effective type of resources that a donor or company could offer, or a combination of all three. It is therefore critical to understand firstly, what are the types of skills and resources that different partners can best bring to a partnership; and secondly, what are the exact needs and what are the capacities for effectively utilising these resources?

One of the strongest trends in corporate partnerships with other sectors is the growing insistence on the part of companies that they should not be seen only

As the US-based Management Institute for Environment and Business conclude in their research on environmental cooperation: "Partnerships are formed among organisations, but succeed because of individuals."

as sources of money, but equally and often even more importantly, as sources of people, premises, products, technical skills and managerial capacities, which can be of immeasurable benefit to other sectors. Equally important is the growing realisation that partners without money often have non-monetary resources, that can be usefully shared for mutual benefit. Linked to this issue is the importance of capacity-building different partners and beneficiaries in order to optimise their ability to understand and respect different needs and capacities.

(vi) Communication

The theme that draws all of the above together is communication. Most other problems can be ironed out if communication between partners and beneficiaries is open, transparent and regular. Accountability is becoming one of the most important issues faced by business, governments and NGOs. The willingness to engage in, and respond to, two-way dialogue with other partners and with stakeholders is fundamental to building long-term trust. Another increasingly important issue is terminology and the need to find words and language which are not paternalistic and which can be understood by different players. Mechanisms that facilitate joint decision-making and conflict resolution also play a key role in good communication.

(vii) Evaluating and celebrating progress

Linked closely to the need to build purposeful partnerships and to be both participatory and accountable, is the need to establish systems to review and evaluate progress. This is often easier said than done, given that many partnerships have qualitative impacts as well as quantitative ones, and these are not easy to measure. However the value of constant assessment and learning cannot be underestimated. Nor can the value of recognising and celebrating progress – however small it may be. Many successful partnerships talk about the importance of having "early wins"; demonstrable examples of benefits and results which can act as a vital motivator to further action.

(viii) Continuous learning and adaptation

Almost all of the partnerships profiled in this publication and the people behind them talk about the need for persistence. The process of moving beyond traditional modes of behaviour and interaction is not an easy one. Building trust between organisations that have either been confrontational, or totally unaware of each other previously, does not happen overnight. The willingness to take risks and to experiment, must be backed by the readiness to either try again, or to try another approach or set of partners if things don't work out. A number of the partnerships profiled emphasise the need to be "learning organisations" and the importance of flexibility and being able to respond and adapt to changing needs, capabilities and circumstances.

Many of the partnerships profiled are only a few years old, a clear indication of how new this cross-sector approach to problem-solving really is. However there are a few organisations that have been around for over 10 years, such as PBSP in the Philippines, Tata Steel's Rural Development Society in India, and Business in the Community in the UK. All have had some major organisational and strategic challenges, and all have persisted and adapted to changing needs, capabilities and circumstances. In doing so, they have not only survived, but have also been able to continue serving their original purpose of bringing business skills, resources and commitment to the greater goals of community and national development, in partnership with the skills and resources of other sectors.

Conclusions and Recommendations

Good corporate citizenship and sustainable development are an absolute must. In a resource business such as BP, license to operate is not a debatable issue. Too few companies are seen as occupying the ethical high ground, but most are regarded as being on the low ground. This is an awful story to hear about the state of our companies today. We have to get these standards up. We are not here to debate whether we should do this. In my view we are here to debate how best to do it, in our businesses at the grassroots level, with encouragement from us all in leadership positions.

Sir David Simon
Chairman BP,
Senior Deputy Chairman PWBLF

The purpose of this publication has been to profile good practice; to emphasise the positive and the possible. In concluding however, it would be naïve and dishonest to suggest that these examples indicate that "all is well with the world." Clearly this is not the case. The scale and complexity of the world's social and environmental problems remain enormous. And the scope and impact of the good practice stories profiled here, and many others like them, are still not enough. There is no time for complacency when more than a billion people still live in absolute poverty, when millions of others are out of work and when inequality and social exclusion is increasing in many countries. There is no time for complacency when climate change, environmental degradation, loss of biodiversity and declining food and water supplies threaten the ecological carrying capacity of our planet. And there is no time for complacency when crime and corruption are still growing, both within the business sector and in society at large.

We know what the economic, environmental and social problems are. The need now is to focus on solutions. At one level the solutions are technology, finance and institutions. Ultimately, however, these are just the "mechanics". The core issue is about changing attitudes, values and approach. It is about thinking and acting in non-traditional ways. It is about a new way of governance – at both a societal and corporate level.

There is a growing need for both countries and companies to be governed in a more transparent, accountable and participatory manner than in the past. At the heart of this approach is the concept of stakeholders. The word has not even appeared in most peoples' dictionaries yet, but it is one that will define societal and corporate relations and organisational structures in the 21st century. Both political and corporate leaders will need to find new ways of listening to, responding to, and working with, each other and with representatives of civil society – individual community leaders, non-governmental organisations and community-based organisations.

The leaders of companies will have to be more responsive than ever before to their primary business stakeholders – customers, employees, investors, suppliers – but also to their secondary stakeholders – communities, governments, NGOs and the general public. They will need to manage a difficult balancing act and often trade-offs, in the search for win-win solutions for the maximum number of participants in their business and societal interactions. And the leaders of countries will also have to be more responsive than ever before to the hopes and fears of their stakeholders – not only the electorate, but also the many people in far too many countries who do not vote at all, and those that cannot vote, such as future generations.

If greater consultation and a more systematic approach to balancing economic success with different stakeholder needs, was a prerequisite to corporate and government decision-making, there would be a much better chance of developing innovative technologies, financial instruments and institutional structures, which could be applied to increasing effectiveness and equity, as well as efficiency.

Two of the factors which would most help business and political leaders in this process are new approaches to measurement and better incentives. As discussed in Section I of this publication, the World Bank and others are researching different ways of measuring national wealth, to accommodate qualitative as well as quantitative aspects. The creation of the UNDP's Human Development Index has been another valuable contribution to the area of measurement in recent years. At the corporate level some companies are looking at measurement methodologies such as full-cost accounting, economic and environmental value-added and accounting for virtual assets. All of this work is vital and should be supported and promoted as extensively as possible.

As the world moves beyond problem identification and toward development of solutions, it is important for the essential contributions of business to become more widely understood. Solutions require awareness, knowledge and resources, together with a drive to find and implement innovative solutions. Clearly, business is in a position to deliver on all counts.

Livio DeSimone
CEO 3M, Chairman WBCSD and
Deputy Chairman PWBLF

In terms of incentives, there is much that can be done both within companies and externally, to encourage more socially and environmentally responsible behaviour. Setting benchmarks and standards against which companies and their employees or business units can operate, and then rewarding progress towards these targets is critical. Within companies, recognition and award schemes can also play a role, not only for employees, but also for other primary stakeholders such as suppliers and contractors. Greater media coverage, national campaigns, and high-profile Presidential or Prime Ministerial Awards for leading companies, can be valuable. Ultimately however it is (a) the behaviour of the market-place – both investors and customers and (b) the under-pinning of a framework of regulatory and fiscal incentives, that will lead to a more consistent approach to driving up standards and motivating business to play its appropriate part in the social and environmental sphere. The debate on how to make this happen, and especially on how to price social and environmental value-added, has already started and can only intensify.

None of these developments are easy to achieve. They will be impossible to achieve without a combination of leadership, dialogue and partnership. Many of the companies, international agencies and NGOs profiled in this publication are already playing a leading role in this process, but their activities need to be scaled-up and replicated – both in terms of increasing the impact of existing partnership initiatives and in terms of getting more players, sectors and countries involved. Some of the ways in which this can be achieved are as follows:

1. Increased emphasis on identifying, studying and rewarding corporate "good practice" and partnership "good practice".

2. Joint efforts by international agencies and business leaders, to encourage national governments to develop fiscal incentives and institutional structures which facilitate national level dialogue and partnership between the public and private sector, and which encourage companies to play an appropriate societal role.

3. Joint awareness-raising and educational campaigns about the benefits and potential of cross-sector partnerships.

4. Identification and/or establishment of joint "demonstration projects" on the ground, such as some of those profiled here.

5. Joint education and capacity-building exercises, based on experiential learning and aimed at educating development professionals, government officials, NGO and business managers.

6. Joint efforts to educate some of tomorrow's leaders by working with schools, universities and student organisations and developing teaching materials, mentoring programmes and other opportunities for today's decision-makers to inspire and inform tomorrow's. If the head of every major company, NGO and government department went to speak to two schools and two universities just once a year, about the positive contribution that different cultures and sectors make to society, and the importance of increased dialogue and partnership between them, this could have a strong multiplier effect for the future.

Ultimately it all comes down to having individual courage and commitment in order to take the risks associated with doing things differently. The people and organisations profiled in this publication, and millions of others like them around the world, are the ones who can make it happen. It is important for each of them to realise that they are not alone; that they are part of a multi-cultural and multi-sector group that is gaining in size and gathering momentum. Above all, it is important to remember that we have come a long way in the last ten years in terms of creating a new vision for corporate citizenship, stakeholder partnership and sustainable development. We can, and must, go even further in the future. It is the only hope we have for a better world and sustainable prosperity for the many, rather than the few.

Appendix 1

BUSINESS AS PARTNERS IN DEVELOPMENT
Good Practices Project

This research project is being undertaken by The Prince of Wales Business Leaders Forum, in co-operation with the World Bank Group and the United Nations Development Programme to identify, analyse and promote examples of how business is working in partnership with public sector institutions, non-governmental organisations and other private sector enterprises, to play a creative and positive role in the process of sustainable development.

The goals of the project are to:

1. **Gather knowledge:** understand what companies are doing to contribute not only to economic growth, but also to wider economic participation, human resource development, social cohesion, environmental improvements and quality of life in the communities and countries where they operate, particularly in developing and transition economies, but also in OECD countries where specific models or mechanisms of public-private partnerships and corporate-community investment may be replicable or adaptable elsewhere.

2. **Provide access:** establish an information system/network to make this knowledge accessible to companies, governments, development institutions, academia, non-governmental organisations, and the media, via written publications, the Internet, conferences, roundtables and media coverage.

3. **Inspire and motivate others to act:** catalyse discussion, establish new standards and guidelines, stimulate new ideas, provide educational materials, and facilitate efforts to expand, improve or scale-up stakeholder partnerships and examples of corporate responsibility which are promoting sustainable development.

The key products of the research project will be:

1. **An inventory of corporate good practice** – drawn from different countries and industry sectors and covering a wide variety of business activities, ranging from: core business practices such as infrastructure development, production, purchasing and supply chain management, distribution and marketing, human resource development, investor relations, government relations, health, safety and environment, and research and development; to community and social investments in areas such as education and training, youth, small-scale and micro-enterprise development, health, public safety, and rural and urban development.

2. **A more detailed analysis of the policies and practices of 20 leading multinational companies from different sectors** – reviewing their overall global management structure, mission statement and key commercial and social activities; profiling two to three of their most outstanding stakeholder partnerships analysing their costs, benefits and potential for replication, adaptation or scaling-up; and assessing the development impacts of each company in five key emerging economies – Poland, South Africa, India, Brazil and Egypt.

3. **A survey of the attitudes of key stakeholder groups on the changing role of business in society** – undertaking a series of surveys and interviews with: local and national politicians, the media, non-governmental and community-based organisations, development professionals, business leaders, academics and youth.

The three publications to be produced in the first year of the project are:

* **Partners in Development: Creating wealth for countries, companies and communities**
* **Partners in Development: Company profiles**
* **Partners in Development: Stakeholder perspectives.**

The most innovative, effective and replicable examples of good practice will also be disseminated electronically, presented at international conferences and regional roundtables, and developed into teaching materials.

WORLD BANK CORPORATE CITIZENSHIP DAY

On September 28, 1996 the World Bank held its first Corporate Citizenship Day as part of the Programme of Seminars preceding the IMF/World Bank Group Annual Meetings.

Attended by over 500 people, the objective of the day was to bring together senior decision-makers from business, NGOs and foundations with their counterparts in the World Bank Group, in order to review good practices and discuss future potential in the area of public-private partnerships for social development.

The day commenced with a breakfast attended by more than 15 of the bank's senior management team and 25 chief executive officers and partnership practitioners from the private sector. This was followed by a plenary session opened by Mr. Wolfensohn the Bank' President, with President Jose Figueres of Costa Rica, Dr. Percy Barnevik, President and CEO of ABB and Sir David Simon, Chairman of British Petroleum making keynote speeches.

The following seminar, moderated by Dr. Rosabeth Moss Kanter from Harvard University, looked in more detail at a few innovative partnerships from around the world, focusing on the opportunities and roles of the private sector. It focused on some key issues, including:

* How does corporate citizenship add value to companies in areas such as license to operate, employee training and development, and corporate reputation?
* How is the impact of being a good corporate citizen measured?
* What has worked in partnership-building among companies, governments and civic organisations?
* How can communities and governments support corporate citizenship?

The panelists represented a wide range of business and community leaders. They were: James Chestnut, the Chief Financial Officer of the Coca-Cola Company; Camilo Bernal, General Manager of Minuto de Dios in Colombia; John Filer, Director of the BOC Group; Nigel Twose, Programme Director of ActionAid; Brian Whittaker, Executive Director of the National Business Initiative in South Africa; and Hani Yamani, Chairman of Centaur Corporation in Switzerland and Executive Director of the Hope Foundation in Saudi Arabia.

The Corporate Citizenship Day closed with a luncheon on Public-Private Partnerships for Youth Development, moderated by David Bell, Chairman of the Financial Times, with the following speakers: Henrique de Campos Meirelles, the COO of BankBoston; William LaMothe, the Chairman Emeritus of the Kellogg Company; Rick Little, the President and CEO of the International Youth Foundation; and Cornelio Marchan, Executive Director of the Fundacion Esquel and Former Minister of Planning in Ecuador.

An Executive Summary of "Business as Partners in Development: Creating Wealth for Countries, Companies and Communities" was produced as background for the day's meetings. The World Bank's Finance and Private Sector Division is now working with the PWBLF and other NGOs that helped to organise the day, such as the International Youth Foundation, to develop a programme of follow-up activities, linked into the "Partners in Development- Good Practices Project."

MEMBERS OF The Prince of Wales Business Leaders Forum

(as at September 1st 1996)

PRINCIPAL SUPPORTERS & BOARD MEMBERS

ABB Asea Brown Boveri Ltd (Switzerland)

BMW AG (Germany)

The BOC Group (UK)

The British Petroleum Company p.l.c. (BP) (UK)

The Coca-Cola Company (USA)

Grand Metropolitan PLC (UK)

ITOCHU Corporation (Japan)

Johnson Matthey PLC (UK)

3M (USA)

SmithKline Beecham plc (UK/USA)

TRW Inc (USA)

Wheelock and Company Limited (Hong Kong)

COUNCIL MEMBERS

Abercrombie & Kent Group (UK/USA)

ALKAN Group (Egypt)

ARTOC Group (Egypt)

Bajaj Auto Ltd (India)

British Gas plc (UK)

Coopers & Lybrand (UK)

D'elegant Holding Ltd (Hong Kong)

DHL Worldwide Express S.A. (USA)

Far Eastern Group (Taiwan)

The Fuji Bank Inc (Japan)

Kolon Group (Korea)

KPMG (UK)

Levi Strauss & Co (USA)

Lorentzen Empreendimentos SA (Brazil)

McKinsey & Company Inc (UK)

Norsk Hydro a.s. (Norway)

Obayashi Corporation (Japan)

Pasona Inc (Japan)

The Perot Group (USA)

Price Waterhouse Europe (UK)

Robert Bosch GmbH (Germany)

Samcrete Egypt (Egypt)

Sedgwick Group plc (UK)

Shobokshi Trading & Development Co (Saudi Arabia)

The Sumitomo Bank, Limited (Japan)

The Tokyo Electric Power Co (Japan)

Toyota Motor Corporation (Japan)

USHA (India) Ltd (India)

U S WEST International (USA)

POLICY ADVISORY GROUP

The Vice-Presidency for Finance and Private Sector Development at the World Bank was created in January 1993 to provide leadership and specialised consulting to other entities of the World Bank Group in setting and implementing the private sector agenda. It groups approximately 200 specialists in:

- **Financial Sector Development** – banking and capital markets.
- **Private Sector Development** – privatisation and restructuring; policy and regulatory frameworks; private provision of infrastructure and micro-finance.
- **Industry and Energy** – oil and gas; telecoms; information technology; power; energy efficiency; renewables and mining. Its principal focus is on the systemic issues and enabling policies that have a major impact on increasing private sector activities – both local and foreign. About 65% of its work is "sold" to the Bank's Regional Vice-Presidencies as cross-support services. The other 35% is policy, dissemination of best practices, training, external partnerships and quality assurance.

Contact: Amy Horng or Amanda Blakely, VPFPD, The World Bank, 1818 H Street N.W., Washington DC 20433, USA

Tel: 1 (202) 473 1598 Fax: 1 (202) 676 9245

e-mail: ahorng@worldbank.org

The HOPE Foundation was established by Mr Hani Yamani two years ago and is funded by 20% of the profit earned by HAZY Investments Ltd. The Foundation is committed to building partnerships for development and recognises the vital role that the private sector can play in this process. It is for this reason that it has agreed to support the work of the World Bank Group on corporate social and environmental responsibility, and has become a member of the project Advisory Group to advise especially on corporate initiatives in the Middle East and Africa.

Contact: Doug Maguire, MIGA, The World Bank, 1818 H Street N.W., Washington DC 20433, USA

Tel: 1 (202) 473 6733 Fax: 1 (202) 522 2650

e-mail: dmaguire@worldbank.org

The Prince of Wales Business Leaders Forum was established in February 1990 as a global network of business leaders from Europe, North and South America, Africa, the Middle East and Asia Pacific. Its goals are to raise awareness of the value of corporate responsibility both to the successful management of international business and to the prosperity of host countries and communities; and to encourage partnership action between business, government, communities, non-governmental organisations and aid agencies, as an effective means of promoting sustainable development. It achieves its goals through a strategy of:

- **Advocacy** – researching and communicating good practice of business-led partnerships in development.
- **Brokerage** – acting as a catalyst to bring together organisations from different sectors to work on specific joint projects.
- **Capacity and institution-building** – running workshops and training programmes.

The Forum works with its member companies and local affiliated organisations in 17 developing and transition countries. It also has strategic alliances with a small number of international development agencies and non-governmental organisations and an International Partnership Network of over 500 "partnership practitioners" drawn from business, non-governmental organisations, community-based organisations, the media, academia, international development agencies and government. It runs the International Hotels Environment Initiative – a programme supported by leading hotel chains and hotel associations around the world.

Contact: Jane Nelson or Karen Gommersall, The Prince of Wales Business Leaders Forum, 15-16 Cornwall Terrace, Regent's Park, London NW1 4QP, UK

Tel: 44 (171) 467 3600 Fax: 44 (171) 467 3610

e-mail: info@pwblf.org.uk

internet site: http://www.oneworld.org/pwblf/

The Private Sector Development Programme at UNDP supports the efforts of UNDP in the area of employment and sustainable livelihoods by providing expertise in the areas of medium, small and micro-enterprise development, and providing expertise on micro-finance. In addition PSDP also supports UNDP Country Office efforts in broader private sector development, including building the institutional fabric for Private Sector Development. As part of its overall strategy, PSDP works as a catalyst to engage the Private Sector for substantive collaboration and resource mobilisation to build Private/Public Partnerships.

Contact: Henry Jackelen, Acting Manager

Tel: 1 (212) 697 9692

e-mail: henry.jackelen@undp.org

or John Tucker, Programme Officer

Tel: 1 (212) 697 4041 Fax: 1 (212) 697 5058

e-mail: john.tucker@undp.org

Index of Case Studies and Profiles

Bibliography

ACKOFF, Russell L. The democratic corporation: a radical prescription for recreating corporate America and rediscovering success. Oxford University Press, 1994.

ADAIR, John. Great leaders. The Talbot Adair Press, 1989.

AIESEC. Educating tomorrow's global business leaders. AIESEC International & The Prince of Wales Business Leaders Forum, 1996.

ALPERSON, Myra. Foundations for a new democracy: corporate social investment in South Africa. Ravan Press, 1995.

ASIAN DEVELOPMENT BANK. Guidelines for social analysis of development projects: operational summary. Asian Development Bank, 1991.

ASIAN DEVELOPMENT BANK. Handbook for incorporation of social dimensions in projects. Asian Development Bank, 1994.

AUSTIN, James E. Managing in developing countries: strategic analysis and operating techniques. Free Press, 1990.

BANURI, Tariq & HOLMBERG, Johan. Governance for sustainable development: a southern perspective. International Institute for Environment and Development, 1992.

BARNET, Richard J & CAVANAGH, J. Global dreams: imperial corporations and the new world order. Simon & Schuster, 1994.

BINSWANGER, Hans P & LANDELL-MILLS, Pierre. The World Bank's strategy for reducing poverty and hunger: a report to the development community. Environmentally Sustainable Development Studies and Monographs series no 4. World Bank, 1995.

BLAIR, Margaret M. Wealth creation and wealth sharing: a colloquium on corporate governance and investments in human capital. Brookings Institute, 1996.

BROCKMAN, Roystan A C & WILLIAMS, Allen. Urban infrastructure finance: a new vision devolution and market-based mechanisms. Asian Development Bank, 1996.

BRUGGER, Ernst, NELSON, Jane, TIMBERLAKE, Lloyd and EDWARDS, Mark. The cutting edge: small business and progress. McGraw, Hill Interamericana de Chile, 1994.

BURKE, Tom & ELKINGTON, John. The Green Capitalists. Victor Gollancz, 1987.

BURKE, Tom & KNIGHT, P, eds. Environment strategy europe 1995/96: sustainable production and consumption. Campden Publishing, 1995.

BUSINESS IN THE COMMUNITY. Directions for the nineties: an action strategy for companies and their partners in community involvement. Business in the Community, 1991.

CANNON, Tom. Corporate responsibility: a textbook on business ethics. governance, environment: roles and responsibility. Pitman, 1994.

CARMICHAEL, Sheena & DRUMMOND, John. Good business: a guide to corporate responsibility and business ethics. Hutchinson, 1989.

CATER, Nick. Relief inc. *World Link*, Jan-Feb 1996. pp90-93.

CAUX ROUND TABLE. Principles for business. Caux Round Table, 1994.

CLARKE, Thomas & MONKHOUSE, Elaine. Rethinking the company. Pitman, 1994.

CLINTON, Bill. Between hope and history: Meeting America's Challenge for the 21st century. Times Books, 1996.

CLUTTERBUCK, David & SNOW, Deborah. Working with the community: a guide to corporate social responsibility. Weidenfeld & Nicholson, 1990.

COLLINS, James C & PORRAS, Jerry I. Built to last: successful habits of visionary companies. Century, 1995.

COMMISSION ON GLOBAL GOVERNANCE. Our global neighbourhood. Oxford University Press, 1995.

CONSULTATIVE BUSINESS MOVEMENT. Building a winning nation: companies and the RDP. Ravan Press, 1994.

CONSULTATIVE BUSINESS MOVEMENT NATIONAL TEAM. Managing change: a guide to the role of business in transition. Ravan Press, 1993.

DALY, Herman E. and COBB, John B. For the common good: redirecting the economy toward community, the environment and a sustainable future. Beacon, 1989.

DAHRENDORF, Ralf, et al. Report on wealth creation and social cohesion in a free society. Commission on Wealth Creation and Social Cohesion, 1995.

DEL ROSSO, Joy Miller. Investing in nutrition with World Bank Assistance. World Bank, 1992.

DENMARK: Ministry of Social Affairs. New partnership for social cohesion: examples from three Danish companies. Ministry of Social Affairs Denmark, 1996.

DE SOTO, Hernando. The other path: the invisible revolution in the third world. Perennial Library, 1989.

DRUCKER, Peter F. Post-capitalist society. Butterworth-Heinemann, 1993.

ELKINGTON, John, KNIGHT, Peter & HAILES, Julia. The green business guide. Victor Gollancz, 1991.

ETZIONI, Amitai. The spirit of community: rights responsibilities and the communitarian agenda. Fontana Press, 1995.

EUROPEAN COMMISSION: Competitiveness Advisory Group. Enhancing European competitiveness: first report to the President of the Commission, the prime ministers and Heads of State June 1995. OOPEC, 1995.

EUROPEAN COMMISSION: Competitiveness Advisory Group. Enhancing European competitiveness: second report to the President of the European Commission, the prime ministers and Heads of State. OOPEC, 1995.

EUROPEAN COMMISSION: Competitiveness Advisory Group. Enhancing European competitiveness: third report to the President of the European Commission, the prime ministers and Heads of State June 1996. OOPEC, 1996.

FAIRCLOUGH, A J. Global corporate citizenship 1995/96. Kensington Publications & The Prince of Wales Business Leaders Forum, 1996.

FAIRCLOUGH, A J. World development aid and joint venture finance 1996/97. Kensington Publications & World Business Council for Sustainable Development, 1996.

FARAKAS, Charles, DE BACKER, Philippe & SHEPPARD, Allen. Maximum leadership: the world's top business leaders discuss how they add value to their companies. Orion, 1995.

FOMBRUN, Charles J. Reputation: realising the value from the corporate image. Harvard Business School Press, 1996.

FOMBRUN, Charles J. Leading corporate change: how the world's foremost companies are launching revolutionary change. McGraw-Hill, 1994.

FOSTER,Timothy R V. 101 great mission statements: how the world's leading companies run their businesses. Kogan Page, 1993.

FREDERICK, William C, POST, James E & DAVIS, Keith. Business and society: corporate strategy, public policy, ethics. 7th ed. McGraw-Hill, 1992.

FRIENDLY, Alfred, ed. Partnerships to progress: the report of the President's Commission on Environmental Quality. PCEQ, 1993.

FUKUYAMA, Francis. Social capital and the global economy. *Foreign Affairs,* Sept/Oct 1995.

FUKUYAMA, Francis. Trust: the social virtues and the creation of prosperity. Hamish Hamilton, 1995.

GALBRAITH, John K. The good society: the humane agenda. Houghton Miflin, 1996.

GIRADET, Herbert. Earthrise: halting destruction, healing the world. Paladin, 1992.

GIRADET, Herbert. The Gaia atlas of cities: new directions for sustainable urban living. Gaia Books, 1992.

GLOBAL CITIZENSHIP: Briefing book. University of Michigan Business School, 1993.

GRAHAM, Edward M. Global corporations and national governments. Institute for International Economics, 1996.

GREAT BRITAIN: Department of the Environment. Partnerships in practice. Department of the Environment, 1994.

GREAT BRITAIN. Competitiveness: creating the enterprise centre of Europe. Cm 3300. HMSO, 1996.

GREEN, Peter Sheldon. Reputation risk management. Pitman, 1992.

HAMEL, Gary & PRAHALAD, C K. Competing for the future. Harvard Business School Press, 1996.

HANDY, Charles. Beyond certainty: the changing worlds of organisations. Random House, 1995.

HARVARD BUSINESS REVIEW. Global strategies: insights from the world's leading thinkers. Harvard Business School Press, 1994.

HARVARD BUSINESS REVIEW. Leaders on leadership. Harvard Business School Press, 1992.

HAWKEN, Paul. The ecology of commerce: how business can save the planet. Weidenfeld and Nicholson, 1993.

HENDERSON, Hazel. Paradigms in progress: life beyond economics. Adamtine Press, 1996.

HENDERSON, Hazel. Building a win-win world: life beyond global economic warfare. Berrett-Koehler, 1996.

HIRST, Paul & THOMPSON, Grahame. Globalisation in question: the international economy and possibilities of governance. Polity Press, 1996.

HITACHI FOUNDATION & JOBS FOR THE FUTURE. Redefining corporate responsibility in a global economy: an agenda for action. Jobs for the Future, 1996.

HOOD, John M. The heroic enterprise: business and the common good. Free Press, 1996.

HORSMAN, Mathew and MARSHALL, Andrew. After the nation state. HarperCollins, 1994.

HUTTON, Will. The state we're in. Vintage, 1996.

INDEPENDENT COMMISSION ON POPULATION AND QUALITY OF LIFE. Caring for the future: making the next decades provide a life worth living. Oxford University Press, 1996.

INTERNATIONAL FINANCE CORPORATION. Annual report 1995. International Finance Corporation, 1995.

INTERNATIONAL FINANCE CORPORATION. Financing private infrastructure projects: emerging trends from IFC's experience. International Finance Corporation, 1994.

INTERNATIONAL FINANCE CORPORATION. Privatisation principles and practice. Lessons of experience series 1. World Bank, 1995

INTERNATIONAL INSTITUTE FOR MANAGEMENT DEVELOPMENT (IMD). The world competitiveness yearbook 1996. IMD, 1996.

JENNINGS, Marie. The guide to good corporate citizenship. Director Books, 1990.

JOHNSON, MIke. Managing in the next millennium. Butterworth-Heinemann, 1995.

KANTER, Rosabeth Moss. Thriving in the global economy. *Harvard Business Review*, Sept-Oct 1995. pp151-160.

KANTER, Rosabeth Moss. World class: thriving locally in the global economy. Simon & Schuster, 1995.

KAY, John. Foundations of corporate success: how business strategies add value. Oxford University Press, 1995.

KAY, John. The good market. *Prospect*, May 1996. pp39-43.

KINGSLEY, Tony & WHITEHEAD, Bradley W. Making environmental partnerships work. *Environment Risk*, April 1993.

KNIGHT, Peter T. Destined to leapfrog: why a revolution in learning will occur in Brazil, Russia and South Africa. Paper prepared for Second International Conference on Distance Learning in Russia. World Bank, 1996.

KORTEN, David C. When corporations rule the world. Kumerian Press & Berrett-Koehler Publishers, 1995.

KRUGMAN, Paul. Pop internationalism. The MIT Press, 1996.

LANDRY, Charles and BIANCHI Franco. The Creative City. Demos.

LEWIS, Jordan D. Partnerships for profit: structuring and managing strategic alliances. Free Press, 1990.

LINTON, Ian. Partnerships for profit. Director Books, 1994.

LOVE, Alexander R. Development co-operation aid in transition: efforts and policies of the members of the Devclopment Assistance Committee. OECD, 1994.

LUZ, Juan Miguel & MONTELIBANO, Teodoro Y. Corporations and communities in a developing country: case studies: Philippines. Philippine Business for Social Progress, 1993.

LYNCH, Robert Porter. Business alliances guide: the hidden competitive weapon. Wiley, 1993.

MAKOWER, Joel. Beyond the bottom line: putting social responsibility to work for your business and the world. Simon & Schuster, 1994.

MANAGEMENT INSTITUTE FOR ENVIRONMENT AND BUSINESS. Environmental partnerships: a field guide for government agencies. Harcourt Brace, 1995.

MANTLE, Clive E & RYAN, Ciaran. Interacting big and small: why South African corporations should get involved in small business development and how. BMI Industrial Consulting, 1994

MARIOTTI, John L. The power of partnerships:the next step beyond TQM, re-engineering and lean production. Blackwell, 1996.

MARSH, Ian, ed. The environmental challenge chapter extract: The environment as a business opportunity by Clem Doherty. Longman Cheshire, 1991.

MAYNARD H & MEHRTENS S The Fourth Wave: Business in the 21st centruy. Berrett Koehler. 1994

McNAUGHTON, Diana & PERLIN, Gary. Private sector development seminar: the finance sector, session 3 of 3. World Bank, 1994

MOBIUS, Mark. The investor's guide to emerging markets. Pitman, 1994.

MOLLER, Kim & RASMUSSEN, Erik, eds. Partnership for new social development: UN World Summit for Social Development. Mandag Morgen Strategic Forum, 1995.

MONKS, Robert A G & MINOW, Nell. Power and accountability. Harper Business, 1991.

MONKS, Robert A G & MINOW, Nell. Corporate governance. Blackwell, 1995.

NAISBITT, John & ABURDENE, Patricia. Re-inventing the corporation: transforming your job and your company for the new information society. Guild Publishing, 1985.

NELLIS, John & ROGER, Neil. Private sector development seminar: increasing private participation, session 2 of 3. World Bank, 1994

NELSON Jane. Business as partners in development: building new bridges for sustainable development in Latin America. Briefing paper prepared for The The Prince of Wales Business Leaders Forum President's review meeting on Latin America. The Prince of Wales Business Leaders Forum, 1995

NELSON Jane ed. New business horizons: the driving forces for business and community partnerships in the 21st century. Briefing paper prepared for International Council Meeting of the The Prince of Wales Business Leaders Forum 1994. First Magazine & The Prince of Wales Business Leaders Forum, 1994.

NELSON Jane ed. Partnerships for African development: business and communities working together in southern Africa. Synergos Institute & The Prince of Wales Business Leaders Forum, 1995

NELSON Jane. Partnerships for progress: sustainable development and corporate citizenship in Asia-Pacific – an Australian business perspective: a report prepared for the Australian meeting of the The Prince of Wales Business Leaders Forum. The Prince of Wales Business Leaders Forum, 1994.

NELSON Jane. Stakeholder partnerships: visionary companies building new forms of partnership to meet the socio-economic and environmental challenges of global change. The Prince of Wales Business Leaders Forum, 1996.

NELSON Jane & SIMPSON Susan. A new spirit of enterprise: business and community partnerships in the transition to a market economy in eastern and central Europe and the CIS. The Prince of Wales Business Leaders Forum, 1994.

NEW CONSUMER. Corporate Social Responsibility in Practice: Research Working Paper Series. 1995

NEW PARTNERSHIPS WORKING GROUP. New partnerships in the Americas: the spirit of Rio. United States Agency for International Development & World Resources Institute, 1994.

OHMAE, Kenrichi. The end of the nation state: the rise and fall of regional economies. Free Press, 1995.

PALABORA FOUNDATION. A corporate contribution to social development in South Africa. Palabora Foundation, 1995.

PEATTIE, Ken. Green marketing. Pitman, 1992.

PORTER, Michael E. Competitive strategy: techniques for analysing industries and competitors. Free Press, 1980.

PORTER, Michael E. The competitive advantage of nations. *Harvard Business Review*, March-April 1990. pp73-93.

PORTER, Michael E. The competitive advantage of the inner city. *Harvard Business Review*, May-June 1995. pp55-71.

PRESIDENT'S COMMISSION ON ENVIRONMENTAL QUALITY. Building successful environmental partnerships: findings from international partnership survey, final report. PCEQ, 1992.

PSACHAROPOULOS, George. Building human capital for better lives. Directions in development series. World Bank, 1996.

PUTNAM, Robert D. Making democracy work: civic traditions in modern Italy. Princeton University Press, 1993.

PUTNAM, Robert D. The prosperous community: social capital and public life. *The American Prospect*, Spring 1993. pp 35-42

RANDEL, Judith & GERMAN, Tony, eds. The reality of aid 1996: an independent review of international aid. Earthscan, 1996

RAY, Michael & RINZLER, Alan, eds. The new paradigm in business: emerging strategies for leadership and organisational change. Tarcher/Perigee, 1993.

REDER, Alan. In pursuit of principle and profit: business success through social responsibility. Tarcher/Putnam, 1994.

REDER, Alan for the Social Venture Network. 75 best business practices for socially responsible companies. Tarcher/Putman books, 1995.

REICH, Robert B. Who is them? *Harvard Business Review*, March-April 1991. pp77-88

REICH, Robert B. The work of nations: preparing ourselves for 21st century capitalism. Knopf, 1991.

RHINESMITH, Stephen H. A manager's guide to globalisation: six keys to success in a changing world. American Society for Training and Development, 1993.

RIFKIN, Jeremy. The end of work: the decline of the global labor force and the dawn of the post-market era. Tarcher/Putman, 1995

ROBINSON, David. Community links: the power of partnership. Business in the Community occasional paper 4. Business in the Community, 1996.

ROYAL SOCIETY FOR THE ENCOURAGEMENT OF ARTS, MANUFACTURES AND COMMERCE (RSA). RSA Inquiry Tomorrow's company: the role of business in a changing world. RSA, 1995

RYRIE, William. First world, third world. Macmillan, 1995.

SAMPSON, Anthony. Company man. HarperCollins, 1995.

SANCHO, Antonio. Policies and programs for social and human development: experiences from developing countries. Institute for Contemporary Studies, 1995.

SCHMIDHEINY, Stephen & BUSINESS COUNCIL FOR SUSTAINABLE DEVELOPMENT. Changing course: a global business perspective on development and the environment. MIT Press, 1992.

SCOTT, Mary & ROTHMAN, Howard. Companies with a conscience: intimate portraits of twelve firms that make a difference. Citadel Press, 1994.

SERAGELDIN, Ismail. Nurturing development: aid and co-operation in today's changing world. Directions in Development series. World Bank, 1995.

SERAGELDIN, Ismail. Sustainability and the wealth of nations: first steps in an ongoing journey. Environmentally Sustainable Development Studies and Monographs series no 5. World Bank, 1996

SERAGELDIN, Ismail. Sustainability as opportunity and the problem of social capital. Brown Journal of World Affairs, Summer-Fall 1996. pp187-202.

SERAGELDIN, Ismail, BARRETT, Richard & MARTIN-BROWN, Joan. The business of sustainable cities: public-private partnerships for creative technical and institutional solutions. Environmentally Sustainable Development Proceedings series no 7. World Bank, 1994.

SERAGELDIN, Ismail, COHEN, Michael, A & LEITMANN, Josef, eds. Enabling sustainable community development. Environmentally Sustainable Development Proceedings series no 8. World Bank, 1994.

SLOAN, Pamela & HILL, Roger. Corporate aboriginal relations: best practice case studies. Hill Sloan Associates, 1995.

SMART, Bruce. Beyond compliance: a new industry view of the environment. World Resources Institute, 1992.

SMITH, Hedrick. Rethinking America. Random House, 1995.

SOLOMON, Robert C. The new world of business: ethics and free enterprise in the global 1990s. Littlefield Adams, 1994.

SPARKES, Russell. The ethical investor: how to make money work for society and the environment as well as for yourself. Harper Collins, 1995.

SPENCER-COOKE, Andrea. From EMAS to SMAS: charting the course from environmental management and auditing to sustainability management: the EPE workbook for implementing sustainability in Europe.

Draft copy. European Partners for the Environment, 1996.

SURVEY OF MULTI-NATIONALS: Big is back. *Economist*, 24 June 1995.

SURVEY OF MULTI-NATIONALS: Everybody's favourite monsters. *Economist*, 27 March 1993.

SURVEY OF SOUTH AFRICA: Coming of age. *Economist*, 20 May 1995.

TAGGERT, James H & McDERMOTT, Michael C. The essence of international business. Essence of Management series. Prentice Hall, 1993.

TAHIJA, Julius. Swapping business skills for oil. *Harvard Business Review*. Sept-Oct 1993. pp4-11

TENNYSON Ros, ed. Dangerous times: exciting times: a series of essays on partnership action for sustainable development in southern Africa. The Prince of Wales Business Leaders Forum, 1994.

TENNYSON, Ros ed. Tools for partnership-building. Partnership Handbook Series no 2. The Prince of Wales Business Leaders Forum, 1994.

TENNYSON, Ros, et al eds. What is partnership?: a collection of essays on the theme of cross-sector partnerships for sustainable development. Partnership Handbook Series no 1. The Prince of Wales Business Leaders Forum, 1994.

THUROW, Lester C. The future of capitalism: how today's economic forces shape tomorrow's world. Morrow, 1996.

UNEP & IPIECA. The oil experience: technology co-operation and capacity building, contributions to Agenda 21. International Petroleum Industry Environmental Conservation Association, 1995.

UNEP, PWBLF & TUFTS UNIVERSITY. Partnerships for sustainable development: the role of business and industry. UNEP & The Prince of Wales Business Leaders Forum, 1994.

UNITED STATES: Department of Commerce, International Trade Administration. The big emerging markets: 1996 outlook and sourcebook. Bernan Press, 1996.

UNITED NATIONS CONFERENCE ON ENVIRONMENT & DEVELOPMENT, Agenda 21. United Nations, 1992.

UNITED NATIONS CONFERENCE ON TRADE AND DEVELOPMENT, Division on Transnational Corporations and Investment. Self-regulation of environmental management: an analysis of guidelines set by world industry associations for their member firms. United Nations, 1996.

UNITED NATIONS DEVELOPMENT PROGRAMME. Human development report 1994. Oxford University Press, 1994.

UNITED NATIONS DEVELOPMENT PROGRAMME. Human development report 1996. Oxford University Press, 1996.

UNITED NATIONS DEVELOPMENT PROGRAMME. United Nations Development Programme private sector guide: creating the action agenda, regional bureau for Africa. UNDP, 1996

UNITED NATIONS ECONOMIC AND SOCIAL COMMISSION FOR ASIA AND THE PACIFIC. Business for development: the HRD approach of the "Thai Business Initiative for Rural Development" (TBIRD). United Nations, 1994.

VAN DER GAAG, Jacques. Private and public initiatives: working together for health and education. Directions in Development series. World Bank, 1995.

VOLKER, Paul et al. Dossier: Globalisation and the nation-state. *World Economic Affairs*, 1(1) Summer 1996. pp29-51.

WATERMAN, Robert. The frontiers of excellence: learning from companies that put people first. Nicholas Brealey, 1994.

WELLS, Phil. The transnational corporation in a host country: policy and practice in developing countries: Premier Tea's quality assurance project. New Consumer Research Working papers, New Consumer, 1995.

WENDT, Henry. Global embrace: corporate challenges in a transitional world. Harper Business, 1993.

WHITTAKER, Brian. Enhancing the Public Contribution of Private Companies. National Business Initiative,1996

WILSON, Graham K. Business and politics: a comparative introduction. Macmillan Education, 1990.

WOLFENSOHN, James D. New directions and new partnerships: address to the World Bank Board of Governors 10 Oct 1995. World Bank, 1995.

WOODS, Peter, et al. Partnerships: work in progress: a guide for organisations of INSIGHT visits. Partnership Handbook Series no 3. The Prince of Wales Business Leaders Forum, 1995.

WORLD BANK. Annual Report 1995. World Bank, 1995.

WORLD BANK. Bureaucrats in business: the economics and politics of government ownership, summary. World Bank Policy Research Report. World Bank, 1995.

WORLD BANK. Claiming the future: choosing prosperity in the Middle East and North Africa. World Bank, 1995.

WORLD BANK: Development Committee. Serving a changing world: report of the task force on multilateral development banks. World Bank, 1996.

WORLD BANK: Environment Department. Mainstreaming the environment: the World Bank Group and the environment since the Rio Earth Summit. World Bank, 1995.

WORLD BANK. Global economic prospects and the developing countries 1996. World Bank, 1996.

WORLD BANK. Governance: The World Bank's Experience, 1994.

WORLD BANK. Investing in people: the World Bank in action. Direction in Development series. World Bank, 1995.

WORLD BANK. Monitoring environmental progress: a report on work in progress. Environmentally Sustainable Development series. World Bank, 1995.

WORLD BANK. Poverty reduction and the World Bank: progress and challenges in the 1990's. World Bank, 1996.

WORLD BANK. World Bank development report 1990: poverty. Oxford University Press, 1990.

WORLD BANK. World Bank participation sourcebook. Environmentally Sustainable Development series. World Bank, 1996.

WORLD BANK. World development report 1996: from plan to market. Oxford University Press, 1996

WORLD BANK. World development report 1995: workers in an integrating world, executive summary. Oxford University Press, 1995.

WORLD COMMISSION ON ENVIRONMENT AND DEVELOPMENT. Our common future. Oxford University Press, 1988.

WORLD WIDE FUND FOR NATURE & NEW ECONOMICS FOUNDATION. Indicators for sustainable development: strategies for use of indicators in national reports to the Commission of Sustainable Development and in the EC Structural Funds Process. WWF & NEF, 1994.

WRIGHT, Robert. What's ahead for the World Bank: interviews on the bank's role in promoting sustainable development. Charles Stewart Mott Foundation, 1995.

Other references include corporate annual reports, corporate social and environmental reports, annual reports of non-governmental organisations.

Acknowledgements

It would have been impossible to produce a publication of this length and scope in such a short period of time without the help and input of many people from around the world.

I would like to thank first and foremost my colleague Alison Beanland, without whom this publication would not have happened. Alison has not only done a wonderful design job, but has offered constant moral support and worked under enormous pressure with a great deal of patience, professionalism and good grace.

Thanks also to:

- My colleagues at The Prince of Wales Business Leaders Forum; our chief executive Robert Davies who has given valuable comments and feedback; everyone who proofed and edited different sections of the document; and especially Olivia Wiwa, Alice Mowlam, Karen Fletcher, Karen Gommersall, Trooper Sanders, Paul Willingham, Andrew Fiddaman, Leda Stott, Susan Simpson, Helen Simms, Kate Cavelle, Leon Taylor and Lana Narancic for all their extra work and support. Readers would have had to endure many more split infinitives and unnecessary superlatives if it had not been for their editing work! Thanks also to my management colleagues.

- Our partners at the World Bank Group – especially Amy Horng, Douglas Maguire, Amanda Blakely, Sabine Perrissin-Fabert, and Anne-Marie Chidzero for their input, and Jean-François Rischard and Elkyn Chaparro for their commitment to our joint research project on *Business as Partners in Development*. Also to Henry Jackelen and John Tucker at UNDP and Hani Yamani of the HOPE Foundation for their support – both intellectual and financial.

- Martin McKay for his help on proofing and sorting out various technical problems and to Mike Coates and his colleagues at Russell Press for their patience, friendliness and professionalism.

- Many people from many organisations and countries have helped with the content of the publication, in most cases at extremely short notice and on the basis of no more than a telephone call. Special thanks to Simon Zadek at the New Economics Foundation, Jon Hobbs at UNEP, Andrea Spencer-Cooke at SustainAbility, Trooper Sanders at the PWBLF, Antony Robbins at CARE International, Hugh Venables at ActionAid and Nick Cater for each writing a case study or article. Different people in the following organisations have willingly shared their information and ideas with me, and in many cases have hosted me on visits to their projects: Business in the Community in the UK; the World Business Council for Sustainable Development; the India Business and Community Partnership; the Business Leaders Forum in Poland; Business for Social Responsibility in the USA; the Thai Business Initiative for Rural Development; Philippine Business for Social Progress; the National Business Initiative in South Africa; the World Business Academy; the Social Venture Network; the Council on Economic Priorities; UNEP; UNDP; UNIDO; ILO; EBRD; WHO; UNICEF; the Empretec programme; Rotary International; AIESEC; the Keidanren in Japan; CERES in the USA; the US Conference Board; the Confederation of Indian Industry; the Canadian Business Council on National Issues; the US President's Council on Sustainable Development; the European Business Network for Social Inclusion; the Synergos Institute; PACT; Transparency International; the UK Government Advisory Council on Business and the Environment; South Africa's National Economic Development and Labour Council (Nedlac); the International Youth Foundation; City Year in the USA; Project HOPE; ACCION International; FUNDES; ActionAid; CARE International; Conservation International; WWF; the World Environment Center; Greenpeace in the UK; the Caux Roundtable and Minnesota Center for Corporate Responsibility; the ICC; the Chemical Manufacturers Association; the Global Environmental Management Initiative (GEMI); European Partners for the Environment; Investors in People in the UK; the Red Cross; the International Network for Environmental management (INEM); Philippine Business for the Environment; the Environmental Forum of southern Africa; the Hong Kong Private Sector Committee on the Environment; Landcare Australia; the Farmers Development Trust in Zimbabwe; the Mega-Cities Project in the USA; EQI in Egypt; Water Aid in the UK; Bombay First in India; the Krakow Development Forum in Poland; the Central Johannesburg Partnership in South Africa; the St

Petersburg Partnership initiative in Russia; Forecom and Açao Comunitária in Brazil; Groundwork in the UK; The Atlanta project in the USA; the Commercial Farmers Union and Agricultural Chemical Industries Association in Zimbabwe; GLOBE; Goals 2000 and the office of the Secretary of Education in the USA; the US Community Empowerment Zone Initiative; the US Departments of State and Commerce; the City Council of Manchester in the UK; the Alexandria Business Association in Egypt; the Get Ahead Foundation, Triple Trust and Izibuko Foundation in South Africa; Opportunity Trust in the UK; Intermediate Technology in the UK; the International Petroleum Industry Environmental Conservation Association (IPIECA) in the UK; the Kenya Management Assistance Programme; Partners for Growth in Zimbabwe; AmCham in Brazil; the Prince's Youth Business Trust in the UK, and its affiliates in India and South Africa; BankBoston; Xerox; RTZ-CRA; Hindustan Lever; Bamburi Portland Cement; Booker Tate; Aracruz Celulose; British Petroleum; the Tata Group; Unilever; Vandenburgh Foods; Eli Lily & Co.; B&Q; Merck & Co.; Johnson & Johnson; Sakal Papers; IBM; SmithKline Beecham; Levi Strauss; US WEST; Coopers & Lybrand; BOC; Toyota; Grand Metropolitan; American Express; the Coca-Cola Company; Gencor; Eskom; Sami Saad; BMW; TRW; KPMG; 3M; ABB; BHP; Citicorp; United Biscuits; Anglo American; San Miguel; Truworths; Chevron; Shell; Price Waterhouse; McKinsey; Telstra; NPI; National Westminster Bank; Golden Hope Plantations; Uni Storebrand; the Sedgwick Group; Monsanto; the Body Shop; the London Benchmarking Group; Norsk Hydro; the Kellogg Company; the Ayala Corporation; Johnson Matthey; Abercrombie & Kent; Wheelock and Co.; Ciba .... and others whom I'm sure I've missed.

There are many other companies and organisations not included in this publication which are undertaking excellent projects and contributing to sustainable development. The case studies that I have profiled cover only a fraction of the activities in this field and represent a collection of the countries, companies and partner organisations that I have come in contact with, or worked with over the past five years. There are probably many others which have equal or better stories to tell, and I hope that these examples will be added to future publications and research on the role of Business as Partners in Development; research which is being undertaken by a growing number of academics and organisations.

In the *Executive Summary*, I wrote that this publication has been produced as part of an on-going journey. For me it has been an important point to pause in my own personal journey; one which started by lecturing agriculture in South Africa, and encountering small-scale farmers eking out livelihoods of a few hundred rand a year, in some of the country's remotest and poorest rural areas, and then, in the space of a few years, moving to work for Citibank in Tokyo, Hong Kong and London, and encountering large-scale investors making millions of dollars a year in some of the world's most cosmopolitan and economically vibrant cities. I could not have encountered two more different worlds even if I had consciously planned it. Yet, despite their differences, I was struck by their inter-connectivity; by the warmth and humanity of the people I met in both of them; and by their common characteristics of resourcefulness, entrepreneurship and ingenuity. This realisation created a set of questions which I've been trying to answer ever since. How can there be so many problems in the world when we have such a wealth of human talent, in such a diversity of locations? How can this talent be harnessed not only to create economic wealth, but also to share it? And how can the process of wealth creation be managed in a way which enhances our natural resources and our social structures rather than destroying them? In the five years since I started working in this field, I have met some truly remarkable and inspirational people who are also asking these and other related questions, and more importantly, doing a myriad of practical things to answer them. Many of these people work in and with the organisations listed above, and they have done much to enrich both my work and my life in general. This publication is really their story and is written as a tribute to them and to the difference they are making in the world.

Jane Nelson